God Alone Is:
Nectar of Bhāgavatam

God Alone Is:
Nectar of Bhāgavatam

Suresh Natarajan

Red Mountain Ashram
Seattle, Washington
RedMountainAshram.org

10 9 8 7 6 5 4 3 2 1
First edition published 2026

ISBN: 979-8-9942201-0-8
Library of Congress PCN: 2026904549

Printed in the United States of America

TABLE OF CONTENTS

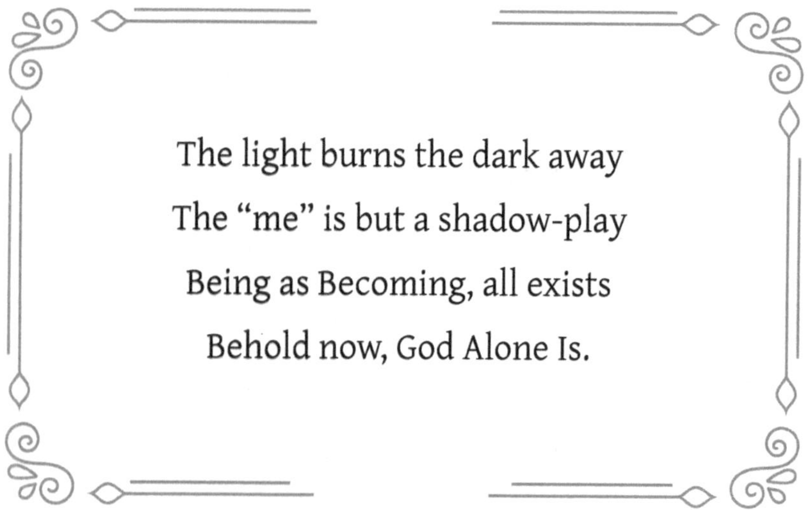

The light burns the dark away

The "me" is but a shadow-play

Being as Becoming, all exists

Behold now, God Alone Is.

PREFACE

ॐ नमो भगवते वासुदेवाय

oṁ namo bhagavate vāsudevaya

Prostrations unto the all-pervading Supreme Being

Human beings have made tremendous strides over the last few centuries in science and technology with pioneering breakthroughs in computing, communication, transportation, medicine etc. This has created unprecedented economic growth and physical comforts. However, with this rapid progress, there has also been an increase in societal disparities, loneliness and isolation leading to depression and other suicidal tendencies creating an inner crisis in the lives of human beings. Then there are wars of aggression, terrorism, pandemics and environmental degradation creating an outer crisis too. The inner and the outer crises are of course linked together as it is the feeling of vacuum within that causes the actions of excesses without, such as over-indulgence, violence etc.

The root of all these crises can be summarized simply as follows. We have made exponential progress in our ability to wield power but have not awakened to the wisdom to wield that power responsibly. The need of the hour then is the wisdom of interconnectedness and oneness of not just all human beings but the entire universe, which alone will usher in true peace and harmony among all beings.

This wisdom is what Srimad Bhāgavatam presents, not as a dry philosophy in abstract terms but as a practical living guide that can be easily adopted by any sincere reader. For this reason, it is the most suitable subject to be studied by young and old alike.

The root of ignorance among humans is the non-recognition of the common Source from which everyone and everything emanates. This ignorance has resulted in individualism, sectarianism, greed, isolation and various other ills of modern society. Scientists intuitively feel the existence of a unifying theory of everything as the all-encompassing framework that fully explains all aspects of the universe. But they are not able to come upon the Source due to the limitations in the perception of the material senses and thinking which is also a material process.

Being a divine work, Srimad Bhāgavatam transcends these limitations effortlessly and presents with great clarity and sweetness the common Source which can also be called God or Almighty. The word Almighty implies that there is no might which can be separate from God. So, right from the subatomic particles all the way to the supernova of the galaxies and everything in between including all animate beings from ants to humans are all expressions of the same Source.

It is into this one unitary Source that Srimad Bhāgavatam begins its inquiry with, in the exact same way as Brahma Sutras, which is the essence of the Vedas:

> *janmādyasya yataḥ*—Let us inquire into That
> of which everything is created.

Then it proceeds to offer the most comprehensive commentary on the Brahma Sutras, written by the same author Vyasa himself. Thus, it carries the distilled wisdom of all the Vedas.

What makes Srimad Bhāgavatam unique with not just unmatched clarity but also with unsurpassed sweetness is that it presents the entire philosophy through the pastimes of the Supreme Being Krishna and His various incarnations and the stories of various devotees. From time immemorial, stories always have held a unique appeal in their seamless ability to distill complex truths into easily consumable forms. And this is especially so with great stories and epics that stand the test of time over millennia as the ones in Bhāgavatam. The rich narrative of pastimes and stories provide the framework within which the deep philosophical discussions find their right place. Thus, it is the cream of all scriptures and also the fountainhead of sweetness.

Knowledge that doesn't lead to love only causes a hardening of the heart. Whereas, in Srimad Bhāgavatam, knowledge (*jnana*) of the most sophisticated philosophy serves as a foundation for the flowering of motiveless love (*ahaituki bhakti*) as the most ecstatic of emotions. Also being a marvel of poetry with the most refined aesthetics, it has served as an inspiration over millennia for innumerable derivative works of literature, art, music, dance and architecture.

Srimad Bhāgavatam is so perfectly arranged that a systematic and sincere study of the work from the beginning till the end will ensure that one is cleansed of all the mental impurities and transported to a transcendental state of peace and love for the Supreme Being and thereby love for all beings of the Universe. This is why it has been hailed as the crown jewel among all scriptures by many great sages and saints who have established the undisputed pre-eminence of Srimad Bhāgavatam among all devotional literature.

A monumental epic of 18,000 verses, Srīmad Bhāgavatam unfolds as a profound dialogue between King Parikshit and the great sage Shuka Brahmam. Spanning twelve large cantos (known as skandhas), it seamlessly integrates deep philosophy through the medium of engaging stories. To navigate its vast spiritual landscape, we offer here a brief summary of the themes explored in each canto.

The First Canto opens with Nārada's instructions to Vyāsa to compose Bhāgavatam and relates Parikshit's curse leading to his seven-day dialogue with Shuka Brahmam. The Second Canto provides a concise summary of the entire teaching. The Third Canto demystifies the creation of the universe, the descent of Varāha Avatar, and Kapila's profound Sāṅkhya philosophy. The Fourth Canto recounts the humbling of Daksha's sacrifice by Shiva and the unwavering devotion of Dhruva. The Fifth Canto glorifies the renunciation and wisdom of Rshabha and Jadabharata. The Sixth Canto reveals the power of causeless Grace through the redemption of Ajāmila and Vrtrāsura. The Seventh Canto heralds the triumph of devotion over tyranny through the story of Prahlāda and Narasimha. The Eighth Canto narrates the deliverance of the elephant Gajendra, the symbolic churning of the ocean, and Bali's surrender to Vāmana. The Ninth Canto chronicles the lineage of righteous kings, including the most auspicious advent of Sri Ram. The Tenth Canto is the very heart of Bhāgavatam dedicated to the nectar-like pastimes of Krishna and Balarām. The Eleventh Canto details Krishna's final instructions to Uddhava, known famously as Uddhava Gītā. The Twelfth Canto concludes with Parikṣhit's blessed liberation and the divine vision of sage Mārkandeya.

Thus, we can see that every canto contains many popular stories and interwoven within them are the most sublime teachings on true wisdom and unconditional devotion. This book contains a selection of verses from each of the twelve cantos in sequential order, highlighting all salient events and instructions, along with a detailed commentary that brings out the symbolism of the stories and the depth of the universal teachings.

Before embarking upon a detailed narration of the various stories and the teachings contained therein, Srimad Bhāgavatam opens with three beautiful introductory verses in the very first chapter of the very first canto which serve as the most comprehensive overview of the entire work itself. So let us dive into this divine work with the detailed introduction in the words of Bhāgavatam itself to the sublime philosophy and the sweet mood of the entire work.

One important point to note as we enter the divine work is that each verse of Bhāgavatam is a meditation unto itself. Therefore, while reading the book from cover to cover will give its own joy, one can also pick any verse from any canto at any time to directly dip into the nectar of devotion and wisdom that leads to true peace and joy of abidance as our true nature of Pure Consciousness.

To recognize the unitary Absolute Power that alone functions through each and every one of us is to attain true victory over ignorance of the false ego. This is the ultimate benediction that Bhāgavatam bestows to one who reads it with humility and love in a prayerful mood.

FIRST CANTO
Introduction and Context

जन्माद्यस्य यतोऽन्वयादितरतश्चार्थेष्वभिज्ञः स्वराट्
तेने ब्रह्म हृदा य आदिकवये मुह्यन्ति यत्सूरयः ।
तेजोवारिमृदां यथा विनिमयो यत्र त्रिसर्गोऽमृषा
धाम्ना स्वेन सदा निरस्तकुहकं सत्यं परं धीमहि ॥ Bh 1.1.1

janmādyasya yato'nvayāditarataścārtheṣvabhijñaḥ svarāṭ
tene brahma hṛdā ya ādikavaye muhyanti yatsūrayaḥ
tejovārimṛdāṁ yathā vinimayo yatra trisargo'mṛṣā
dhāmnā svena sadā nirastakuhakaṁ satyaṁ paraṁ dhīmahi

We meditate upon the Transcendent Absolute Truth
from whom springs forth the creation, sustenance
and dissolution of the universe. As the all-pervading
Consciousness who is totally independent, He is present
in all that exists and yet distinct from everything. He
revealed to the heart of the first seer the import of Vedic
wisdom which can delude even the sages. The material
creation made of threefold gunas appears in Him alone as
though real, just as the fiery rays of the sun cause water
to appear in a mirage. Being eternally self-effulgent, He
is ever free of the illusion (Maya) of the material world.
We meditate upon Him, the Supreme Being.

Srimad Bhāgavatam is hailed as the perfect scripture composed by Vyasa that is the distilled essence of all the Vedas, and it fittingly begins with the most perfect invocation by going to the heart of all inquiries as to the source of this universe. And it affirms the source to be the Supreme Truth (*satyaṁ paraṁ*) that is Consciousness (*abhijñaḥ*). It is also totally independent (*svarāṭ*), being the cause of all causes. Thereby it transcends the idea of God as the mere Creator and ascribes creation, sustenance and dissolution of the universe to the Supreme Being. In other words, everything comes from, remains in and goes back to the Supreme Being.

The verse describes the Supreme Being as beyond all limitations including the debate of impersonal or personal God. He is described both as the impersonal Presence that pervades all of existence and the personal Being who taught the essence of the Vedas to Brahma, the first created entity. The personal aspect of the Supreme Being is later described with sublime sweetness as Krishna, the all-attractive, along with His glorious pastimes through various Avatars.

Also, the transient and illusory nature of the universe is explained through the simile of water appearing in a mirage. All of creation is seen to be made of the three gunas or modes (namely *sattva, rajas, tamas*—purity, passion and ignorance) and it is later explained comprehensively that by ascending to the mode of purity, one eventually transcends all three gunas to the realization of the Supreme Being. In fact, the very structure of Bhāgavatam is ideally organized for this process of ascension to purity through the first nine cantos before entering the transcendental pastimes of Krishna in the tenth canto.

Finally, the entire verse is given in the form of the Gayatri mantra which is the greatest mantra of all the Vedas with the invocation, *dhimahi*. Reading and listening to Srimad Bhāgavatam with an attitude of humility that is free of criticism illuminates the intellect, brings clarity to the mind and awakens love in the heart.

धर्मः प्रोज्झितकैतवोऽत्र परमो निर्मत्सराणां सतां
वेद्यं वास्तवमत्र वस्तु शिवदं तापत्रयोन्मूलनम् ।
श्रीमद्भागवते महामुनिकृते किं वा परैरीश्वरः
सद्यो हृद्यवरुध्यतेऽत्र कृतिभिः शुश्रूषुभिस्तत्क्षणात्
॥ Bh 1.1.2

dharmaḥ projjhitakaitavo'tra paramo nirmatsarāṇāṁ satāṁ
vedyaṁ vāstavamatra vastu śivadaṁ tāpatrayonmūlanam
śrīmadbhāgavate mahāmunikṛte kiṁ vā parairīśvaraḥ
sadyo hṛdyavarudhyate'tra kṛtibhiḥ śuśrūṣubhistatkṣaṇāt

Free of any deception in religiosity born of ulterior motives and desires, Srimad Bhāgavatam compiled by the great sage Vyasa expounds the highest truth for the pure at heart. It bestows auspiciousness and uproots the threefold miseries (caused by one's own body/mind, other living entities and acts of nature respectively). Thus, Bhāgavatam alone is sufficient for God-realization. Simply by hearing its message with sincerity, that very instant one can establish in their heart the truth of the Supreme Being, who is unknowable by all other means.

Deception in religiosity is rooted in being attached to desires and outcomes. In general, all activities (religious or secular) are found to be motivated by desires of various kinds. They can be broadly classified as desires for financial security (*artha*), sense gratification (*kāma*), virtuous living (*dharma*) and finally liberation or freedom from the egoic self (*moksha*).

As long as we are stuck in the first two desires of security and pleasure, it is no different from animal life. While we may engage in sophisticated instruments of security and variegated avenues of pleasure, it still remains only rooted in the conception of bodily identification as all animals do. The role of religion in the realm of these two desires is to only guide people away from fulfilling them in an unregulated manner which leads to over-indulgence, disease and depression. Through such guidance and regulation, it helps us live according to dharma where human life truly begins.

Dharma is the recognition that we are part of an interconnected universe with all our fellow beings. Therefore, it encourages activities such as sharing, giving, being truthful, non-violence, non-coveting etc. Many injunctions and commandments of various religions are toward molding one's life in the platform of dharma. While this is a beginning to one's religious life, it too is found to be beset with attachment to various fragmentary causes—political, social, national, religious, environmental etc. Underlying all of it is the identification as an egoic self that is still caught in comparison, judgment, envy, pride etc. Thus, all acts of religiosity motivated by the desire for virtuous living are still limiting.

The recognition then that the root of suffering is the egoic identification and hence the desire to be free of it is the last category of desire called liberation (*moksha*). This causes one to strive toward removing the root of egoic identity. And yet, the very desire to be free of the ego is ultimately the ego coming through the back door. It is the thief posing as a cop to catch the thief and will never be caught. Therefore, even acts of religiosity motivated by the desire for liberation, however pious they may be, are still found, upon keen insight, to be ultimately binding.

Thus, all the four desires are ultimately rooted in comparison and desirous of an outcome in time which only leads to frustration and falling prey to false teachings and teachers. Thus, the highest message of the Vedas which is called Vedanta (lit. the end of all knowledge) is to transcend all desires, including the desire for liberation. This is the platform of true love or devotion (*bhakti*) that Srimad Bhāgavatam presents in the most comprehensive manner.

The last important point of this verse is the need to hear the message keenly, with humility and sincerity. An earnest attitude toward listening to this work is the only pre-requisite necessary to reap the supreme benefit of Srimad Bhāgavatam which is a direct realization in the heart of the truth of the Supreme Being and the flowering of love toward Him and thereby all fellow beings.

Srimad Bhāgavatam is the highest expression of Vyasa's vast spiritual treasure. It will be told in subsequent chapters that Vyasa was not fully satisfied after compiling the four Vedas, the great epic Mahābhārata and also the commentary of all Upanishads known as the Brahma Sutras. Narada pointed out that the glorification of loving devotion toward the Supreme Being as the pinnacle of all philosophical inquiry is the lacuna in his body of work. That prompted Vyasa to compose this Srimad Bhāgavatam as an expression of the most sublime philosophy through the platform of motiveless love.

निगमकल्पतरोर्गलितं फलं शुकमुखादमृतद्रवसंयुतम् ।
पिबत भागवतं रसमालयं मुहुरहो रसिका भुवि भावुकाः ॥
Bh 1.1.3

nigama kalpa taror galitaṁ phalaṁ śhuka mukhād amṛta drava saṁyutam
pibata bhāgavataṁ rasamālayam muhuraho rasikā bhuvi bhāvukāḥ

Oh, devotees who relish a taste for divine love! Bhāgavatam is the fully ripened fruit of the wish-yielding tree of Vedic wisdom flowing from the lips of the great sage Shuka. It is full of the immortal nectar of supreme bliss and perfect in every way. Go on drinking this nectar of unalloyed sweetness again and again.

This is the last introductory verse before the dialogues and the stories of Srimad Bhāgavatam unfold. After presenting the supreme position of Bhāgavatam as the cream of the highest philosophy of the Vedas, the mood of the entire work is made clear in this verse. It is not a dry exposition of abstract philosophy that only touches the intellect but filled with sweet exchanges of divine love that goes straight to the heart.

By addressing the listeners as those with taste for divine love, it is made clear that it is not a sophisticated intellect but a tender heart that is necessary to approach this work. Vedas are compared to a wish-yielding tree as they present a regulated way of living to fulfill desires of all kinds and Bhāgavatam represents the ripened fruit of this tree as it provides the nectar of loving devotion that transcends all desires. And what's more it comes from the mouth of the sage Shuka, an enlightened being who ever relishes the nectar of devotion. Just as a fruit pecked by a parrot is known to be extra sweet, similarly this ripened fruit of devotion is all the more sweet being pecked by the sage Shuka whose name itself means parrot.

An important word in this verse is *rasa* which also represents the various moods of devotion. The five most prominent moods or rasa are later described in detail in Srimad Bhāgavatam as increasing levels of sweetness with well-known examples illustrated through stories:

1. *shānta* (peaceful reverence) exemplified by Prahlada
2. *dāsya* (loving service) exemplified by Hanuman
3. *sakhya* (close friendship) exemplified by Arjuna and Uddhava
4. *vātsalya* (parental affection) exemplified by Yashoda and Nanda
5. *mādhurya* (sweet intimacy) exemplified by Radha and Rukmini

The common factor of all the five rasas is devotional love or bhakti, and the object of each rasa is the Source or the fountainhead of truth, wisdom and love that is Krishna. So, the entire essence of Srimad Bhāgavatam can be summed up as realizing the one true Source, through the mood of loving devotion that cleanses the mind and enables us to abide in our innate nature of peace, harmony and love.

वेत्य त्वं सौम्य तत्सर्वं तत्त्वतस्तदनुग्रहात् ।
ब्रूयुः स्निग्धस्य शिष्यस्य गुरवो गुह्यमप्युत ॥ Bh 1.1.8

vettha tvaṁ saumya tat sarvaṁ tattvatas tad anugrahāt
brūyuḥ snigdhasya shishyasya guravo guhyam apyuta

Oh Sūta, being very pure in heart, you have earned the Grace of the sages and learned Bhāgavatam. Because teachers confide the most profound secrets only to their beloved students.

After the first three introductory verses on the essence, glory and mood of this great work, Bhāgavatam begins with a conversation among a congregation of sages in a sacred forest known as Naimisharanya (near present day Lucknow, India). The sages perform a long *yajna* (fire sacrifice) there, headed by the sage Shaunaka. Sūta Maharshi who is an expert in Puranas, arrives there and the sages offer their respects to him. When Shuka Brahmam narrated Bhāgavatam to Parikshit on the banks of Ganga, there was a distinguished assembly of listeners. One among them was Sūta, who learned it by heart, so Shaunaka and the sages ask Sūta to narrate the same to them so that every day after completing the *yajna*, they can spend the evenings soaking in the nectar of Bhāgavatam. In this verse, an important quality of how Sūta learned Bhāgavatam and in turn, how we have to approach such a work is given. It is mentioned that he learned by being pure at heart, thereby making clear that it is not a logical intellect but a pure heart that is the most essential prerequisite. As Krishna says in the Bhagavad Gita, "You can learn the Truth by inquiring with an attitude of humility and devotion" (*tad viddhi praṇipātena paripraśhnena sevayā*—BG 4.34). It is a great art to listen in this manner, neither with blind faith nor an attitude of challenge, but with genuine curiosity and reverence while inquiring and posing questions. The most confidential and profound wisdom of Self-realization is revealed to us only when there is love and reverence for the teacher and the teaching. Therein lies the guidance for us on how to approach Bhāgavatam or Gita or any such work of the highest wisdom—with purity, love and humility while also inquiring, questioning and verifying inwardly, which is the true meaning of *shraddha*.

भूरीणि भूरिकर्माणि श्रोतव्यानि विभागशः ।
अतः साधोऽत्र यत्सारं समुद्धृत्य मनीषया ।
ब्रूहि भद्रायभूतानां येनात्मा सुप्रसीदति ॥ Bh 1.1.11

bhūrīṇi bhūri karmāṇi śhrotavyāni vibhāgaśhaḥ
ataḥ sādho'tra yat sāram samuddhṛtya manīṣhayā
brūhi bhadrāya bhūtānām yenātmā suprasīdati

The scriptures are numerous with various prescriptions of rituals and voluminous with many parts requiring a very long time to study. Therefore, being most benevolent, draw out with your keen insight and teach the quintessence (that is Bhāgavatam) by which the heart will be satisfied.

The Vedas are a vast body of literature with various divisions such as Samhitas (hymns and prayers), Brahmanas (rituals and sacrifices), Aranyakas (inner meaning of rituals), Upanishads (wisdom of the sages) along with six Vedangas (grammar, prosody etc.), four Upavedas (ayurveda etc.), Sutras or aphorisms (brahma sutra, dharma sutra etc.), Smritis or codes of living (manu smrti etc.), two Itihasas or grand epics (Ramāyana and Mahabharata) and eighteen primary Puranas. Thus, they are extremely voluminous, diverse and prescribe various levels of teachings based on the stage of life, proclivity, interest, time and place. However, because of that vast diversity, they are also extremely bewildering. Therefore, the sages in Naimisharanya ask Sūta to relate only the quintessence of all the Vedas, which is Bhāgavatam, as it gives us the timeless wisdom that is applicable to everyone and by which the highest purpose of peace and love is realized in the heart.

यत्पादसंश्रया: सूत मुनय: प्रशमायना: ।
सद्य: पुनन्त्युपस्पृष्टा: स्वर्धुन्यापोऽनुसेवया ॥ Bh 1.1.15

yat pāda saṁśhrayāḥ sūta munayaḥ praśhamāyanāḥ
sadyaḥ punantyupaspṛṣhṭāḥ svardhunyāpo 'nusevayā

Sages who have taken shelter in the Supreme Being and therefore ever abide in perfect equanimity purify anyone who comes in contact with them even once. Whereas even the celestial waters of Ganga cleanse the heart only by long and sustained contact.

The greatness of association with sages and holy gathering, known as Satsang, is glorified in this verse by Shaunaka. Because a sage is completely free of the sense of "me" and "mine" he is a visible manifestation of the Divine. While everyone is a manifestation of the Divine in truth, it is not visible because of the covering of the ego. The world can be visualized as a room full of mirrors covered by dust with an occasional mirror here and there that is completely clean. All mirrors are equally capable of reflecting light and yet only the ones that are free of dust can actually do so. Similarly, all beings are manifestations of the same Divine. Yet only the sage who is free of the dust of the ego shines as that Light. We see in him our own reflection as well as the pure manifestation of the Divine. Therefore, having contact with sages and being in Satsang enables us to instantly have a glimpse into who we really are, while going to sacred places and bathing in holy waters etc. can only gradually cleanse the heart. So the easiest boat to cross the ocean of suffering is through Satsang. We can have Satsang not just through physical contact but also through virtual contact with sages such as by reading Bhāgavatam and listening to the discourse of a true sage. Therefore, we have to always prioritize Satsang as the highest form of association over all other frivolous associations that drag us down further into egoic identification. The unique power of Satsang is glorified repeatedly in Bhāgavatam as the single most important portal into Truth.

अथाख्याहिहरेर्धीमन्नवतारकथाः शुभाः ।
लीला विदधतः स्वैरमीश्वरस्यात्ममायया ॥ Bh 1.1.18

athākhyāhiharerdhīmannavatāra kathāḥ śhubhāḥ
līlā vidadhataḥ svairamīśhvarasyaatmamāyayā

O wise Sūta, please narrate the blessed stories of the descents of the Supreme Being who enacts various pastimes by his own Yogamaya (divine potency).

After glorifying the virtues of Satsang, especially with a great being like Sūta well versed in Bhāgavatam, Shaunaka asks him to recount the glorious pastimes of the Supreme Being through all His Avatars (descents). The Supreme Being is the ground of Pure Consciousness and also the Source of the entire Universe through His own Maya. Furthermore, He takes Avatars into the Universe in various forms to establish dharma and bestow loving devotion through His transcendental names, forms and pastimes. Therefore, Shaunaka says that there is no easier way to purify one's heart than to hear the glorious exploits of the Lord and His playful pastimes. So, he requests Sūta to narrate all such pastimes and specifically His most complete descent (*purna avatāra*) as Krishna along with Balaram, which is most delightful to hear at every step for listeners with a taste for sweetness. He concludes by stating that in this age of Kali (lit. age of conflict), there is no easier way to cross over the turbulent ocean of suffering than to listen to the glories of Krishna and Bhāgavatam as a whole and thus reverently requests Sūta to narrate the Bhāgavatam. Accordingly, Sūta will begin his blessed narration in the following verses.

यं प्रव्रजन्तमनुपेतमपेतकृत्यंद्वैपायनो विरहकातर आजुहाव ।
पुत्रेति तन्मयतया तरवोऽभिनेदुस्तं सर्वभूतहृदयं मुनिमानतोऽस्मि
‖ Bh 1.2.2

yaṁ pravrajantam anupetam apetakṛtyaṁ dvaipāyano
virahakātara ājuhāva
putreti tanmayatayā taravo'bhinedustaṁ sarvabhūtahṛdayaṁ
munim ānato'smi

The sage Vyasa saw his son Shuka walk away all alone with the intent of leading the life of a recluse, though he had not yet been initiated with the sacred thread and had not performed any religious rituals. So, Vyasa called out, "O, My son" with an agitated heart feeling separation from his beloved son. But the son kept on walking while all the trees turned around as it were, filled as they were with the presence of Shuka. I bow to that great sage Shuka who is one with the Universe and thus present in the hearts of all.

Sūta begins his response to the queries of the sages headed by Shaunaka by first offering his obeisances to the great sage Shuka Brahmam, through whose narration to Parikshit, Sūta too listened and learned Bhāgavatam. This is a very famous verse to glorify Shuka Brahmam and his supreme state of renunciation and wisdom. When he was just a young lad of barely sixteen, it is said that Shuka Brahmam was already completely free of the false idea of "me" and "mine" and therefore felt one with the entire Universe. He did not have any inclination toward religious rituals starting with sacred thread ceremony etc. that are normally done at his age. He instead walked away from his house as a recluse with total renunciation. His father, the great sage Vyasa, who is himself of the greatest stature among the Rishis and who has composed the great epics and Puranas, still had a trace of attachment to his son and therefore called out to his son as he walked away. Shuka on the other hand, free of all attachments and abiding in the Supreme Being who animates all of creation, kept walking, while all the trees felt one with Shuka and responded to the call of Vyasa by turning around. Sūta thus brings out poetically in a dramatic way the supreme inner state of the great sage Shuka who is the speaker of Bhāgavatam. Thereby, he both offers his gratitude to Shuka Brahmam for narrating Bhāgavatam as well as bringing out the greatness of the work by revealing the sublime state of the speaker of Bhāgavatam. It is often said that one can judge a tree by its fruits. Here, it is the other way around where one can judge the fruit (Bhāgavatam) by the quality of the tree (Shuka) who produced it.

यः स्वानुभावमखिलश्रुतिसारमेकमध्यात्मदीपमतितितीर्षतां तमोऽन्धम् ।
संसारिणां करुणयाह पुराणगुह्यं तं व्याससूनुमुपयामि गुरुं मुनीनाम् ॥ Bh 1.2.3

yaḥ svānubhāvam akhilaśhrutisāram ekam adhyātmadīpam atititīrṣhatāṁ tamo'ndham
saṁsāriṇāṁ karuṇayāha purāṇaguhyaṁ taṁ vyāsasūnum upayāmi guruṁ munīnām

My obeisances unto the teacher of all sages, the son of Vyasa, who has out of his compassion given this most glorious and mystical Bhāgavatam which is the essence of all Vedas. It is a unique light illuminating spiritual wisdom for all those caught in material bondage and seeking to transcend this darkness of ignorance.

Sūta offers another beautiful prayer to the main speaker of Bhāgavatam, Shuka Brahmam, while glorifying the greatness of Bhāgavatam again. Śhuka Brahmam being completely free of any attachment and one with the Divine had no desire to accomplish anything whatsoever and yet narrated this voluminous work of Bhāgavatam with 18,000 verses only out of compassion for all beings caught in the false attachment to "me" and "mine," which is the material bondage and the darkness of ignorance. Transcending this darkness requires the light of wisdom that not merely appeals to the intellect but goes directly to the heart. This is the unique nature of Bhāgavatam where the highest philosophy of Self-realization is soaked in the nectar of loving devotion through stories. Unlike dialectical discourses, stories bypass the mind and go to the heart. To hear the narration of the Avatars and pastimes of Bhagavan and the lives of great Bhagavatas brings the Truth home as a living reality that is at once profound and heart melting. What is considered to be a very confidential wisdom of the Upanishads and the Vedas is made easily accessible for anyone without any prior qualifications to simply listen and be transformed. That is the greatness of Bhāgavatam itself and of Shuka Brahmam who narrated it in the most perfect manner.

नारायणं नमस्कृत्य नरं चैव नरोत्तमम् ।
देवीं सरस्वतीं व्यासं ततो जयमुदीरयेत् ॥ Bh 1.2.4

nārāyaṇaṁ namaskṛtya naraṁ chaiva narottamam
devīṁ sarasvatīṁ vyāsaṁ tato jayam udīrayet

After offering obeisances to the divine sages Narayana and Nara, the Supreme Person Krishna, Mother Saraswati and the sage Vyasa, one should recite this sacred work that bestows victory in all endeavors.

After glorifying Shuka Brahmam who narrated the uniquely sublime Bhāgavatam, Sūta Maharshi prescribes the way to read Bhāgavatam and the purpose of doing so. Bhāgavatam is begun by offering obeisances to the Supreme Being who pervades the entire universe, who manifests as the divine sages Narayana and Nara, who descended as the Supreme Person Krishna, who manifests as Mother Saraswati, the very power of learning itself, and the great sage Vyasa who authored Bhāgavatam. The purpose for reading Bhāgavatam is mentioned as victory (*jayam*). The victory of all victories is to be free of the false sense of "me" that is associated with the body/mind and be free of the fear of death which can only affect the body. To recognize the unitary Absolute Power that alone functions through each and every one of us is to attain true victory over ignorance of the false ego. This is the ultimate benediction that Bhāgavatam bestows to one who reads it with humility and love in a prayerful mood.

स वै पुंसां परो धर्मो यतो भक्तिरधोक्षजे ।
अहैतुक्यप्रतिहता ययात्मा सुप्रसीदति ॥
वासुदेवे भगवति भक्तियोगः प्रयोजितः ।
जनयत्याशु वैराग्यं ज्ञानं च यदहैतुकम् ॥ Bh 1.2.6–7

sa vai puṁsāṁ paro dharmo yato bhaktiradhokṣhaje
ahaitukyapratihatā yayātmā suprasīdati
vāsudeve bhagavati bhaktiyogaḥ prayojitaḥ
janayatyāśhu vairāgyaṁ jñānaṁ cha yad ahaitukam

That alone is the supreme duty of all, from which follows unconditional and unobstructed loving devotion to the Transcendent Being and the true Self is pleased. Loving connection with the Source who is Vasudeva speedily awakens dispassion and wisdom.

The highest purpose of human life is to recognize the Source of our existence from which all energy flows and to be in tune with the Source, called *adhokshaja* or the Transcendent. The Supreme Being as Pure Consciousness is the Source of all existence, and His energy is the all-pervading Controller of all activities as the Divine Will. Since all sensory activities, including thought, are only enabled by Him, it is not possible to perceive Him through the sensory activities. Therefore, He is called the Transcendent Being. To have unconditional and unobstructed loving devotion is to surrender to the Divine

Will every moment, thus being in total acceptance of "what is" and responding with undivided attention. Such a state of total and unconditional love naturally awakens dispassion and true wisdom. The Source is referred to as Vasudeva because He resides everywhere. As Krishna says in the Gita: "The mark of a great soul and a realized being is to surrender unto Me, seeing everything as Vasudeva" (*bahūnāṁ janmanām ante jñānavān māṁ prapadyate vasudevaḥ sarvam iti sa mahātmā sudurlabhaḥ*—BG 7.19).

वदन्ति तत्त्वविदस्तत्त्वं यज्ज्ञानमद्वयम् ।
ब्रह्मेति परमात्मेति भगवानिति शब्द्यते ॥
तच्छ्रद्दधाना मुनयो ज्ञानवैराग्ययुक्तया ।
पश्यन्त्यात्मनि चात्मानं भक्त्या श्रुतगृहीतया ॥
Bh 1.2.11–12

vadanti tattattvavidastattvaṁ yajjñānamadvayam
brahmeti paramātmeti bhagavān iti śhabdyate
tachchhraddadhānā munayo jñānavairāgyayuktayā
paśhyantyātmani chātmānaṁ bhaktyā śhrutagṛhītayā

The knowers of Truth declare only such wisdom that is free of duality as Truth that is called Brahman, Paramatma and Bhagavan. Sages filled with dedication perceive that Truth as their own Self in their heart through devotion coupled with wisdom and dispassion, realized through pure listening.

In this famous verse, Sūta describes the very essence of Truth as that wisdom which is free of duality. Knowledge generally has the duality of the knower and the known or the subject and the object. But the wisdom that reveals both the subject and the object as essentially only expressions of the unitary Divine Will rooted in the Supreme Being is the highest wisdom. This unitary Source is known as the all-pervading infinite Brahman. It appears within everyone as the indwelling Spirit that illuminates and yet remains unaffected by the activities of the body and mind. This indwelling Spirit is known as Paramatma. It appears in embodied manifestation in the form of Avatars and great enlightened beings as Bhagavan. Further, this Truth is realized by the one who listens with total *shraddha* (sincerity and dedication along with confidence in oneself and the teachings) to the pointers in works such as Bhāgavatam and thus gets blessed with not just intellectual knowledge but wisdom that awakens the heart through loving devotion. That leads to the realization that there is nothing other than the Supreme Being, with everything, everywhere, every moment only an expression of the Divine Will that comes forth from the Supreme Being.

तस्मादेकेन मनसा भगवान् सात्वतां पति: ।
श्रोतव्य: कीर्तितव्यश्च ध्येय: पूज्यश्च नित्यदा ॥
यदनुध्यासिना युक्ता: कर्मग्रन्थिनिबन्धनम् ।
छिन्दन्ति कोविदास्तस्य को न कुर्यात्कथारतिम् ॥ Bh 1.2.14-15

tasmādekena manasā bhagavān sātvatāṁ patiḥ
shrotavyaḥ kīrtitavyaśhcha dhyeyaḥ pūjyaśhcha nityadā
yadanudhyāsinā yuktāḥ karmagranthinibandhanam
chindanti kovidāstasya ko na kuryātkathāratim

Therefore, with a single pointed mind, one ought to hear, glorify, meditate upon and worship the Lord, who is the protector of the devotees. The wise ones who are armed with the sword of constant meditation upon Him

cut asunder the hard knot of karma. Who then would not take delight in listening about the Lord?

Having described the essential nature of the Supreme Truth as both the all-pervading Infinite Being as well as the indwelling Spirit, Sūta Maharshi states that one therefore ought to listen to this teaching with single pointed attention. It is by listening that the fog of confusion clears away and Truth shines forth. Therefore, listening with total attention is the most important first step, which is also the last step, as it comprises all other processes mentioned such as glorification, meditation and worship. To give full attention to the teachings about the Supreme Being is to glorify, meditate upon and worship the Supreme Being. This can be done every moment through the constant inquiry into the Source of all activities, whatever one might be engaged in. If we recognize that all the physical and mental activities at any given moment happen only through the Intelligence that pervades every cell of our body, then we are free of the false sense of doership. The only doer of all actions is that Intelligence that is operating in infinite ways in our bodies and in every aspect of the universe. This frees us of the hard knot of karma which is only sustained through the fiction of an individual egoic doer. Therefore, anyone interested in being free of suffering which rises due to the false ego in the form of anxiety, comparison, envy, worry etc. would do well to listen to this teaching that removes the very root of the false ego.

शुश्रूषो: श्रद्दधानस्य वासुदेवकथारुचि: ।
स्यान्महत्सेवया विप्रा: पुण्यतीर्थनिषेवणात् ॥
शृण्वतां स्वकथा: कृष्ण: पुण्यश्रवणकीर्तन: ।
हृद्यन्त:स्थो ह्यभद्राणि विधुनोति सुहृत्सताम् ॥ Bh 1.2.16-17

shushrūṣhoḥ shraddadhānasya Vasudevakathāruciḥ
syānmahatsevayā viprāḥ puṇyatīrthaniṣhevaṇāt
shṛnvatāṁ svakathāḥ kṛṣhṇaḥ puṇyashravaṇakīrtanaḥ
hṛdyantaḥstho hyabhadrāṇi vidhunoti suhṛtsatām

By resorting to holy places of pilgrimage, one obtains the blessing of serving exalted beings and thereby develops a relish for listening to the pastimes and teachings of Krishna who abides in the Heart, is a friend of the virtuous, and removes the inauspicious tendencies of those who listen about Him.

Bhāgavatam is said to be the sound incarnation of Krishna. Therefore, listening to Bhāgavatam which contains the pastimes and teachings of Krishna, removes all the inauspicious tendencies which are rooted in the false ego. Such evil tendencies are innumerable as seen in the world and yet they all have only one root—the false ego that causes comparison, greed, envy, covetousness and all other such tendencies. So, the intelligent way is to not try and remove each one of these tendencies but to go to the very root and see the false sense of me which dissolves everything, in the very moment of clear perception. That is the essence of Bhāgavatam. Further, Sūta Maharshi says that one can develop the taste for listening to Bhāgavatam and such teachings only by association with exalted beings. This is the purpose of visiting holy places—to get an opportunity to meet with saintly beings and loosen egoic attachment. Also in this verse, it is hinted that while outer pilgrimages to holy places are sacred indeed, the holiest site of pilgrimage is our own Heart where the Supreme Being ever shines as Pure Consciousness.

One can make this pilgrimage wherever one is and thus be cleansed of egoic attachment.

नष्टप्रायेष्वभद्रेषु नित्यं भागवतसेवया ।
भगवत्युत्तमश्लोके भक्तिर्भवति नैष्ठिकी ॥
तदा रजस्तमोभावाः कामलोभादयश्च ये ।
चेत एतैरनाविद्धं स्थितं सत्त्वे प्रसीदति ॥ Bh 1.2.18-19

nashṭa prāyeshu abhadreshu nityam bhāgavata sevayā
bhagavati uttamashloke bhaktir bhavati naishṭhikī
tadā rajastamobhāvāḥ kāmalobhādayaśhcha ye
cheta etairanāviddhaṁ sthitaṁ sattve prasīdati

All inauspiciousness is removed by constantly offering service to Bhāgavatam that brings forth abiding and unflinching loving devotion toward Bhagavan, the Supreme Being, of the most supreme glory. Then the mind, freed of the inner enemies such as lust and greed born out of the modes of passion and ignorance, remains situated in purity and goodness that gives true happiness.

Serving Bhāgavatam eternally removes all negative tendencies effortlessly and bestows unconditional love for all beings. What does it mean to serve Bhāgavatam? It has many layers of meaning—reading or listening to the text of Bhāgavatam daily, serving the great Bhagavatas (devotees) and surrendering to the Supreme Source or Bhagavan. By doing so, the modes of passion (*rajas*) and ignorance (*tamas*) lose their effect and one is freed of the six inner enemies (*arishadvarga*) of lust, anger, greed, arrogance, delusion and envy. This situates us in the mode of goodness (*sattva*) which bestows true happiness that is equanimity and peace.

एवं प्रसन्नमनसो भगवद्भक्तियोगतः ।
भगवत्तत्त्वविज्ञानं मुक्तसङ्गस्य जायते ॥
भिद्यते हृदयग्रन्थिश्छिद्यन्ते सर्वसंशयाः ।
क्षीयन्ते चास्य कर्माणि दृष्ट एवात्मनीश्वरे ॥ Bh 1.2.20-21

evaṁ prasannamanaso bhagavadbhaktiyogataḥ
bhagavattattvavijñānaṁ muktasaṅgasya jāyate
bhidyate hṛdayagranthiśhchhidyante sarvasaṁshayāḥ
kṣhīyante chāsya karmāṇi dṛṣhṭa evātmanīśhvare

When one is free of attachment and has loving devotion to the Lord, the mind is filled with peace, and one realizes the essential truth of God. The moment one sees God as one's own true Self, the knot of ignorance in the heart is removed, all doubts are cut asunder and the entire stock of karmas gets destroyed.

The mind affected by the modes of passion and ignorance is disturbed and not in peace. By listening to Bhāgavatam and by surrendering to Bhagavan as the Supreme Controller, the mind is freed of passion and ignorance and gets situated in purity which leads to a pleasing disposition and freedom from attachment. This awakens true loving devotion toward the Supreme Being as the essence of the entire universe and true realization of God flowers in the heart, not as a conceptual idea or an intellectual abstraction but as the living Presence. This is to see God as our true Self that removes the knot of ignorance in the heart which is the false ego identification with the body and its activities as "me." When this false ego goes, all doubts are dispersed because all doubts are rooted in the doubter which is the false ego itself. So, when the doubter is seen as false, all doubts vanish. And similarly, the entire stock of karma also goes when the false idea of doership goes. All actions are then seen as an expression of the Divine Will, with no individual doer thereof. This results in freedom from any bondage of karmas while activities go on perfectly with total attention.

पार्थिवाद्दारुणो धूमस्तस्मादग्निस्त्रयीमयः ।
तमसस्तु रजस्तस्मात्सत्त्वं यद्ब्रह्मदर्शनम् ॥
भेजिरे मुनयोऽथाग्रे भगवन्तमधोक्षजम् ।
सत्त्वं विशुद्धं क्षेमाय कल्पन्ते येऽनु तानिह ॥ Bh 1.2.24-25

pārthivāddāruṇo dhūmastasmādagnistrayīmayaḥ
tamasastu rajastasmātsattvaṁ yadbrahmadarśanam
bhejire munayo'thāgre bhagavantamadhokṣhajam
sattvaṁ viśhuddhaṁ kṣhemāya kalpante ye'nu tāniha

Just as smoke is more active and thus superior to inert wood and superior to smoke is fire that is essential for Vedic sacrifices, even so *rajas* is superior to *tamas* and higher still is *sattva* that helps one realize Brahman. Of yore, sages adored the Supreme Transcendent Being who is pure *sattva* for the highest benefit and even now those who follow them attain blessedness.

First, a clear gradation of the three modes of material nature is described. Even though wood contains smoke and fire in a latent form, only when heat is applied, first smoke comes out and after a while, fire manifests out of the inert wood. Similarly, when the heat of penance is applied, the inert mode of dullness or laziness (*tamas*) is overcome with the mode of activity and passion (*rajas*). And when the mode of passion is refined by engaging toward dharmic activities, then it is overcome with the mode of purity and goodness (*sattva*) which enables realization of the Supreme Truth as Brahman, the all-pervading Infinite Being, described as transcendent to all the senses. All activities of the senses take place only due to the illumination of Pure Consciousness that is the essence of Brahman. The great sages of the yore fully dedicated themselves to realizing Him by ascending to the mode of purity and perceiving only the Supreme Being as the essence of all. This way shown by the sages is open to everyone at all times and all places as it only requires inner purification and clear perception of the Truth which is independent of time and space, ever available here and now.

वासुदेवपरा वेदा वासुदेवपरा मखा: ।
वासुदेवपरा योगा वासुदेवपरा: क्रिया: ॥
वासुदेवपरं ज्ञानं वासुदेवपरं तप: ।
वासुदेवपरो धर्मो वासुदेवपरा गति: ॥ Bh 1.2.28–29

vāsudeva parā vedā vāsudeva parā makhāḥ
vāsudeva parā yogā vāsudeva parāḥ kriyāḥ
vāsudeva paraṁ jñānaṁ vāsudeva paraṁ tapaḥ
vāsudeva paro dharmo vāsudeva parā gatiḥ

The all-pervading Supreme Being Vasudeva is the subject of all Vedas, the goal of all sacrifices, the object of all Yoga, the essence of all activities, the supreme wisdom, the highest austerity, the greatest virtue and the supreme abode.

Sūta Maharshi, after responding to the questions of the Rishis, by giving a summary of the entire wisdom of Bhāgavatam, the glory of listening to it that results in purification of the mind and leads to the realization of the Supreme Being, now culminates his response with two powerful verses. Vāsudeva means the One who is the son of Vasudeva in His personal aspect and also, He who is everything in His impersonal aspect. As Krishna mentions in the Gita, to realize that Vāsudeva pervades everywhere is the highest and rarest wisdom (*bahūnām janmanām ante jñānavān mām prapadyate / vāsudevaḥ sarvam iti sa mahātmā sudurlabhaḥ*—BG 7.19). Therefore, Sūta Maharshi invokes Vāsudeva as the only purpose of all seemingly diverse aspects of spiritual life—to realize the Supreme Being as the all-pervading Consciousness (Brahman) abiding within as the true Self (Paramatma) and descending out of His Grace in various forms (Bhagavan). The study of all scriptures is only to realize Vāsudeva, the Absolute. All sacrifices are only to deny the false ego and behold Vāsudeva within and without. The purpose of all Yoga is to remove the illusory separateness, seeing the union of everything in Vāsudeva. All austerities are only to purify the mind of the dust of ignorance about Vāsudeva. Therefore, true transcendental wisdom, the highest virtue and the greatest austerity is all to realize Vāsudeva. Thus, the supreme destination of all—not separated by time and space, but here and now—is Vāsudeva.

तया विलसितेष्वेषु गुणेषु गुणवानिव ।
अन्तःप्रविष्ट आभाति विज्ञानेन विजृम्भितः ॥
यथा ह्यवहितो वह्निर्दारुष्वेकः स्वयोनिषु ।
नानेव भाति विश्वात्मा भूतेषु च तथा पुमान् ॥ Bh 1.2.31-32

tayā vilasiteshveshu guṇeshu guṇavāniva
antaḥpravishṭa ābhāti vijñānena vijṛmbhitaḥ
yathā hyavahito vahnirdārushvekaḥ svayonihṣhu
nāneva bhāti viśhvātmā bhūteshu cha tathā pumān

Having entered into the three gunas that have been evolved by Maya, He appears as possessed of the gunas, while being essentially Pure Consciousness. Just as fire appears as many inhering in different logs of wood, so does the Self of the Universe appear as many, manifesting in different beings.

Having concluded that the Supreme Being Vāsudeva is the essence of all spiritual practices, Sūta Maharshi ends this discourse to the Rishis by stating that although He is transcendent to the material energy with its three gunas, it is from Him alone that this material energy comes forth to evolve this creation. Therefore, the material energy, which is also known as Maya, is both real and unreal at the same time. It is real because of its essence being one with the Supreme Being. And as the forms it assumes are constantly changing and impermanent, it is unreal. He remains thus both within and beyond this material universe. Every form that appears within this universe is only a modification of the same material energy, which is none other than the true Self of the universe alone as Pure Consciousness. Just as fire appears in various shapes and intensities when different logs of wood are burned and yet all fire is essentially the same, He appears in various forms as various beings and yet their essence is the same. It is the unitary material energy alone that animates all the senses, mind, sense objects and all the bodies. Hence, it is He alone who creates this universe, descends into the universe in various forms of life, protects all beings and dissolves them as Time.

जगृहे पौरुषं रूपं भगवान्महदादिभि: ।
सम्भूतं षोडशकलमादौ लोकसिसृक्षया ॥
एतन्नानावताराणां निधानं बीजमव्ययम् ।
यस्यांशांशेन सृज्यन्ते देवतिर्यङ्‌नरादय: ॥ Bh 1.3.1,5

jagṛhe pauruṣaṁ rūpaṁ bhagavānmahadādibhiḥ
sambhūtaṁ ṣhoḍaśhakalamādau lokasisṛkṣhayā
etannānāvatārāṇāṁ nidhānaṁ bījamavyayam
yasyāṁśhāṁśhena sṛjyante devatiryaṅNaradayaḥ

In the beginning, with the intent of evolving the universe, the Lord assumed the form of the Primal Being consisting of sixteen principles along with Cosmic Intelligence. This form of the Lord is the imperishable seed of the various Avatars as well as the source of all humans and other life forms.

The Primal Being called Purusha is the Cosmic form made of sixteen principles which are the five elements of space, air, fire, water and soil, the five senses of cognition, the five senses of action and the mind. All of these come forth from the Cosmic Intelligence called *mahat* which is the universal order reflected through the perfect laws of physics observable in matter. The creative energy known as Brahma comes forth from the Primal Being. The whole universe is thus seen as the body of the One Supreme Being with infinite heads, eyes, ears and limbs. From the Supreme Being who has evolved the whole Universe as His body, also come forth various Avatars who are either partial or full manifestations of the Lord. All beings from humans to various life forms come forth from the same Source. Having described the Source of all Avatars, now Sūta Maharshi will give an account of all the key Avatars.

अवतारा ह्यसङ्ख्येया हरे: सत्त्वनिधेर्द्विजा: ।
यथाविदासिन: कुल्या: सरस: स्यु: सहस्रश: ॥ Bh 1.3.26

avatārā hyasaṅkhyeyā hareḥ sattvanidherdvijāḥ
yathāvidāsinaḥ kulyāḥ sarasaḥ syuḥ sahasraśhaḥ

Avatars of the Lord who is the storehouse of purity are countless indeed like rivulets flowing from an inexhaustible lake.

Sūta Maharshi gives an account of the various Avatars of the Lord in a series of verses. Each of these Avatars and their various activities, as well as the symbolism behind them, is covered in the subsequent cantos of Bhāgavatam in detail. Here are all the Avatars in the order listed by Sūta in the first canto:

1. The four young Kumaras (Sanaka, Sanātana, Sanandana, Sanatkumāra)
2. The Divine Boar, Varāha
3. The celestial sage Nārada
4. The sages Nara and Nārāyana
5. Kapila who taught Sānkhya
6. The great sage Dattātreya
7. Yajna as the embodiment of sacrifice
8. Rshabha who is the model of renunciation
9. King Prthu after whom earth is called Prthvi
10. The Divine Fish, Matsya, who guided the ark of Manu

11. The Divine Tortoise, Kurma
12. Dhanwantari, the source of all medicine and healing
13. Mohini, the most attractive feminine form to bewilder the demons
14. Narasimha who protected dear Prahlāda
15. Vāmana who became Trivikrama to bestow Grace on Bali
16. Parashurāma to destroy all evil kings
17. Vyāsa to organize the Vedas
18. Sri Rāma who did unimaginable feats
19, 20. Balarāma and Krishna to relieve the burden of earth
21. Buddha to correct those blindly attached to rituals
22. Kalki to re-establish order at the end of Kali Yuga

As seen above, the order is much larger than the standard ten Avatars and is still not exhaustive and hence Sūta concludes by stating that the number of Avatars are in fact countless like rivulets flowing from an inexhaustible lake.

एतद्रूपं भगवतो ह्यरूपस्य चिदात्मनः ।
मायागुणैर्विरचितं महदादिभिरात्मनि ॥ Bh 1.3.30

etad rūpaṁ bhagavato hyarūpasya chidātmanaḥ
māyāguṇairvirachitaṁ mahadādibhirātmani

The manifest Cosmic form of the Supreme Being, who is beyond all forms and of the essence of Pure Consciousness, evolved out of His Maya through the principle of Cosmic Intelligence (mahat) that is superimposed on Him.

Just as clouds appear in the sky and dust particles are found in air, it is said that the Universe appears on the substrate of Pure Consciousness. The clouds that appear and disappear do not affect the sky just as the dust particles that are carried by the air do not affect the air itself. Similarly, the various forms of the universe which are projected by the material energy made of Cosmic Intelligence (*mahat*) does not affect the substrate of Pure Consciousness which is the essence of the Supreme Being. When one identifies with one's material form and the various other forms as separate beings due to ignorance, then it results in egoic attachment and resultant suffering. When one sees clearly that all the forms are simply an expression of the unitary material energy of the Supreme Being, then one is not deluded by the multitude of forms. This is the true dawn of wisdom.

इदं भागवतं नाम पुराणं ब्रह्मसम्मितम् ।
उत्तमश्लोकचरितं चकार भगवानृषिः ।।
निःश्रेयसाय लोकस्य धन्यं स्वस्त्ययनं महत् ।
तदिदं ग्राह्यामास सुतमात्मवतां वरम् ।। Bh 1.3.40-41

idaṁ bhāgavataṁ nāma purāṇaṁ brahmasammitam
uttamaśhlokacharitaṁ chakāra bhagavān ṛṣiḥ
niḥśhreyasāya lokasya dhanyaṁ svastyayanaṁ mahat
tadidaṁ grāhayāmāsa sūtamātmavatāṁ varam

The divine sage Vyasa composed this great Bhāgavatam which is the essence of all Vedas and details the activities of the Supreme Being of excellent glory. He taught this blessed and great scripture to his son Shuka Brahmam, the foremost among the Self-realized, for the highest good of humanity.

Sūta Maharshi glorifies the greatness of Bhāgavatam which is considered as an Avatar in the sound form of Krishna Himself. It is the cream extracted from all the Vedas and taught by Vyasa to his son, the great Shuka Brahmam. Sūta Maharshi further adds that when Shuka Brahmam taught this great Purana to Parikshit on the banks of Ganga, there assembled a congregation of sages, and he was also one among them and learned it by heart through the grace of Shuka Brahmam. The Bhāgavatam details the essence of Self-knowledge by revealing that the conscious spark found in each being as the *jiva* (individualized consciousness) is none other than Bhagavan, the Universal Consciousness, the essence of the Supreme Being. This Self-knowledge cannot be gained by dialectical skills but only through an attitude of humility and loving devotion. He concludes that anyone who listens to Bhāgavatam is very lucky indeed as it naturally creates unconditional love for the Supreme Being and for all beings in the Universe.

दृष्ट्वानुयान्तमृषिमात्मजमप्यनग्रं देव्यो ह्रिया परिदधुर्न सुतस्य चित्रम् ।
तद्वीक्ष्य पृच्छति मुनौ जगदुस्तवास्ति स्त्रीपुम्भिदा न तु सुतस्य विविक्तदृषे: ॥ Bh 1.4.5

dṛṣhtvānuyāntamṛṣhimātmajamapyanagnaṁ devyo hriyā
paridadhurna sūtasya chitram
tadvīkṣhya pṛchchhati munau jagadustavāsti strīpumbhidā na tu
sūtasya viviktadṛṣhteḥ

Vyasa followed his son Shuka Brahmam and went past a group of ladies bathing in a lake. They covered

themselves out of modesty when Vyasa walked by, though they didn't when Shuka Brahmam walked by earlier. Noticing the strange behavior, the sage asked the reason and the lady's said Vyasa was still alive to gender differences while the son Shuka Brahmam had no difference in his vision.

After listening to the summary of Bhāgavatam narrated by Sūta Maharshi, the Rishis headed by Shaunaka are curious as to how Shuka Brahmam came to learn Bhāgavatam from Vyasa and narrate the same to Parikshit. In the process, Shuka Brahmam is glorified as the great Yogi who views all alike with no diversity in his mind, exclusively seeing God everywhere. Shuka Brahmam left home while very young and set out as a recluse. On the way, a few ladies who were bathing in a lake saw Shuka Brahmam walk by, and could perceive his total child-like purity, so they never bothered to cover themselves. Whereas his father Vyasa, though a great sage himself, went behind him with a slight trace of attachment toward his son and when he walked past the lake, the ladies covered themselves. Further it is also said that Shuka Brahmam would not stay at any one place for too long but just kept moving, happy and content with whatever came his way. Therefore, the sages headed by Shaunaka are curious as to how such a supremely renounced Shuka Brahmam, who revels in his own being, happened to narrate the entire Bhāgavatam.

शिवाय लोकस्य भवाय भूतये य उत्तमश्लोकपरायणा जना: ।
जीवन्ति नात्मार्थमसौ पराश्रयं मुमोच निर्विद्य कुत: कलेवरम् ।।
Bh 1.4.12

śivāya lokasya bhavāya bhūtaye ya uttamaśhlokaparāyaṇā janāḥ jīvanti nātmārthamasau parāśhrayaṁ mumocha nirvidya kutaḥ kalevaram

Those who are surrendered to the Supreme Being of excellent fame live only for the welfare, auspiciousness and prosperity of the world and not for their own sake. Parikshit being such a devotee and a support for others, why did he cast off his body?

The one who is devoid of the sense of "me" and "mine" is free of narrow self-interest and his actions naturally promote auspiciousness and welfare for all. Parikshit was such a person, and his very presence was conducive for the welfare of the world. He was the undisputed emperor and set the perfect example of how one can discharge the greatest responsibilities in the world while being a householder and fully devoted to the Supreme Being. Therefore, the Rishis express their doubt as to why he would cast off his body by fasting unto death by the river Ganga while listening to Bhāgavatam from Shuka Brahmam. The previous question on how Shuka Brahmam came to narrate Bhāgavatam and this question on how Parikshit came to listen to Bhāgavatam will now be answered in detail by Sūta Maharshi for the rest of the first skandha, thus providing the context for the main dialogue of Bhāgavatam that begins with the second skandha.

किं वा भागवता धर्मा न प्रायेण निरूपिताः ।
प्रियाः परमहंसानां त एव ह्यच्युतप्रियाः ॥ Bh 1.4.31

kiṁ vā bhāgavatā dharmā na prāyeṇa nirūpitāḥ
priyāḥ paramahaṁsānāṁ ta eva hyacyutapriyāḥ

Perhaps I am not satisfied because I have not fully expounded on the virtues of loving devotion and surrender to the Supreme Being, which is dear to the great sages and the Infallible Lord.

Sūta Maharshi narrates the story of how Vyasa came to compose Bhāgavatam. One day, after taking an early morning bath in the sacred river Saraswati, he sat in contemplation near the river. He had already organized the Vedas into four portions and taught it to four different sages for preservation through their lineages, written the great Mahabharata and the Brahma Sutras, which is a collection of aphorisms on the highest essence of Vedanta and composed many Puranas. Still, he felt a lacuna in him, and he was inquiring into the reason for it. The realization dawned upon him that none of the works he had composed showed the most direct way of loving surrender to the all-pervading Supreme Being. Loving devotion and surrender alone is dear to the sages endowed with the highest degree of wisdom known as *paramahamsa* (divine swans) as well as to Krishna Himself who is known as Achyuta or the Infallible.

भवतानुदितप्रायं यशो भगवतोऽमलम् ।
येनैवासौ न तुष्येत मन्ये तद्दर्शनं खिलम् ॥
यथा धर्मादयश्चार्था मुनिवर्यानुकीर्तिता: ।
न तथा वासुदेवस्य महिमा ह्यनुवर्णित: ॥ Bh 1.5.8-9

bhavatānuditaprāyaṁ yaśho bhagavato'malam
yenaivāsau na tuṣhyeta manye taddarśhanaṁ khilam
yathā dharmādayaśhchārthā munivaryānukīrtitāḥ
na tathā vāsudevasya mahimā hyanuvarṇitaḥ

You have failed to adequately sing the stainless glory of the Lord. That wisdom which does not speak of the Supreme Being is deficient. You have not fully described the glory of the all-pervading Lord as you have done with other subjects such as dharma.

As Vyasa was contemplating upon his dissatisfaction, the great sage Narada came there, and Vyasa received him with honor. Narada then inquired of Vyasa's wellbeing and he revealed his sense of lacuna in his humongous body of work. Narada promptly responded by pointing out that the glorification of the all-pervading Supreme Being Vasudeva was missing in his work. Vyasa had written extensively about dharma or righteous living and also about moksha or liberation. But the one who is free of the false sense of ego is beyond both righteousness and liberation, only perceiving the Supreme Being as the essence of the whole universe and glorifying Him alone through thought, word and action. Thus, Narada exhorted Vyasa to write about such a state of loving devotion which is the essence of Bhāgavatam.

तद्वाग्विसर्गो जनताघविप्लवो यस्मिन् प्रतिश्लोकमबद्धवत्यपि ।
नामान्यनन्तस्य यशोऽङ्कितानि यत् शृण्वन्ति गायन्ति गृणन्ति
साधव: ॥ Bh 1.5.11

tadvāgvisargo janatāghaviplavo yasmin pratiśhlokam abaddhavatyapi
nāmānyanantasya yaśho'ṅkitāni yat śhṛṇvanti gāyanti gṛṇanti sādhavaḥ

Speech, though faulty in diction, if it glorifies the Infinite Lord, it wipes out all impurities. Thus, the saintly beings love to hear, sing and repeat such compositions.

Narada now narrates to Vyasa the importance of content over style and expression. He says that if one can speak with great figurative expressions in a very refined and stylistic language on mundane topics unrelated to the Absolute Truth, then such speech is found entertaining only by men of low intelligence just like crows that wallow on dirty leavings. Whereas speech that is focused on the highest wisdom and coming straight from the heart and not a mere intellectual discourse, gives true delight to the sages and the devotees, just as swans living in the pure Manasarovar lake consume only the purest food. Thus, Narada impresses upon the importance of the purity of the content in speech rather than the ability to impress an audience with rhetorical flourishes.

नैष्कर्म्यमप्यच्युतभाववर्जितं न शोभते ज्ञानमलं निरञ्जनम् ।
कुतः पुनः शश्वदभद्रमीश्वरे न चार्पितं कर्म यदप्यकारणम् ॥
Bh 1.5.12

naiṣkarmyamapyacyutabhāvavarjitaṁ na śobhate jñānamalaṁ nirañjanam
kutaḥ punaḥ śhaśhvadabhadramīśhvare na chārpitaṁ karma yadapyakāraṇam

Wisdom that may be free of any blemish, or action without any attachment does not adorn one with Truth if it is devoid of heartfelt loving devotion, what to speak then of action with desire that only causes sorrow.

Normally it is said that there are two ways of realizing the Truth—through wisdom (jnana yoga) or action without any attachment (karma yoga). In the third chapter of Gita, Krishna mentions the two ways as suited for those drawn to contemplation, and those drawn to action respectively. However, Narada here adds that both those ways have to be based on the foundation of heartfelt loving devotion. True wisdom flowers only when one sees that everything is an expression of the divine energy including one's own body and mind and abides free of the false sense of ego. True karma yoga flowers only when one realizes that every action gets the results ordained by the divine energy and is not under the control of the apparent doer. Thus, both require a recognition of the all-pervading divine energy, not through intellectual understanding but by heartfelt surrender. In this way, Narada teaches that the essential prerequisite for both jnana and karma yoga is bhakti or unconditional love alone.

ततोऽन्यथा किञ्चन यद्विवक्षतः पृथग्दृशस्तत्कृतरूपनामभिः ।
न कर्हिचित्क्वापि च दुःस्थिता मतिर्लभेत वाताहतनौरिवास्पदम् ॥
Bh 1.5.14

tato'nyathā kiñchana yadvivakṣhataḥ
pṛthagdṛśhastatkṛtarūpanāmabhiḥ
na karhichitkvāpi cha duḥsthitā matirlabheta
vātāhatanaurivāspadam

The one who talks about mundane topics falls into the trap of seeing separation through names and forms and his mind finds no rest just as a boat caught in a strong wind.

Narada exhorts Vyasa, who is already endowed with sacred wisdom and a steadfast resolve, to focus only on writing about the teachings and pastimes of the Supreme Being, that can bring liberation to the sincere listener. He says here that instead, if one focuses on mundane topics about people and events, then one gets caught in the illusion of diversity and sees manifold names and forms as separate entities rather than seeing everyone and everything as an expression of the one divine energy. Narada gently points to Vyasa that even reading the great epic Mahabharata authored by Vyasa that focused primarily on dharma could result in men being drawn to the sense of separate ego that adheres to prescriptions and injunctions. Therefore, the highest wisdom needs to be pointed out by Vyasa, which is the essence of Bhāgavatam that everyone is nothing other than a spark of the divine energy of the Supreme Being.

इदं हि विश्वं भगवानिवेतरो यतो जगत्स्थाननिरोधसम्भवाः ।
तद्धि स्वयं वेद भवांस्तथापि ते प्रादेशमात्रं भवतः प्रदर्शितम् ॥
Bh 1.5.20

idaṁ hi viśhvaṁ bhagavānivetaro yato
jagatsthānanirodhasambhavāḥ
taddhi svayaṁ veda bhavāṁstathāpi te prādeśhamātraṁ
bhavataḥ pradarśhitam

This universe is none other than the Supreme Being, who is responsible for its creation, sustenance and dissolution. Oh Vyasa, I am only pointing out to you what you know by yourself.

After stating that one's speech and compositions ought to focus on the highest Truth which alone is conducive to sweetness and not any mundane topics, Narada now starts instructing on the essence of Bhāgavatam. Vyasa, being a self-realized sage, only needs a brief pointer to bring out what is already within him, so Narada simply states that the entire universe is none other than the Supreme Being. As long as we seek God as an entity separate from the Universe either in time and space (such as heaven or paradise) or in a particular state (such as enlightenment), we are creating a duality which blinds us to the truth that God is omnipresent here and now as the essence of the entire universe. As Krishna teaches in the Gita, the one who sees everything as God (*vāsudeva sarvamiti*) is the one truly situated in wisdom. That's exactly what Narada points to Vyasa in this beautiful verse by tersely stating that "this very universe is Bhagavan" (*idaṁ hi viśhvaṁ bhagavān*). Internalizing these four words puts an end to all seeking and leaves one in the simple state of total acceptance and love of what is.

इदं हि पुंसस्तपसः श्रुतस्य वा स्विष्टस्य सूक्तस्य च बुद्धिदत्तयोः ।
अविच्युतोऽर्थः कविभिर्निरूपितो यदुत्तमश्लोकगुणानुवर्णनम् ॥
Bh 1.5.22

idaṁ hi puṁsastapasaḥ śhrutasya vā sviṣṭasya sūktasya cha
buddhidattayoḥ
avichyuto'rthaḥ kavibhirnirūpito
yaduttamaśhlokaguṇānuvarṇanam

The wise have declared the abiding purpose of all austerities, scriptural knowledge, sacrifices, chanting,

clarity of intellect and charitable activities to be the realization of the Supreme Being.

Narada reminds Vyasa that he is already a ray of the Supreme Being as is every single atom of the universe. Furthermore, the purpose of Vyasa's very appearance is to share the highest wisdom of the all-pervading Absolute. Narada then says that Vyasa has thus far described all the various spiritual practices in the greatest detail. By organizing and teaching the Vedas, by writing the aphorisms of Brahma Sutras, by authoring Mahabharat etc. Vyasa has detailed the various austerities, limits of scriptural knowledge, all kinds of Vedic sacrifices, mantras to be chanted and the correct intonation to chant them with, discerning wisdom that gives clarity to the intellect and various kinds of charitable activities. Narada now tells Vyasa that he has one last work remaining which is to make clear that the purpose of all spiritual practices has only one end—the realization of the Supreme Being as the only Truth there is. And that is the ultimate purpose to actualize by authoring Bhāgavatam, the crown jewel of all his works.

तस्मिंस्तदा लब्धरुचेर्महामते प्रियश्रवस्यस्खलिता मतिर्मम ।
ययाहमेतत्सदसत्स्वमायया पश्ये मयि ब्रह्मणि कल्पितं परे ॥
Bh 1.5.27

tasmiṁstadā labdharuchermahāmate priyaśhravasyaskhalitā matirmama
yayāhametatsadasatsvamāyayā paśhye mayi brahmaṇi kalpitaṁ pare

When I developed an affinity for the Supreme Being, my mind got firmly established in Him, thus perceiving clearly that the whole world of gross and subtle forms are only appearing in the Absolute through Maya.

Now Narada recounts his back story of how he became realized through association with great sages. He was living as the child of a maid servant in a village where a group of sages stopped for the rainy season. Narada, even as a young boy, was not interested in the normal childish activities but was drawn to the sages and took to serving them daily with their chores. Pleased with the boy's service, the sages blessed him with the Grace of the highest wisdom through discourses on the teachings and pastimes of Krishna. By listening to them with rapt attention, Narada says that he developed an affinity and perceived the truth that the entire universe is only a projection of divine energy. Thus, Narada brings out the greatness of Satsang, through which alone and not through any other practices, he was able to gain the highest realization.

ज्ञानं गुह्यतमं यत्तत्साक्षाद्भगवतोदितम् ।
अन्ववोचन् गमिष्यन्तः कृपया दीनवत्सलाः ॥ Bh 1.5.30

jñānaṁ guhyatamaṁ yattatsākṣhādbhagavatoditam
anvavochan gamiṣhyantaḥ kṛpayā dīnavatsalāḥ

The sages, who are most compassionate to the afflicted, graciously impart the most esoteric wisdom that has been directly revealed by the Supreme Being.

Narada was blessed with the association of the great sages whom he served as a young child when they stayed in his village for the rainy season. The sages are full of compassion for everyone and especially those who are sincere, humble and afflicted in any way. Narada, being a poor child of a maid servant and full of faith in the sages, was therefore fully able to partake of the grace of the sages. They imparted to him the most esoteric wisdom that awakens the Presence of the Supreme Being in one's heart. This wisdom is the direct teaching that the individual self that identifies with the body as "me" is the false ego and in truth, everything is an expression of the one undivided energy. All the animate beings and inanimate objects, all capacities and abilities, all perceptions and activities are only an expression of the same energy of the Supreme Being that operates from the subatomic to the super galactic realms. Narada was taught this supreme wisdom that naturally engenders unconditional love and surrender to the Supreme Being and thereby he realized the glory of Vasudeva (the all-pervading Lord).

नमो भगवते तुभ्यं वासुदेवाय धीमहि ।
प्रद्युम्नायानिरुद्धाय नमः सङ्कर्षणाय च ॥ Bh 1.5.37

namo bhagavate tubhyaṁ vāsudevaya dhīmahi
pradyumnāyāniruddhāya namaḥ saṅkarṣhaṇāya cha

Obeisance to You, O Vasudeva, we meditate upon You. Obeisance also to Pradyumna, Aniruddha and Sankarshana.

This is a simple and beautiful prayer invoking what is known as the four aspects (*chatur vyuha*) of the Supreme Being and comes many times in Bhāgavatam. Vasudeva is the primary all-pervading Being who descends as the complete Avatar of Krishna, the son of Vasudeva. Sankarshana is the plenary expansion of the Absolute representing the principle of Grace (*guru tattva*), who descends as Balaram, the brother of Krishna. Pradyumna and Aniruddha are the partial expansions representing the mind and the ego, who descend as Krishna's son and grandson respectively. The same four descended as the divine brothers Ram, Lakshman, Bharat and Shatrughna respectively. The four aspects indicate that nothing is apart from the Supreme, including the ego that creates the attachment of "me" and "mine." Therefore, one cannot overcome the ego by any effort or struggle but by simply recognizing it as an expression of the divine energy and such a recognition naturally leads to the falling away of the ego on its own.

तदा तदहमीशस्य भक्तानां शमभीप्सतः ।
अनुग्रहं मन्यमानः प्रातिष्ठं दिशमुत्तराम् ॥ Bh 1.6.10

tadā tadahamīshasya bhaktānāṁ shamabhīpsataḥ
anugrahaṁ manyamānaḥ prātiṣṭhaṁ dishamuttarām

I took the calamity as the Grace of the Lord who always wishes the best for His devotees and set out in a northerly direction.

Narada continues his story upon being asked by Vyasa as to what happened after the sages departed. Narada continued to stay in the village with his mother, who worked as a servant-maid and struggled to make ends meet. One night as she left the house to milk a cow, she got bitten by a snake and died suddenly. Narada, being already situated in the wisdom received from the sages that everything happens as ordained by the Supreme like puppets in the hands of puppeteer, accepted this calamity of losing his only caretaker as Grace. This is the true mark of wisdom that is not simply an intellectual abstraction but shines as clarity when challenges arise. Far from being grief-stricken or feeling helpless, Narada simply took it as a benediction to leave the village, being now free of all worldly responsibilities.

नामान्यनन्तस्य हतत्रपः पठन् गुह्यानि भद्राणि कृतानि च स्मरन् ।
गां पर्यटंस्तुष्टमना गतस्पृहः कालं प्रतीक्षन् विमदो विमत्सरः ।।
Bh 1.6.27

nāmānyanantasya hatatrapaḥ paṭhan guhyāni bhadrāṇi kṛtāni cha smaran
gāṁ paryaṭaṁstuṣhṭamanā gatuspṛhaḥ kālaṁ pratīkṣhan vimado vimatsaraḥ

Shaking off all self-conscious shyness, I started chanting the most auspicious names and singing the most mysterious pastimes of the Infinite Being. Rid of all cravings, free from vanity and jealousy, and content at heart, I roam about around the globe.

After Narada left his village, he walked through many villages, towns and forests, lakes and mountains, seeing the beauty of nature as an expression of divine energy. Then he found a solitary place to meditate and got fully settled in God-realization. After that, he simply moved around singing the glories of the Infinite Lord, free of all symptoms of the egoic separative identity. The symptoms of the separate "me" are rooted in being self-conscious which is the identification with the body and the mind as a fixed entity and imagining others to be fixed entities. In this false sense of separation between me and others rises shyness, vanity, jealousy and all other sources of strife and suffering. Narada, being free of this separative structure of "me," was naturally free of all egoic symptoms, thus roamed the globe freely and spread auspiciousness wherever he went.

यमादिभिर्योगपथैः कामलोभहतो मुहुः ।
मुकुन्दसेवया यद्त्तथात्माद्धा न शाम्यति ॥ Bh 1.6.36

yamādibhiryogapathaiḥ kāmalobhahato muhuḥ
mukundasevayā yadvat tathātmāddhā na śāmyati

A heart smitten with lust and greed does not attain peace so surely by recourse to practices of Yoga, controlling the mind etc. as through total surrender to Mukunda, the Supreme bestower of liberation.

All negative qualities such as lust and greed are fundamentally rooted in the sense of false separation between me and others. Most spiritual practices that concede this false assumption of a separative egoic structure and then prescribe various methods and techniques to control the mind, the senses etc. are not removing the root problem. They only make the separative structure a more pleasant experience at best but the seed of suffering remains untouched. Therefore, Narada says it is through total surrender to the all-pervading Being as the only reality that one gets freed of this separative structure. The direct realization that everyone and everything including the seeker of liberation is only an expression of the Divine removes the desire to even attain liberation as a future goal, as all that is present here and now is only the Divine. There is nobody other than the Infinite Being, to even have the desire for liberation. This recognition is true liberation (*mukti*) that is realized by the Grace of the Infinite Lord, hence called Mukunda (the one who bestows *mukti*).

यया सम्मोहितो जीव आत्मानं त्रिगुणात्मकम् ।
परोऽपि मनुतेऽनर्थं तत्कृतं चाभिपद्यते ॥
अनर्थोपशमं साक्षाद्भक्तियोगमधोक्षजे ।
लोकस्याजानतो विद्वांश्चक्रे सात्वतसंहिताम् ॥ Bh 1.7.5-6

yayā sammohito jīva ātmānaṁ triguṇātmakam
paro'pi manute'nartham tatkṛtaṁ chābhipadyate
anarthopaśhamaṁ sākṣhādbhaktiyogamadhokṣhaje
lokasyājānato vidvāṁśhchakre sātvatasaṁhitām

Deluded by Maya, the apparent individual identifies with the three gunas that make up the body/mind and suffers due to this identification. Knowing that total surrender unto the Supreme Being who is beyond all sense perceptions is the direct means to remove this suffering, the sage Vyasa composed Bhāgavatam for the benefit of everyone.

After Narada instructed Vyasa to compose Bhāgavatam by teaching the essence of complete surrender, he took leave and went his way singing the glories of the Lord as always. Then Vyasa sat down in his Ashram by the western bank of the Saraswati River and collecting his mind, started to compose the great epic of Bhāgavatam. The entire purpose of Bhāgavatam is laid out in these two verses by a description of the core problem of all conditioned beings which is the false sense of self or "me" that branches into so many sufferings and the direct way out of it through total surrender. This surrender is the recognition that all that exists is only the Absolute who takes infinite forms and brings about the ending of the false "me" that never began in reality. Therefore, it is not to surrender one's possessions or desires, but the very notion that there is a separate self who has possessions or desires. Such total surrender is non-different from the highest non-dual wisdom that God alone is. This is the entire essence of Bhāgavatam.

आत्मारामाश्च मुनयो निर्ग्रन्था अप्युरुक्रमे ।
कुर्वन्त्यहैतुकीं भक्तिमित्थम्भूतगुणो हरि: ॥ Bh 1.7.10

ātmārāmāśhcha munayo nirgranthā apyurukrame
kurvantyahaitukīṁ bhaktimitthambhūtaguṇo hariḥ

Even sages whose knot of ignorance has been cut asunder and who delight only in Pure Being are always in causeless loving devotion to the Supreme.

After Vyasa composed the entire Bhāgavatam, he taught this voluminous work to his son Shuka, the totally realized boy sage, who then narrated it to Parikshit. When this was related by Sūta Maharshi to Shaunaka, Shaunaka expresses the doubt as to why a great sage like Shuka free of any attachment whatsoever would master a voluminous work such as Bhāgavatam. In response, Sūta says that even great sages whose knot of ignorance which is the false separation as a fixed "me" has been removed are always in motiveless loving devotion to the Supreme. Normally devotion has a motive (*hetu*) due to the gunas that the apparent individual identifies with. Ignorance (*tamas*) leads to dark motives, passion (*rajas*) leads to wealth or pleasure motives, and goodness (*sattva*) leads to motives of knowledge or liberation. But the one who is not identified with the body/mind as "me" such as Shuka is not associated with any gunas and therefore has no motives. Yet such a sage has unconditional, motiveless love (*ahaituki bhakti*) of the Supreme as simply the essence of all that is. The Supreme is referred to in this verse as Hari, a most lovely name that means "One who takes away the ego."

पाहि पाहि महायोगिन् देवदेव जगत्पते ।
नान्यं त्वदभयं पश्ये यत्र मृत्युः परस्परम् ।। Bh 1.8.9

pāhi pāhi mahāyogin devadeva jagatpate
nānyaṁ tvadabhayaṁ paśhye yatra mṛtyuḥ parasparam

Protect me, O greatest Yogi. Save me, O Supreme Lord of the Universe. I see no protection here in this world where everyone is death personified to each other.

The actual dialogue of Bhāgavatam between the narrator Shuka Brahmam and the listener Parikshit begins only with the second skandha. This entire first skandha sets up the context for the great dialogue between Shuka Brahmam and Parikshit. The story of Parikshit begins with the end of the Mahabharat war when almost everyone is killed on both sides and Pandavas have won. Ashwatthama, one of the few surviving warriors, who fought alongside the Kauravas decides to take revenge by killing all the descendants of Pandavas. First, he kills all their surviving sons while they are asleep in the camp. For this heinous act, he is caught by Arjuna and about to be killed but let go after being forgiven by the compassionate Draupadi as Ashwattama is the son of their teacher Drona. Being thus freed, Ashwattama still harbors revenge and now decides to kill the last descendent Parikshit who is still in the womb of Uttara. Parikshit is the grandson of Arjuna and the son of the already slain Abhimanyu. When Uttara is attacked by a fire missile launched by Ashwattama, she comes to Krishna for protection with this prayer. What is most significant about the prayer is her statement that everyone is death personified to each other, except the Supreme Being Krishna. Because everyone is identified with the false ego as "me" to the body/mind, they are constantly afraid of death. Only the Pure Being who eternally exists as the source and the ground of all is the true refuge. Thus, Uttara in her moment of great peril reveals her wisdom and surrender and hence she turns not to the Pandavas who are the greatest warriors but only to Krishna. Accordingly, Krishna protects Parikshit in Uttara's womb from the missile sent by Ashwatthama.

Kunti's Prayers

After Parikshit is thus saved by Krishna, Kunti is deeply moved by the ever-present Grace of Krishna and offers a very moving set of prayers to Him with a radically different approach toward the attitude of suffering.

Kunti is the mother of the five Pandavas who have gone through untold suffering while living in accordance with the right dharma and are ever devoted to their friend, philosopher and guide—Krishna. She has seen her husband die prematurely, then her five sons attempted to be killed by their envious Kaurava cousins by poison, fire and many other wicked means, their wife humiliated and their kingdom stolen. And each time, Krishna came to their rescue and removed their suffering by his presence, counsel and grace.

Then there was the Mahabharat war when almost everyone got killed on both sides and Pandavas won with Krishna's guidance and instructions to Arjuna through the immortal teaching of Bhagavad Gita that removed his confusion. After the war ended, Ashwatthama, one of the few surviving warriors, decided to take revenge by killing all the descendants of Pandavas. First, he killed the sons of Pandavas while they were asleep and later attempted to kill Parikshit in Uttara's womb and was saved by Krishna.

Kunti, having witnessed every single suffering and Krishna coming to their aid each time, upon this last act of Grace by Krishna in saving Parikshit, pours her heart out in the form of beautiful prayers expressing the most sublime love for the Divine.

The oft-quoted and most significant among Kunti's prayers is her appeal to Krishna to give them suffering at each step so her mind turns inward in a mood of total surrender to Krishna who manifests Himself to remove their suffering:

Suffering is an inevitable part of the human experience. It is an inescapable aspect of life in the physical realm that comes in three ways primarily—caused by one's own body and mind, by other people and by acts of nature. It is often viewed as something to be avoided and yet it is the greatest catalyst for spiritual awakening. Thus, Kunti instructs through her prayers on the right way to view suffering.

Like a sharp whack that wakes us from a dangerous slumber, suffering jolts us out of our complacency and forces us to confront the impermanent nature of existence. In this light, suffering becomes a form of grace, guiding us towards self-realization and freedom from identification with the ever-changing phenomena of body and mind.

As we deepen our understanding, we begin to see the world differently. We recognize the miraculous intelligence that permeates all of creation—from the intricate workings of our bodies to the long and complex cycles of nature. We come to understand that both joy and sorrow, birth and death, are part of a grand cosmic dance.

By embracing suffering as a teacher and viewing life as a divine play, we can approach our journey with light and love. We learn to take each moment as it comes, neither struggling against nor clinging to our experiences. In this way, suffering becomes not just bearable, but truly transformative—a bridge that leads us from our limited human perspective to the boundless expanse of our divine nature.

Hence Kunti, with great wisdom born out of experience, expresses a most profound truth in her prayers by not asking for any favor except suffering itself. It is through suffering at each step that she has realized the Truth of Being as Krishna to bestow the Grace of wisdom and peace.

Here are all the verses of the beautiful prayers of Kunti with a simple versified translation:

नमस्ये पुरुषं त्वाद्यमीश्वरं प्रकृतेः परम् ।
अलक्ष्यं सर्वभूतानामन्तर्बहिरवस्थितम् ॥ Bh 1.8.18

namasye purusham tvādyam īshvaram prakṛteh param
alakshyam sarvabhūtānāmantarbahiravasthitam

I offer my obeisances to You, the Primordial Being Transcending all of material nature

Abiding within all living entities and without
Invisible and incomprehensible

मायाजवनिकाच्छन्नमज्ञाधोक्षजमव्ययम् ।
न लक्ष्यसे मूढदृशा नटो नाट्यधरो यथा ॥ Bh 1.8.19

māyājavanikāchchhannamajñādhokṣhajamavyayam
na lakṣhyase mūḍhadṛśhā naṭo nāṭyadharo yathā

Veiled by the curtain of Maya
Beyond sense perceptions and Imperishable
Unrecognized even while seen by the ignorant
Like an actor playing a part in disguise

तथा परमहंसानां मुनीनाममलात्मनाम् ।
भक्तियोगविधानार्थं कथं पश्येम हि स्त्रिय: ॥ Bh 1.8.20

tathā paramahaṁsānāṁ munīnāmamalātmanām
bhaktiyogavidhānārthaṁ kathaṁ paśhyema hi striyaḥ

You descend to engender loving devotion
Even in the great sages of wisdom
Abiding in stillness with a pure mind
What to speak of women like us

कृष्णाय वासुदेवाय देवकीनन्दनाय च ।
नन्दगोपकुमाराय गोविन्दाय नमो नम: ॥ Bh 1.8.21

kṛṣhṇāya vāsudevaya devakīnandanāya cha
nandagopakumārāya govindāya namo namaḥ

Obeisances to You, O Krishna, O Govinda
All-pervading Vāsudeva
Delight of Mother Devaki
Foster Son of the cowherd chief Nanda

नम: पङ्कजनाभाय नम: पङ्कजमालिने ।
नम: पङ्कजनेत्राय नमस्ते पङ्कजाङ्घ्रये ॥ Bh 1.8.22

namaḥ paṅkajanābhāya namaḥ paṅkajamāline
namaḥ paṅkajanetrāya namaste paṅkajāṅghraye

Obeisance to You whose navel is adorned with a lotus
Obeisance to You who wears a garland of lotus
Obeisance to You whose eyes are like lotus
Obeisance to You whose feet are like lotus

यथा हृषीकेश खलेन देवकी कंसेन रुद्धातिचिरं शुचार्पिता ।
विमोचिताहं च सहात्मजा विभो त्वयैव नाथेन मुहुर्विपद्गणात् ॥
Bh 1.8.23

yathā hṛṣhīkeśha khalena devakī kaṁsena ruddhātichiraṁ
śhuchārpitā
vimochitāhaṁ cha sahātmajā vibho tvayaiva nāthena
muhurvipadgaṇāt

O Hrishikesh, Lord of the senses
As You liberated Your Mother Devaki
Imprisoned by Kamsa for long, overcome by grief
You repeatedly saved me and my sons too

विषान्महाग्नेः पुरुषाददर्शनादसत्सभाया वनवासकृच्छ्रतः ।
मृधे मृधेऽनेकमहारथास्त्रतो द्रौण्यस्त्रतश्चास्म हरेऽभिरक्षिताः ॥
Bh 1.8.24

*viṣhānmahāgneḥ puruṣhādadarśhanādasatsabhāyā
vanavāsakṛchchhrataḥ
mṛdhe mṛdhe'nekamahārathāstrato drauṇyastrataśchāsma
hare'bhirakṣhitāḥ*

From poison, huge fire, demons and the wicked
From perils in forest, missiles in battles
From the terrible weapon of the son of Drona
You've protected us repeatedly, O Lord

विपदः सन्तु ताः शश्वत्तत्र तत्र जगद्गुरो ।
भवतो दर्शनं यत्स्यादपुनर्भवदर्शनम् ॥ Bh 1.8.25

*vipadaḥ santu tāḥ śhaśhvattatra tatra jagadguro
bhavato darśhanaṁ yatsyādapunarbhavadarśhanam*

May calamities befall us at every step forever
O Teacher of the entire world
For adversity blesses with Your vision
And uproots the egoic desire of becoming

जन्मैश्वर्यश्रुतश्रीभिरेधमानमदः पुमान् ।
नैवार्हत्यभिधातुं वै त्वामकिञ्चनगोचरम् ॥ Bh 1.8.26

*janmaiśhvaryaśhrutaśhrībhiredhamānamadaḥ pumān
naivārhatyabhidhātuṁ vai tvāmakiñchanagocharam*

Pedigree, power, learning and affluence
Only serve to swell the pride of man
Making him unable to surrender unto You
Being available only to those free of any attachment

नमोऽकिञ्चनवित्ताय निवृत्तगुणवृत्तये ।
आत्मारामाय शान्ताय कैवल्यपतये नम: ।। Bh 1.8.27

namo'kiñchanavittāya nivṛttaguṇavṛttaye
ātmārāmāya śhāntāya kaivalyapataye namaḥ

You are the wealth of the one free of attachment
You are beyond the modes of material nature
You remain perfectly calm and blissful in Your Self
You are the bestower of Liberation
My obeisances unto You

मन्ये त्वां कालमीशानमनादिनिधनं विभुम् ।
समं चरन्तं सर्वत्र भूतानां यन्मिथ: कलि: ।। Bh 1.8.28

manye tvāṁ kālamīśhānamanādinidhanaṁ vibhum
samaṁ charantaṁ sarvatra bhūtānāṁ yanmithaḥ kaliḥ

You are Time, the Almighty Ruler
With no beginning or end
Moving alike among all beings
And yet causing delusion among them by your Maya

न वेद कश्चिद्भगवंश्चिकीर्षितं तवेहमानस्य नृणां विडम्बनम् ।
न यस्य कश्चिद्दयितोऽस्ति कर्हिचिद् द्वेष्यश्च यस्मिन् विषमा
मतिर्नृणाम् ।। Bh 1.8.29

na veda kaśhchidbhagavaṁśhchikīrṣhitaṁ tavehamānasya nṛṇāṁ viḍambanam
na yasya kaśhchiddayito'sti karhichid dveṣhyaśhcha yasmin viṣhamā matirnṛṇām

None can fathom Your ways of acting
None is dear or loathsome to You
It is only those deluded by ignorance
That think of You as separate

जन्म कर्म च विश्वात्मन्नजस्याकर्तुरात्मनः ।
तिर्यङ्नृषिषु याद:सु तदत्यन्तविडम्बनम् ॥ Bh 1.8.30

janma karma cha viśhvātmannajasyākarturātmanaḥ
tiryaṅnṛṣhiṣhu yādaḥsu tadatyantaviḍambanam

You are the Soul of the Universe
Devoid of birth and actions
Yet engaging in birth, actions among us
Your descents are a mere sport

गोप्यादे त्वयि कृतागसि दाम तावद् या ते
दशाश्रुकलिलाञ्जनसम्भ्रमाक्षम् ।
वक्त्रं निनीय भयभावनया स्थितस्य सा मां विमोहयति भीरपि
यद्विभेति ॥ Bh 1.8.31

gopyādade tvayi kṛtāgasi dāma tāvad yā te
daśhāśhrukalilāñjanasambhramākṣham
vaktraṁ ninīya bhayabhāvanayā sthitasya sā māṁ vimohayati
bhīrapi yadbibheti

When Mother Yashoda took a cord to bind You
You stood as Baby Krishna with eyes rolling
As if full of fear and flowing with tears
While fear itself is afraid of You
Bewildering thus one and all

केचिदाहुरजं जातं पुण्यश्लोकस्य कीर्तये ।
यदो: प्रियस्यान्ववाये मलयस्येव चन्दनम् ॥ Bh 1.8.32

kechidāhurajaṁ jātaṁ puṇyaśhlokasya kīrtaye
yadoḥ priyasyānvavāye malayasyeva chandanam

Though Unborn, Your descent enhances the glory of the
    Yadus
As a sandal tree brings fragrance to a whole mountain

अपरे वसुदेवस्य देवक्यां याचितोऽभ्यगात् ।
अजस्त्वमस्य क्षेमाय वधाय च सुरद्विषाम् ॥ Bh 1.8.33

apare vāsudevasya devakyāṁ yāchito'bhyagāt
ajastvamasya kṣhemāya vadhāya ca suradviṣhām

Though Unborn, You are born of Devaki and Vasudeva
For protecting the virtuous and annihilating the wicked

भारावतारणायान्ये भुवो नाव इवोदधौ ।
सीदन्त्या भूरिभारेण जातो ह्यात्मभुवार्थित: ॥ Bh 1.8.34

bhārāvatāraṇāyānye bhuvo nāva ivodadhau
sīdantyā bhūribhāreṇa jāto hyātmabhuvārthitaḥ

Though Unborn, You have appeared due to the prayer of
the virtuous
To relieve the burden of Earth suffering the weight of the
wicked

भवेऽस्मिन् क्लिश्यमानानामविद्याकामकर्मभिः ।
श्रवणस्मरणार्हाणि करिष्यन्निति केचन ॥ Bh 1.8.35

bhave'smin kliśhyamānānāmavidyākāmakarmabhiḥ
shravaṇasmaraṇārhāṇi kariṣhyanniti kechana

Though Unborn, You have descended in the world
To perform glorious deeds, that by simply listening
Removes ignorance, grief and selfishness

शृण्वन्ति गायन्ति गृणन्त्यभीक्ष्णशः स्मरन्ति नन्दन्ति तवेहितं जनाः
।
त एव पश्यन्त्यचिरेण तावकं भवप्रवाहोपरमं पदाम्बुजम् ॥
Bh 1.8.36

shṛṇvanti gāyanti gṛṇantyabhīkṣhṇaśhaḥ smaranti nandanti
tavehitaṁ janāḥ
ta eva paśhyantyachireṇa tāvakaṁ bhavapravāhoparamaṁ
padāmbujam

Those who listen, sing, contemplate on Your deeds
Behold before long Your lotus feet, the ground of Being
Putting an end to the stream of suffering

अथ विश्वेश विश्वात्मन् विश्वमूर्ते स्वकेषु मे ।
स्नेहपाशमिमं छिन्धि दृढं पाण्डुषु वृष्णिषु ॥ Bh 1.8.41

atha viśhveśha viśhvātman viśhvamūrte svakeshu me
snehapāśhamimaṁ chhindhi dṛḍhaṁ pāṇḍushu vṛshṇishu

You are the Lord of the Universe
Nay, the Soul of the Universe
Nay, the very Universe Itself
Pray cut my bonds of attachment

त्वयि मेऽनन्यविषया मतिर्मधुपतेऽसकृत् ।
रतिमुद्वहताद्दधा गङ्गेवौघमुदन्वति ॥ Bh 1.8.42

tvayi me'nanyavishayā matirmadhupate'sakṛt
ratimudvahatādaddhā gaṅgevaughamudanvati

As Ganga incessantly pours her waters into the ocean
Let my stream of thoughts constantly flow toward You
**   alone**

श्रीकृष्ण कृष्णसख वृष्ण्यृषभावनिध्रुग् राजन्यवंशदहनानपवर्गवीर्य
।
गोविन्द गोद्विजसुरार्तिहरावतार योगेश्वराखिलगुरो भगवन्नमस्ते ॥
Bh 1.8.43

śrīkṛshṇa kṛshṇasakha vṛshṇyṛshabhāvanidhrug rājanyavaṁśhad
ahanānapavargavīrya
govinda godvijasurārtiharāvatāra yogeśhvarākhilaguro
bhagavannamaste

O Krishna, O Friend of Arjuna, O Govinda
You are fire that burns the wicked
Your prowess is infinite

**Your descent relieves the distress of the pious
Obeisance to You, O Master of Yoga, Teacher of all**

Thus conclude the beautiful prayers of Kunti. Bhāgavatam has many prayers by many elevated beings each with a different mood of love and wisdom. Among them, these prayers of Kunti hold a special significance.

Bhishma's Prayers

Next comes the glorious event of Bhishma's departure preceded by his prayers to Krishna, who accompanies Pandavas to bless Bhishma lying in the battlefield.

Bhishma was the patriarch of the Kuru clan who fought an internecine war (Mahabharat) due to the envy of one set of cousins (the evil Kauravas) against the other (the virtuous Pandavas). The Pandavas with Arjuna as the main warrior were surrendered to the Supreme Lord Krishna who out of His great compassion became the charioteer for His dear friend Arjuna. Prior to the war, Krishna makes a vow that He will only be the charioteer and will not lift any weapon in the war.

Bhishma, due to his oath of loyalty to the Kauravas, headed by Duryodhana, fought on the other side of the war against his beloved Arjuna and the Pandavas. And yet, Bhishma also fully surrendered his heart to Krishna. This led to the predicament of Arjuna to take arms against his own grandfather and many other relatives and friends. When Arjuna felt great confusion and turmoil due to his attachment, Krishna famously taught the timeless message of Bhagavad Gita.

Once the war began with unmatched intensity and destruction, one of the moving duels was the one directly between Arjuna and Bhishma. Arjuna, being his beloved grandson, Bhishma is accused by Duryodhana of going soft on him. To prove him wrong, Bhishma made a vow that he'd fight with such ferocity that Krishna would break his own vow and be forced to take weapons against Bhishma to protect His dear friend Arjuna.

Krishna, being well aware of the vow made by Bhishma and now having to choose between keeping His vow or His devotee Bhishma's, chose to break His own to keep the honor of His devotee, thus showing that he is bound by the love of His devotees. So, Krishna picked a chariot wheel as if to hurl it against Bhishma. Seeing this, Bhishma was moved to tears, knowing full well the intent of Krishna to let him keep this word out of His compassion. Krishna thus enacts one of his pastimes by seemingly picking up the wheel and dropping it on Arjuna's plea. Eventually the battle continued until Arjuna prevailed over Bhishma.

When Bhishma was defeated, he fell to the ground but chose to die at the time of his choosing due to a boon. And since the auspicious northerly movement of the Sun (*uttarayana*) was just weeks away, Bhishma decided to wait for the right hour to depart the world. As typical of any great warrior, he'd resolved to win or die in the battlefield, so Arjuna, the matchless archer, made a bed of arrows for Bhishma to rest right there on the battlefield.

Finally, the appointed hour came when the northerly movement of the Sun began. By then, the war was over, the Pandavas had won with a decisive victory and ascended the throne. They all now came to the battlefield, along with Krishna Himself, to witness the glorious departure of Bhishma.

At this hour of his death, he first answered all the questions of the Pandavas on the right dharma for all men in general and the royals in particular. Then he finally poured out his heart to Krishna, the Supreme Avatar, in what is famously known as Bhishma Stuti.

Bhishma, through these prayers, beautifully synthesizes the philosophical wisdom of Oneness with heartfelt devotion and unconditional love. Bhishma first presents the ontological position of Krishna in a concise way. Then, he goes to recount the various pastimes of Krishna including and especially the ones involving the battle Bhishma waged with the Lord on the opposing side.

Bhishma was uniquely fortunate to see the form of Krishna as Parthasarathy (charioteer of Arjuna) by directly facing Him, unlike Arjuna himself who was seated behind Krishna on the chariot. So, Bhishma very movingly invokes through these prayers the various visions he encountered during the war that are imprinted in his heart with love.

Reading these prayers while envisioning the scene of the battlefield and entering the heart of pure devotion of Bhishma can effortlessly awaken love for the Supreme Being and remove the sense of me and mine, which is the only veil that prevents the realization of our true nature as *Sat-Chit-Ananda* (Eternal, Conscious and Blissful).

Here are all the verses of the profound prayers of Bhishma with a simple versified translation:

इति मतिरुपकल्पिता वितृष्णा भगवति सात्वतपुङ्गवे विभूम्नि ।
स्वसुखमुपगते क्वचिद्विहर्तुं प्रकृतिमुपेयुषि यद्भवप्रवाहः ॥
Bh 1.9.32

iti matirupakalpitā vitṛṣṇā bhagavati sātvatapuṅgave vibhūmni
svasukhamupagate kvachidvihartuṁ prakṛtimupeyuṣhi
yadbhavapravāhaḥ

I offer my mind, freed of all desires, on the eve of my
    departure
To the Supreme Lord, the Leader of all devotees
Ever blissful in His eternal Self
Who at times for the transcendental joy of devotees
Descends into the world of matter that streams forth
    only from Him

त्रिभुवनकमनं तमालवर्णं रविकरगौरवराम्बरं दधाने ।
वपुरलककुलावृताननाब्जं विजयसखे रतिरस्तु मेऽनवद्या ॥
Bh 1.9.33

*tribhuvanakamanaṁ tamālavarṇaṁ ravikaragauravarāmbaraṁ
dadhāne
vapuralakakulāvṛtānanābjaṁ vijayasakhe ratirastu me'navadyā*

May I cherish motiveless love for that friend of Vijaya
    (Arjuna)
The most desirable Being of all the three worlds
Dark blue in complexion like a bay leaf tree
Wearing silk that shines like the golden rays of the sun
His lotus like face with curly locks floating about

युधि तुरगरजोविधूम्रविष्वक्कचलुलितश्रमवार्यलङ्कृतास्ये ।
मम निशितशरैर्विभिद्यमानत्वचि विलसत्कवचेऽस्तु कृष्ण आत्मा
॥ Bh 1.9.34

*yudhi
turagarajovidhūmraviṣhvakkachalulitaśhramavāryalaṅkṛtāsye
mama niśhitaśharairvibhidyamānatvachi vilasatkavache'stu
kṛṣhṇa ātmā*

May my body, mind and soul rest in Krishna
His face decorated with beads of sweat in the battlefield
Covered with scattered hair turned ashen with the dust
     of the horses' hoofs
Skin, though protected with a shining armor, pierced by
     my sharp arrows

सपदि सखिवचो निशम्य मध्ये निजपरयोर्बलयो रथं निवेश्य ।
स्थितवति परसैनिकायुरक्षणा हृतवति पार्थसखे रतिर्ममास्तु ॥
Bh 1.9.35

sapadi sakhivacho niśhamya madhye nijaparayorbalayo ratham niveśhya
sthitavati parasainikāyurakṣhṇā hṛtavati pārthasakhe ratirmamāstu

May my love be exclusively for the dear friend of Pārtha
     (Arjuna)
The Infallible Krishna who as per the words of His dear
     friend
Entered and established the chariot between the
     opposing forces
Shortening the life spans of the enemies by simply
     glancing at them

व्यवहितपृतनामुखं निरीक्ष्य स्वजनवधाद्विमुखस्य दोषबुद्ध्या ।
कुमतिमहरदात्मविद्यया यश्चरणरति: परमस्य तस्य मेऽस्तु ॥
Bh 1.9.36

vyavahitapṛtanāmukhaṁ nirīkṣhya svajanavadhādvimukhasya doṣhabuddhyā
kumatimaharadātmavidyayā yaśhcharaṇaratiḥ paramasya tasya me'stu

May my love be for the feet of the Transcendent Lord
    Imparting the timeless teaching of Self-knowledge
To remove the ignorance of His friend Arjuna on the
    battlefield
That arose due to Arjuna's delusion upon seeing the
    troops arrayed
Reluctant as he was to slay his kinsmen due to
    attachment

स्वनिगममपहाय मत्प्रतिज्ञामृतमधिकर्तुमवप्लुतो रथस्थः ।
धृतरथचरणोऽभ्ययाच्चलद्गुर्हरिरिव हन्तुमिभं गतोत्तरीयः ॥
Bh 1.9.37

svanigamamapahāya matpratijñāmṛtamadhikartumavapluto rathasthaḥ
dhṛtarathacharaṇo'bhyayāchchaladgurharariva hantumibhaṁ gatottarīyaḥ

Breaking His own vow not to take up arms during the
    Great War
To fulfill my vow that my fight would force Him to take
    up a weapon
He jumped down from His chariot
Charging toward me like a lion about to kill an elephant
    With earth beneath trembling and His upper garment
    flying away

शितविशिखहतो विशीर्णदंशः क्षतजपरिप्लुत आततायिनो मे ।
प्रसभमभिससार मद्वधार्थं स भवतु मे भगवान् गतिर्मुकुन्दः ॥
Bh 1.9.38

*shitavishikhahato vishīrṇadaṁśaḥ kshatajaparipluta ātatāyino me
prasabhamabhisasāra madvadhārthaṁ sa bhavatu me bhagavān
gatirmukundaḥ*

**May my destination be Lord Mukunda, the Bestower of
    liberation
Who charged at me, as if angry to kill the aggressor I was
    When His shield got broken
His transcendent body seemingly wounded
Blood flowing from the piercing of my sharp arrows**

विजयरथकुटुम्ब आत्ततोत्रे धृतहयरश्मिनि तच्छ्रियेक्षणीये ।
भगवति रतिरस्तु मे मुमूर्षोर्यमिह निरीक्ष्य हता गताः स्वरूपम् ॥
Bh 1.9.39

*vijayarathakuṭumbha āttatotre dhṛtahayaraśhmini
tachchhriyekṣhaṇīye
bhagavati ratirastu me mumūrṣhoryamiha nirīkṣhya hatā gatāḥ
svarūpam*

**May my love be, at this moment of death, in the Supreme
    Lord
Who took on the role of the charioteer for Vijaya (Arjuna)
With the whip in one hand and the horses' reins in the
    other
Upon looking at Him so charming
Those who died in the battlefield attained their eternal
    nature**

ललितगतिविलासवल्गुहासप्रणयनिरीक्षणकल्पितोरुमाना: ।
कृतमनुकृतवत्य उन्मदान्धा: प्रकृतिमगन् किल यस्य गोपवध्व: ॥
Bh 1.9.40

*lalitagativilāsavalguhāsapranayanirikshanakalpitorumānāḥ
krtamanukrtavatya unmadāndhāḥ prakrtimagan kila yasya
gopavadhvaḥ*

Beholding His charming gait and playful actions
His bewitching smile and loving glances
And imitating His movements in mad ecstasy
When He disappeared from their midst
Blessed with perfection were the cowherd damsels

मुनिगणनृपवर्यसङ्कुलेऽन्त:सदसि युधिष्ठिरराजसूय एषाम् ।
अर्हणमुपपेद ईक्षणीयो मम दृशिगोचर एष आविरात्मा ॥
Bh 1.9.41

*muniganan̄rpavaryasankule'ntaḥsadasi yudhiṣṭhirarājasūya eṣām
arhaṇamupapeda īkshanīyo mama dṛśhigochara eṣha āvirātmā*

In the assembly of sages and kings at the royal sacrifice
    of Yudhishthira
He who attracted everyone's eyes and was worshiped by
    all
A sight that I was able to behold with my own eyes
Now has appeared before me at this moment

तमिममहमजं शरीरभाजां हृदि हृदि धिष्ठितमात्मकल्पितानाम् ।
प्रतिदृशमिव नैकधार्कमेकं समधिगतोऽस्मि विधूतभेदमोह: ॥
Bh 1.9.42

tamimamahamajaṁ śharīrabhājāṁ hṛdi hṛdi
dhiṣhṭhitamātmakalpitānām
pratidṛśhamiva naikadhārkamekaṁ samadhigato'smi
vidhūtabhedamohaḥ

Having shaken off all delusions of differences
I have realized Him as the One, the Unborn
Who is enthroned in the heart of every conditioned being
Even as the Sun, though one, appears differently to every
eye

Thus conclude the final prayers of Bhishma, known as Bhishma Stuti. One of the finest examples of the sublime fusion of devotion and wisdom found recurring in Bhāgavatam that harmonizes the Personal and Impersonal aspects of the Divine seamlessly, are presented by these prayers. After offering these prayers, Bhishma gloriously departed this world in the presence of Krishna, the Pandavas, various great sages, all of whom marked the momentous occasion with absolute silence.

स वा अयं यत्पदमत्र सूरयो जितेन्द्रिया निर्जितमातरिश्वनः ।
पश्यन्ति भक्त्युत्कलितामलात्मना नन्वेष सत्त्वं परिमार्ष्टुमर्हति ॥
Bh 1.10.23

sa vā ayaṁ yatpadamatra sūrayo jitendriyā nirjitamātariśhvanaḥ
paśhyanti bhaktyutkalitāmalātmanā nanveṣha sattvaṁ
parimārṣhṭumarhati

Krishna is the same Supreme Spirit whose reality is
perceived only by seers who have regulated their senses
and life energy, with a mind yearning for His vision and

are cleansed of all impurities through devotion by His Grace.

After Bhishma's blessed departure, everyone returned to the kingdom and with Krishna's blessings, Yudhishthira began ruling the kingdom righteously. All the people, other living beings and all of nature were free of afflictions and flourished in abundance. After spending a few months there, Krishna took leave to go back to Dwaraka. All the residents found it exceedingly difficult to forgo His company and yet came to see Him off, restraining their tears of affection. Various musical instruments were played and the city of Hastinapur was decked up to give Krishna a royal farewell as His chariot proceeded through the streets. A few wise women seeing the procession discussed among themselves about the true nature of Krishna as the Eternal Being descended on Earth to eradicate the wicked and bestow Grace on the pious. They glorified Him as the Source of the Universe who brings forth material energy with Time and sustains all, while His true essence is known only to the pure hearted sages.

एतदीशनमीशस्य प्रकृतिस्थोऽपि तद्गुणैः ।
न युज्यते सदात्मस्थैर्यथा बुद्धिस्तदाश्रया ॥ Bh 1.11.38

etadīshanam īshasya prakṛtistho'pi tadguṇaiḥ
na yujyate sadātmasthairyathā buddhistadāshrayā

The divinity of the Lord is such that, even though abiding in material nature, He never gets tainted by the modes of material energy. Anyone fully surrendered unto Him too similarly remains unaffected by the material energy.

Krishna, after leaving Hastinapur and proceeding through various territories and being honored at each stop, finally reachedDwarakaandblewHisconchPanchajanya.Immediately recognizing the auspicious sound, all the residents sallied forth to meet Him and offered Him gifts, just as one offers light to the sun. They expressed their grief of separation thus far and the immense joy of beholding Him again. The city was decked up with flags and banners and sprinkled with scented waters to welcome Him. Balaram along with parents and elders left the palace in chariots accompanied by elephants to welcome back Krishna. The consorts of Krishna were overjoyed to see Him after long and embraced Him. Yet amidst all this pomp and festivities, nothing could disturb His serenity. In the Gita, Krishna describes the One who is ever still within (*sthitaprajna*) whatever the outer circumstances. In Bhāgavatam, Krishna demonstrates it by His own activities under various such circumstances.

भवद्विधा भागवतास्तीर्थभूताः स्वयं विभो ।
तीर्थीकुर्वन्ति तीर्थानि स्वान्तःस्थेन गदाभृता ॥ Bh 1.13.10

bhavadvidhā bhāgavatāstīrthabhūtāḥ svayaṁ vibho
tīrthīkurvanti tīrthāni svāntaḥsthena gadābhṛtā

A pure being (Bhagavata) is verily a sacred spot himself. And it is such beings who make the sacred places sacred by the living presence of the Supreme Being in their hearts.

Vidura, who went on long pilgrimage for many years, returned to Hastinapur and was welcomed by King Yudhishthira and everyone in the palace with great joy. Having met with Uddhava and then the sage Maitreya, Vidura was now established in unwavering devotion to the Supreme Being within. Yudhishthira therefore glorified the nature of a Bhagavata like Vidura in this verse. Bhagavata is one who totally abides in Bhagavan. And the whole of Bhāgavatam is nothing but a chronicle of the activities and teachings of Bhagavan and the Bhagavatas such as Vidura. For, Bhagavatas are walking sacred sites, carrying the holy presence of the Divine everywhere they go. And it is only due to such beings that the sacred places are themselves consecrated. Even the great holy rivers like Ganga are blessed by the contact of the sages and Bhagavatas. Through their purity, austerities and by their very presence, they bestow sacred places with true sacredness. This is why the most important pilgrimage one can make is to meet with such pure beings wherever they are.

मा कञ्चन शुचो राजन् यदीश्वरवशं जगत् ।
लोका: सपाला यस्येमे वहन्ति बलिमीशितु: ।
स संयुनक्ति भूतानि स एव वियुनक्ति च ॥ Bh 1.13.40

mā kañchana śhucho rājan yadīśhvaravaśhaṁ jagat
lokāḥ sapālā yasyeme vahanti balimīśhituḥ
sa saṁyunakti bhūtāni sa eva viyunakti cha

Grieve not for anybody, for the world is under the control of the Supreme Controller. It is unto Him that all these worlds and the rulers offer homage. It is He alone who unites and then parts living beings from one another.

Vidura came to Hastinapur for only one reason—to bestow Grace upon his elder brother Dhrtarashtra by taking him away from a life of slumber and ignorance. Though

Dhrtarasthra was complicit in all the evils committed against the Pandavas,Vidura points out that he is now shamelessly enjoying their hospitality in the palace rather than going to solitude and making proper use of the remaining time in realizing God. These words of Vidura awaken Dhrtarashtra and he along with wife Gandhari leave the palace overnight with Vidura to retire to solitude on the banks of Ganga. Not finding them in the palace the next morning, the virtuous Yudhishthira is grief-stricken and worried about his old uncles. Narada comes to advise Yudhishthira not to grieve as everyone is brought together and separated by the Divine Will as ordained. Just as a child brings toys together to play and then separates them after a while or a river brings together logs of wood in its stream and separates them, so do living beings come together and get separated by the Supreme Controller. Seeing this clearly as the natural order of life brings total acceptance and peace, and one cherishes all relationships without any possessiveness or grief.

तदिदं भगवान् राजन्नेक आत्मात्मनां स्वदृक् ।
अन्तरोऽनन्तरो भाति पश्य तं माययोरुधा ॥ Bh 1.13.47

tadidaṁ bhagavān rājanneka ātmātmanāṁ svadṛk
antaro'nantaro bhāti paśhya taṁ māyayorudhā

All this is the One self-effulgent Supreme Being, the Self of all. It is He who appears as the subject and the object. Perceive Him alone as manifested in diverse forms through Maya.

In this one verse, the entire truth of Bhāgavatam is summarized beautifully with the simple expression "All this is Bhagavan" (*tad idaṁ bhagavān*) or to put it plainly, God alone is. Everyone, everything, everywhere, every moment is only an expression of the unitary Divine Energy with its three modes (*sattva, rajas, tamas* or goodness, passion and ignorance) and five elements (space, air, fire, water, soil), all subject to Time and destiny. And this unitary Divine Energy has as its Source in the One Supreme Being who is unborn, inscrutable and eternal. Through the core ignorance which is the apparent subject/object division in all perceptions and actions, we falsely presume that there is a separate persistent "me" sitting within the body as the subject that interacts with others as the object. While in reality, there is only the ever dynamic unitary energy manifesting in everyone as the body/ mind that is constantly in flux, so there are no others. Hence, it is pointed out that He alone appears as all the diverse forms and the false division between the observer and the observed is only an illusion.

नोत्तमश्लोकवार्तानां जुषतां तत्कथामृतम् । स्यात्सम्भ्रमोऽन्तकालेऽपि स्मरतां तत्पदाम्बुजम् ॥ Bh 1.18.4

nottamaślokavārtānāṁ juṣhatāṁ tatkathāmṛtam
syātsambhramo'ntakāle'pi smaratāṁ tatpadāmbujam

No delusion arises even at the last moment in the one who listens only to speech glorifying the Supreme Being, His nectar-like stories and is ever devoted to His lotus feet.

All delusion is rooted in the false conception of separative identities and the attachments they engender. The way out of delusion is to be free of the sense of "me" and "mine" through God-realization which is the recognition that the Absolute Being alone manifests as all forms. Listening and contemplating exclusively upon this wisdom revealed through teachings and stories removes the fear of death which is said to be the root of all fears. The experience structure of "me" as the body/mind constantly wants to acquire more experiences due to the false sense of separation and therefore lives perpetually with the fear of the end of experience which is the fear of death. When the very experience structure is seen as illusory and the body/mind is seen as an expression of the unitary Divine energy with no separate self, then the fear of death ceases and there is no delusion even in the last moment as this verse points out. This echoes a similar verse in the Gita where Krishna also declares that the one who abides in Him even at the last moment is liberated in God-realization undoubtedly (*antakāle cha mām eva smaran muktvā kalevaram / yaḥ prayāti sa madbhāvaṁ yāti nāstyatra sanśhayaḥ*—BG 8.5).

तुलयाम लवेनापि न स्वर्गं नापुनर्भवम् ।
भगवत्सङ्गिसङ्गस्य मर्त्यानां किमुताशिषः ॥ Bh 1.18.13

*tulayāma lavenāpi na svargaṁ nāpunarbhavam
bhagavatsaṅgisaṅgasya martyānāṁ kim utāśhiṣhaḥ*

**One cannot compare even a moment's association
of those surrendered unto the Supreme Being with
heavenly pleasures or freedom from transmigration,
much less the petty desires of the mortals.**

Of all aids in one's spiritual journey, most paramount is the right association with the fully surrendered beings whose greatness cannot be overstated. Such right association with those who are fully surrendered unto the Absolute, free of the false ego and ever abiding in Truth is called Satsang, literally meaning confluence (*sang*) with Truth (*sat*). The very association with them brings about all the qualities necessary for the flowering of wisdom and divine love such as sincerity, discernment and dispassion. All heavenly pleasures are petty in comparison because they are temporary in nature. And even the desire for freedom from transmigration is rooted in the false sense of self that seeks liberation. Whereas, Satsang in its truest sense uproots the very "me" that seeks to be liberated through time and bestows the timeless freedom here and now. This is captured poetically by Adi Shankara while describing the glory of Satsang as that which leads to dispassion, which in turn leads to removal of delusion, which in turn leads to a still mind, which in turn leads to freedom while living (*satsangatve nissangatvam / nissangatve nirmohatvam / nirmohatve nishchalatattvam / nishcalatattve jivanmuktiḥ*—Bhaja Govindam).

प्रायशः साधवो लोके परैर्द्वन्द्वेषु योजिताः ।
न व्यथन्ति न हृष्यन्ति यत आत्माऽगुणाश्रयः ॥ Bh 1.18.40

prāyaśhaḥ sādhavo loke parairdvandveṣhu yojitāḥ
na vyathanti na hṛṣhyanti yata ātmā'guṇāshrayaḥ

The holy men when subject to the pairs of opposites in the world neither grieve nor rejoice, as they abide as the Pure Being that is beyond the modes of material nature.

The world is always full of pairs of opposites such as heat and cold, pleasure and pain, highs and lows etc. which is the nature of the material energy. If one is identified with these dualities, then one is tossed upside down by the emotions of both grief and excitement. The material energy starting with the physical body, the adjuncts such as memory, intellect, thoughts, emotions and relationships be it family, friends, possessions, career, nation etc. are all constantly bringing forth pairs of opposites. When the sense of "me" is taken to be the body and its adjuncts and the sense of "mine" is attached to all its relationships, then the resultant dualities cause feelings of grief and excitement, pleasure and pain, gain and loss etc. But if they are seen as the ever changing, impermanent flow of material energy and not identified with, then one remains equanimous to outer situations, while abiding in inner stillness. As Krishna instructs in the Gita, being equanimous whether it be pleasure or pain, profit or loss, victory or defeat is the way of right action (*sukhaduḥkhe same kṛitvā lābhālābhau jayājayau*—BG 2.38). Such equanimity in the midst of pairs of opposites is the true essence of Yoga.

तत्राभवद्भगवान् व्यासपुत्रो यदृच्छया गामटमानोऽनपेक्ष: ।
अलक्ष्यलिङ्गो निजलाभतुष्टो वृतश्च बालैरवधूतवेष: ॥
Bh 1.19.25

tatrābhavad bhagavān vyāsaputro yadṛchchhayā
gāmaṭamāno'napekṣhaḥ
alakṣhyaliṅgo nijalābhatuṣhto vṛtaścha bālairavadhūtaveṣhaḥ

There arrived the divine sage Shuka, son of Vyasa, wandering about the earth at will without any expectation, with no marks of any kind, fully content in Self-realization, surrounded by children and in the garb of a total ascetic with no attachments.

After King Parikshit learns that he is going to face death in seven days, he retires to the banks of Ganga, and many sages assemble around him. As Parikshit addresses the sages with the question of what is the purpose of human life in general and of one facing death in particular, there walks in by divine happenstance the great sage Shuka Brahmam, son of Vyasa. He is only sixteen years old, very handsome and radiant, perfectly situated in Self-realization and with no attachments or desires whatsoever. He is not identified with any grades or divisions of society, being beyond all such identification (*ativarṇāshrami*). Children are naturally drawn to the child-like purity of the great sage and therefore surround him wherever he goes. He is not known to linger anywhere, being constantly on the move, wandering the earth and happens to arrive at the holy assembly gathered around the extraordinary circumstances of the king awaiting death. Everyone there, though much senior to him by age, rises to express their reverence and Parikshit too after glorifying the greatness of Shuka Brahmam poses the question again to him as the first skandha ends. Shuka Brahmam's response to the question for the next seven days till the death of Parikshit is the content of the entire Bhāgavatam over the remaining eleven Skandhas.

SECOND CANTO
Teaching Summarized

एतावान् सांख्ययोगाभ्यां स्वधर्मपरिनिष्ठया ।
जन्मलाभः परः पुंसामन्ते नारायणस्मृतिः ॥
प्रायेण मुनयो राजन्निवृत्ता विधिषेधतः ।
नैर्गुण्यस्था रमन्ते स्म गुणानुकथने हरेः ॥ Bh 2.1.6-7

etāvān sāṅkhya-yogābhyāṁ svadharma pariniṣṭhayā
janma lābhaḥ paraḥ puṁsām ante nārāyaṇa smṛtih
prāyeṇa munayo rājan nivṛttā vidhi-ṣhedhataḥ
nairguṇyasthā ramante sma guṇānukathane hareḥ

By engaging in one's duties with a firm abidance in the wisdom of discernment of the impermanent (*sānkhya*) as well as total acceptance of the fruits of all actions (*karma yoga*), one attains the highest perfection of human life which is the loving remembrance of the Supreme Being. Even sages who are established in the Absolute and are beyond the sphere of injunctions take delight in the virtues and pastimes of Hari.

Shuka Brahmam begins his teachings by pointing out the highest purpose of human life is to abide free of ego in the all-pervading Supreme Being. Here, Shuka Brahmam invokes the most sacred name for the Absolute as Nārāyana, that has many beautiful meanings such as "One resting in the causal waters," "Refuge of all beings" and "Eternal Being." The glory of the very name Nārāyana comes forth many verses later and in the sixth canto through the story of Ajāmila. The way to realize the Absolute is summarized as either through the wisdom of self-inquiry that is referred to as *sānkhya yoga* or the total acceptance or loving surrender that is referred to as *karma yoga.* This exactly mirrors what Krishna teaches in the Gita as well: "The two ways leading to realization are the way of wisdom of discernment for those inclined toward contemplation and the way of acting free of doership for those engaging in action" (*loke'smin dvividha nishtha pura prokta mayanagha / jnanayogena sankhyanam karmayogena yoginam —* BG 3.3). Also, there is the reference to the true meaning of divine pastimes (*lila*) which are both the means and the end as they remove our impurities through listening, and they give delight even to the sages abiding in purity. Another sacred and oft-repeated name of the Absolute invoked here is Hari that means "One who takes away the ego."

एतन्निर्विद्यमानानामिच्छतामकुतोभयम् ।
योगिनां नृप निर्णीतं हरेर्नामानुकीर्तनम् ॥ Bh 2.1.11

etan nirvidyamānānām icchatām akutobhayam
yoginām nṛpa nirṇītaṁ harer nāmānukīrtanam

The holy names of Hari have been concluded as the best means and the end for those who see the impermanence of the world and seek the fearless state of Truth, as well as for the realized beings that are abiding in the Truth.

Just as listening to Hari Katha (divine pastimes) was glorified earlier as the means and the end, Hari Nam (holy names) is glorified in this verse. Both are accessible easily through the ears wherever one is and do not require any rituals, instructions, qualifications etc. They cleanse the heart effortlessly of false identifications and reveal the Truth of the One Supreme Being within and without.

किं प्रमत्तस्य बहुभिः परोक्षैर्हायनैरिह ।
वरं मुहूर्तं विदितं घटते श्रेयसे यतः ॥ Bh 2.1.12

kiṁ pramattasya bahubhiḥ parokṣhair hāyanair iha
varaṁ muhūrtaṁ viditaṁ ghaṭate śhreyase yataḥ

What is the use of long years of life that slip away in ignorance? Far more valuable is even an hour spent consciously, endeavoring for the highest perfection of human life.

The highest perfection of human life is to recognize that everyone, everything, everywhere, is a unique expression of the Divine Intelligence and therefore be free of any covetousness or fear and abide in unconditional love toward one and all. Thus, God is the most immediate truth of our being but thought creates an illusion of being million miles away. This illusory distance seems real as long as we waste our time contemplating upon the mundane affairs of the world. On the other hand, even a short time spent in conscious company immediately lifts the veil and awakens the heart.

अन्तकाले तु पुरुष आगते गतसाध्वसः ।
छिन्द्यादसङ्गशस्त्रेण स्पृहां देहेऽनु ये च तम् ॥ Bh 2.1.15

*antakāle tu puruṣha āgate gata sādhvasaḥ
chindyād asaṅga śhastreṇa spṛhāṁ dehe'nu ye ca tam*

With the sword of detachment, one ought to cut the false identification with the body and its connections and thereby be free of the fear of death.

It is rightly observed in psychology that all fears are rooted in the fear of death. This fear is due to false identification with the body and its connections, relations, possessions as "me" and "mine." The sword of detachment is the wisdom that everything including the body functions is due to the one indivisible energy that pervades the whole universe in various forms. The source of this energy is called the Supreme Being. This verse also mirrors the teaching of Krishna in the Gita exhorting one to cut down the tree of false attachment to the ephemeral with the sword of detachment (*asaṅgaśhastreṇa dṛidhena chhittvā—BG 15.3*)

अभ्यसेन्मनसा शुद्धं त्रिवृद्ब्रह्माक्षरं परम् ।
मनो यच्छेज्जितश्वासो ब्रह्मबीजमविस्मरन् ॥ Bh 2.1.17

*abhyasenmanasā śhuddhaṁ trivṛd brahmākṣaraṁ param
mano yacchejitaśhvāso brahmabījam avismaran*

Sitting still and erect in a clean place, one must focus on the holy Pranava of three parts (A, U, M) with the breath and the mind regulated and not fall out of attention to the sound OM, the seed of all wisdom.

Shuka Brahmam teaches Parikshit a simple meditation that is applicable for everyone, needing no special initiation or qualification. It is simply to align the incoming and outgoing breath with the sound OM, the most mystical of all sounds, and sit in stillness. In Gita too, Krishna says "I am OM among all Vedas" (*praṇavaḥ sarva vedeshu*—BG 7.8), showing the supreme importance of the sound OM. This meditation can be done every day through alignment of breath and sound to be free of the chattering of the mind.

नियच्छेद्विषयेभ्योऽक्षान्मनसा बुद्धिसारथि: ।
मन: कर्मभिराक्षिप्तं शुभार्थे धारयेद्धिया ॥ Bh 2.1.18

niyacched vishayebhyo'kṣhān manasā buddhi sārathiḥ
manaḥ karmabhir ākṣhiptaṁ śhubhārthe dhārayed dhiyā

With reason as the charioteer (guide), one ought to withdraw attachment to sense objects in the mind and let the mind, that is prone to getting caught in unnecessary activities, fix the attention on the most auspicious Supreme Being, ever present within and without.

The simile of the chariot found in the Gita and in the Katha Upanishad is of the embodied being as the rider in a chariot whose horses are the senses, the reins are the mind and intellect is the charioteer. If the charioteer is holding the reins and guiding properly, then the rider in the chariot has a purposeful journey. Else the horses (senses) go after whatever they please (sense objects) and the rider is dragged along. This is also the symbolism of Krishna as the perfect charioteer teaching Arjuna, the rider.

तत्रैकावयवं ध्यायेदव्युच्छिन्नेन चेतसा ।
मनो निर्विषयं युक्त्वा ततः किञ्चन न स्मरेत् ।
पदं तत्परमं विष्णोर्मनो यत्र प्रसीदति ॥ Bh 2.1.19

tatraikāvayavaṁ dhyāyed avyucchinnena cetasā
mano nirviṣhayaṁ yuktvā tataḥ kiñcana na smaret
padaṁ tat paramaṁ viṣhṇor mano yatra prasīdati

With a focused mind, one ought to meditate on any aspect of the Supreme Being, while being aware of all His aspects. With the mind withdrawn from all worldly concerns, one ought to be completely absorbed in Him such that there is no thought of anything else. Such a state is the supreme reality of the all-pervading Vishnu, realizing which, the mind is flooded with the ecstasy of divine love.

The three main aspects of the Supreme Being are described as Brahman, Paramatma and Bhagavan. Brahman is the Infinite Being that manifests as the Cosmic form of the entire universe. Paramatma is the in-dwelling pure awareness in the heart of all beings. Bhagavan is the sweet descents (Avatars) with form, name, pastimes and holy abodes (*rūpa, nāma, līlā, dhāma*). Meditating on any of the three aspects of Brahman, Paramatma or Bhagavan takes one to the realization of the all-pervading reality of Vishnu and to see Him in everyone and everything with love. The word Vishnu literally means One who pervades everything (*vyāpayati iti vishnuḥ*).

रजस्तमोभ्यामाक्षिप्तं विमूढं मन आत्मनः ।
यच्छेद्धारणया धीरो हन्ति या तत्कृतं मलम् ॥ Bh 2.1.20

rajas tamobhyām ākṣhiptaṁ vimūḍhaṁ mana ātmanaḥ
yacched dhāraṇayā dhīro hanti yā tat kṛtaṁ malam

When the mind is disturbed by tendencies in the form of passion (*rajas*) and dullness (*tamas*), one of steady intelligence ought to be free of it through alert awareness and curb them from causing impurity within.

Tendencies of the mind that propel one toward unnecessary activities and excitement (*rajas*) or idle consumption of junk food or content and excessive sleep (*tamas*), cause impurities due to unconscious identification with them as "mine." Being in alert awareness as and when such tendencies rise up ensures they are not unconsciously identified with and acted upon. This is the way of living in meditation throughout the day by being consciously aware of every movement of thought within.

यस्यां सन्धार्यमाणायां योगिनो भक्तिलक्षण: ।
आशु सम्पद्यते योग आश्रयं भद्रमीक्षत: ।। Bh 2.1.21

yasyāṁ sandhāryamāṇāyāṁ yogino bhakti lakshaṇaḥ
āshu sampadyate yoga āshrayaṁ bhadram īkṣhataḥ

Through steady and alert meditation, the Yogi beholds very soon the most auspicious Supreme Being within and without. This is the state of true Yoga that is characterized by loving devotion (*bhakti*).

Being in steady and alert awareness is to not unconsciously identify with the tendencies of the mind. Then one soon recognizes that everyone and everything is an expression of the one Cosmic Intelligence which is the material energy (*prakrti*) of the Supreme Being (*purusha*). He alone abides in the hearts of all as pure Consciousness (*paramatma*) and is ever available for loving relationships as Bhagavan through holy names, forms and pastimes. Thus, beholding Him alone within and without as the only truth is the most auspicious vision. This is the highest conception of Yoga (oneness). It brings about unconditional love and equanimity in all situations as Krishna says in the Gita (*samatvam yoga uchyate*—BG 2.48).

जितासनो जितश्वासो जितसङ्गो जितेन्द्रिय: ।
स्थूले भगवतो रूपे मन: सन्धारयेद्‌धिया ॥ Bh 2.1.23

jitāsano jitaśhvāso jitasaṅgo jitendriyaḥ
sthūle bhagavato rūpe manaḥ sandhārayeddhiyā

Having a steady posture, regulating the breath, free of attachment and with senses regulated, one ought to focus the mind on the Cosmic form of Bhagavan with the help of reason.

After Shuka Brahmam gives an overview of the purpose of human life as realizing Bhagavan as the source and sustenance of all and the process of realizing it through devotion and wisdom, Parikshit asks Shuka Brahmam to elaborate further on how and what to meditate upon, that removes the impurities of the mind speedily. Shuka Brahmam begins his response by first emphasizing the regulation of the physical aspects—posture, breath and senses, that correspond to the limbs of Yoga—Asana, Pranayama and Pratyahara. This ensures the energy flow of the body is channelized toward a higher purpose rather than being dissipated. Then he mentions the need to be free of attachment which is best cultivated through right association or Satsang. With this foundation, he says one ought to focus on the Cosmic form of Bhagavan rationally. This Cosmic form will be described in the coming verses.

विशेषस्तस्य देहोऽयं स्थविष्ठश्च स्थवीयसाम् ।
यत्रेदं दृश्यते विश्वं भूतं भव्यं भवच्च सत् ।। Bh 2.1.24

visheshas tasya deho'yaṁ sthavishṭhash cha sthavīyasām
yatredaṁ drśhyate vishvaṁ bhūtaṁ bhavyaṁ bhavachcha sat

The Cosmic body of the Supreme Being is the directly perceived infinite form of the Universe here, with all its past, present and future.

The three aspects of the Supreme Being as described earlier are the infinite Brahman, the indwelling Paramatman and the personal Bhagavan. Shuka Brahmam describes all three aspects in great detail throughout Bhāgavatam. First, he begins with the infinite universal aspect as it is directly perceived by our senses. Recognizing the Cosmic Intelligence (*mahat*) as the only source behind the functioning of the universe through all of space and all of time (past, present and future) removes the false idea of taking the body as one's self and the false sense of doership to activities happening through the movement of time. The key is to see the whole universe as One Cosmic Body (*virāt*) of the Supreme Being, interconnected and functioning with tremendous intelligence, with our body/mind like a cell in this Universal Body.

अण्डकोशे शरीरेऽस्मिन् सप्तावरणसंयुते ।
वैराज: पुरुषो योऽसौ भगवान् धारणाश्रय: ॥ Bh 2.1.25

aṇḍakośhe śharīre'smin saptāvaraṇa saṁyute
vairājaḥ puruṣho yo'sau bhagavān dhāraṇāśhrayaḥ

With the entire universe made of seven sheaths as His cosmic body, the Supreme Being appears in His gigantic (*virāt*) form. He is our object of meditation.

The seven sheaths of the universe (from gross to subtle) are the five elements—earth, water, fire, air, space—of the manifest creation, the Cosmic Intelligence (*mahat tattva*) and primordial material energy (*mūla prakrti*). From the Supreme Being who is pure consciousness (*sat-chit-ananda*), comes forth the primordial material energy and cosmic intelligence that in turn brings forth with perfect order the elements and their laws of functioning. Thus, the seven sheaths that form the entire universe are seen as the body of the Supreme Being. Just as consciousness residing in our heart animates our individual body, the universal consciousness animates the universal body. Just as our body is made of trillions of cells that are all interconnected to form one unit, the universe is made of trillions of beings that are all interconnected to form one unit—the cosmic (*virāt*) body. Thus, the object of meditation is to recognize the one Universal Being in whom we all reside. This is a rational vision that awakens true intelligence, automatically removes covetousness, comparison and conflict, and situates us in unconditional love toward all.

इयानसावीश्वरविग्रहस्य यः सन्निवेषः कथितो मया ते ।
सन्धार्यतेऽस्मिन् वपुषि स्थविष्ठे मनः स्वबुद्ध्या न यतोऽस्ति
किञ्चित् ॥ Bh 2.1.38

*iyānasāvīśhvaravigrahasya yaḥ sanniveśhaḥ kathito mayā te
sandhāryate'smin vapuṣhi sthaviṣhṭhe manaḥ svabuddhyā na
yato'sti kiñcit*

**The magnitude and constitution of the cosmic body of
the Supreme Being has been explained by me to you.
With the clarity of intellect that nothing exists outside
His cosmic form, the mind ought to focus on the all-
pervading universal form of Supreme Being.**

Shuka Brahmam describes in a set of verses the various
aspects of the Cosmic Being (*virāt purusha*) that includes all
regions of the universe, all classes of beings—animate and
inanimate, all activities, all potencies, all qualities—righteous
and unrighteous, all wisdom and the mighty time that
devours everything. This is the correct understanding of
Almighty—that there is no might apart from Him. Clarity
of intellect is thus to see that everyone and everything is
His energy alone, because all that is manifest is made of the
same elements and is only a play of the elements—gross and
subtle. This clarity is true meditation because it awakens
unconditional acceptance of "what is," with no resistance
within. And it helps actions automatically come forth, out of
acceptance and love, rather than resistance and anxiety. All
suffering and evil is rooted only in the darkness of ignorance
which causes the false attachment to "me" and "mine."
Therefore, the right response is to be rooted in the wisdom
of the one Cosmic Being who alone appears in infinitely

diverse yet unique forms and in this way, one can act from this ground in all situations, be it gentle or tough love as the situation demands.

स सर्वधीवृत्त्यनुभूतसर्व आत्मा यथा स्वप्रजनेक्षितैक: ।
तं सत्यमानन्दनिधिं भजेत नान्यत्र सज्जेद् यत आत्मपात: ॥
Bh 2.1.39

sa sarva dhī vṛtti anubhūta sarva ātmā yathā svapna
janekṣhitaikaḥ
taṁ satyam ānandanidhiṁ bhajeta nānyatra sajjed yata ātma
pātaḥ

Just as all experiences of every character in a dream are perceived by the same dreamer, the indwelling Awareness perceives all the variegated experiences of everyone through their respective mental faculties. That alone is the Supreme Self of all, the Absolute Truth and the storehouse of bliss, that one ought to be devoted to. Getting attached to anything else causes a fall into the false ego.

When dreams happen during sleep, the script of the entire dream happens with its own intelligence and there is also the effortless awareness of the entire dream. Both the events of the dream and the awareness of the dream do not happen through individual will. Similar is the waking experience too if observed carefully, the events of the world happen through the cosmic intelligence (*mahat tattva*) as explained in the preceding verses by Shuka Brahmam. Now he points to the spontaneous Awareness of all the events of the world in each one of us. While the events are variegated and diverse and each embodied being is unique in manifestation, the Awareness is common to all. This Awareness is the Supreme Self of all—*ātmā*. Hence Krishna says in the Gita: "I am the indwelling Self of all" (*aham ātmā gudākesha sarva bhutāshaya sthitaḥ*—BG 10.20). To sum it up, it is the material energy of Bhagavan that manifests as the universe, and He alone perceives this entire manifestation as pure Awareness. Therefore, nothing exists apart from Him. He is the eternal Truth and the storehouse of bliss, being pure Awareness that is unchanging and ever peaceful, unaffected by the ups and downs of life. To devote oneself to this recognition is to be free and live and act from the platform of love. To get attached to any fragment within the manifest universe—whether it be body, people, idea, nation etc.—is to lose sight of Him and fall into suffering. Thus, Shuka Brahmam summarizes beautifully the whole essence of the highest wisdom as his first discourse.

अतः कविर्नामसु यावदर्थः स्यादप्रमत्तो व्यवसायबुद्धिः ।
सिद्धेऽन्यथार्थे न यतेत तत्र परिश्रमं तत्र समीक्षमाणः ॥ Bh 2.2.3

ataḥ kavirnāmasu yāvadarthaḥ syādapramatto vyavasāyabuddhiḥ
siddhe'nyathārthe na yateta tatra pariśhramaṁ tatra
samīkṣhamāṇaḥ

To realize the highest perfection of human life, a wise person ought to engage with the material world, made of just names, only for the essential needs of life. He ought to be steadily fixed in his clarity of intelligence and never endeavor for unnecessary things, clearly perceiving that it only entails fruitless labor.

The purpose of human life is to recognize the Supreme Being as the source, sustenance and essence of all, and thereby live with freedom, fearlessness and love, seeing Him in all. Now Shuka Brahmam instructs the way of living to realize this wisdom. He says that this unfailing vision comes through meditation and being steadily fixed in this wisdom with intelligence (*vyavasāya buddhi*). As Krishna says in the Gita that being fixed in intelligence leads to clarity and one-pointedness (*vyavasāyātmikā buddhirekeha kurunandana*—BG 2.41). Whereas the one with an unsteady mind goes in many random directions. Therefore, one ought to not get distracted by even the words of Vedas, let alone other sources of knowledge. Even the flowery words of Vedas (*yām imām pushpitām vācham*—BG 2.42) can bewilder us by leading us to unnecessary activities, desire for material pleasures and heavenly realms which are all temporary in nature. What then to speak of worldly philosophies? Such activities only sap the vital energy and spirit by causing us to wander as in a dream behind fleeting pleasures of objects and experiences. Therefore, Shuka Brahmam advises here to minimize our material needs and free up time and energy for the higher order principle. This is the Vedic dictum of "simple living, high thinking." Living as simply as possible frees up time and energy for transcendental activities.

एवं स्वचित्ते स्वत एव सिद्ध आत्मा प्रियोऽर्थो भगवाननन्तः ।
तं निर्वृतो नियतार्थो भजेत संसारहेतूपरमश्च यत्र ॥ Bh 2.2.6

evaṁ svachitte svata eva siddha ātmā priyo'rtho bhagavān anantaḥ
taṁ nirvṛto niyatārtho bhajeta saṁsāra hetū paramaśhca yatra

Being clear and composed with purpose, one ought to adore the Supreme Being, who is infinite and resides in the heart as the beloved Self of all, the self-evident

In the last few verses, Shuka Brahmam instructed on the need to live simply. Minimizing our needs and not running behind those who are caught in attachment to wealth, Shuka Brahmam points to all the great resources available in nature that is bountiful and asks if the Supreme Lord ever denies protection to those who surrender unto Him fully and therefore, why do we worry so much about our material needs. This finds its beautiful echo later in the teachings of Jesus too: "Do not the birds of the sky get fed? Does not the grass of the field get clothed with flowers? Why do you worry about tomorrow?" Shuka Brahmam thus points to the need for living simply with total clarity in purpose and being composed to adoring the Supreme Being. Shuka Brahmam highlights clearly the nature of the Supreme Being being both the infinite (*ananta*) and self-evident as the indwelling beloved Self (*siddha ātmā priya*). To see Him as the only Truth in us, in everyone and in everything is to be free, fearless and have love toward all. He adds forcefully that to not recognize this Truth but simply be caught in sense pleasures is to live the life of a beast. Hence, he emphasizes again that the purpose of human life is to awaken to the Absolute Truth as described in this verse.

केचित् स्वदेहान्तर्हृदयावकाशे प्रादेशमात्रं पुरुषं वसन्तम् ।
चतुर्भुजं कञ्जरथाङ्गशङ्खगदाधरं धारणया स्मरन्ति ॥
Bh 2.2.8

kechit svadehāntar hṛdayāvakāśhe prādeśhamātraṁ puruṣhaṁ vasantam
chaturbhujaṁ kañja rathāṅga śhaṅkha gadādharaṁ dhāraṇayā smaranti

Some fix their mind in meditation upon the form of the Supreme Being with four arms bearing lotus, discus, conch and mace, in the heart space of their own body.

As already mentioned by Bhāgavatam, the three aspects of the Supreme Being are Brahman, Paramatma and Bhagavan. Shuka Brahmam first described Him as Brahman, the all-pervasive and infinite Cosmic Being. Then, he described Him as the indwelling pure Awareness who is the Self of all beings. Now he describes Him as the personal form of Bhagavan which is conducive for visual meditation. Every aspect of the form is transcendental and is replete with beautiful symbolism. Here the four arms carrying lotus, discus, conch and mace are mentioned. The conch of Krishna represents the Source of all creation. When the conch is blown, it makes the primordial sound OM. From OM, proceeds the five elements and thus His conch is called Pānchajanya (birth of five). The spinning discus represents Time. It is called Sudarshana (beautiful to behold) because movement of time through sunrise, sunset, and change of seasons is very pleasing to behold. And yet it cuts life with every passing moment and hence the most deadly weapon. One who is attached to the body is killed by Sudarshana, that is Time. The mace represents the knocks in the form of suffering given by Bhagavan that are blessings in disguise, as they are wake up calls to get out of the slumber of Maya which is false attachment to "me" and "mine." And the lotus represents the ultimate purpose of life—for the heart to flower in purity and love.

यावन्न जायेत परावरेऽस्मिन्विश्वेश्वरे द्रष्टरि भक्तियोग: ।
तावत् स्थवीय: पुरुषस्य रूपं क्रियावसाने प्रयत: स्मरेत ॥
Bh 2.2.14

yāvan na jāyeta parāvare'smin vishveshvare drashtari bhaktiyogaḥ
tāvat sthavīyaḥ puruṣhasya rūpaṁ kriyāvasāne prayataḥ smareta

Till the mind gets fixed through devotion to the all-witnessing Supreme Being, one ought to contemplate on the Cosmic form of the Lord as manifest in the world of names and forms.

The Cosmic form of the Lord is the vision that everything, everyone, everywhere is the expression of the same material energy (*prakrti*) of the Supreme Being. This is rationally ascertained through inquiry as already described by Shuka Brahmam. This eventually flowers into devotion in the heart to the all-witnessing Supreme Being within. That is the purpose of spiritual life, to go beyond just an intellectual understanding of the Source of the universe into a flowering of the heart in purity and love by devotional connection (*bhakti yoga*) to the same Source as the essence of everyone's existence. A great aid for such bhakti yoga is the transcendent form with four arms (*chaturbhuja*) with all its symbolism as described earlier of the Supreme Being who is beyond all material names and forms.

मनः स्वबुद्ध्यामलया नियम्य क्षेत्रज्ञ एतां निनयेत् तमात्मनि ।
आत्मानमात्मन्यवरुध्य धीरो लब्धोपशान्तिर्विरमेत कृत्यात् ॥
Bh 2.2.16

manaḥ svabuddhyāmalayā niyamya kṣhetrajña etāṁ ninayet tamātmani
ātmānamātmanyavarudhya dhīro labdhopaśhāntirvirameta kṛtyāt

One ought to regulate the mind with a clear intellect and recognize the light illuminating the mind within. Then, recognize this light of pure Consciousness as the true Self which is the one Supreme Consciousness and thereby abide in lasting peace, free of the false sense of doership.

After describing the Cosmic universal form, the indwelling Awareness and the transcendental Name with form as the three aspects of the Supreme Being, Shuka Brahmam now brings out the essence of inquiry which leads to Self-realization. Having a steady posture (*sthiram sukham āsanam*) and calm breathing, he instructs that one ought to sit in meditation with the mind not wandering in time and space. Then with an intellect made clear through reason, the mind ought to be freed of the sense of difference by recognizing that everything within and without is an expression of the One material energy. Then the mind has to be drawn to the ever-present light within that illuminates all activities of the body and the mind. The field of activity (*kshetra*) is matter as the body and mind. The knower of the field (*kshetrajña*) is the spirit as the Awareness. Thus, Krishna says in the Gita that this knower in every field is He alone: "Know Me as the knower of all fields" (*kshetrajñaṁ chāpi māṁ viddhi sarvakshetreshu bhārata*—BG 13.2). And then Shuka Brahmam guides us to recognize that this knower itself as pure Consciousness, which is the true Self of all, just as Krishna says in the Gita: "I am the Self abiding in the hearts of all" (*aham ātmā gudākeśha sarva bhutaśhaya sthitaḥ*—BG 10.20). To summarize, all activities of matter are His energy alone. The knower of all the activities is He alone. The source of the knower itself as the Self is again He alone. And that source is the same in all as the Universal source of all. Therefore, everything is the play of Him as Pure Consciousness (*sat chit ānanda vigraha*). This realization leads to peace, freedom from ego, and action without attachment.

न ह्यतोऽन्य: शिव: पन्था विशत: संसृताविह ।
वासुदेवे भगवति भक्तियोगो यतो भवेत् ॥ Bh 2.2.33

na hyato'nyaḥ śhivaḥ panthā viśhataḥ saṁsṛtāv iha
vāsudeve bhagavati bhakti yogo yato bhavet

For the one who wants to be free of suffering, there is no blessed path other than that which makes for loving devotion to the Supreme Being, Vāsudeva.

After describing the essence of Self-realization which is God-realization, Shuka Brahmam describes the Yogic process of raising the Kundalini energy through the seven chakras—*mulādhāra* at the base of the spine, *swādhishthāna* at the lower abdomen, *manipuraka* at the navel, *anāhata* at the heart, *vishuddhi* at the throat, *ājna* between the eyebrows and *sahasrāra* at the crown of the head. He also describes the various *siddhis* (supernatural powers) that Yogis can acquire and also the ability to visit subtler realms of consciousness. All these realms and the Yogic process to ascend to these regions are described in the Vedas. However, all these experiences are fraught with danger and unless the Yogi is very advanced, it can result in falling down due to attachment to experiences and siddhis. Therefore, after describing the Yogic process in detail for completion, Shuka Brahmam brings us back to the safest, most auspicious and blessed way of loving devotion to the Supreme Being. Vāsudeva is the most prominent Name used in Bhāgavatam for the Supreme Being, from the very first invocation. All three aspects of the Supreme Being—Brahman, Paramātma and Bhagavān—are covered by the one Name, Vāsudeva. The word *vasa* means residence. The one who resides everywhere as Brahman is Vāsudeva. The one who resides in the heart as Paramātma is Vāsudeva. The one who incarnates as the son of Vasudeva as Bhagavān is Vāsudeva (*krishnastu bhagavān swayam*). To recognize and surrender to the all-pervading Supreme Being as Vāsudeva is bhakti yoga, the most blessed path of freedom from suffering. This direct recognition that He alone exists takes us beyond even the goal of moksha and enables one to live and act in full loving presence here and now.

भगवान् ब्रह्म कात्स्न्र्येन त्रिरन्वीक्ष्य मनीषया ।
तदध्यवस्यत् कूटस्थो रतिरात्मन् यतो भवेत् ॥ Bh 2.2.34

bhagavān brahma kārtsnyena trir anvīkṣhya manīṣhayā
tad adhyavasyat kūṭastho ratir ātman yato bhavet

The first born Brahmā, after thoroughly studying all the scriptures with a keen intellect, concluded that having exclusive love for Him who is the Supreme Self in our Heart is the highest perfection of all virtues.

Shuka Brahmam, after describing all aspects of spiritual wisdom and practices, gives the final conclusion, which is to have exclusive love for the Supreme Self of all who abides in our Heart. This mirrors the conclusion given by Krishna in the Gita as well. After 18 chapters and 700 verses, Krishna summarizes the entire teaching in one verse by instructing Arjuna to simply surrender unto Him as the Only Truth (*sarva dharmān parityajya mām ekaṁ śharaṇaṁ vraja—BG 18.66*). Such surrender is not out of blind faith but out of clarity of wisdom that He alone exists. All of self inquiry is to only lead to this blessed state of surrender and love. Further Shuka Brahmam adds that this is the conclusion of studying all scriptures as ascertained by the first created being Brahma and thus all the sages henceforth. One of the subtle traps of the ego is to keep acquiring knowledge of scriptures and get caught in intellectual abstractions that only bewilder the mind. This is declared by a beautiful Upanishadic verse that the Supreme Self is not realized by listening to eloquent discourses, intellectual abstractions, listening to various scriptures etc. (*nāyamātmā pravachanena labhyo na medhayā na bahunā śhrutena—Katha Upanishad 1.2.33*). Bhāgavatam therefore teaches us the sweet way of pure hearted love rooted in wisdom, seeing everyone and everything as expressions of the one divine energy (*prakrti*) whose very ground is the Supreme Being.

भगवान् सर्वभूतेषु लक्षितः स्वात्मना हरिः ।
दृश्यैर्बुद्ध्यादिभिर्द्रष्टा लक्षणैरनुमापकैः ॥ Bh 2.2.35

*bhagavān sarva-bhūteṣhu lakṣhitaḥ svātmanā hariḥ
dṛśhyair buddhyādibhir draṣhṭā lakṣhaṇair anumāpakaiḥ*

The Supreme Being Hari alone abides as the very Self of all beings. Inquiring into the nature of phenomenal experiences and the intellect leads us to infer the presence of the true Seer within as the Light of Awareness.

When we inquire into all our experiences such as seeing, hearing etc., we can infer two facts. One is that there is tremendous intelligence involved in every experience. The other is that there is a spontaneous awareness of all experiences. The intelligence aspect comes from the one energy that pervades the universe. Just the simple act of how our eyes see objects reveals the tremendous intelligence underlying the rendition of images in our brain. This is why robotic vision for instance is such a hard problem even with all the computing power at our disposal. The same is true of the experiences of sound, smell, taste and touch. Even the functioning of the intellect, which is normally conflated with intelligence, is so remarkably complex with so many facets that come together for the experience of cognition. All this points to the humble recognition that everything we experience is not "our" doing but happens by the Supreme Intelligence. Then there is the ground of Awareness in which all these experiences unfold. Unlike machines, there is an undercurrent of Awareness beneath all experiences. This Awareness is the only unchanging truth of our Being while everything else keeps changing. This is the presence of Bhagavan as our existence which is conscious (*sat-chit*) and our very Self. Shuka Brahmam uses the beautiful name Hari in this verse for Bhagavan. Hari means "One who takes away." What does He take away? The false sense of "me" and "mine." If we realize the truth of our Self as Him and the truth of all activities as His energy, then we are free of "me" and "mine." We see only Him in everyone and everything. This is the confluence of jnana (wisdom) and bhakti (love).

तस्मात् सर्वात्मना राजन् हरि: सर्वत्र सर्वदा ।
श्रोतव्य: कीर्तितव्यश्च स्मर्तव्यो भगवान्नृणाम् ।। Bh 2.2.36

tasmāt sarvātmanā rājan hariḥ sarvatra sarvadā
shrotavyaḥ kīrtitavyaścha smartavyo bhagavān nṛṇām

Therefore, everyone ought to listen, recite and ruminate upon the Supreme Being Hari alone, seeing Him in all beings, all places and at all times.

Shuka Brahmam has brought us, through a rational inquiry into all outer phenomena and our inner self, to the realization of the Supreme Being Hari, the One who removes the ego, as the ever-existent Truth (*sat*) who is pure consciousness (*chit*) and ever blissful (*ananda*). Now he gives us the process of deepening this realization. He begins with "therefore" (*tasmāt*) to indicate that having gained total conviction that this is the highest truth, one has to live one's life in accordance with this realization, which is the foundation of unconditional love, that transcends all desires including the desire for liberation. To live and act out of this platform of love is the highest purpose of life. To abide by this and not fall prey to the false sense of ego that rises due to past conditioning (*vāsanā*), Shuka Brahmam gives three processes. It is to listen, recite or glorify, and ruminate upon Him. Listening to Bhāgavatam, Gita or such texts is the first process because it gives us this message that is both most ancient and ever fresh. Parikshit is the finest example of such listening. To recite these texts, to talk or discuss is to glorify Him is the next process. Shuka Brahmam is the finest example of such recitation or glorification. To ruminate upon Him through contemplation is the third process. The great devotee Prahlada is the finest example of such constant remembrance. These are processes of loving devotion.

There are in fact totally nine such processes that Prahlada himself describes later in the 7th skandha: *shravanam kīrtanam viṣṇoḥ smaraṇam pāda sevanam archanam vandanam dāsyam sakhyam ātma nivedanam* (Bh 7.5.23).

The first three as already mentioned are:
1. listening (like Parikshit)
2. reciting or glorifying Him (like Shuka Brahmam)
3. ruminating only upon Him (like Prahlada).

The next three are for worship:
4. adoring His lotus feet (like Mahalakshmi)
5. offering prayers (like Prthu)
6. humbly falling prostrate (like Akrura).

The final three are in the mood of living:
7. as a servant to Him (like Hanuman)
8. as a dear friend of Him (like Arjuna or Uddhava)
9. in total self surrender to Him (like Bali or the Gopis of Vrndavan).

Bhāgavatam will beautifully expand upon all these nine processes with the nine example devotees mentioned here and many more, deepening further the realization that Shuka Brahmam has brought us to. This enables us to see Him in all beings, all places and at all times as mentioned in this verse.

This is the highest perfection of life where we live and act with great energy out of love.

पिबन्ति ये भगवत आत्मनः सतां कथामृतं श्रवणपुटेषु सम्भृतम् ।
पुनन्ति ते विषयविदूषिताशयं व्रजन्ति तच्चरणसरोरुहान्तिकम् ॥
Bh 2.2.37

pibanti ye bhagavata ātmanaḥ satāṁ kathāmṛtaṁ śhravaṇa-puṭeshu sambhṛtam
punanti te vishaya-vidūṣhitāśhayaṁ vrajanti taccharaṇa saroruhāntikam

Those who drink through their ears the nectar-like activities of the Supreme Being, the Soul of the universe, have their heart purified of the dirt caused due to attachment to sense objects and they thus abide in His lotus feet.

Of the nine processes of devotion outlined in the previous verse, the first and foremost is *shravanam* (listening). Shuka Brahmam emphasizes it here by stating that if one simply listens with reverence to the nectar-like activities of Bhagavan, that alone is sufficient to remove the contamination due to the past conditioning of attachment to objects and experiences. It purifies the heart effortlessly by mere listening. The activities of Bhagavan include His direct teachings, His pastimes through various Avatars, the stories of various Bhagavatas fully surrendered unto Him and the way His Grace works in their lives. All of these are indeed exclusively covered in the Bhāgavatam. The conclusion is therefore that by just listening to Bhāgavatam with love every day, one can be free of all false attachments and abide in the Supreme Being who is the only Truth.

अकामः सर्वकामो वा मोक्षकाम उदारधी: ।
तीव्रेण भक्तियोगेन यजेत पुरुषं परम् ॥ Bh 2.3.10

akāmaḥ sarva kāmo vā mokṣha kāma udāra dhīḥ
tīvreṇa bhakti yogena yajeta puruṣham param

The one with discerning intelligence—whether he has no desire at all or driven by all kinds of desires including liberation—ought to only worship the One Supreme Being with intense loving devotion.

It is the general propensity of people to imagine many "gods" or sources of power and blessings, and worship different deities to fulfill desires. This is true of people of all religions, whether it be going after the Vedic pantheon or visiting the shrines of various saints and mystics. To clarify this, Shuka Brahmam lists all the various deities of the Vedic pantheon that people believe have the powers to give wealth, learning, progeny, strength, long life, prestige etc. He then concludes that one with true wisdom recognizes that there is only One ultimate Source of all powers and blessings. The beginning of wisdom is to seek fulfillment of all desires (*sarva kāmaḥ*) in the Supreme Being who is Almighty and to see the temporary nature of all desires, including seeking liberation. Liberation (*mokṣha kāmaḥ*) from desires is a more evolved desire and to inquire as to who is seeking liberation Sund realize that if God is truly Almighty, then every might comes only from Him and therefore the very "I" that seeks even liberation is His energy alone is the culmination of wisdom. This mirrors what

Krishna says in the Gita: "Four types of pious people worship Me—those who seek to remove distress, those who seek worldly possessions, those who seek knowledge, and those situated in wisdom" (*chatur vidhā bhajante mām janāḥ sukṛitino'rjuna / ārto jijñāsur arthārthī jñānī cha bharatarṣhabha*—BG 7.16). The first two types are motivated by worldly desires (*sarva kāmaḥ*), the third type by knowledge (*mokṣha kāmaḥ*) and the last alone are situated in wisdom free of all desires (*akāmaḥ*). Only when we recognize the Supreme Being as the Almighty who bestows everything, we are free of all desires and situated in unconditional love.

एतावानेव यजतामिह निःश्रेयसोदयः ।
भगवत्यचलो भावो यद् भागवतसंगतः ॥ Bh 2.3.11

etāvāneva yajatāmiha niḥśhreyasodayaḥ
bhagavatyachalo bhāvo yad bhāgavatasaṅgataḥ

All those who worship partial deities can attain the highest benediction only through steady and unwavering devotion to the Supreme Being, that comes through association with devotees.

As already outlined by Shuka Brahmam, wisdom begins with recognizing the Source of the entire manifest universe as the One Supreme Being and not be caught in fragmentary devotion to partial deities. Krishna emphasizes this in Gita as well: "The fruit attained by people of limited understanding who worship partial deities is perishable, whereas My devotees realize Me, the Supreme Being" (*antavat tu phalaṁ teṣhāṁ tad bhavati alpa medhasām devān deva yajo yānti mad bhaktā yānti mām api*—BG 7.23). Therefore, Shuka Brahmam says the highest benediction is attained by steady, unwavering (*achala*) devotion. Constant wavering (*chanchala*) is the nature of the mind. To steady and still the mind is essential to realize the highest wisdom. Shuka Brahmam gives the best way to go from wavering to steady mind—by associating with Bhagavatas (devotees). This is the secret to lift us up, by being in constant association (Satsang) with the sacred. And the most prominent among all Satsang activities is to listen to such teachings as Bhāgavatam and Bhagavad Gita, which automatically purifies and steadies the mind in wisdom.

ज्ञानं यदाप्रतिनिवृत्त गुणोर्मिचक्रमात्मप्रसाद उत यत्र गुणेष्वसङ्गः ।
कैवल्यसम्मतपथस्त्वथ भक्तियोगः को निर्वृतो हरिकथासु रतिं न कुर्यात् ।। Bh 2.3.12

jñānaṁ yadāpratinivṛtta guṇormichakram ātmaprasāda uta yatra guṇeshvasaṅgah
kaivalyasammata pathastvatha bhakti yogah ko nirvṛto
harikathāsu ratiṁ na kuryāt

Listening to the discourses on the Supreme Being Hari sets at rest the waves of passion in the mind, purifies the heart filling it with joy, creates a natural distaste for fleeting pleasures and awakens loving devotion which is the blessed way to freedom and beatitude. Having once tasted this supreme joy, who would cease taking delight in listening to such discourses?

Having concluded that true wisdom begins with recognizing the source and essence of all as the Supreme Being, Shuka Brahmam glorifies the power of listening to discourses on the Supreme Being. This includes listening to the direct teachings of Bhagavan as found in Bhagavad Gita and the detailed accounts of the various Avatars, sages, devotees as found in Bhāgavatam. Simply listening to such discourses with reverence (*shraddhā*) gives us a glimpse into the highest potential of human life. Having once tasted this, the waves of passion for fleeting objects and experiences start receding and are seen as trivial, not worth investing precious energy into. Thus dispassion (*vairāgya*) naturally awakens, not by controlling desires, but by giving the highest taste of divine love that makes all worldly desires seem petty. That is why the Supreme Being is referred to in this verse as Hari, the One who takes away all petty desires. This happens without any effort when the mind turns toward Him by association with devotees. This is the way of freedom (*kaivalya*) that is taught by Bhāgavatam that gives us the unique blessing of this sweet divine love. That is why Bhāgavatam is considered to be the direct sound form (*shabda swarupa*) of the Supreme Being.

आयुर्हरति वै पुंसामुद्यन्नस्तं च यत्रसौ ।
तस्यर्ते यत्क्षणो नीत उत्तमश्लोकवार्तया ॥ Bh 2.3.17

āyurharati vai puṁsāmudyannastaṁ cha yannasau
tasyarte yatkṣhaṇo nīta uttamaśhloka vārtayā

The sun, rising and setting every day, steals away the life of all humans except the ones properly utilizing the time in the discourses on the Supreme Being.

The sage Shaunaka is pleased to listen to the narration of Sūta in Naimisharanya on the discourse of Shuka Brahmam's teachings to Parikshit. He glorifies the greatness of the speaker and the listener that naturally elevates the quality of the conversation. Shuka Brahmam is the son of Vyasa ever devoted to Vasudeva (*vaiyāsakiśhcha bhagavān vāsudeva parāyaṇaḥ*). Parikshit is a great Bhagavata devoted to Krishna, even his childhood play was spent in games about Krishna's pastimes. So Shaunka says it is natural that sublime talks saturated with the glories of the Supreme Being alone take place in the assembly in Haridwar. He says otherwise when we waste our time in idle talk and gossip, time is ticking away and we waste precious human life in frivolous pursuits. And the sun comes around every day, leaving us shorter of breath and one day closer to death. Therefore, Bhāgavatam instructs in this verse that it is important that we utilize time judiciously in realizing the highest purpose of human life, by listening to such transcendental discourses, contemplating upon them and living by their light.

तदश्मसारं हृदयं बतेदं यद् गृह्यमाणैर्हरिनामधेयैः ।
न विक्रियेताथ यदा विकारो नेत्रे जलं गात्ररुहेषु हर्षः ॥
Bh 2.3.24

tadaśhmasāraṁ hṛdayaṁ batedaṁ yad
gṛhyamāṇairharināmadheyaiḥ
na vikriyetātha yadā vikāro netre jalaṁ gātraruheṣhu harṣhaḥ

The heart ought to be not hard like stone but melt in divine love with tears upon hearing the holy names and discourses of the Supreme Being Hari.

After stating that time steals away the lives of those engaged in frivolous pursuits, the sage Shaunaka points out the essence of what distinguishes human life from other life forms. He asks very pointedly, "Don't the trees live? Don't bellows breathe? Don't animals eat and copulate? How is a human different from a swine or a donkey if he is only interested in eating and working hard for it?" He answers by saying that every organ of cognition or action—eyes, ears, tongue, smell, hands, feet, head—that is not engaged in transcendental activities is just a burden to oneself. Therefore, he concludes in this verse that to truly actualize human birth, one has to listen to the holy names and discourses on the Supreme Being Hari (the One who takes away the ego), not with the mind but with one's heart that melts in divine love. And the great secret is that this highest perfection of human life is achieved simply through engaging the senses, mainly ears and tongue, listening and speaking on the most sublime topic of God-realization. As Krishna says in the Gita: "The ones with minds fixed and lives surrendered unto Me enlighten each other through conversing about Me and remain ever content and blissful" (*mat chittā mad gata prāṇā bodhayantaḥ parasparam / kathayantaśhcha māṁ nityaṁ tuṣhyanti cha ramanti cha*—BG 10.9).

अथाभिधेह्यङ्ग मनोऽनुकूलं प्रभाषसे भागवतप्रधानः ।
यदाह वैयासकिरात्मविद्याविशारदो नृपतिं साधु पृष्ट: ॥
Bh 2.3.25

athābhidhehyaṅga mano'nukūlaṁ prabhāṣhase bhāgavata pradhānaḥ
yad āha vaiyāsakir ātma vidyā viśhārado nṛpatiṁ sādhu pṛṣhṭaḥ

Dear Sūta, what you speak is therefore most pleasing to the mind. Please narrate to us more of what Shuka Brahmam, the greatest among Bhāgavatas and the most

perfect in the wisdom of the Supreme Self, spoke in response to the excellent question of the king Parikshit.

Expressing his joy at listening to the conversation between Shuka Brahmam and Parikshit and glorifying such listening as the highest perfection of human life in the past few verses, Shaunaka now exhorts Sūta to continue with the narration. He refers to Shuka Brahmam as Vaiyāsaki, the son of the great Vyasa, who is both the greatest devotee and the most perfect in the wisdom of the Supreme Self (*ātma vidyā*). From this we see that there is no distinction between devotion and wisdom at the highest level. The perfection of devotion is wisdom. The perfection of wisdom is devotion. If they are seen as separate, it is fragmentary and not fully mature yet. Shuka Brahmam represents the perfect ideal of the oneness of devotion and wisdom. The questioner Parikshit also is an advanced being putting forth excellent questions and listening with his heart. This dialogue thus makes for the most sublime conversation to listen to and hence Shaunaka says it is most pleasing to the mind.

संस्थां विज्ञाय संन्यस्य कर्म त्रैवर्गिकं च यत् । वासुदेवे भगवति आत्मभावं दृढं गतः ॥ Bh 2.4.4

saṁsthāṁ vijñāya sannyasya karma traivargikaṁ cha yat
vāsudeve bhagavati ātma bhāvaṁ dṛdhaṁ gataḥ

Being free of attachment to the threefold pursuit (*dharma, artha, kāma*), Parkshit was firmly established in the realization of his true Self as the Supreme Being Vasudeva.

Sūta continues the narration of the dialogue between Shuka Brahmam and Parikshit by describing the mood of the listener, Parikshit. After describing the qualities of the speaker in the last verse, he now describes the listener as one who's already freed of all attachments due to listening to the discourse of Shuka Brahmam. Being a pious king and very devoted to Krishna right from childhood, Parikshit shook off whatever attachment remained in him as the sense of mine (*mamatā*) toward body, relations, property, kingdom etc. Therefore, he was free of attachment to the pursuit of wealth, comforts or even virtue. He was firmly established in the realization that his true Self is the all-pervading Supreme Being, Vasudeva (One who resides everywhere). As has been revealed in the Gita: "The mark of a true great soul and a realized being is to surrender unto Me, seeing everything as Vasudeva" (*bahūnāṁ janmanām ante jñānavān māṁ prapadyate / vāsudevaḥ sarvam iti sa mahātmā sudurlabhaḥ*—BG 7.19).

नमः परस्मै पुरुषाय भूयसे सदुद्भवस्थाननिरोधलीलया ।
गृहीतशक्तित्रितयाय देहिनामन्तर्भवायानुपलक्ष्यवर्त्मने ॥
Bh 2.4.12

namaḥ parasmai puruṣhāya bhūyase sad udbhava sthāna nirodha līlayā
gṛhīta śhakti tritayāya dehinām
antarbhavāyānupalakṣyavartmane

Obeisances to the Supreme Being of infinite glory, who takes on the three powers of creation, sustenance and dissolution of the universe as His divine play. He is the Inner Controller whose true nature cannot be comprehended through the intellect.

This marks the beginning of the response of Shuka Brahmam to Parikshit's question on the mystery of creation, sustenance and dissolution of the Universe. His response begins not as an intellectual analysis but in a prayerful mood, declaring the Supreme Being is beyond the comprehension of the intellect. Because the intellect is a tiny spark of the infinite energy of the Universe, it is quite preposterous to assume that one can understand all the mysteries of the Universe through the intellect. With all the great advances in science and technology, we only have a very limited understanding of how even our body functions with such tremendous intelligence at all levels. Therefore, quite appropriately Shuka Brahmam says that the infinite glory of the Supreme Being who has the powers of creation, sustenance and dissolution of the universe that goes on cyclically cannot be comprehended by the intellect but can only be surrendered to with love.

भूयो नमः सद्वृजिनच्छिदेऽसतामसम्भवायाखिलसत्त्वमूर्तये ।
पुंसां पुनः पारमहंस्य आश्रमे व्यवस्थितानामनुमृग्यदाशुषे ॥
Bh 2.4.13

bhūyo namaḥ sad vṛjinachchhide asatām asambhavāya akhila sattva mūrtaye
puṁsāṁ punaḥ pāramahaṁsya āśhrame vyavasthitānām anumṛgya dāśhuṣhe

I again offer my obeisances to He who is the universal Truth, who roots out the sorrow of the pious, obstructs the growth of the wicked and confers the highest state of freedom to those who have perfect discernment.

Shuka Brahmam continues to reveal the nature of the Supreme Being as the one universal and absolute Truth through this prayer. First, he states that the sorrow of the pious is rooted out through wisdom of the Supreme Being. The nature of the world is to cause suffering due to its very impermanence. Hence suffering is inevitable at the material level. To root out sorrow or suffering is therefore not by eradicating outer suffering but by bestowing inner wisdom that helps us dissociate from the impermanence. All grand plans of the most wicked have been brought to nought by Time, which is the very form of Bhagavan. Thus, Krishna declares while revealing His Cosmic Form in the Gita, "I am Time, the destroyer of all" (*kalo'smi loka kshaya krt*—BG 11.32). And finally, He confers the highest state of freedom for the ones with perfect discernment. They are called *paramahamsa* (Supreme Swan) that refers to the mythical bird that can separate milk from water. Similarly, the one who can discern and separate the eternal substrate of Being from the impermanent play of becoming is *paramahamsa* among humans, and through this discernment is bestowed the supreme state of freedom.

नमो नमस्तेऽस्त्वृषभाय सात्वतां विदूरकाष्ठाय मुहुः कुयोगिनाम् ।
निरस्तसाम्यातिशयेन राधसा स्वधामनि ब्रह्मणि रंस्यते नमः ॥
Bh 2.4.14

namo namaste'stu ṛṣhabhāya sātvatāṁ vidūra kāṣhṭhāya muhuḥ kuyoginām
nirasta sāmyātiśhayena rādhasā svadhāmani brahmaṇi raṁsyate namaḥ

My obeisances to the Supreme Being who reveals Himself to the devotees but is out of the reach of those devoid

of devotion. Being unequaled and unsurpassed, He delights in His own essence as the Infinite Consciousness (Brahman).

Shuka Brahmam here emphasizes that one cannot realize the Truth of the Supreme Being through a logical process of analysis however sophisticated. It requires a heart of devotion to perceive that He is not merely an object of understanding but the very Subject in which all understanding takes place. The true Subject is the very sense of Being in our heart—the Supreme Self of all, who is Infinite Consciousness (Brahman). Being indivisible and non-dual, there can be nothing equal or surpassing Him. Normally, delight or joy is found to be in duality such as when one enjoys a sense object. But such delight is always temporary, requiring an externally manifest object which cannot last forever. Whereas the true delight or joy can be found only in one's own essence as Pure Consciousness who is devoid of any duality and doesn't require any external object. Therefore, such delight is the highest, supreme bliss of Bhagavan that is everlasting.

यत्कीर्तनं यत्स्मरणं यदीक्षणं यद्वन्दनं यच्छ्रवणं यदर्हणम् ।
लोकस्य सद्यो विधुनोति कल्मषं तस्मै सुभद्रश्रवसे नमो नमः ॥
Bh 2.4.15

yatkīrtanaṁ yatsmaraṇaṁ yadīkṣhaṇaṁ yadvandanaṁ
yacchravaṇaṁ yadarhaṇam
lokasya sadyo vidhunoti kalmaṣhaṁ tasmai subhadra śhravase
namo namaḥ

Obeisances to the Supreme Being of most auspicious renown. By glorifying, contemplating, beholding,

greeting and adoring Him, one is cleansed of all impurities in the mind and realizes Him.

This next verse points out that the only obstacle to realizing Him and tasting the everlasting joy of His essence is the impurity in the mind, the root of which is the sense of me and mine. Therefore, Shuka Brahmam gives the process of realizing Him who is our true Self in this prayer as the One who can be perceived, listened to, contemplated upon, worshiped and glorified through Holy names and forms. And by engaging in this process, one is cleansed of the impurities of the mind and is freed of the attachment to body/mind as me and mind and the true Self that abides ever in our Heart shines forth. This is the essence of God-realization or Self-realization.

विचक्षणा यच्चरणोपसादनात् सङ्गं व्युदस्योभयतोऽन्तरात्मनः ।
विन्दन्ति हि ब्रह्मगतिं गतक्लमास्तस्मै सुभद्रश्रवसे नमो नमः ॥
Bh 2.4.16

vicakṣhaṇā yachcharaṇopasādanāt saṅgam vyudasyobhayato'ntar ātmanaḥ
vindanti hi brahmagatim gataklamās tasmai subhadra śhravase namo namaḥ

Obeisances to the Supreme Being of most auspicious renown. By surrendering unto Him, the wise ones shake off their attachment to this world or the other world and thereby realize the true Self as the Infinite Being (Brahman).

To surrender unto the Supreme Being is to see that His energy alone manifests as all names and forms in all of time and space. This removes the delusion of being caught in the identification of the body/mind as me and the resulting duality of attachment to hold onto and fear losing what is "mine." It also removes the projected ideals of an afterlife or even liberation for the same false "me" which is only an invention of thought as an escape mechanism from facing the truth of this moment. Instead, if we see that everyone and everything here and now is sacred and divine, then we are situated in total acceptance and love. There is no desire to escape from here and now, project any afterlife, future state of enlightenment etc. That's why Bhāgavatam always emphasizes that true bhakti is to transcend even the desire for liberation.

तपस्विनो दानपरा यशस्विनो मनस्विनो मन्त्रविदः सुमङ्गलाः ।
क्षेमं न विन्दन्ति विना यदर्पणं तस्मै सुभद्रश्रवसे नमो नमः ॥
Bh 2.4.17

tapasvino dānaparā yaśhasvino manasvino mantravidaḥ sumaṅgalāḥ
kṣhemaṁ na vindanti vinā yadarpaṇaṁ tasmai subhadra śhravase namo namaḥ

Obeisances to the Supreme Being of most auspicious renown. Even those engaged in austerities and charity, having high repute, with their mind under control, expert in sacred chants and righteous in conduct, do not attain blessedness without surrendering unto Him.

The material energy of the Supreme Being is of three modes (*sattva, rajas, tamas* or goodness, passion, dullness) and the only source of all activities. Of the three modes, clearly *sattva* is the superior mode of living that results in activities rooted in goodness such as austerity, charity, sacred chants, righteous conduct etc. Such living results in an agitation free mind and a high reputation in the world. Yet even these pious actions result in bondage, when done out of a false sense of doership. It subjects one to feelings of pride and superiority and is vulnerable to flattery. Then, what to speak of actions out of *rajas* or *tamas* which are even more binding. Therefore, Shuka Brahmam points out that it is not just good actions, but the wisdom that everything is done only by the One Supreme Being through His material energy that frees us from bondage and suffering. This establishes us in the blessed state of peace here and now.

स एष आत्मात्मवतामधीश्वरस्त्रयीमयो धर्ममयस्तपोमयः ।
गतव्यलीकैरजशङ्करादिभिर्वितर्क्यलिङ्गो भगवान् प्रसीदताम्
॥ Bh 2.4.19

sa eṣha ātmātmavatām adhīśhvarastrayīmayo
dharmamayastapomayaḥ
gatavyalīkair ajaśhaṅkarādibhirvitarkyaliṅgo bhagavān
prasīdatām

May the Lord, who is the Self of the wise sages, who manifests as the Vedas, Dharma and all austerities and who is adored by all sincere devotees, bestow Grace upon me.

Shuka Brahmam continues his prayer that is steeped in wisdom by invoking the Grace of the Supreme Being who is the Lord of all activities that are five-fold—creation (*srishti*), sustenance (*sthiti*), dissolution (*samhāra*), veiling (*tirodhāna*) and grace (*anugraha*). The first three are clearly seen everywhere in the cosmic cycle, life cycle, and in the cycle of day and night. Every waking is a creation and sleep a dissolution. Every birth is a creation and death a dissolution. And the whole cosmos goes through creation and dissolution. Sustenance is what maintains the activities of the day, of one's life, of the whole cosmos. Veiling is the ignorance found in all beings by nature that causes identification with me and mine based on the bodily conception. Grace removes this ignorance and situates us in true wisdom. While the first four happen automatically for everyone, Grace is revealed only to the sincere devotees. Therefore, Shuka Brahmam invokes the Grace of Bhagavan in this prayer. He describes Bhagavan as the Self of the wise sages because, even though He is the Self of all, only the wise sages realize the Truth and see Him as their very Self. It is the Supreme Being who manifests as the Vedas or all knowledge, Dharma or all righteousness and Tapas or all austerities.

यदङ्घ्र्यभिध्यानसमाधिधौतयाधियानुपश्यन्ति हि तत्त्वमात्मनः ।
वदन्ति चैतत् कवयो यथारुचं स मे मुकुन्दो भगवान् प्रसीदताम् ॥
Bh 2.4.21

yadaṅghryabhidhyāna samādhi dhautayā dhiyānupaśhyanti hi tattvam ātmanaḥ
vadanti chaitat kavayo yathāruchaṁ sa me mukundo bhagavān prasīdatām

May Lord Mukunda, contemplating upon whom the wise realize the Truth with intellect purified through meditation and describe Him each according to their own predilection, bestow Grace upon me.

Shuka Brahmam continues to invoke Grace by describing Him as the one whose contemplation purifies our intellect and liberates us. Thus, He is known as Mukunda—One who bestows *mukti* (liberation). When we contemplate upon the Source of our very being and that of the whole universe, we transcend petty thoughts, gossip and worries. Thereby the intellect is purified. Both scientific and spiritual inquiry are ultimately directed only toward that which can explain everything and has an elevating effect. However, spiritual inquiry goes inward to find the Source within our very Heart and situates us in silent meditation (*samādhi*). This helps us realize the Truth here and now as our very existence. The ones who have thus realized describe Him each according to their cultural conditioning and taste. Therefore, we don't find any two sages describing God in the same way. To see past such differences in descriptions into the underlying commonality removes comparisons or judgments which is essential for wisdom to dawn.

भूतैर्महद्भिर्य इमाः पुरो विभुर्निर्माय शेते यदमूषु पूरुष: ।
भुङ्क्ते गुणान् षोडश षोडशात्मक: सोऽलङ्कृषीष्ट भगवान्
वचांसि मे ॥ Bh 2.4.23

bhūtairmahadbhirya imāḥ puro vibhurnirmāya śhete yadamūṣhu pūruṣhaḥ
bhuṅkte guṇān ṣhoḍaśha ṣhoḍaśhātmakaḥ so'laṅkṛṣhīṣhṭa bhagavān vachāṁsi me

Having spawned all the beings out of the five elements, the all-pervading Supreme Being indwells as the Self, and is endowed with sixteen instruments, enjoying their sixteen objects. May He shine forth through my speech.

The five elements of space, air, fire, water and soil come forth from the Cosmic Intelligence of the Supreme Being, and they spawn all animate and inanimate beings. All living entities are made of these five elements as are all objects of the universe. The underlying essence or the true Self of all beings is the very same Supreme Being as Pure Consciousness. Among human beings, the Cosmic Intelligence expands as sixteen instruments—the five senses of cognition (sight, sound, smell, taste and touch), the five senses of action (speech, holding, moving, copulation and excretion), the five vital airs of the body (*prāna, apāna, samāna, udāna, vyāna*) that govern various bodily functions of breathing, digestion, blood circulation etc. and the sixteenth is the mind. They go forth to enjoy their respective objects of cognition, action, bodily functions and thoughts. Thus, every activity of human beings is conducted by the Cosmic Intelligence through the power of Prakrti (material energy) in the field of Purusha (indwelling Awareness). To falsely take ownership of any activity of the senses, body or mind as "mine" is the root of ignorance. All functions happen spontaneously due to the Cosmic Intelligence that pervades the whole universe and manifests as precise laws of physics. Thus, Shuka Brahmam points out the highest wisdom that all actions are performed and enjoyed not by us, but through each of us by the One Supreme Being. This is beautifully declared by Krishna in the Gita: "Realizing Me alone as the enjoyer of all activities, the Supreme Lord of all the worlds and the true friend of all living beings, one attains peace" (*bhoktāraṁ yajña tapasām sarvaloka maheśhvaram suhridaṁ sarva bhūtānāṁ jñātvā māṁ śhāntim ṛichchhati—BG 5.29*).

नमस्तस्मै भगवते वासुदेवाय वेधसे ।
पपुर्ज्ञानमयं सौम्या यन्मुखाम्बुरुहासवम् ॥ Bh 2.4.24

namas tasmai bhagavate vāsudevaya vedhase
papurjñānamayaṁ saumyā yanmukhāmburuhāsavam

Obeisances to the all-knowing sage Vyasa who is non-different from the Supreme Being Vasudeva and from whose lotus-like lips has come forth the nectar of wisdom for us to drink.

Here Shuka Brahmam glorifies his father and teacher Vyasa who composed and taught the nectar Bhāgavatam to Shuka Brahmam. That's the nectar that Shuka Brahmam shared with Parikshit and we are all now able to partake of. Shuka Brahmam henceforth concludes this prayer, most appropriately, to the Supreme Being with an expression of gratitude to his Guru and father Vyasa who is himself an empowered Avatar of the Lord. After this, Shuka Brahmam proceeds to relate a dialogue between Narada and Brahmā which will answer Parikshit's question on the topic of creation in greater detail.

यद्रूपं यदधिष्ठानं यतः सृष्टमिदं प्रभो ।
यत्संस्थं यत्परं यच्च तत् तत्त्वं वद तत्त्वतः ॥ Bh 2.5.2

yad rūpam yad adhiṣhṭhānam yataḥ sṛṣhṭam idaṁ prabho
yat saṁstham yat param yachcha tat tattvaṁ vada tattvataḥ

(Narada addressing Brahmā) Oh father, please tell me in essence the truth about this universe as to its nature, its underlying substrate, how it is created, how it is maintained and what is transcendent to it.

Shuka Brahmam relates a dialogue between the divine sage Narada and his father Brahmā as it directly addresses the question posed by Parikshit about the mystery of creation. Narada begins by offering his obeisances to his father Brahmā who embodies the creative energy that brings forth this universe and makes a thorough inquiry on all aspects of the universe. Narada sets an example of how to question one's teacher with both reverence and curiosity. As Krishna says in the Gita, "Learn the Truth by approaching Guru and question with reverence" (*tad viddhi praṇipātena paripraśhnena sevayā*—BG 4.34). Narada further tells Brahma that being the creative power of the entire universe of all animate beings and inanimate objects, he ought to know everything clearly. He further asks, please tell me how you are able to bring forth the elements of the universe, who empowers you and what is the source of your knowledge? Narada adds that since you are found to practice penance yourself to bring forth the universe, it is clear that there is One higher than you, so please instruct about Him. God is many times described as the Creator but here Narada inquires about the very act of creation itself that seems to be grounded in a Truth more foundational because it is followed by sustenance and then dissolution at all levels. Every thought, every being, every culture, every planet and the whole cosmos goes through the same threefold cycle of creation, sustenance and dissolution. What underlies this cycle from the microcosm to the macrocosm is the penetrating inquiry of Narada.

येन स्वरोचिषा विश्वं रोचितं रोचयाम्यहम् ।
यथार्कोऽग्निर्यथा सोमो यथर्क्षग्रहतारकाः ॥ Bh 2.5.11

yena svarochiṣhā viśhvaṁ rochitaṁ rochayāmyaham
yathārko'gnir yathā somo yatharksha graha tārakāḥ

(Brahmā responds to Narada) I bring forth this universe only by the power of the self-effulgent Supreme Being, just as the moon and other planets provide illumination that comes only by the illumination of the sun.

After lauding the inquiry of Narada as being beneficial to all beings and pleased that it reveals the glory of the Supreme Being, Brahmā responds by stating that indeed it appears as if he creates the universe until one knows the real Source. He gives a beautiful example of how moonlight or other shiny objects reflect the light of the sun and are seen in its light. All other sources of light powered by electricity are also produced directly or indirectly only due to the sun's energy. So, while there seem to be many sources of light, in fact there is only one, the sun. Similarly, while there seems to be the creative, sustaining, dissolving energies and various natural forces of the universe, in fact there is only one Source of all.

तस्मै नमो भगवते वासुदेवाय धीमहि ।
यन्मायया दुर्जयया मां वदन्ति जगद्गुरुम् ॥ Bh 2.5.12

tasmai namo bhagavate vāsudevaya dhīmahi
yanmāyayā durjayayā māṁ vadanti jagadgurum

My obeisances to that Source who is Vasudeva, upon whom I meditate. Deluded by His Maya that is hard

to penetrate, people speak of me as the creator of the universe.

In this verse, Brahmā addresses that Supreme Source as Vasudeva and offers his prayers to Him. One who resides everywhere is Vasudeva and therefore He is the substrate upon which all creation, sustenance and dissolution happens. It is by His Maya that people are deluded into ignorance and ascribe doership to various individuals starting from Brahmā. And it is by His Grace that wisdom dawns. Therefore, Brahmā offers his obeisances and meditates (*dhīmahi*) upon Him before beginning his detailed response on the mystery of creation.

विलज्जमानया यस्य स्थातुमीक्षापथेऽमुया ।
विमोहिता विकत्थन्ते ममाहमिति दुर्धियः ॥ Bh 2.5.13

vilajjamānayā yasya sthātum īkṣāpathe'muyā
vimohitā vikatthante mamāham iti durdhiyaḥ

Bewildered by Maya, the ignorant one's prattle on about "mine" and "me," though this Maya is too shy to stand the look of the Lord even once.

The false sense of ownership and doership as "mine" and "me" (*mama aham*) with reference to one's possessions and activities is only due to lack of inquiry into oneself. The sense of "mine" causes blinding attachment toward people, places, objects, ideas, feelings etc. And what underlies it is the sense of "me" ascribed to the activities of the body and mind. This results in various dualities tossing us about and causing suffering, such as pride and guilt, vulnerability to flattery and insult, excitement and depression. When we inquire as to who is the doer, we find that actions are rooted in thoughts, and thoughts spring up from the ground of Existence-Consciousness (*sat-chit*). We only have to carefully look at the genesis of one thought within to see that it rises from a field of energy with its own power. And this power is rooted in the ever-present Consciousness, our true Being as the Lord within. Hence Brahma says that if we turn to the Lord within, then Maya cannot have hold in the form of "mine" and "me." The bewildering potency of Maya can survive only in darkness which is ignorance. As Krishna says in the Gita, "Only the ignorant ones think "I am the doer," being deluded by ego" (*ahankāra vimūḍhātmā kartāham iti manyate*—BG 3.27). Therefore, if we shine the light of wisdom, then Maya is too shy to face the light and runs away. So, the import is that to be free of "mine" and "me" is to turn within to face the Lord ever abiding as our true Self and the Source of all our activities.

द्रव्यं कर्म च कालश्च स्वभावो जीव एव च ।
वासुदेवात्परो ब्रह्मन्न च चान्योऽर्थोऽस्ति तत्त्वतः ॥ Bh 2.5.14

dravyaṁ karma cha kālaśhcha svabhāvo jīva eva cha
vāsudevat paro brahman na chānyo'rtho'sti tattvataḥ

In Truth, the various material elements, activities, Time, nature of animate beings or inanimate objects, and all individual beings are all none other than Vasudeva, the Supreme Being.

Brahma in this verse declares the supreme truth that the apparent multiplicity of various phenomena is nothing but the unique and infinite expressions of the One Source, who is the Self of all. The entire universe of elements engages in various activities through the movement of Time, each according to their unique nature. If we trace the Source of all this multiplicity, we come upon the ground of Being who is Vasudeva, the all-pervading Supreme Being. Krishna declares in the Gita, "A great being is one who sees everything as Me, Vasudeva" (*vāsudevaḥ sarvam iti sa mahātmā su-durlabhaḥ*—BG 7.19).

नारायणपरा वेदा देवा नारायणाङ्गजाः ।
नारायणपरा लोका नारायणपरा मखाः ॥
नारायणपरो योगो नारायणपरं तपः ।
नारायणपरं ज्ञानं नारायणपरा गतिः ॥ Bh 2.5.15-16

nārāyaṇa parā vedā devā nārāyaṇāṅgajāḥ
nārāyaṇa parā lokā nārāyaṇa parā makhāḥ
nārāyaṇa paro yogo nārāyaṇa paraṁ tapaḥ
nārāyaṇa paraṁ jñānaṁ nārāyaṇa parā gatiḥ

The Supreme Being Nārāyaṇa is the subject of all Vedas, the source of all deities, the realms of existence, the goal of all sacrifices, the object of all Yoga, the essence of all austerities, the transcendental wisdom, and the supreme realization to be attained.

Brahma now offers a pair of verses that are at once filled with sublime devotion and highest wisdom. The Supreme Being is called as Nārāyaṇa because all humans (*nara*) have their ultimate refuge (*ayana*) in Him. It is one of the most sacred names of the Lord that has its own power and hence Brahma invokes multiple times with great devotion. With each invocation, Brahma covers an aspect of spiritual life that seem very diverse and yet has one purpose—realizing the

Supreme Being as the only Truth, known as the all-pervading Consciousness (Brahman) abiding within as the true Self (Paramatma) and descending out of His Grace in various forms (Bhagavan). Study of all scriptures (Vedas) is only to realize Nārāyaṇa, as Krishna declares in the Gita: "I alone am meant to be known through all Vedas" (*vedaiśhcha sarvair aham eva vedyaḥ*—BG 15.15). All deities worshipped in various ways are only aspects of Nārāyaṇa. All the realms of existence one may perceive or imagine are only in Nārāyaṇa. All sacrifices are only to deny the false ego and behold Nārāyaṇa. The purpose of all Yoga is to only remove the illusory separateness, seeing the oneness of everything as Nārāyaṇa. All austerities are only to purify the mind of the dust of ignorance about Nārāyaṇa. Therefore, true transcendental wisdom is Nārāyaṇa. The ultimate refuge of all is Nārāyaṇa.

तस्यापि द्रष्टुरीशस्य कूटस्थस्याखिलात्मनः ।
सृज्यं सृजामि सृष्टोऽहमीक्षयैवाभिचोदितः ॥ Bh 2.5.17

tasyāpi drashtur īshasya kūtasthasyākhilātmanah
srjyam srjāmi srshto'ham īkshayaivābhichoditah

The Supreme Being is at once the Seer and the Controller, unchanging as the Self of the Universe. It is He who creates everything, while I (Brahma) appear to create.

The Seer (*drashtā*) and the Controller (*īsha*) represent the Consciousness and Energy aspect of the Supreme Being. As the screen of Consciousness, He is the pure Seer. As the Energy that animates the dance of forms on the screen, He is the Controller. Therefore, the unmanifest and the manifest are both Him alone. Thus, He is the essence and the Self of the Universe. He alone creates, sustains and dissolves everything which is the entire gamut of all activities. So, Brahma says that any appearance of separate doership or creation of any activity of the whole cosmos is only an appearance, for the real doer is the Supreme Being alone. This is exactly as Krishna says in the Gita to Arjuna, "Simply be My instrument" (*nimitta mātram bhava savyasāchin*—BG 11.33). Arjuna is the greatest archer who is ambidextrous, hence called *savyasāchin.* And yet Krishna tells him that Arjuna is a mere instrument. Brahma who evolves all of creation, says that he too is a mere instrument. Thus, we can see the silliness of claiming doership for petty deeds, when such great beings acknowledge they are mere instruments.

सत्त्वं रजस्तम इति निर्गुणस्य गुणास्त्रयः ।
स्थितिसर्गनिरोधेषु गृहीता माययया विभोः ॥ Bh 2.5.18

sattvaṁ rajas tama iti nirguṇasya guṇāstrayaḥ
sthiti sarga nirodheṣhu gṛhītā māyayā vibhoḥ

The Lord is infinite and beyond the three modes of nature. It is His Maya that assumes the three modes for the threefold activities of creation, sustenance and dissolution.

The three modes of nature (*sattva, rajas, tamas* or goodness, passion, dullness) enable the said threefold activities of creation, sustenance and dissolution. These modes are attributes of the material energy called Maya that engage in all activities. And yet He is beyond the three modes of nature, and unaffected by the activities of His energy. This mystery of causing all activities to happen and yet being totally unaffected by the activities can be understood with an example. The sun causes various activities on earth to happen and in fact, no activity would be possible without the energy of the sun. Yet the sun remains unaffected by all the activities on earth. In a similar manner, the presence of the Supreme Being as Pure Consciousness (*sat-chit*) brings forth the energy that makes all activities possible. And yet He remains unaffected by activities, being transcendent to them all.

कार्यकारणकर्तृत्वे द्रव्यज्ञानक्रियाश्रया: ।
बध्नन्ति नित्यदा मुक्तं मायिनं पुरुषं गुणा: ॥ Bh 2.5.19

kārya kāraṇa kartṛtve dravya jñāna kriyāśhrayāḥ
badhnanti nityadā muktaṁ māyinaṁ puruṣhaṁ guṇāḥ

The modes of nature engage as agents of action, through the material elements, knowledge and capacity to act, taking the form of cause and effect and a false sense of doership, thus binds the eternally free being.

All actions require the coordination of three factors—the material elements (*dravya*) needed for the action, the knowledge (*jñāna*) required to engage in the action and the capacity to execute (*kriyā*) the action. Taking the simple example of preparing a meal, it requires the ingredients to cook, the knowledge of the recipe as well as the physical capacity to cook using the recipe and the ingredients. These three factors are seen as required for every single action, from the most mundane to the most difficult. And through these three factors, actions manifest in the form of cause and effect (*kārya kāraṇa*). All this is done by the agency of the three modes of nature alone. It is the modes of nature that constitute all material elements, the memory cells that store knowledge and the physical body with its energy to act. This is succinctly stated by Krishna in the Gita: "All activities are carried out by the modes of nature" (*prakṛteḥ kriyamāṇāni guṇaiḥ karmāṇi sarvaśhaḥ*—BG 3.27). But in addition to doing all the activities, the modes of nature acting through the mind also project a false sense of doership of every activity. Thus, they not only act, but also bind us into egoic identification. Therefore, to let them act while being free of the bondage of doership is the key to freedom. Every action happens only with the three factors mentioned earlier. And the sense of doership is only a post facto appropriation of the doing by the false ego. Hence to be alert and aware of this false ownership of actions is the way to be free of it. This enables actions to be carried out with natural intelligence and clarity.

स एष भगवाल्लिङ्गैस्त्रिभिरेतैरधोक्षजः ।
स्वलक्षितगतिर्ब्रह्मन् सर्वेषां मम चेश्वरः ॥ Bh 2.5.20

sa eṣha bhagavān liṅgaistribhiretair adhokṣhajaḥ
svalakṣhita gatirbrahman sarveṣhāṁ mama cheśhvaraḥ

The Supreme Being transcends sense perception and is ever beyond cognition by the three modes of nature. He is the Controller of everyone, including myself.

While the three modes of nature engage in all activities, their very Source is the Supreme Being, untouched by the three modes and transcendent to them. Therefore, He cannot be cognized through the three modes of nature and remains beyond the senses including the mind. This is why all attempts to know Him through the mind only result in frustration. True wisdom then is to simply surrender unto Him as the Supreme Controller of all activities and recognize Him as the true Self of all entities, from Brahma down to an ant.

काळं कर्म स्वभावं च मायेशो मायया स्वया ।
आत्मन् यदृच्छया प्राप्तं विबुभूषुरुपाददे ॥ Bh 2.5.21

kālaṁ karma svabhāvaṁ cha māyeśho māyayā svayā
ātman yadṛchchhayā prāptaṁ vibubhūṣhur upādade

With the intent to become many, the Lord of Maya took on the form of Time along with the activities and innate dispositions of the beings to be created through His own Maya and brought forth creation.

Brahma now explains the process of creation beginning with this verse. He says that the power of Maya that is inherent in the Supreme Being who is Pure Consciousness comes forth first as Time, the most essential aspect of becoming. Along with Time, Maya also brings forth the various potentialities of activities and innate dispositions of all the beings to be created. Then, Time disturbs the equilibrium of the three gunas and thus brings forth the Cosmic Intelligence (*mahat*). Then Brahma goes on to describe in the next few verses, the sequence of creation starting from Cosmic Intelligence. First, space is evolved which is characterized by sound and hence the primordial state of creation is the sound Om. Then comes air characterized by touch followed by fire characterized by sight, water characterized by taste and soil characterized by smell. Then comes forth the senses of cognition and organs of action. And lastly, the faculties of memory, intellect and ego. In this way, the various phenomena of the universe are manifested, and they come together to form the Cosmic Body (*virāt puruṣa*). Thus, the whole universe is one interconnected body of the Supreme Being that comes forth by His own Maya. Recognizing this interconnected nature of the entire universe is essential to being free of false separation and in true love of everyone including oneself.

तदा संहृत्य चान्योन्यं भगवच्छक्तिचोदिताः ।
सदसत्त्वमुपादाय चोभयं ससृजुर्ह्यदः ॥ Bh 2.5.33

tadā saṁhatya chānyonyaṁ bhagavachchhakti choditāḥ
sadasattvam upādāya chobhayaṁ sasṛjurhyadaḥ

Impelled by the power of the Supreme Being, the various phenomena come together assuming the role of causes and effects, thus producing both the Universe and the individual.

After bringing forth Time, the five elements, modes of perception, various dispositions and activities, the power of the Supreme Being brings them all together as the perfectly intelligent network of causes and effects. This manifests the various individual beings from a single-celled organism to the most complex human beings. And all these beings are part of the one interconnected universe which is the Cosmic Being. Thus, in the manifest form, the Lord is described as the very Universe itself with infinite eyes, arms and feet. This conception is all inclusive, covering all realms of existence, all types of beings, all propensities and so on. Therefore, everyone and everything is a unique expression of the Cosmic Being with nobody inferior or superior. Also, this understanding of uniqueness of each being transcends the artificial idea of equality, thus embracing and celebrating the infinite diversity of creation. Further, to see everything as a part of the Cosmic Being in the Universal form is to see God here and now by affirming life as inherently divine rather than escaping life to find God. As Krishna declares in the Gita: "The one who sees Me everywhere and sees everything in Me is never lost" (*yo mām pashyati sarvatra sarvaṁ cha mayi pashyati—*BG 6.30). This divine vision of seeing God everywhere is actualized by the understanding that the whole Universe is the manifest intelligence of the Supreme Being as described here in Bhāgavatam.

सर्वं पुरुष एवेदं भूतं भव्यं भवच्च यत् ।
तेनेदमावृतं विश्वं वितस्तिमधितिष्ठति ॥ Bh 2.6.15

sarvaṁ puruṣha evedaṁ bhūtaṁ bhavyaṁ bhavachcha yat
tenedamāvṛtaṁ viśhvaṁ vitastimadhitiṣhṭhati

All this universe, with its past, present and future, is none other than the Supreme. It is all pervaded by Him through only a small span of His Being.

Brahma continues with his narration to Narada on the glories of the Supreme Being. After describing the various phenomena of the material universe such as seven essential ingredients of all bodies, the seven Vedic meters, the six tastes, the five airs (*prāṇa*) and so on, as expressions of the one indivisible Cosmic Being, Brahma summarizes by stating that all this universe through all of time is none other than Him. Every phenomenon from the microscopic to the galactic is manifest only through the movement of Time. Therefore, to recognize that the past, present and future (*bhuta bhavya bhavat*) is pervaded by Him alone is all inclusive of every aspect of the universe. Further, it is all pervaded only by a small span of His Being since the Power that brings forth this universe is only an aspect of the eternal Being and the Supreme Being remains unaffected by it. It is similar to how daytime activities on earth are only a small portion of the grandeur of the sun that remains unaffected by the earthly activities.

सोऽमृतस्याभयस्येशो मर्त्यमन्नं यदत्यगात् ।
महिमैष ततो ब्रह्मन् पुरुषस्य दुरत्यय: ॥ Bh 2.6.17

so'mṛtasyābhayasyeśho martyamannaṁ yadatyagāt
mahimaiṣha tato brahman puruṣhasya duratyayaḥ

He is the Lord of immortality and fearlessness, transcendent to death as well as all fruitive actions. Hence nobody can fathom the glory of the Supreme Being.

As Pure Consciousness that is free of birth or death, He is immortal and therefore to realize Him is the state of fearlessness. As long as we are identified with the born, there is fear. When we recognize the Unborn that is unaffected by birth, death and activities of all that is born, there is fearlessness. Therefore, one cannot know Him through the activities of the mind or intellect which are also of the nature of being born. Only when we cease to identify with them, can we recognize the substrate Truth of the glory of the Unborn. This is done by engaging in any activity without the false identification that "I am the doer" but instead let the doing happen through the body and mind with its own power being free of any egoic identification.

सृती विचक्रमे विश्वङ्‌साशनानशने उभे ।
यदविद्या च विद्या च पुरुषस्तूभयाश्रयः ॥ Bh 2.6.20

sṛtī vicakrame viśhvaṅsāśhanānaśhane ubhe
yad avidyā cha vidyā cha puruṣhastūbhayāśhrayaḥ

The scriptures speak of two ways of living—the way of mindless action due to ignorance and the way of contemplative action due to wisdom. All beings resort to one of these two ways, the former by those who seek fleeting gratification and the latter by those who seek to be free. Both the ways have the Supreme Being as the substrate ground of support.

Ignorance (*avidyā*) leads to unconscious living and acting out the unconscious patterns of the ego that lead to fleeting gratifications, inevitably followed by suffering that one then blames on fate. Wisdom (*vidyā*) leads to conscious living through awareness of unconscious patterns of the ego and thus being free of such patterns that otherwise take one down the alley of suffering. Both these ways of living are ultimately rooted in the Supreme Being alone, as both ignorance and wisdom are two aspects of His own Maya. Both these ways are available in the world to all human beings. They are described in the scriptures respectively through elaborate rituals that one takes up due to desire for pleasure, heavenly realms etc. and through the wisdom of Self-realization. The one who seeks to be free of suffering due to unconscious living awakens to the wisdom of Self-realization.

नारायणे भगवति तदिदं विश्वमाहितम् ।
गृहीतमायोरुगुणः सर्गादावगुणः स्वतः ॥ Bh 2.6.30

*nārāyaṇe bhagavati tad idaṁ viśhvamāhitam
gṛhītamāyoruguṇaḥ sargādāvaguṇaḥ svataḥ*

This universe rests on the support of the Supreme Being Narayana, who though transcendent to the modes of material energy, apparently takes on the various modes through His own Maya.

The example of the sun acting through the energy of the sunlight while remaining impervious to all activities on earth describes the apparent conundrum of the Supreme Being acting through His material energy while also transcendent to it. Therefore, if we recognize the truth that the ground of all our activities is the Supreme Being and the energy of all our activities is His expression, then we are free of the interloper in the form of the false ego. This enables us to neither get caught in the web of activities mindlessly nor attempt to escape them through false projections of future heaven or liberation but to engage in activities here and now with clarity and wisdom.

इति तेऽभिहितं तात यथेदमनुपृच्छसि ।
नान्यद्भगवतः किंचिद्भाव्यं सदसदात्मकम् ॥ Bh 2.6.32

*iti te 'bhihitaṁ tāta yathedam anupṛchchhasi
nānyad bhagavataḥ kiñchid bhāvyaṁ sadasadātmakam*

Thus, I have answered your inquiry about creation. In essence, there is nothing other than Supreme Being in the manifest universe, existing as cause or effect.

Narada's inquiry of creation has been answered in detail by Brahma. Brahma began with the manifestation of Cosmic Intelligence, that comes forth from the material energy of the Supreme Being due to Time. Then he described the five elements coming forth starting from the subtlest to the gross, i.e. space, air, fire, water and soil, and their corresponding subtle objects of sound, touch, sight, taste and smell and the organs of cognition to perceive them as also the organs of action to act upon them. And finally, Brahma described how all these elements came together as a network of causes and effects, with each effect becoming the next cause and manifesting the entire Universe as the Cosmic Being with the apparent multitude of individual beings. Brahma also mentioned the two ways of ignorance and wisdom that are both part of the Maya of the Supreme Being. Thus, Narada's query has been comprehensively answered by Brahma by summarizing that there is nothing other than Him that is present either as a cause or an effect in this Universe as the Supreme Being is the cause of all causes (*sarva kāraṇa kāraṇam*).

नतोऽस्म्यहं तच्चरणं समीयुषां भवच्छिदं स्वस्त्ययनं सुमङ्गलम् ।
यो ह्यात्ममायाविभवं स्म पर्यगाद् यथा नभः स्वान्तमथापरे कुतः ॥
Bh 2.6.35

nato'smyahaṁ tachcharaṇaṁ samīyuṣhāṁ bhavachchhidaṁ
svastyayanaṁ sumaṅgalam

yo hyātmamāyāvibhavaṁ sma paryagād yathā nabhaḥ svāntam athāpare kutaḥ

I offer obeisances unto His most auspicious feet that ends the false sense of separation for those who take refuge in Him. Just as the sky does not know its limits, there are limits to His energy. How can anyone else then know it?

Brahma now offers a prayer steeped in the wisdom of self-realization to the all-encompassing Supreme Being. By taking refuge in Him and thus recognizing that Bhagavan alone through His material energy takes the form of all causes and effects and thereby all activities at the individual and cosmic level, one is freed of the false sense of doership and separation as "me" and "mine." Thus, one is situated in wisdom through true surrender. Furthermore, Brahma says that His material energy constantly expands in His presence that Bhagavan Himself cannot estimate the limits of His Maya. This is validated by physics today that the universe seems to be expanding faster than the speed of light. Therefore, Brahma teaches that any attempt to know Him as an object of knowledge is futile because the scope of such knowledge is infinite and ever expanding. Hence Brahma directs to the way of surrender which is to simply recognize that nothing exists apart from Him. This enables one to engage in purposeful action without any sense of ownership of the doing or entitlement to its results, thus living and acting with true freedom here and now.

यस्यावतारकर्माणि गायन्ति ह्यस्मदादयः ।
न यं विदन्ति तत्त्वेन तस्मै भगवते नमः ॥ Bh 2.6.37

yasyāvatārakarmāṇi gāyanti hyasmadādayaḥ
na yaṁ vidanti tattvena tasmai bhagavate namaḥ

Obeisances to the Supreme Being whose Avatars and exploits are glorified by many, though nobody can know Him in entirety.

After describing the mystery of creation and the nature of the Supreme Being as limitless and thus unknowable, Brahma brings forth the glory of His Avatars which are specifically meant to relate to the Infinite through the finite mind. Because the Avatars have names, forms and pastimes, they enable one to contemplate upon and connect with the Absolute. This is the special purpose and mystery of Avatars. The outward purpose of Avatars is to establish dharma as revealed by Krishna in the Gita (*dharma sansthāpanārthāya sambhavāmi yuge yuge*—BG 4.8). The inner purpose of Avatars is to bestow name, form and pastimes that enable loving devotion to the Infinite Lord. Thus, one's heart is purified by invoking and glorifying Him who is Unknowable through the various enchanting pastimes. So rather than making futile attempts to know Him, Brahma recommends that one can take this sweet way of recounting His pastimes in the form of various Avatars. From the third skandha onward, Bhāgavatam will describe the various pastimes of the Avatars leading up to the sweetest of all, those of Krishna.

स एष आद्यः पुरुषः कल्पे कल्पे सृजत्यजः ।
आत्मात्मन्यात्मनात्मानं स संयच्छति पाति च ॥ Bh 2.6.38

sa eṣha ādyaḥ puruṣhaḥ kalpe kalpe sṛjaty ajaḥ
ātmātmanyātmanātmānaṁ sa saṁyachchhati pāti cha

The Primordial Being who is Unborn as the Self, in His Self by His Self, creates, maintains and dissolves His Self as the Universe, cycle after cycle.

As the Primordial Being, He alone exists before creation as the Unborn (*ajaḥ*). Thus, He is the only Self. And in His own Self, by the energy of His own Self, He creates the Universe which is His own Self. In this way, Brahma summarizes through a beautiful alliteration on the word *ātmā* (Self) that the substrate of the Universe, the material cause of the Universe, the efficient cause of the Universe and the manifest effect as the Universe are all Him alone. Thus, Bhāgavatam brings forth in so many fresh ways the simple Truth that God alone is. Further, as Brahma intends to segue into the topic of Avatars, he refers to Him as Unborn as Krishna Himself states in the Gita while describing the mystery of His Avatars: "Though Unborn and Imperishable, as the Lord of all entities, I appear through my own Maya" (*ajo'pi sannavyayātmā bhūtānām īśhvaro'pi san / prakṛitiṁ svām adhiṣhṭhāya sambhavāmi ātma māyayā*—BG 4.6).

विशुद्धं केवलं ज्ञानं प्रत्यक् सम्यगवस्थितम् ।
सत्यं पूर्णमनाद्यन्तं निर्गुणं नित्यमद्वयम् ॥ Bh 2.6.39

viśhuddhaṁ kevalam jñānaṁ pratyak samyagavasthitam
satyaṁ pūrṇam anādyantaṁ nirguṇaṁ nityam advayam

The Supreme Being is pure, unalloyed Consciousness abiding within as the Self of all. He is ever true and complete, with no beginning or end, beyond all attributes, eternal and non-dual.

Brahma captures all aspects of the Supreme Being in this one verse. The Supreme Being is the very Consciousness that underlies all activities of the mind and body, remaining unaffected by those activities and, ever pure and unalloyed. Only the content of Consciousness can acquire the dirt of egoic desires, fears, worries, envy etc. But He who holds the content is ever pure and unalloyed Consciousness, who abides as the true Self of all. When we inquire as to "who am I" and strip away all that comes and goes, what remains is the Supreme Being as our ever-true Self. He is also ever complete as nothing can be added or taken away from the truth of the Pure Being. He is ever present, without any beginning or end. He transcends all attributes that can only affect the manifest world of names and forms. All dualities of cold and heat, pleasure and pain etc. can be experienced only within the content of Consciousness. But as Pure Consciousness itself, He transcends all such dualities too and is ever non-dual.

ऋषे विदन्ति मुनयः प्रशान्तात्मेन्द्रियाशयाः ।
यदा तदेवासत्तर्कैस्तिरोधीयेत विप्लुतम् ॥ Bh 2.6.40

ṛṣhe vidanti munayaḥ praśhāntātmendriyāśhayāḥ
yadā tadevāsattarkaistirodhīyeta viplutam

Those who are given to contemplation realize Him by regulating their body, mind and senses. But for those who try to find Him through arguments and debates, He remains elusive and hidden.

After describing the essential nature of the Supreme Being, Brahma succinctly describes the way to realize Him. It is by contemplating and inquiring within, being aware of and free of egoic thought patterns, regulating the body, the mind and the senses through discipline and living with clarity in all aspects of our life—physical, emotional, relationships, work etc. Instead, if we engage in abstract arguments and debates while not clearing the ground through conscious living, He remains hidden. Therefore, one has to integrate clarity and authenticity into all aspects of living rather than compartmentalizing "spirituality" as another fragmentary activity. Only then can one actualize the Truth of the Supreme Being here and now.

प्राधान्यतो यानृष आमनन्ति लीलावतारान् पुरुषस्य भूम्नः ।
आपीयतां कर्णकषायशोषानानुक्रमिष्ये त इमान् सुपेशान् ॥
Bh 2.6.45

*prādhānyato yānṛsha āmananti līlāvatārān purushasya bhūmnaḥ
āpīyatāṁ karṇakashāyaśhoshānanukramishye ta imān supeśhān*

The scriptures have described the chief among the sportful descents of the Supreme Being and I shall now narrate those delightful stories. One can easily clean all the impurities within by drinking the nectar of these stories to the heart's content through one's ears.

After describing the Supreme Being as the Infinite and all-pervading cosmos as well as the indwelling pure Awareness, now Brahma describes Him in the sweetest and most relatable form of Avatars. As the Infinite being and as the indwelling Awareness, He is beyond all names, attributes and contemplation. Any attempt to understand the Supreme Being in His impersonal form as the Infinite and the substrate Awareness will only prove to be a futile exercise for the limited mind which always operates through the subject-object duality. Therefore, to bestow on sincere devotees the means to relate to Him through name, form, pastimes and holy abodes (*rūpa, nāma, līlā, dhāma*), He takes on the descents or Avatars. Simply listening to the stories of each Avatar effortlessly stills the mind, purifies the heart and awakens unconditional love. So, Brahma now will proceed to describe all the Avatars briefly as a teaser, while the rest of Bhāgavatam will elaborate on the detailed stories and teachings of each Avatar.

विद्धः सपत्न्युदितपत्रिभिरन्ति राज्ञो बालोऽपि सन्नुपगतस्तपसे वनानि ।
तस्मा अदाद् ध्रुवगतिं गृणते प्रसन्नो दिव्याः स्तुवन्ति मुनयो यदुपर्यधस्तात् ॥ Bh 2.7.8

viddhaḥ sapatnyuditapatribhiranti rājño bālo'pi
sannupagatastapase vanāni
tasmā adād dhruvagatiṁ gṛṇate prasanno divyāḥ stuvanti
munayo yad uparyadhastāt

Pierced by the sharp words of his stepmother in the presence of his royal father, Dhruva, though still a child, went to the woods to practice severe penance. Pleased with his penance, the Lord appeared and bestowed upon Dhruva the eternal abode of a pole star which is extolled by all the sages.

Brahma begins a beautiful summary account of all the Avatars of Bhagavan. While the ten principal Avatars are well known as Dashavatar, Brahma describes many more, though not exhaustively, as they are countless. This verse describes the seventh among them in the following order.

First, he describes Varaha, the divine Boar who symbolizes the principle of sacrifice and restores earth to its order.

Second, he mentions Suyajna who held the position of Indra in the first epoch (Manvantara).

Third, the great sage Kapila, born to Mother Devahuti who teaches her the perfect wisdom of Sankhya. In the Gita, Krishna mentions Kapila as the highest among all perfected beings (*siddhānāṁ kapilo muniḥ*—BG 10.26).

Fourth, the Avatar of Dattatreya who is given (*Datta*) as a boon to sage Atri as a son (*Atreya*). Dattatreya is a great jñānī who taught the Avadhuta Gita (the song of the free one).

Fifth, the set of four brothers Sanaka, Sanātana, Sanandana and Sanatkumāra who are forever young, steeped in God-realization thus embodying the truth that only those who are children at heart enter the kingdom of God.

Sixth, the twin sages Nara and Narayana who are ever in penance in Badrinath. They represent the perfect man (Nara) and God (Narayana) who again come forth as Arjuna and Krishna to present the perfect dialogue between man and God.

Seventh, the descent of the Lord for the child devotee Dhruva described in this verse. Dhruva, the son of king Uttānapāda and grandson of Manu, is wounded by the words of his stepmother Suruchi who is more dear to the king than his Mother Suniti. So, his mother instructs Dhruva to take refuge in the Supreme Lord who is the only true refuge. Accordingly, Dhruva departs to the forest and meets Narada on the way. Narada first tests the resoluteness and earnestness of the boy and after being fully convinced, gives the blessed instructions on where to meditate, how to meditate, and what to meditate upon. Dhruva accordingly engages in austere penance by the banks of Yamuna that pleases the Supreme Being who descends and bestows His Grace. Dhruva offers the most beautiful prayers to the Lord and is blessed with the boon of having as an eternal abode a star by his name (Dhruva Nakshatra). Apart from being a beautiful story, it is rich in symbolism. Suniti represents righteousness, Suruchi represents sense gratification. The king drawn to Suruchi represents the mind. Dhruva, born to Suniti, represents the inner spirit of renunciation, when awakened beholds the Divine within.

त्रैपिष्टपोरुभयहा स नृसिंहरूपं कृत्वा भ्रमद्भ्रुकुटिदंष्ट्रकरालवक्त्र
म् ।
दैत्येन्द्रमाशु गदयाभिपतन्तमारादूरौ निपात्य विददार नखैः
स्फुरन्तम् ‖ Bh 2.7.14

traipiṣhṭaporubhayahā sa nṛsiṁharūpaṁ kṛtvā
bhramadbhrukuṭidaṁṣhṭrakarālavaktram
daityendramāśhu gadayābhipatantamārādūrau nipātya vidadāra
nakhaiḥ sphurantam

In order to dispel the great fear of the demigods, the Lord took the form of Narasimha, looking frightful with restless eyebrows and terrible jaws. When the demon Hiranyakashipu attacked Him with a mace, the Lord seized and threw him upon His thighs and ripped him apart with His sharp nails.

Brahma continues the narration of the various Avatars of the Lord.

Eighth, King Prthu who appeared in the dynasty of Dhruva. Prthu was the first king to rule over an extensive portion of earth and to harvest its rich resources for the welfare of all beings. Henceforth, earth has been called Prthvi.

Ninth, the great renunciate Rshabha who though born in a royal dynasty, walked away from all attachment with a thoroughly composed mind, looking upon everyone as the same Divine energy, and attained the state of Paramahamsa (Supreme Wisdom).

Tenth, Hayagriva who is Veda personified and represents all sacrifices and is invoked as the basis for all knowledge (*ādhāram sarva vidyānām hayagrīvam upāsmahe*).

Eleventh, Matsya (Fish) who guided Manu to take all living entities in a giant boat during an apocalyptic deluge and also rescued the Vedas from the deluge. This symbolizes the Supreme Being as the guide for all living entities to navigate the chaos of the world.

Twelfth, Kurma (Tortoise) who supported Mount Mandara which was used by the demigods and demons to churn the ocean of milk to get nectar. This churning represents the churning in the mind with its good (demigod) and evil (demon) tendencies and the substrate of the mind that supports the very churning as the Supreme Being.

Thirteenth, the famous Narasimha Avatar as the Man-Lion described in this verse. The demon Hiranyakashipu considered himself invincible and got boons that he thought would make him immortal. His son Prahlada, however, being a pure devotee of the Lord, instructed his father to worship the Supreme Being that irritated the demon. After trying unsuccessfully to change Prahlada, the demon decides to kill his son, then the Lord appears in the frightful form of Narasimha and tears apart the demon, while working around all the boons he acquired. Hiranya means gold and Kashipu means a soft bed, thus the demon symbolizes the ego addicted to wealth and pleasure. All the boons he got are the plans that the ego makes for the future that gets thwarted by the Divine Will. Narasimha is at once ferocious toward the evil Hiranyakashipu and most benevolent toward the pious Prahlada, symbolizing that He simultaneously destroys evil tendencies and fosters loving devotion.

अन्तःसरस्युरुबलेन पदे गृहीतो ग्राहेण यूथपतिरम्बुजहस्त आर्तः ।
आहेदमादिपुरुषाखिललोकनाथ तीर्थश्रवः श्रवणमङ्गलनामधेय ॥
श्रुत्वा हरिस्तमरणार्थिनमप्रमेयश्चक्रायुधः पतगराजभुजाधिरूढः ।
चक्रेण नक्रवदनं विनिपाट्य तस्मादधस्ते प्रगृह्य भगवान् कृपयोज्जहार ॥ Bh 2.7.15-16

antaḥ sarasyurubalena pade gṛhīto grāheṇa yūthapatir
ambujahasta ārtaḥ
āhedam ādipuruṣākhilalokanātha tīrthaśravaḥ
śravaṇamaṅgalanāmadheya
śrutvā haristam araṇārthinam aprameyaśchakrāyudhaḥ
patagarāja bhujādhirūḍhaḥ
chakreṇa nakravadanaṁ vinipāṭya tasmād dhaste pragṛhya
bhagavān kṛpayojjahāra

With his foot seized inside a lake by an alligator of immense strength, the famous leader of the elephants, Gajendra, felt distressed and holding up a lotus in his trunk, called out, "O Primordial Being, O Protector of all the worlds, O Lord of sacred renown whose names are auspicious to hear!" Hearing this, the infinite Lord Hari appeared with His discus Sudarshana mounted on the divine eagle Garuda and severed the head of the alligator and rescued the elephant who sought His refuge.

This is the fourteen Avatar narrated by Brahma. In a beautiful mountainous island, there lived Gajendra, the king of elephants, with his herd and lording over the whole region with strength and vigor. One day, as he was sporting in the waters of a beautiful lake, his leg got caught by an alligator and was unable to free himself. Nobody else from his family or friends could come to his rescue and only watched helplessly while he struggled in pain. In that moment of utter despair, the seed of devotion from his past life awoke in him and he turned to the Supreme Lord to take refuge. Settling his mind in the heart with clarity, Gajendra offered the most sublime prayer of surrender to the Lord, describing with great depth and love the infinite glory of the Supreme Lord. In doing so, he lost his desire to prolong his life but only to realize the Supreme Being and attain His eternal abode. The Lord heard this prayer and out of His supreme compassion, descended in His transcendent form and killed the alligator with His divine Sudarshana Chakra to liberate Gajendra. The symbolism shown by the story is beautiful, where the elephant is the giant ego that wants to play in the waters of sense pleasure but gets inevitably seized by the alligator of suffering. But when the ego surrenders fully, the suffering is removed through the weapon of wisdom (Sudarshana). The way Gajendra calls out to the Lord from the depth of his heart as "Adi Purusha"—Oh Primordial Being, whose very remembrance is greater than all the holy pilgrimage sites, is very moving and evocative of the mood of surrender. This story of Gajendra Moksham is so blessed that Shuka Brahmam says simply listening to or remembering it purifies one's mind and removes the fear of death through total surrender to the Lord.

ज्यायान् गुणैरवरजोऽप्यदिते: सुतानां लोकान् विचक्रम इमान् यदधाधियज्ञ: ।
क्ष्मां वामनेन जगृहे त्रिपदच्छलेन याञ्चामृते पथि चरन् प्रभुभिर्न चाल्य: ॥ Bh 2.7.17

jyāyān guṇairavarajo'pyaditeḥ sutanām lokān vichakrama imān yadathādhiyajñaḥ
kṣmām vāmanena jagṛhe tripadachchhalena yāchñām ṛte pathi charan prabhubhir na chālyaḥ

Born as the youngest son of Aditi, the Lord presiding over all sacrifices appeared as Vamana, the foremost in all virtues. He covered all the worlds in His three strides after king Bali promised to grant Him three paces of land. Thus, by soliciting Bali, the Lord demonstrated the greatness of the king who stuck to the path of righteousness.

This is the fifteenth Avatar in the order narrated by Brahma. In this Avatar, the Lord appeared as the son of Aditi and Kashyapa as a dwarf boy, Vamana. He went to Bali's sacrifice where everyone was completely overwhelmed by His radiance. Being offered to ask for any boon by Bali, Lord Vamana asks Bali for three paces of land. Bali agrees and is about to offer the boon when his Guru Shukracharya objects by revealing to Bali that the one who has come as the dwarf is none other than the Supreme Being and He will snatch away everything with His three strides. Bali respectfully disregards his own Guru because he has given his word already to Vamana and now it has to be kept all the more so, knowing that it is Bhagavan. Once Bali solemnizes his offering, Bhagavan takes His Cosmic Form as the Infinite Lord and with one stride, measures all of earth with the subterranean regions and a second stride to cover all of heaven. Now there is not an atom left for His third stride. Bhagavan then tests Bali by saying that he has failed to keep his word as there is no place left for His third stride. Bali, in a sublime act of self-surrender, offers his head for the third stride with great composure, seeing it as a blessing. Then Bhagavan reveals that He has only bestowed His Grace to Bali by removing all his possessions and has demonstrated the greatness of Bali's supreme surrender at the time of unparalleled adversity. This is again rich in symbolism showing that all of one's waking state (earth) and dream state (heaven) as well as the very "me" that perceives the waking and dream worlds are only the Supreme Being. To recognize this is to surrender all possessions to Him and gain the blessing of eternal life in Him.

अस्मत्प्रसादसुमुखः कलया कलेश इक्ष्वाकुवंश अवतीर्य गुरोर्निदेशे ।
तिष्ठन् वनं सदयितानुज आविवेश यस्मिन् विरुध्य दशकन्धर आर्तिमाच्छत् ॥ Bh 2.7.23

*asmatprasādasumukhaḥ kalayā kaleśa ikṣhvākuvaṁśha avatīrya guror nideśhe
tiṣṭhan vanaṁ sadayitānuja āviveśha yasmin virudhya daśhakandhara ārtim ārchchhat*

Ever disposed to shower His Grace, the Lord took His descent in the dynasty of Ikshwaku as Sri Ram along with His expansions (Bharat, Laskhman, Shatrughna) and in deference to His father's command, went in exile to the forest with His consort Sita and younger brother

Lakshman. Then he encountered and eliminated the ten-headed monster Ravana to restore order.

Brahma continues with his narration of the many Avatars of the Supreme Being, leading up to a summary of the entire Ramayana in one compact verse.

Sixteenth, the divine Swan (Hamsa) who gave instructions to Narada.

Seventeenth, Dhanvantri who came to provide the science of healing and Ayurveda.

Eighteenth, the intense Avatar of Parashurama who came to destroy the warriors (Kshatriyas) who turned away from protecting righteousness (dharma).

Nineteenth, the glorious Avatar of Sri Ram. The most awe-inspiring pastimes of Ram was originally narrated by the sage Valmiki in his magnum opus of 24,000 verses which brings out the essence of Ram as the perfect man (Purushottama) and an embodiment of dharma. In addition to being an account of the event as they happened (*itihāsa*), the story is steeped in symbolism. The Divine (Ram) descends into the jungle (creation) along with the jiva (Sita), equipped with an intellect to discern (Lakshman). There, the ten senses (ten headed Ravana) offer temptation of material pleasure (golden deer) to the jiva, who falls for it ignoring the line of discernment drawn by the intellect, and gets caught in material bondage (Lanka). As the jiva deeply pines for re-union, the Divine sets forth to reclaim the jiva from the clutches of ignorance. The key instrument of the Divine is the totally surrendered mind (Hanuman) that has an unimaginable potential to remove all obstacles. The material bondage of Lanka has as its reigning quality passionate desire (rajas/Ravana) but also two other brothers—sloth (tamas/Kumbhakarna) and goodness (sattva/

Vibhishana). Once Hanuman sets fire to Lanka, i.e. the totally surrendered mind burns desire, the outcome of the war is assured. And with the final victory of Ram over Ravana comes the joyous reunion of Sita back in the throne of Ayodhya (no yuddha or conflict).

भूमेः सुरेतरवरूथविमर्दितायाः क्लेशव्ययाय कलया सितकृष्णकेशः ।
जातः करिष्यति जनानुपलक्ष्यमार्गः कर्माणि चात्ममहिमोपनिबन्धनानि ॥ Bh 2.7.26

bhūmeḥ suretaravarūthavimarditāyāḥ kleśhavyayāya kalayā sita-kṛṣhṇa-keśhaḥ
jātaḥ kariṣhyati janānupalakṣhyamārgaḥ karmāṇi chātmamahimopanibandhanāni

In order to relieve the burden on earth due to the armies of demoniac kings, the Lord will appear as Krishna along with His expansion Balaram and perform such great feats that are superhuman and incomprehensible.

Brahma comes to the glorious descent of Balaram and Krishna as the twentieth and the twenty first Avatars. In the first skandha itself, while describing all the Avatars, it was mentioned that Krishna is the Supreme Being Himself descending with His complete opulences (*krishnastu bhagavān swayam*). The Supreme Being is known as Vāsudeva who Himself descends as Krishna and His primary expansion is Sankarshana who descends before Him as Balaram, the elder brother. The descent of the Lord is outwardly for the destruction of evil kings and establishing dharma. But the inner purpose is to foster devotion through His most glorious names, forms and pastimes which are especially sweet and superhuman at the same time. The story of the appearance of Krishna and Balaram itself is utmost miraculous and auspicious to listen to. After Vasudeva and Devaki get married, Devaki's brother Kamsa hears a prophecy that he shall be killed by the eighth son of Devaki. So, he proceeds to kill his own sister. But Vasudeva pleads to spare her life by offering up his sons to Kamsa as they are born. The evil Kamsa kills the first six sons of Vasudeva and Devaki. Then, Balaram enters Devaki's womb as the seventh son. Krishna instructs His divine energy Yogamaya to transfer Balaram to Rohini's womb and then for herself to be born as the daughter of Yashoda and Nanda. Krishna enters Devaki's womb at the same time making her radiant. On the auspicious Rohini nakshatra and eighth day of lunar fortnight marked as Ashtami, with the whole universe celebrating, Sweet Lord Krishna appears first in the original form and then transforms into a little baby. Facilitated by Yogamaya, Vasudeva carries Krishna across Yamuna to the house of Nanda and Yashoda, and brings back Yogamaya who has appeared as the baby girl to Mathura. Kamsa is informed of the birth and tries to kill this baby too. However, She slips out of his grasp and reveals Her transcendent form and proclaims that Kamsa's killer is elsewhere, leaving him utterly fearful. Meanwhile the appearance of Krishna along with Balaram are celebrated with great festivities by Nanda, Yashoda and the cowherds.

गृह्णीत यद्यदुपबन्धममुष्य माता शुल्ब सुतस्य न तु तत्तदमुष्य माति ।
यज्जृम्भतोऽस्य वदने भुवनानि गोपी संवीक्ष्य शङ्कितमनाः प्रतिबोधितासीत् ॥ Bh 2.7.30

gṛhṇīta yadyadupabandhamamuṣhya mātā śhulbaṁ sutasya na tu
tattadamuṣhya māti
yajjṛmbhato'sya vadane bhuvanāni gopī saṁvīkhṣya
śhaṅkitamanāḥ pratibodhitāsīt

Mother Yashoda tries to bind Krishna with ropes ever increasing in length that still fall short every time. And when Yashoda beholds the universe in His mouth, she is filled with wonder with the sense of His supreme divinity.

Brahma narrates a few of the most wonderful pastimes of Krishna before moving on to completing the account of the remaining Avatars. He mainly shares the pastimes of Vrndavan that are the sweetest, most well-known and often sung to bring the highest mood of devotion. After mentioning how Krishna killed many demons such as Putana, Trnavrata etc. playfully, Brahma here recounts the famous pastime as Damodara (One who has a rope around His waist). Once, while Mother Yashoda was churning butter, Krishna came to her hungry for milk. She feeds Him but then hears the milk boiling over so she runs to the stove, before finishing the feeding. Krishna feigns anger at this, first breaking a pot of curds and then stealing and eating butter. Yashoda decides to punish Him by binding Him with a rope but is unable to do so, no matter how long a rope she brings. Finally, when Yashoda gives up and looks at Him with love, Krishna allows Himself to be bound by the rope. This symbolizes the attempt by a spiritual seeker to capture the Truth which remains elusive, if one tries to grasp it through the intellect or mystical practices. But the moment we stop trying to capture and surrender unto Him, then He is available to us here and now.

Brahma then relates another lila of Krishna eating dirt and chastised by Yashoda, He denies it. When asked to open the mouth, He reveals the whole universe within His mouth, thus demonstrating that the entire manifest creation is simply held within Him as Pure Consciousness.

क्रीडन् वने निशि निशाकररश्मिगौर्यां रासोन्मुखः
कलपदायतमूर्च्छितेन ।
उद्दीपितस्मररुजां व्रजभृद्वधूनां हर्तुर्हरिष्यति शिरो धनदानुगस्य ॥
Bh 2.7.33

krīḍan vane niśi niśākara raśmi gauryāṁ rāsonmukhaḥ kala padāyata-mūrcchitena
uddīpitasmararujāṁ vrajabhṛdvadhūnāṁ hartur hariṣyati śhiro dhanadānugasya

Sporting in the forests of Vrndavan on a night bright with the rays of the full moon, He pours out a sweet melody from His flute that kindles the flame of love in the hearts of the young Gopis of Vraja as prelude to the Rāsa dance.

Brahma narrates more of the wonderful pastimes of Krishna, including subduing the poisonous serpent Kaliya from Yamuna as well as holding up the Govardhana mountain to protect the residents of Vrndavan from the torrential downpours of Indra. Then, Brahma arrives at the sweetest of Krishna's pastimes in this verse, the most intimate and auspicious Rāsa dance with the Gopis of Vrndavan. On a beautiful autumn full moon night (Sharad Purnima), Krishna plays His enchanting flute drawing out the Gopis to the forest from their homes, leaving whatever they were doing. Krishna first tests the

Gopis by asking them to go back to their homes. When they offer a heartfelt prayer expressing their intense longing to be only with Him, He obliges them with His intimate association. The Gopis momentarily feel proud of it and Krishna instantly disappears, causing the Gopis to search for Him tracing His footprints through the forest. Unable to find Him, they gather in the moonlit banks of Yamuna and pour their hearts out in the most sublime song of Divine Love called the Gopi Gitam. When they are at the peak of intense longing, Krishna suddenly appears in their midst and enraptures them all. Their bliss knows no bounds as they surround Him with love. Removing their agony of separation, Krishna starts the most blessed Rāsa Lila dance, the pinnacle of the most intimate form of devotion that bestows Grace and awakens divine love in the hearts of beings for all of posterity.

कालेन मीलितधियामवमृश्य नृणां स्तोकायुषां स्वनिगमो बत दूरपारः ।
आविर्हितस्त्वनुयुगं स हि सत्यवत्यां वेददुमं विटपशो विभजिष्यति स्म ॥ Bh 2.7.36

kālena mīlitadhiyāmavamṛśhya nṝṇāṁ stokāyuṣhāṁ svanigamo bata dūrapāraḥ
āvirhitastvanuyugaṁ sa hi satyavatyāṁ vedadrumaṁ viṭapaśho vibhajiṣhyati sma

By flux of time, as the intelligence of men gets dwarfed and life becomes shorter and the entire Vedas with its import cannot be grasped easily, the Lord descends as Vedavyasa, son of Satyavati, to assort and organize Vedas into many branches.

Brahma continues with his narration of the Avatars and lists the great Vedavyasa as the twenty second in the list. The Vedas are revealed scriptures with no human authorship and hence called *shruti* (listened). They have been passed down through disciplic succession via oral transmission alone. This requires a monumental ability to learn and memorize as Vedas are a vast body of knowledge with various divisions such as Samhitas (hymns), Brahmanas (rituals), Aranyakas (meanings of rituals) and Upanishads (wisdom of Vedanta), along with the six Vedangas (grammar, prosody etc.), four Upavedas (ayurveda etc.), Smritis (codes of living) etc. Since it was found that the human ability to commit such voluminous works to memory degenerates with time, Vyasa, a partial expansion of the Lord, divided the Vedas into four branches(Rig, Sama, Yajur and Atharva), so each lineage can focus only on their respective branch. In addition, Vyasa composed Brahma Sutras (aphorisms on Truth), the great epic Mahabharata and the Puranas. The crown jewel among the Puranas is this very Bhāgavatam that he composed at Narada's instruction to consummate his life's work.

Brahma recounts the great Buddha as the twenty third Avatar, who came to stop mindless ritualism and turn within to realize the Truth.

And finally, as the twenty fourth Avatar, Brahma mentions that at the end of Kali Yuga when unrighteousness reigns supreme, the Lord will appear as Kalki to destroy the wicked and re-establish dharma.

Thus, Brahma gives an account of twenty-four Avatars, rather than the usual ten (Dashavatar), which is still not exhaustive as His Avatars are countless (*avatārā hi asaṅkhyeyā*—Bh 1.3.26).

येषां स एष भगवान् दययेदनन्तः सर्वात्मनाश्रितपदो यदि निर्व्यलीकम् ।
ते दुस्तरामतितरन्ति च देवमायां नैषां ममाहमिति धीः श्वशृगालभक्ष्ये ॥ Bh 2.7.42

*yeṣhāṁ sa eṣha bhagavān dayayedanantaḥ sarvātmanāśhritapado
yadi nirvyalīkam
te dustarām atitaranti cha devamāyāṁ naiṣhāṁ mamāham iti
dhīḥ śhva-śhṛgālabhakṣhye*

Only by taking refuge in the infinite Supreme Being with one's whole self in a guileless, child-like manner can one cross over this most difficult and deluding power of Maya by His Grace. And it is possible only by not taking the impermanent body and its possessions to be "me" and "mine."

After concluding the narration of all the Avatars, Brahma then glorifies the infinite powers and potencies of the Supreme Being who manifests as the sages, the principles of righteousness along with sacrifice and penance, as well as the demons and the principles of unrighteousness. Brahma concludes that nobody can enumerate the powers of the Lord, a task more impossible than counting all the particles on the earth. Therefore, the only way to cross over this ocean of Maya is to not attempt to understand Him through intellectual speculation but to simply surrender unto Him, as an innocent child does with the parent. This requires a total freedom from the sense of "me" and "mine" which is the source of all guile, expectations, fears etc. If one is child-like, then there is a natural flow of ease and freedom in actions that is effortless. That is the secret to be ever in the field of

Grace here and now, and actualize one's fullest potential with a spirit of playful spontaneity.

शश्वत् प्रशान्तमभयं प्रतिबोधमात्रं शुद्धं समं सदसतः परमात्मतत्त्वम् ।
शब्दो न यत्र पुरुकारकवान् क्रियार्थो माया परैत्यभिमुखे च विलज्जमाना ॥ Bh 2.7.47

*shashvat prashāntam abhayam pratibodhamātram shuddham
samam sadasataḥ paramātmatattvam
shabdo na yatra purukārakavān kriyārtho māyā
paraityabhimukhe cha vilajjamānā*

The Supreme Being is ever most serene, fearless of the nature of Pure Consciousness. He is pure, same toward all beings, beyond cause and effect, beyond the reach of words, beyond the fruits of actions. The illusory Maya cannot stand in His presence.

The Supreme Being, as Pure Consciousness, is ever peaceful, being unaffected by any happenings in the world much as the light in the room is unaffected by what's happening in the room. Therefore, there is no scope for fear or covetousness of any kind. Just as the light illuminates all aspects of the room equally, He is the same toward all beings. Every event, word, thought of every being is illuminated by Him alone as Pure Consciousness. He is beyond cause and effect as they operate only in the realm of Time which itself is secondary to and only an appearance within Pure Consciousness. He is beyond the reach of words as all pointers to Him never capture Him due to His infinite nature. As Taittiriya Upanishad puts it poetically, words come back empty handed along with the mind when they try to reach Him (*yato vācho nivartante aprāpya manasā saha*). The illusory Maya that causes the false separation of "mine" and "me" goes away when the unitary nature of Absolute Truth is perceived. Therefore, the exhortation of Brahma is to not engage in verbal speculation about God but simply see Him as everything, everywhere and act out of this ground of sacredness each moment.

तद् वै पदं भगवतः परमस्य पुंसो ब्रह्मेति यद् विदुरजस्रसुखं विशोकम् ।
सध्र्यङ् नियम्य यतयो यमकर्तहेतिं जह्युः स्वराडिव निपानखनित्रमिन्द्रः ॥ Bh 2.7.48

tad vai padaṁ bhagavataḥ paramasya puṁso brahmeti yad vidurajasrasukhaṁ viśhokam
sadhryaṅ niyamya yatayo yamakartahetiṁ jahyuḥsvarāḍ iva nipānakhanitram indraḥ

The essential nature of the Supreme Being is realized by the wise as the Absolute Brahman, ever free from sorrow and of the nature of eternal bliss. Having fixed their mind on Him, ascetics neglect even the practices of discernment, just as Indra who controls rain has no use for digging wells.

The one who has completely surrendered oneself has no need for practicing even discernment (*viveka*) as the fruit of all discernment is included in surrender to the Supreme being. Indra, the deity who controls rain, has no need for digging wells to get water. Similarly, if one is fully surrendered here and now unto the all-pervading Supreme Being as the source and sustenance that animates each moment of our lives, then the practices of discernment, dispassion etc. as ways to remove the false ego are not necessary as one lives in the clarity that He alone functions through everyone and everything, every moment. Such surrender to the Supreme Being comes forth in an even sweeter way through unconditional love for Him as a divine manifestation, such as the love of the Gopis for Krishna. Being thus surrendered unto Him gives the true realization of Him as the Absolute Brahman whose nature is free of sorrow and ever in bliss. It is in the mind brooding upon the past, resisting what has happened or speculating about the future, worrying and anxious about what is yet to happen that sorrow is created. If we recognize the Supreme Being as the source of all actions and totally accept everything as perfectly ordained and act from such total acceptance, there is total attention to here and now. That is freedom from sorrow. And such a total, alert presence as now is eternal because the future arrives only as now. Therefore, eternal bliss is not to be wrongly understood as bliss for all of time to come which is only a projection of the mind. It is simply to be in total attention now, as each moment unfolds only as now. This is the true realization of the essential nature of the Supreme Being.

स श्रेयसामपि विभुर्भगवान् यतोऽस्य भावस्वभावविहितस्य सतः प्रसिद्धिः ।
देहे स्वधातुविगमेऽनुविशीर्यमाणे व्योमेव तत्र पुरुषो न विशीर्यतेऽजः ॥ Bh 2.7.49

sa shreyasām api vibhur bhagavān yato'sya
bhāvasvabhāvavihitasya satah prasiddhih
dehe svadhātuvigame'nuvishīryamāṇe vyomeva tatra puruṣho na
vishīryate'jah

It is the Supreme Being who bestows all the fruits of actions. He alone inspires all activities performed in accordance with the natural disposition of everyone. And even when the body gets dissolved, as the constituent elements disintegrate, the Unborn dwelling in it remains unaffected, much like space.

It is normally presumed that we are the cause or author of our activities and the effect or fruit of the activities is determined by the cause. Brahma dispels both myths in this verse. The cause of all activities is the natural disposition (*svabhāva*) of everyone, which is constantly changing due to the various influences and impressions around us. This natural disposition, which is dynamically evolving due to the divine energy of countless interactions, brings forth the impulse to perform any activity. The effect which is the fruit of the activity seems apparently determined by the cause but in truth only as ordained by the same divine energy. Thus, both the cause and effect of all activities is the Supreme Being alone. Further, what remains unaffected by the constant dynamism in the realm of activities up to and even beyond the disintegration of the body is the Pure Awareness within, which is the essence of the Supreme Being. Just as space in a building is unaffected when it is torn down, the Pure Awareness within remains unaffected even when the body dissolves. That is the Unborn and ever present Supreme Being as the true Self of all. Thus, all activities are done by His energy through everyone, and He abides as the true Self of everyone. Seeing this clearly removes the false sense of "me" so that one can act with full attention as the perfect instrument of God.

सोऽयं तेऽभिहितस्तात भगवान् विश्वभावनः ।
समासेन हरेर्नान्यदन्यस्मात् सदसच्च यत् ॥
इदं भागवतं नाम यन्मे भगवतोदितम् ।
संग्रहोऽयं विभूतीनां त्वमेतद् विपुलीकुरु ॥ Bh 2.7.50-51

so'yaṁ te'bhihitastāta bhagavān viśhvabhāvanaḥ
samāsena harernānyadanyasmāt sadasachcha yat
idaṁ bhāgavataṁ nāma yanme bhagavatoditam
saṅgraho'yaṁ vibhūtīnāṁ tvametad vipulī kuru

Thus, have I told you briefly about the Lord who creates the universe by His very thought. Whatever exists as cause or effect is no other than the Supreme Being Hari. This is the Bhāgavatam that the Lord instructed me that describes His glories in summary that you can expand upon.

Brahma thus concludes his narration to Narada after describing how creation came forth from the Supreme Being as His own projection, an account of His various descents as Avatars in His own creation and finally His essential nature. In this verse, he sums up by saying whatever exists as cause or effect is none other than Him. We already saw in the last verse how every effect of action is as ordained by Him and the very cause of actions is His own energy. Therefore, the entire summary of the teaching is that nothing exists apart from Him. Brahma says that this is Bhāgavatam in a nutshell that was revealed directly by the Lord. Later in this skandha, we will see this essence of Bhāgavatam presented in four compact verses known as the Chatushloki Bhāgavatam. Brahma then tells Narada to expand upon these teachings which Narada then instructs to Vyasa, who in turn taught his son Shuka

Brahmam who is now narrating Bhāgavatam. Thus, we can see that the wisdom of Bhāgavatam can be revealed in just one verse or it can be expanded upon as 18,000 verses as it came through Shuka Brahmam. Each amplification of Bhāgavatam is meant to further develop devotion to the Lord who is the Universal Spirit that sustains all. Brahma concludes by stating that the one who describes or listens to this message with reverence is never deluded by ignorance. That is the resultant fruit of this great work of Bhāgavatam.

शृण्वतः श्रद्दधया नित्यं गृणतश्च स्वचेष्टितम् ।
कालेन नातिदीर्घेण भगवान् विशते हृदि ॥
प्रविष्टः कर्णरन्ध्रेण स्वानां भावसरोरुहम् ।
धुनोति शमलं कृष्णाः सलिलस्य यथा शरत् ॥ Bh 2.8.4-5

shṛṇvataḥ shraddhayā nityaṁ gṛṇatashcha svacheshṭitam
kālena nātidīrgheṇa bhagavān vishate hṛdi
praviṣṭaḥ karṇarandhreṇa svānāṁ bhāvasaroruham
dhunoti shamalaṁ kṛshṇaḥ salilasya yathā sharat

If one listens daily with reverence to His glories and also narrates them, in the heart of such a person, the Supreme Being shines before long. Entering through the cavities of the ears into the lotus of the heart, Krishna rids one of all impurities just as autumn turns all rivers clear.

After listening to Brahma's discourse to Narada as narrated by Shuka Brahmam, Parikshit now speaks by first glorifying the greatness of just listening to this nectar of wisdom. Parikshit has only a week left to live and therefore he is listening with complete attention to every word of Shuka

Brahmam, thus setting an example. And he reveals his own experience of the Lord shining in the heart clearly by such listening. Though Bhagavan shines forth ever in the hearts of all as mentioned repeatedly in Bhāgavatam and in Gita as well (*sarvasya chāhaṁ hṛdi sanniviṣṭaḥ*—BG 15.15), He is as though covered by the cloud of the ego. Listening to the teaching with reverence daily removes the cloud of impurities so that the ever present Supreme Being shines forth clearly. This is akin to how the sun is ever present and yet we say that the sun has come when the clouds clear out or dawn breaks. Of all the various processes of meditation, listening with total attention (*shravanam*) is the primary, as this is how wisdom enters into the mind and awakens the heart. And it has already been mentioned that the very text of Bhāgavatam is another form of Bhagavan as Krishna. Hence Parikshit poetically states that Krishna goes into the heart through the cavities of the ears. Just as all the mud and debris flowing into the rivers due to monsoon rains are cleared out by the arrival of autumn, the muck accumulated due to the ego is cleared out by Krishna entering the heart in the form of Bhāgavatam.

धौतात्मा पुरुषः कृष्णपादमूलं न मुञ्चति । मुक्त सर्वपरिक्लेशः पान्यः स्वशरणं यथा ॥ Bh 2.8.6

dhautātmā puruṣhaḥ kṛṣṇapādamūlaṁ na muñchati
muktasarvaparikleśhaḥ pānthaḥ sva-śharaṇaṁ yathā

He, whose heart is purified and rid of all afflictions (through listening to Bhāgavatam) never leaves the lotus feet of Krishna who abides in the heart, just as a weary traveler who returns home after a long and tedious journey does not leave his home.

Everyone is constantly running here and there looking for scraps of pleasure while the fountainhead of true happiness abides in our very heart, which is our true home. But it is covered by layers and layers of accumulated dirt through conditioning of all kinds. Therefore, if one listens with sincerity and reverence to the message of Bhāgavatam daily, then as mentioned in the previous verse, all the dirt gets removed and the heart shines forth like a crystal-clear river during autumn. And the presence of Krishna as Pure Consciousness shines forth in a clear heart. Having discovered our home as the very heart where the Lord resides, we have no need to go elsewhere. To abide in our heart is to live consciously every moment. Here it is important to note that the Supreme Being abides in our heart as the dynamic presence of Pure Consciousness, not as a static entity. God or Truth is not a fixed entity to be acquired at one point in time but a dynamic presence that is revealed through conscious living each moment. To not leave our heart where the Lord resides is to live with alert awareness here and now.

अत्र प्रमाणं हि भवान् परमेष्ठी यथात्मभूः ।
अपरे चानुतिष्ठन्ति पूर्वेषां पूर्वजैः कृतम् ॥ Bh 2.8.25

atra pramāṇaṁ hi bhavān parameṣhṭhī yathātmabhūḥ
apare chānutiṣhṭhanti pūrveṣhāṁ pūrvajaiḥ kṛtam

You are an authority on the entire Vedic wisdom like Brahma and therefore worthy of inquiring from. Others blindly follow what has been done by the ancestors without inquiring.

Parikshit, after describing the fruits of listening to the narration of Bhāgavatam thus far, seeks more of the nectar from Shuka Brahmam by asking a series of questions on the nature of karma, time with its divisions and cycles, realms of the universe, the effects of the gunas, the propensities of people and the stages of life, the way of dharma, the mystery of Avatars etc. The answers to all these questions form the rest of Bhāgavatam. Parikshit concludes his inquiries by stating that one ought to live life, not by blindly following traditions, but by approaching a genuine authority to truly understand and live accordingly. Shuka Brahmam is the greatest authority as already described in the first skandha due to his great wisdom and complete freedom from any egoic identification. Therefore, the instruction here is to neither blindly accept traditions nor to speculate but seek a genuine authority such as a teacher like Shuka Brahmam to learn a scripture like Bhāgavatam with an attitude of humility and curiosity.

आत्ममायामृते राजन् परस्यानुभवात्मनः ।
न घटेतार्थसम्बन्धः स्वप्रद्रष्टुरिवाञ्जसा ॥
बहुरूप इवाभाति मायया बहुरूपया ।
रममाणो गुणेष्वस्या ममाहमिति मन्यते ॥ Bh 2.9.1-2

ātmamāyāmṛte rājan parasyānubhavātmanaḥ
na ghaṭetārthasambandhaḥ svapnadraṣṭurivāñjasā
bahurūpa ivābhāti māyayā bahurūpayā
ramamāṇo guṇeshvasyā mamāhamiti manyate

The connection of the Supreme Being as Pure Consciousness to the world of matter projected through Maya is similar to the connection of the sleeping man

with his dream. It is due to the multi-faceted Maya that there is a diversity of forms and when one gets attached to the objects of the world, it leads to the sense of "me" and "mine."

After Parikshit asks a series of questions, Shuka Brahmam starts expounding the great Bhāgavatam which was learned by him from his father Vyasa. Shuka Brahmam begins his response here by giving the supreme wisdom of Bhāgavatam that the world of matter is projected by the Divine Will which is also known as Maya. This is similar to how we perceive a dream world while asleep as a projection of the mind. The dream world can be said to be neither true because it is transient nor false because it seems real while it is happening. Same with the waking world that is projected by the divine energy of the Supreme Being. Hence rather than speculate as to whether the world is real or illusory, the wise simply accept it as it is, as the projection of the Divine Will that pervades the entire universe. However, if one gets attached to the objects of the world starting with the body and the mind, then it leads to the bondage of "I" and "mine." If we recognize the Source as the one energy that pervades the whole world and makes everything function, then one is rid of the attachment to "I" and "mine" by seeing that the body and the mind are constantly changing as an expression of the divine energy just as the entire universe.

स चिन्तयन् द्व्यक्षरमेकदाम्भस्युपाशृणोद् द्विर्गदितं वचो विभुः ।
स्पर्शेषु यत्षोडशमेकविंशं निष्किञ्चनानां नृप यद् धनं विदुः ॥
Bh 2.9.6

sa chintayan dvyakṣharamekadāmbhasyupāśhṛṇod dvirgaditaṁ vacho vibhuḥ
sparśheṣu yat ṣhoḍaśhamekaviṁśhaṁ niṣhkiñchanānāṁ nṛpa yad dhanaṁ viduḥ

While absorbed in contemplation, Brahma hears two syllables —the sixteenth (त/*ta*) and the twenty first (प/*pa*) consonants—together uttered twice. It signifies that, which is the wealth of those. who do not possess anything.

Shuka Brahmam now proceeds to narrate how Brahma came to receive the teaching of Bhāgavatam in the first place. In the beginning, Brahma was said to have been in contemplation on how to proceed with the act of creation. At that time, he heard a word of two syllables (*tapa*) coming out of nowhere and it was repeated twice. Sanskrit language has five groups of five primary consonants each beginning with *ka, cha, ṭa, ta, pa* and this consonant order is the same in all Indian languages. Therefore, the sixteenth and the twenty first form together the word *tapa* which is the root for penance. Brahma is thus instructed to engage in penance to attain clarity before embarking upon creation. This is in fact an instruction for all of us to act from the ground of clarity rather than just acting fast and breaking things, which causes a lot of chaos. Penance is mentioned as the wealth of those who don't possess anything which is rightly understood as free of being possessive. In this way, Brahma is exhorted to engage in penance so that he can recognize the principle by which right action can come forth.

प्रत्यादिष्टं मया तत्र त्वयि कर्मविमोहिते ।
तपो मे हृदयं साक्षादात्माहं तपसोऽनघ ॥
सृजामि तपसैवेदं ग्रसामि तपसा पुनः ।
बिभर्मि तपसा विश्वं वीर्यं मे दुश्चरं तपः ॥ Bh 2.9.22-23

pratyādiṣhṭaṁ mayā tatra tvayi karmavimohite
tapo me hṛdayaṁ sākṣhādātmāhaṁ tapaso'nagha
sṛjāmi tapasaivedaṁ grasāmi tapasā punaḥ
bibharmi tapasā viśhvaṁ vīryaṁ me duśhcharaṁ tapaḥ

"I commanded you to do penance because you were confused on how to go about creation. Penance is My very heart, O sinless one. And I am the soul of penance. It is by penance that I create this universe, maintain it and dissolve it. Penance is my prowess that is indeed hard to practice."

After Brahma engaged in penance for a long time, the Supreme Being appeared in His divine form, revealing His Supreme abode which is the Heart, free of all afflictions, fears and delusions. It is transcendent to all the three gunas and beyond the all-destroying Time and all effects of Maya. Brahma was moved upon beholding the vision of the Lord showering His Grace as the source of all divine potencies. The Lord pleased with the penance of Brahma spoke to him who was now full of love and bliss and fit to receive instructions to begin creation of living entities. He first glorified penance as the way to go about any activity with clarity. Because penance is the very essence of the Absolute Truth, it is penance that is behind creation, maintenance and dissolution of the whole universe. And it is true for every small activity too. As Krishna instructs in the Bhagavad Gita (Ch17), penance involves austerity of body, speech and mind. Cleanliness, simplicity, celibacy and non-violence is the penance of the body. Penance of speech is speaking words of wisdom through words that are truthful, pleasant and beneficial. Serenity, regulation, gentleness, silence and purity constitute the penance of the mind. Thus, engaging in penance of the body, speech and mind can and ought to be done every moment to be free of confusion, abide in Truth and gain clarity in action. Hence Bhagavan says penance is His very essence as the revealer of Truth in the Heart.

अहमेवासमेवाग्रे नान्यद् यत् सदसत् परम् ।
पश्चादहं यदेतच्च योऽवशिष्येत सोऽस्म्यहम् ॥ Bh 2.9.32

ahamevāsamevāgre nānyad yat sadasat param
paśchād ahaṁ yadetachcha yo'vaśiṣhyeta so'smyaham

Prior to creation, I alone existed in my absolute state. Other than Me, there was nothing gross or subtle, nor the cause for both. Upon creation, I alone exist in the form of this phenomenal universe. After dissolution, I alone exist as that which remains.

Bhagavan gives Brahma the entire essence of Bhāgavatam in four verses, known as the *Chatushloki* Bhāgavatam. This is the first of the four verses. Here the Lord declares that His absolute state as Pure Consciousness precedes the manifest universe with space, time and causality. The entire dance of the cosmos happens due to the material energy known as Prakrti that comes forth from the one Source which exists in the absolute state, prior to creation. The seed of creation lies dormant in Pure Consciousness and wakes up to spawn each cycle of creation and then is withdrawn at the end of the cycle, much like a spider spins a web out of itself, sports in it and takes it back into itself. Therefore, in the beginning prior to creation, in the middle during the dance of creation, and in the end after creation is dissolved, only the Supreme Being exists. To recognize this truth is to be free of "me" and "other." This is true yoga which is equanimity, true bhakti which is unconditional love and true jnana which is realization of the Supreme Being as the Self of all.

ऋतेऽर्थं यत् प्रतीयेत न प्रतीयेत चात्मनि ।
तद्विद्यादात्मनो मायां यथाभासो यथा तमः ॥ Bh 2.9.33

ṛte 'rthaṁ yat pratīyeta na pratīyeta chātmani
tadvidyādātmano māyāṁ yathābhāso yathā tamaḥ

That which makes it possible for something inexplicable to appear in My Being like a fleeting appearance and obscures My Being like an eclipse, is to be regarded as My Maya.

After describing the nature of Being in the first verse of the Chatushloki Bhāgavatam, in this verse, the Supreme Being describes the nature of His energy that makes all manifestations or becoming possible. This energy is called Maya which means that it is fleeting, constantly changing and causing delusion. Everything is constantly evolving every moment in the dynamic dance of creation of what is. And yet when one tries to hold onto anything as "mine" or "me," it causes delusion. Another meaning of Maya is that it can be measured. Due to the appearance of time and space, there is the possibility of measuring anything that manifests. Whereas the Unborn Supreme Being is the source of all manifestation and therefore immeasurable (*aprameya*). Maya is also known as the Divine Will—the power that makes every activity happen and is constantly expanding at all levels. So, if we recognize this as the only doer of all activities, then the process of becoming unfolds perfectly without any false sense of attachment or doership.

यथा महान्ति भूतानि भूतेषूच्चावचेष्वनु ।
प्रविष्टान्यप्रविष्टानि तथा तेषु न तेष्वहम् ॥ Bh 2.9.34

yathā mahānti bhūtāni bhūteshūccāvaceṣhvanu
praviṣhṭānyapraviṣhṭāni tathā teṣhu na teṣhvaham

Just as the five elements can be said to be within the living entities, both great and small, and also the living entities can be said to be within the elements, similarly I can be said to be within the living entities and the living entities can be said to be within Me.

The five elements of earth, water, fire, air and space are found within our bodies and that of all living entities. At the same time, we live surrounded by the five elements that make up this planet and beyond. In the same way, in this third verse of Chatushloki Bhāgavatam, it is made clear that the Supreme Being is both the indwelling spirit and the all-pervading cosmic energy. Therefore, any inquiry into the nature of Self within and into the nature of the observable universe without will have to come to the same Truth. In fact, the observer and the observed are ultimately non-different and of the same essence. The scientists inquire into the observed universe with its various phenomena but as quantum physics has shown, ultimately the observed cannot be studied as separate from the observer. On the contrary, many who take up spiritual inquiry focus exclusively within, while not recognizing the divine nature of the universe and wanting to escape from the world. But here, it is made beautifully clear that the Supreme Being dwells within and without, inside and outside. Therefore, the inner is the outer. This powerful realization can make every activity divine, every moment a meditation.

एतावदेव जिज्ञास्यं तत्त्वजिज्ञासुनात्मनः ।
अन्वयव्यतिरेकाभ्यां यत् स्यात् सर्वत्र सर्वदा ॥ Bh 2.9.35

etāvadeva jijñāsyaṁ tattvajijñāsunātmanaḥ
anvayavyatirekābhyāṁ yat syāt sarvatra sarvadā

He who is keen to realize the Supreme Self, who exists everywhere and forever, can inquire into and ascertain it either through the negative or the positive process.

After describing the truth of both Being and Becoming as the One Supreme Being who is both Pure Consciousness and the all-pervading cosmic energy, in this final verse of Chatushloki Bhāgavatam, the way to realize Him is given as through either a negative or positive process. The negative process is what the Upanishads call *"neti neti"* ("not this, not this") which is to discard all that is impermanent as false. This reveals the ever-present, unchanging substrate of Awareness, in which the appearance and disappearance of all worldly phenomena take place. This corresponds to jnana yoga. The positive process is where every phenomenon and every action is seen as happening through divine agency and therefore every action and all the results are surrendered unto the Supreme

Being. This corresponds to karma yoga. This is as Krishna describes in the Gita that the two ways to realize the Truth are jnana yoga through reflection and karma yoga through action (*loke'smin dvividhā niṣṭhā purā proktā mayānagha / jñānayogena sāṅkhyānāṁ karmayogena yoginām*—BG 3.3). And what underlies both jnana yoga and karma yoga is the attitude of loving devotion which is bhakti. Thus, Chatushloki Bhāgavatam aptly contains the entire teaching both in terms of the ontological nature of the Divine as well as the practical means of realization.

अत्र सर्गो विसर्गश्च स्थानं पोषणमूतय: ।
मन्वन्तरेशानुकथा निरोधो मुक्तिराश्रय: ॥ Bh 2.10.1

*atra sargo visargaśhcha sthānaṁ poṣhaṇam ūtayaḥ
manvantareśhānukathā nirodho muktir āśhrayaḥ*

The ten topics covered in the Bhāgavatam are creation, sub-creation, order, grace, desire, epochs, divine stories, stillness, freedom and abidance.

Comments:

After narrating the Chatushloki Bhāgavatam in summary as revealed to Brahma, and how it was passed on from Brahma to Narada, then to Vyasa and then himself, Shuka Brahmam now speaks of the comprehensive wisdom contained in the expanded form of Bhāgavatam. These are addressed as ten topics, one in each skandha, thus forming the topics of the third through the twelfth skandha:

1. Creation (*sarga*) is the primary expansion of the Divine Will as the Cosmic Intelligence and the material elements.

2. Sub-creation (*visarga*) is the coming forth of life—various plants and trees, animal species an humans.
3. Order (*sthānaṁ*) is the perfect arrangement of the Universe as observed through laws of physics.
4. Grace (*poshaṇam*) is the aspect of creation that is conducive to freedom.
5. Desires (*ūtayaḥ*) in the form of attachment that brings about bondage.
6. Epochs (*manvantara*) are Manvantaras or civilizations with various kings and emperors.
7. Stories (*īshānukathā*) are mainly of the descents of the Lord and His devotees.
8. Stillness (*nirodha*) is that which brings about total absorption of the mind.
9. Freedom (*mukti*) is to be liberated from false identification of the mind.
10. Abidance (*āshraya*) is to be totally established in the state of freedom.

नास्य कर्मणि जन्मादौ परस्यानुविधीयते ।
कर्तृत्वप्रतिषेधार्थं माययारोपितं हि तत् ॥ Bh 2.10.45

nāsya karmaṇi janmādau parasyānuvidhīyate
kartṛtvapratiṣedhārtham māyayāropitam hi tat

The Supreme Being has no doership in relation to the creation and other activities connected with this universe. They are ascribed to Him only as a superimposition of Maya with a view to deny individual doership.

After detailing the ten topics covered in Bhāgavatam, Shuka Brahmam explains again the emergence of the Cosmic Being (*virāt*) as the form of universe itself comprising the elements, activities, energy and Time. All of this is the Divine Will that comes forth from the Supreme Being to manifest the creation of this universe. It is also known as Maya composed of three gunas that make all activities happen. It arises not out of any volition of the Supreme Being but only as a natural effect of His presence. Just as the sun has no volition to do all the activities that are carried forth by sunlight and yet without sunlight, no activity is possible, similarly the Supreme Being is free of any volition or sense of doership and yet without Him, no activity is possible. Every action done by everyone, every moment, everywhere, happens only through this Divine Will but ignorance makes us imagine to be the doer. Only to remove such ignorance with its false notion of the individual will, the Divine Will is ascribed as that of God. But in truth, it comes forth on its own simply in the presence of the Supreme Being as *sat-chit-ananda* (Existence Consciousness and Bliss) with no active volition. A clear understanding of this truth enables us to simply see this universe as a play which goes on perfectly in which each of our roles carry on as ordained, while our essential nature is that of the Supreme Being, whoever remains unaffected and free.

THIRD CANTO
Right Discernment

स मुहूर्तमभूत्तूष्णीं कृष्णाङ्घ्रि सुधया भृशम् ।
तीव्रेण भक्तियोगेन निमग्नः साधु निर्वृतः ॥ Bh 3.2.4

sa muhūrtamabhūttūṣṇīṁ kṛṣṇāṅghrisudhayā bhṛśham
tīvreṇa bhaktiyogena nimagnaḥ sādhu nirvṛtaḥ

Completely immersed in the nectar of remembrance of Krishna and flooded with bliss of intense loving devotion, Uddhava remained silent for an hour.

While on his peregrinations, Vidura meets with Uddhava, the dear friend of Krishna and lovingly asks after Krishna's welfare in Dwaraka. However, Krishna had just departed Earth and Uddhava is on his way to Badrinath to spend the rest of his life there as instructed by Krishna. Upon being asked about Krishna, Uddhava is instantly transported to an ecstatic mood of loving devotion and flooded with transcendental bliss that he is unable to speak a word and remains silent for an hour as tears well up and roll down his cheeks. By totally losing himself in the Beloved, Uddhava is effortlessly free of any sense of "me" in the pinnacle of loving devotion. Then he slowly starts to tell Vidura of Krisha's departure and also recounts all His pastimes on Earth all the way from His divine appearance till the moment of departure. Upon hearing the moving account and the news of departure of Krishna, Vidura too is deeply affected and established in ecstatic love and bliss.

यतोऽप्राप्य न्यवर्तन्त वाचश्च मनसा सह ।
अहं चान्य इमे देवास्तस्मै भगवते नमः ॥ Bh 3.6.40

yato'prāpya nyavartanta vāchaśhcha manasā saha
ahaṁ chānya ime devāstasmai bhagavate namaḥ

Obeisance to the Supreme Being, ever beyond the reach of speech, mind, ego and the powerful demigods who all return disappointed while attempting to capture Him.

The manifest creation of the whole Universe is described as the Cosmic Body of the Absolute by the sage Maitreya. This is the same as the *vishwarupa* or the Cosmic Form as revealed by Krishna in the Bhagavad Gita with all living entities, planets and galaxies as interconnected parts of the One Universal Being. Just as each part of the body is unique in its function and works harmoniously together with all other parts for the overall health of the body, similarly the right dharma of each individual is to recognize the inherent uniqueness of all and co-operate together in harmony. It is in being free of the false identification as "me" and acting from a spontaneous attitude of love and service toward all that one can realize the Supreme Being. Instead, as this verse declares, if one is caught in the separation of "me," then any attempt to realize the Supreme using one's faculties of speech, mind, intellect and ego come back empty handed. This exactly mirrors the beautiful verse of Taittriya Upanishad: "That from which speech and mind come back empty" (*yato vācho nivartante aprāpya manasā saha*). A wave, being part of the ocean, cannot ever "understand" the ocean but being made of the same water, it is already one with the ocean. Similarly, being already one with the Divine, any attempt to "understand" the Divine only causes disappointment. By simply surrendering to the Divine, unconditionally loving every wave of the Divine, one is already that.

स वै निवृत्तिधर्मेण वासुदेवानुकम्पया ।
भगवद्भक्तियोगेन तिरोधत्ते शनैरिह ॥ Bh 3.7.12

sa vai nivṛttidharmeṇa vāsudevanukampayā
bhagavadbhaktiyogena tirodhatte śhanairiha

The false identification (with "me" and "mine") disappears through work done without any attachment, through the Grace of the Lord and loving devotion.

The default mode of functioning in most interactions for many people is rooted in the attitude of "what's in it for me." This is due to the false identification of oneself with the body/mind as "me" and anything associated with it as "mine," while everyone and everything else is seen as "other." This division breeds comparison, envy, manipulation, anger, greed, pride, inferiority and many other complexes and resultant suffering. And this attitude continues with one's desire for liberation or mokṣha as a goal for the "me to attain." Transcending this pettiness is the highest purpose of human life or else we live akin to animals but with more sophisticated instruments to further the egoic identification. Therefore, Bhāgavatam instructs that to be free of this root cause of suffering which is false identification is by doing work without attachment. When we switch the inner attitude from "what's in it for me" to "how can I be of service" in each interaction, the attachment of self gives way to love for everyone. This invokes Grace of the Lord Vasudeva, the One who abides everywhere, and the flowering of true loving devotion which makes the false identification disappear completely including the desire for liberation.

दैवेन ते हतधियो भवतः प्रसङ्गात्सर्वाशुभोपशमनाद्विमुखेन्द्रिया ये ।
कुर्वन्ति कामसुखलेशलवाय दीना लोभाभिभूतमनसोऽकुशलानि शश्वत् ॥ Bh 3.9.7

daivena te hatadhiyo bhavataḥ
prasaṅgātsarvāśhubhopaśhamanād vimukhendriyā ye
kurvanti kāmasukhaleśhalavāya dīnā
lobhābhibhūtamanaso'kuśhalāni śhaśhvat

Activities connected with listening and glorifying the Supreme Being remove all inauspicious tendencies. Yet those who are robbed of good sense do not engage in such activities and only focus on unwholesome pursuits due to desire for fleeting sense gratification.

The activities that one engages in and the association one keeps are very powerful indeed in determining the course of life. If we have the right association or Satsang, it draws us toward the right activities which are wholesome, auspicious and conducive for peace and true happiness. It leads to discussions that elevate and result in clarity to put things into the right perspective. This brings forth true discernment (*viveka*) and disinterest (*vairāgya*) toward fleeting pleasures, and most importantly, an earnest reverence (*shraddhā*) awakens for the Absolute and unconditional love for all. But those who are drawn to the wrong association end up wasting their lives, focusing on sense gratification and not realizing the highest purpose of human life. They are caught in pettiness, greed, envy and insecurity, feel disconnected and empty within and try to cover it up with constant self-gratification with no taste for serving others. Therefore, the most important pointer of Bhāgavatam repeatedly is to always have the right association which automatically leads to the right activities and the right way of living.

नातिप्रसीदति तथोपचितोपचारैराराधितः सुरगणैर्हृदि बद्धकामैः ।
यत्सर्वभूतदययासदलभ्ययैको नानाजनेष्ववहितः सुहृदन्तरात्मा ॥
Bh 3.9.12

nātiprasīdati tathopachitopachārairārādhitaḥ suragaṇairhṛdi
baddhakāmaiḥ
yatsarvabhūtadayayāsadalabhyayaiko nānājaneṣvavahitaḥ
suhṛdantarātmā

The Supreme Being is One without a second, the well-wisher and the inner Self of all beings seated in their heart. He is not as pleased with pompous worship using abundant materials by those bound with desires in their heart as with those who are compassionate toward all beings and free of malice.

The meaning of true worship and the essence of loving devotion (*bhakti*) is clearly defined in this verse. When one is bound with desires in one's heart and engages in worship to fulfill such desires, then even if one is the most powerful being or a demigod and can engage in very opulent worship with all kinds of paraphernalia, such a display of devotion is not pleasing to the Lord. Whereas, if one has a heart full of compassion for all beings, then one is naturally free of all selfish desires including the desire for liberation. As indicated in this verse, He is One without a second, and being so, who is ever separate from Him to even seek liberation? When this realization dawns that He alone is manifest as all beings and situated in the hearts as the indwelling presence "I am," then the natural response is unconditional love, compassion and service toward all beings. This is declared as the most pleasing and sublime form of devotion.

कालोऽयं परमाण्वादिर्द्विपरार्धान्त ईश्वरः ।
नैवेशितुं प्रभुर्भूम्न ईश्वरो धाममानिनाम् ॥ Bh 3.11.38

kālo'yaṁ paramāṇvādirdviparārdhānta īśvaraḥ
naiveśituṁ prabhur bhūmna īśvaro dhāmamāninām

The all-powerful Time ranging from the smallest measure to eons has no control over the Supreme Being. It holds sway only on those who have identified themselves with the body.

Time is a fundamental aspect of the material energy that manifests as the entire Universe. Everything within the scope of the material energy is subject to Time that consumes all. And yet, the very Source of Time who is the Absolute Being is beyond the influence of Time by definition. Only the body and the mind are ever under the influence of Time. Our true essence is non-different and also beyond the influence of Time. The body goes through growth, maturation, decay and death. The mind, which is a collection of memories, experiences and knowledge also constantly goes through change and decay. Thus, the body and the mind are always in the process of becoming. Whereas the essence of our true nature is free of any becoming and is ever abiding as Pure Being. It is only due to false identification with the body and mind that we wrongly imagine ourselves subject to becoming. When we recognize that the body and the mind are simply an expression of the material energy that goes through Time as designed, and the Source or the substrate of the material energy as the Absolute Being is ever free of Time, then there is the instant recognition of the inherent freedom here and now.

नमो नमस्तेऽखिलमन्त्रदेवताद्रव्याय सर्वक्रतवे क्रियात्मने ।
वैराग्यभक्त्यात्मजयानुभावितज्ञानाय विद्यागुरवे नमो नमः ॥
Bh 3.13.39

namo namaste'khilamantradevatādravyāya sarvakratave kriyātmane
vairāgyabhaktyātmajayānubhāvitajñānāya vidyāgurave namo namaḥ

Obeisances to the One who is the embodiment of all mantras chanted, all deities honored and all materials employed in sacrifices and all activities. Obeisances to the One who is the embodiment of wisdom realized through dispassion, devotion and regulation of the mind, and who is also the Teacher who imparts this wisdom.

This verse glorifies the most auspicious Varaha Avatar, the descent of the Lord in the form of a wild boar. When the demon Hiranyaksha takes Earth and submerges it in the ocean, Varaha Avatar descends to kill the demon and restore Earth back to its original place. This whole episode is beautifully symbolic in nature. Hiranyaksha represents greed and selfishness that causes one's world to be submerged in chaos (which is the ocean). And Varaha Avatar embodies the principle of *yajna* or sacrifice (make sacred). By transcending the selfishness of "me" and "mine," one's world is retrieved from chaos and restored back to order. Therefore, this verse aptly glorifies the Varaha Avatar as the embodiment of the highest principle of sacrifice with all its incantations and processes as well as the essence of sacrifice which is dispassion, devotion and wisdom. Thus, the true meaning of invoking and worshiping Varaha Avatar is to awaken the spirit of sacrifice within us which leads to realization and causes divine love to flower.

परं प्रधानं पुरुषं महान्तं कालं कविं त्रिवृतं लोकपालम् ।
आत्मानुभूत्यानुगतप्रपञ्चं स्वच्छन्दशक्तिं कपिलं प्रपद्ये ॥
Bh 3.24.33

param pradhānam puruṣam mahāntam kālam kavim trivṛtam lokapālam
ātmānubhūtyānugataprapañcham svachchhandaśhaktim kapilam prapadye

I take refuge in Kapila, the embodiment of the Supreme and the all-witnessing Seer, all potencies are in Him, who appears as Primordial Matter, the Cosmic Intelligence, Time, threefold energy and dissolves everything unto Himself.

Kapila is an Avatar of the Supreme Being who teaches Sankhya Yoga to His Mother Devahuti, which will be the main topic of the rest of this third skandha. He is born to the sage Kardama and his wife Devahuti and hailed as the greatest among the perfect beings known as Siddhas. While recounting His various glorious manifestations in the Bhagavad Gita, Krishna says "I am Kapila among all the perfect beings" (*siddhānāṁ kapilo muniḥ*—BG 10.26). Upon His birth, the sage Kardama offers a prayer to his own son knowing that Him to be the Avatar of the Supreme. Kapila is glorified as the descent of the Absolute Being who is the repository of all powers, the unitary Source of all energy which appears as Time and Space and is responsible for every aspect of material creation as well as its dissolution.

मनो ब्रह्मणि युञ्जानो यत्तत्सदसतः परम् ।
गुणावभासे विगुण एकभक्त्यानुभाविते ॥
निरहंकृतिर्निर्ममश्च निर्द्वन्द्वः समदृक् स्वदृक् ।
प्रत्यक्प्रशान्तधीर्धीरः प्रशान्तोर्मिरिवोदधिः ॥ Bh 3.24.43-44

mano brahmaṇi yuñjāno yattatsadasataḥ param
guṇāvabhāse viguṇa ekabhaktyānubhāvite
nirahaṅkṛtirnirmamaścha nirdvandvaḥ samadṛk svadṛk
pratyakpraśhāntadhīrdhīraḥ praśhāntormirivodadhiḥ

The sage Kardama fixed his mind on Brahman (the Absolute) who is beyond all cause and effect and all attributes, and yet is the Source of all, realized through exclusive devotion. Free of "me" and "mine" and all pairs of opposites, viewing all with the same eye, his mind turned within and was perfectly composed like an ocean without waves.

The sage Kardama, after glorifying Kapila who appeared as his son, left to be in solitude. The way the sage got free of the bondage of the ego through single pointed devotion and discernment is described here. The Absolute transcends the apparent world of cause and effect, while being its very Source. But the idea of "me" and "mine" that takes false ownership of the body/mind and all its possessions and activities causes ignorance and bondage. Through exclusive devotion, the sage was freed of this false idea and he viewed everyone and everything with the same eye. The correct vision is to see that all activities of the body/mind as well as that of everyone and everything is happening spontaneously by the same material energy. This is to see God in everyone and everyone in God, thereby perceiving the truth that God alone exists as the all-pervading Reality. The sage was established in this vision and freed of all desire and malice, his mind was still like an ocean without waves. Such a composed mind with equanimity toward all is the symptom of Self-realization.

त एते साधवः साध्वि सर्वसङ्गविवर्जिताः ।
सङ्गस्तेष्वथ ते प्रार्थ्यः सङ्गदोषहरा हि ते ॥ Bh 3.25.24

ta ete sādhavaḥ sādhvi sarvasaṅgavivarjitāḥ
saṅgasteṣhvatha te prārthyaḥ saṅgadoṣhaharā hi te

Association must be sought with saints who are free of all attachments as they counteract all the pernicious effects of one's attachments.

Kapila is raised by His Mother Devahuti who recognizes the divinity of her son. She asks her son how to be free of cravings of the mind and the senses which are the root of all suffering. Kapila replies that the way to be free of suffering is through contemplation and devotion toward the Supreme Being. It removes the impurities of the mind rooted in "me" and "mine," which alone causes comparison, covetousness, fear and hence all suffering. Contemplation, devotion and dispassion are awakened most effortlessly by association with saints who are compassionate, composed and equanimous at all times. Being free of all attachments and selfishness, the saints by their association raise the frequency of those in their company, removing all false attachments, and immersing everyone around in the current of peace. Therefore, Kapila instructs that the first step toward Self-realization is to seek the company of saints. This can be done either in person or through reading of great works such as Bhāgavatam which is a detailed chronicle of various saints, their activities and teachings.

अनिमित्ता भागवती भक्ति: सिद्धेर्गरीयसी ।
जरयत्याशु या कोशं निगीर्णमनलो यथा ॥ Bh 3.25.33

animittā bhāgavatī bhaktiḥ siddhergarīyasī
jarayatyāshu yā kosham nigīrṇamanalo yathā

Motiveless devotion to the Supreme Being is superior to even seeking liberation. It speedily dissolves the ego as the digestive fire dissolves the food that is consumed.

After hearing the glory of Satsang, Devahuti asks Kapila about what is the right kind of devotion that helps one be free of the false identification of "me." Kapila answers her directly by saying that devotion free of any motive—including the motive of liberation—is the highest form of devotion. When one consumes food, there is no effort needed to digest the food as the digestive fire dissolves the food instantly. This very process is divine intelligence at work as Krishna says in the Gita: "I am the fire of digestion in the bodies of all beings that digests four kinds of food" (*aham vaiśhvānaro bhūtvā prāṇinām deham āśhritaḥ / prāṇāpāna samāyuktaḥ pachāmyannam chaturvidham*—BG 15.14). Kapila here states that just as the divine intelligence in the form of the digestive fire dissolves all food, divine love that is motiveless dissolves the ego instantly. When there is any motive including that of liberation, it is only for the false "me." When there is the recognition that God alone exists, then there is nobody separate to seek liberation. There is only motiveless, unconditional love for God and all creation as divine.

एवं पराभिध्यानेन कर्तृत्वं प्रकृतेः पुमान् ।
कर्मसु क्रियमाणेषु गुणैरात्मनि मन्यते ।। Bh 3.26.6

evam parābhidhyānena kartṛtvam prakṛteḥ pumān
karmasu kriyamāṇeshu guṇair ātmani manyate

By identifying with the material energy, one attributes the doership of actions which are performed by the modes of material nature onto himself.

Kapila now instructs his Mother Devahuti on the wisdom of discernment that is known as Sankhya Yoga that liberates one from ignorance. The Supreme Being, also known as *Purusha*, is the eternal substrate of all of existence as Pure Consciousness. The material energy, also known as *Prakrti*, comes forth from the Supreme Being and manifests the entire Universe through its three modes of *sattva, rajas, tamas.*

And it is the material energy that performs every action at all levels from the subatomic to the supergalactic. However, the Consciousness in the living beings gets identified with the material energy and creates a false sense of "me" which then assumes doership of all actions of the body. Because of this core ignorance, there is bondage and suffering. To be free of suffering is to completely recognize this false identification and see the illusion of the egoic identity as "me." As Krishna instructs in the Gita: "All activities are done by the modes of material nature. But due to the ignorance of egoic identification, one considers oneself to be the doer." (*prakriteḥ kriyamāṇāni guṇaiḥ karmāṇi sarvaśaḥ / ahankāravimūḍhātmā kartāham iti manyate—BG 3.27*). When one recognizes through inquiring within that the ego or "me" is only an illusion, then all actions are seen as done by the Divine energy with no false sense of doership and the ensuing suffering.

प्रकृतिस्थोऽपि पुरुषो नाज्यते प्राकृतैर्गुणैः ।
अविकारादकर्तृत्वान्निर्गुणत्वाज्जलार्कवत् ॥ Bh 3.27.1

prakṛtistho'pi puruṣho nājyate prākṛtairguṇaiḥ
avikārādakartṛtvānnirguṇatvājjalārkavat

Just as the sun reflected in water, remains unaffected by the attributes of water, the Supreme Being, though abiding in the material body, remains unaffected by its attributes, being changeless, free of doership and devoid of attributes.

When we see the sun reflected inside a pot of water, the light of the reflected sun illuminates the water but none of the attributes of the water, such as coolness, ripples etc. affect the sunlight. In the same way, the Supreme Self (*paramātma*) abides as Pure Consciousness in the hearts of all beings and illuminates all activities of the body. And yet, none of the qualities or activities of the body which are performed by the material energy affect the Supreme Self. When the false ego rises as "me" and due to delusion imagines itself to be the doer and experiencer of all actions, it undergoes suffering. When one is not living a conscious life, one identifies as the doer and perceiver much like the one dreaming while asleep identifies with the dream character and suffers. But when one is alert, awake and living consciously, then one is freed of this false identification, much like the one who wakes up from a dream.

तस्मादिमां स्वां प्रकृतिं दैवीं सदसदात्मिकाम् ।
दुर्विभाव्यां पराभाव्य स्वरूपेणावतिष्ठते ॥ Bh 3.28.44

tasmād imāṁ svāṁ prakṛtiṁ daivīṁ sadasadātmikām
durvibhāvyāṁ parābhāvya svarūpeṇāvatiṣṭhate

By transcending identification with the divine material energy, which is normally difficult to transcend, being the cause and effect of all, one realizes one's true essence.

By regulating the body and mind through moderate diet, being calm and composed, friendly toward all, having steadiness of posture and breath, speaking the truth and living austerely with purity, one can engage in true meditation that results in transcending identification with "me" and "mine." The false identification with the body and the mind, its possessions and activities are due to the material energy which manifests as both the cause and the effect of all actions. It is both the subject and the object, the observer and the observed. And yet one identifies wrongly with the subject as "me" due to the power of the material energy and the attachments it causes that is difficult to transcend. But when one is fully surrendered through loving devotion and the wisdom of discernment, then one is free of all false identification and transcends the "me." This reveals one's true essence (*svarūpa*) to be that of the all-pervading Supreme Being who abides in the hearts of all.

मद्गुणश्रुतिमात्रेण मयि सर्वगुहाशये ।
मनोगतिरविच्छिन्ना यथा गङ्गाम्भसोऽम्बुधौ ॥
लक्षणं भक्तियोगस्य निर्गुणस्य ह्युदाहृतम् ।
अहैतुक्यव्यवहिता या भक्तिः पुरुषोत्तमे ॥ Bh 3.29.11–12

madguṇaśhrutimātreṇa mayi sarvaguhāśhaye
manogatiravichchhinnā yathā gaṅgāmbhaso'mbudhau
lakṣhaṇaṁ bhaktiyogasya nirguṇasya hyudāhṛtam
ahaitukyavyavahitā yā bhaktiḥ puruṣhottame

Just as the waters of Ganges flow toward the ocean with motiveless love, the uninterrupted flow of the mind toward the Supreme Being, dwelling in the hearts of all, is the true characteristic of pure devotion that transcends the three modes of nature.

Kapila describes the nature of pure motiveless devotion which is distinct from devotion colored by motives. The modes (*gunas*) of nature are threefold as *tamas* (ignorance), *rajas* (passion) and *sattva* (goodness), devotion that is tainted by these modes is also threefold. Devotion in the mode of *tamas* is full of anger and jealousy, dividing people into us and them based on faith and engaging in acts of violence. Devotion in the mode of *rajas* is rooted in desire for fame, power, pleasures etc. Devotion in the mode of *sattva* is aimed at removal of sins and focused on discharging one's duty. So, while there is an increasing gradation of purity in the three modes as clearly seen in the world, they all share a sense of separation seeing God as distinct from "me," motivated by what "I" desire from God. Whereas pure loving devotion as described by Kapila is that which is free of this sense of separation, seeing God as the essence of one and all. It is free of the egoic "me" and recognizes everything as God's will. Therefore, such pure devotion is a continuous flow of unconditional love with no personal motive but only interested in serving God in all His infinite forms as everyone, everywhere and in every moment.

सम्यग्दर्शनया बुद्ध्या योगवैराग्ययुक्तया ।
मायाविरचिते लोके चरेऩ्यस्य कलेवरम् ॥ Bh 3.31.48

samyagdarśhanayā buddhyā yogavairāgyayuktayā
māyāvirachite loke carennyasya kalevaram

Endowed with the right vision and clarity, situated in equanimity and dispassion, one can move about in this illusory world freely without identifying with the body.

After teaching wisdom (*jnāna*) through discernment of the eternal and the impermanent as well as loving devotion (*bhakti*) untainted by personal motives, Kapila teaches dispassion (*vairāgya*), the third critical component of Self-realization. He instructs that if one does not heed to the wisdom of discernment and love for the Supreme, then one gets caught in the illusory world by going after frivolous pursuits that are all destroyed by Time. Being attached to the body, relations, wealth etc., one is overcome by anxiety and gets caught in wrong associations, unnecessary efforts, frustration, envy, greed, etc. Thus, the whole life wastes away but even death approaches, one is foolishly caught in attachment and repeats the same pattern over and over. Therefore, Kapila instructs that one ought to be careful with the association one keeps and have dispassion towards the impermanent. Minimizing activities in the worldly realm only for sustenance purposes, one can devote time and energy toward awakening which is the Vedic dictum of "simple living and high thinking." This gives clarity, right vision and equanimity (which is true Yoga), and one can be liberated here and now.

ज्ञानयोगश्च मन्निष्ठो नैर्गुण्यो भक्तिलक्षणः ।
द्वयोरप्येक एवार्थो भगवच्छब्दलक्षणः ॥ Bh 3.32.32

jñānayogaśhcha mannishtho nairgunyo bhaktilakshanah
dvayorapyeka evārtho bhagavachchhabdalakshanah

The way of wisdom and the way of unconditional devotion both have the same meaning which is the essence of the word Bhagavan.

After summarizing in detail, the way of wisdom (*jnana*), which is right discernment and the way of unconditional loving devotion (*bhakti*) which is free of any personal motive, Kapila concludes his teachings by emphatically declaring that both are essentially the same. Wisdom and divine love are two sides of the same coin and seeing them as distinct from each other is ignorance. Kapila makes it clear through the discourse on

Sankhya Yoga to Mother Devahuti that mere philosophical understanding through knowledge of texts is not true wisdom and mere sentimentality toward a sectarian conception of the Supreme Being is not true devotion. Instead, the true essence of wisdom and devotion is the clear perception of the falsity of "me" and "mine" and the recognition of the all-pervading Presence of the Supreme Being. This results in inner peace and the outer expression of unconditional love toward all. Such true peace and love are the very essence of the word Bhagavan.

श्रद्दधानाय भक्ताय विनीतायानसूयवे ।
भूतेषु कृतमैत्राय शुश्रूषाभिरताय च ॥
बहिर्जातविरागाय शान्तचित्ताय दीयताम् ।
निर्मत्सराय शुचये यस्याहं प्रेयसां प्रियः ॥ Bh 3.32.41–42

shraddadhānāya bhaktāya vinītāyānasūyave
bhūteṣhu kṛtamaitrāya shushrūṣhābhiratāya cha
bahirjātavirāgāya shāntachittāya dīyatām
nirmatsarāya shuchaye yasyāhaṁ preyasāṁ priyaḥ

This wisdom is to be imparted to the one full of reverence who is a true devotee, humble, non-envious, friendly toward all beings, eager to serve all, detached, serene and pure, regarding the Supreme Being alone as the dearest.

As the conclusion to the most comprehensive discourse on spiritual wisdom, Kapila states the qualification that makes one eligible to receive this wisdom. The first and the most important is the attitude of reverence called *shraddhā* which is a multi-layered word that means total confidence in the teaching and the teacher, and the sincerity to test it out for oneself earnestly, rather than just accepting or rejecting it out of faith. This attitude automatically manifests all the other qualities mentioned in these verses as it is the foundation for any learning, especially the supreme wisdom of Self-realization. Hence Krishna also states in the Gita that the one with this attitude of reverence attains realization (*shraddhāvān labhate jñānam*—BG 4.39). It brings forth true humility, which is the absence of ego, freedom from comparison with others which is the root of envy, natural attitude of friendliness and service toward all, detachment from worldly objects and experiences, true peace within and unconditional love of the Divine.

तं त्वामहं ब्रह्म परं पुमांसं प्रत्यक्स्रोतस्यात्मनि संविभाव्यम् ।
स्वतेजसा ध्वस्तगुणप्रवाहं वन्दे विष्णुं कपिलं वेदगर्भम् ॥
Bh 3.33.8

tam tvāmahaṁ brahma paraṁ pumāṁsaṁ pratyaksrotasyātmani saṁvibhāvyam
svatejasā dhvastaguṇapravāhaṁ vande viṣhṇuṁ kapilaṁ vedagarbham

I offer my obeisances to Kapila, who is the Supreme Being, who can be realized only by turning the mind within, who brings an end to the stream of material bondage by His effulgence, who is the all-pervading Vishnu, the source of all Vedas.

Upon the conclusion of the teachings by her son Kapila, Devahuti, with her veil of ignorance removed, offers a prayer to her son for being her Guru. She recognizes her son to be the Avatar of the Supreme Being who is the source of inconceivable powers that carry on the creation, sustenance and dissolution of the universe. She is amazed that she was fortunate to give birth to such a glorious son who has descended to show the way of Self-realization. So, she aptly glorifies Kapila as the all-pervading Supreme Essence who brought forth all the Vedas and by realizing whom, one's attachment to matter made of threefold attributes is removed when one inquires within. Thus, praised by Devahuti, Kapila instructs her to abide by the way shown to her while he takes leave and proceeds to live by a far-off ocean in solitude. Devahuti applies herself to a meditative life of wisdom and devotion as instructed by Kapila and her mind merges in the Divine with no trace of ego, to be eternally free. Thus, ends the most auspicious teachings of Kapila which also marks the end of the third canto.

FOURTH CANTO
Loving Devotion

सत्त्वं विशुद्धं वसुदेवशब्दितं यदीयते तत्र पुमानपावृतः ।
सत्त्वे च तस्मिन्भगवान्वासुदेवो ह्यधोक्षजो मे नमसा विधीयते ॥
Bh 4.3.23

sattvaṁ viśhuddhaṁ vasudevaśhabditaṁ yadīyate tatra
pumānapāvṛtaḥ
sattve ca tasmin bhagavān vāsudevo hyadhokṣhajo me namasā
vidhīyate

The absolutely pure mind is called "Vasudeva" because it is there that the Supreme Being is realized in His full glory as Vāsudeva, who is beyond sense perception.

Krishna is born as the son of Vasudeva and hence is called Vāsudeva. As with every single episode of the pastimes of Krishna, the very name is symbolic of the deeper Truth. Vāsudeva is the One who abides everywhere. As Krishna declares in the Gita, the greatest among the wise perceive that Vāsudeva is everything (*vāsudeva sarvam iti*—BG 7.19) and that realization is born only in a pure mind, which is signified by the word Vasudeva. Thus, Krishna's appearance as the son of Vasudeva symbolizes the dawn of God-realization in a pure mind. The pure mind is one that is free from the dirt of ego. All impurities of the mind such as envy, greed, anger, etc. are rooted only in the core ignorance of the ego sense of "me" and "mine." When this dirt is removed through total attention, then the mind is pure and realization of the Divine shines forth. That is the essence of this beautiful verse of Bhāgavatam.

त्वमेव भगवन्नेतच्छिवशक्त्यो: स्वरूपयो: ।
विश्वं सृजसि पास्यत्सि क्रीडन्नूर्णपटो यथा ॥ Bh 4.6.43

tvam eva bhagavannetachchhivaśhaktyoḥ svarūpayoḥ
viśhvaṁ sṛjasi pāsyatsi krīḍannūrṇapaṭo yathā

Carrying on Your sport as Shiva and Shakti, who are essentially one, You create, maintain and dissolve this universe, just as the spider spins a cobweb out of itself, preserves it and takes it back into itself.

The well-known episode of Daksha *yajna* (sacrificial performance) destroyed by Lord Shiva is covered in depth in Bhāgavatam. Daksha conducted a great *yajna* during which he disrespected Shiva with vile words while Shiva just sat calmly and then left silently. Daksha was puffed up with pride and conducted another massive sacrifice to which everyone was invited except Lord Shiva. Sati, the consort of Lord Shiva and Daksha's daughter, wanted to attend the sacrifice though uninvited and made a plea to Shiva. Shiva advised Sati on the inappropriateness of going to any event organized by the vain and arrogant who are caught in egoic identification. Despite Shiva's counsel, Sati went to the Daksha Yajna and encountered great disrespect, so through a Yogic process, she gave up her body that was born through Daksha. Shiva came to know of her sacrifice and destroyed the yajna of Daksha and removed his pride entirely. Brahma then offers prayers to Shiva by glorifying Him as the One who creates, sustains and dissolves the Universe. The whole episode has a beautiful symbolism. Daksha represents the ego that is caught in doership and engages in grand activities for sense gratification, ignoring Shiva who is the Source from which all activities manifest. All egoic undertakings ultimately result in destruction as everything is taken away by Time. So the teaching is to recognize the Source of all activities as the Divine and to act without the sense of doership or else it only ends in suffering.

यथा पुमान्न स्वाङ्गेषु शिरःपाण्यादिषु क्वचित् ।
पारक्यबुद्धिं कुरुते एवं भूतेषु मत्परः ॥ Bh 4.7.53

yathā pumānna svāṅgeshu śhirahpāṇyādiṣuh kvachit
pārakyabuddhiṁ kurute evaṁ bhūteṣhu matparaḥ

Just as a man never conceives of his own head, hands and other limbs as belonging to anyone else, even so one who is surrendered to the Supreme does not regard one's fellow creatures as separate from oneself.

1. Each part of the body is unique in its function and distinct from the other, yet they are not separate but belong to one whole unit as an interconnected organism. If one part of the body is affected, various other parts of the body automatically do what is necessary to heal the affected part. This is the natural state of a healthy body. Similarly, the whole universe is one interconnected Cosmic Body of the Supreme made of each one

of us, all living forms, all inanimate objects—each unique and distinct,yet not separate. The sense of separation is the false notion of ego as "me" that causes one to ascribe difference in agency as various selves. The correct vision is to be free of this sense of separation by seeing that it is only projected by thought. It is the image put together by thought that overlays itself on every interaction to feed this separation. When there is no movement of the past rising as images built over time, then there is only the truth of "what is" as one unitary movement. So, to be alert every moment to any rising self-image and not identifying with it is the key to being free of the false sense of separation.

तमेव वत्साश्रय भृत्यवत्सलं मुमुक्षुभिर्मृग्यपदाब्जपद्धतिम् ।
अनन्यभावे निजधर्मभाविते मनस्यवस्थाप्य भजस्व पूरुषम् ॥
Bh 4.8.22

tameva vatsāśhraya bhṛtyavatsalaṁ
mumukṣhubhirmṛgyapadābjapaddhatim
ananyabhāve nijadharmabhāvite manasyavasthāpya bhajasva
pūruṣham

Take refuge in Him who is fond of His devotees and whose lotus feet are sought after by seekers of liberation. Fixing Him in the mind and being purified by exclusive devotion, surrender unto the Supreme Being.

King Uttānapāda had two wives, Suniti and Suruchi, and of them, the younger Suruchi was the more beloved of the king. One day, the stepmother Suruchi insulted Dhruva, who was born of Suniti, for simply seeking to climb onto the lap of his father. The boy went to his mother sobbing, and the wise Suniti consoled him and asked him to turn his attention to the Supreme Father of all. She asked him to consider the insult of the stepmother as a blessing and adore the Supreme Lord through exclusive, single-pointed devotion. The story symbolizes Suniti as the way of righteousness and Suruchi as the way of sense gratification. The king is drawn to Suruchi as the ego that enjoys sense gratification. The righteous counsel represented by Suniti is to take every challenge as a blessing to realize the highest purpose of life, which is Self-realization through surrendering the false ego. Dhruva, who is an embodiment of *shraddha* (dedication), is thus instructed to turn to the Supreme Being which he does with total sincerity.

योऽन्तः प्रविश्य मम वाचमिमां प्रसुप्तां सञ्जीवयत्यखिलशक्तिधरः स्वधाम्ना ।
अन्यांश्च हस्तचरणश्रवणत्वगादीन् प्राणान्नमो भगवते पुरुषाय तुभ्यम् ॥ Bh 4.9.6

yo'ntaḥ praviśhya mama vāchamimāṁ prasuptāṁ
sañjīvayatyakhilaśhaktidharaḥ svadhāmnā
anyāṁśhcha hastacharaṇaśhravaṇatvagādīn prāṇānnamo
bhagavate puruṣhāya tubhyam

Obeisances unto You, the wielder of all potencies. Having entered within me, You have awakened my dormant speech, hands, feet, ears, touch and the life force.

Dhruva goes to the forest and meets with Narada who instructs him on meditation and initiates Dhruva into the most sacred twelve syllable mantra:

ॐ नमो भगवते वासुदेवाय
oṁ namo bhagavate vāsudevaya

The mantra invokes the all-pervading Supreme Being and is given by the merciful Narada to everyone reading or listening to this portion of Bhāgavatam freely. Dhruva commits to the meditation with the mantra given by Narada and after six months of austere penance is blessed with the vision of the Supreme Lord Narayana. Overawed by the vision of the lord, he is speechless with his eyes full of tears. Then his speech awakens by the Lord touching Dhruva's face with His conch that makes Dhruva utter this very famous and oft-quoted prayer of Bhāgavatam. It reveals that every faculty one possesses—speech, locomotion, listening, the tactile sense and the very life force—is only due to the Cosmic Intelligence of the One Supreme Being. While we take for granted all these faculties, each one of them is a miracle in itself and functions due to such precise intelligence operating in the body. That miracle is the Presence of the Universal Being within us every moment that Dhruva invokes in this beautiful prayer.

त्वं नित्यमुक्तपरिशुद्धविबुद्ध आत्मा कूटस्थ आदिपुरुषो भगवांस्त्रयधीश: ।
यद्बुद्ध्यवस्थितिमखण्डितया स्वदृष्टया द्रष्टा स्थितावधिमखो व्यतिरिक्त आस्से ॥ Bh 4.9.15

tvaṁ nityamuktapariśhuddhavibuddha ātmā kūṭastha ādipuruṣho bhagavāṁs tryadhīśhaḥ
yadbuddhyavasthitimakhaṇḍitayā svadṛṣhṭyā drasṭā sthitāvadhimakho vyatirikta āsse

You are eternally free, all pure and all-knowing Self, the immutable, most ancient Being, possessed of all divine attributes and the controller of the three gunas with unobstructed vision, the Lord of all sacrifices and unknowable to the individual self.

Dhruva glorifies the Supreme Being as the source of the entire Cosmic Intelligence made of the three gunas that pervade the entire creation in various diverse forms. Only due to ignorance, people get strongly caught in the sense of individuality and hanker after various desires. But once they recognize the Truth by meditating upon the essence of one's true nature, all desires including the seeking of liberation come to an end. Therefore, Dhruva prays that there may be constant fellowship with those that are pure hearted and Self-realized through total surrender of their ego, so that one can be free of all attachments and abide in the Supreme Being who is the Self of all. After offering these beautiful prayers, Dhruva is blessed to go back to the kingdom and eventually rules righteously for many years and then ascends to his own pole star (*dhruva nakshatra*) as an eternal abode in the interstellar sphere.

यदा रतिर्ब्रह्मणि नैष्ठिकी पुमानाचार्यवान् ज्ञानविरागरंहसा ।
दहत्यवीर्यं हृदयं जीवकोशं पञ्चात्मकं योनिमिवोत्थितोऽग्निः ॥
Bh 4.22.26

yadā ratirbrahmaṇi naiṣṭhikī pumānāchāryavān
jñānavirāgaraṁhasā
dahatyavīryaṁ hṛdayaṁ jīvakoshaṁ pañchātmakaṁ
yonimivotthito'gniḥ

When the love for the Supreme Being gets firmly established, one resorts to a worthy teacher, and like the fire consuming the very source from which it originates, the mind, made of the five subtle elements that acts as the veil of the ego, dissolves freed of its latent desires by the force of wisdom and dispassion.

King Prthu is a descendant of Dhruva Maharaj and a very righteous king who is said to be the first to bring large portions of Earth under his dominion and hence Earth is called *prthvi*. Once the young sage Sanatkumara with his divine brothers visited the palace of Prthu. The king welcomed him with great love and honor stating that truly a place is hallowed only by the visit of sages who ever abide in the Absolute. Then he requested the sage Sanatkumara to instruct everyone assembled on Self-realization. The very conduct and query of the king reflects the highest culture that comes forth from the ground of right *dharma*. The sage was pleased by the inquiry and praised the king for elevating the conversation for the benefit of all. He instructed that the absence of attachment to anything other than the Supreme Being and abiding love for the Supreme Being which is the Pure Self is the essence of all scriptures. That love comes forth through sincerity, inquisitiveness, association with the saintly, non-violence, non-hoarding, non-covetousness, chastity, endurance of opposites, study, purity and devotion. When love for the Absolute Truth is firmly established through these qualities, the right Guru comes along and bestows the wisdom that dissolves the ego completely by freeing it of all images of the past.

दग्धाशयो मुक्तसमस्ततद्गुणो नैवात्मनो बहिरन्तर्विचष्टे ।
परात्मनोर्यद्व्यवधानं पुरस्तात् स्वप्ने यथा पुरुषस्तद्विनाशे ॥
Bh 4.22.27

dagdhāśhayo muktasamastatadguṇo naivātmano
bahirantarvicaṣhṭe
parātmanoryadvyavadhānaṁ purastāt svapne yathā
puruṣhastadvināśhe

When the veil of the ego that covers the Pure Self has been dissolved, one is freed of all ignorance and no longer perceives division between the inner and the outer, just as one whose dream has been broken no longer sees the images of the dream.

Sage Sanatkumara continues to instruct Prthu that due to firm love for the Supreme Being, when one comes in contact with the right Guru, then the veil of the ego gets dissolved. The veil is that which covers up the indwelling Pure Being and gives the false sense of "me" that is built as the self-image stored in the memory through knowledge and experiences. What we think we are, is nothing but a set of memories from the past which intervenes as the false self in every interaction due to unconscious identification with it. When this wrong identification is removed by the light of wisdom, then there is pure perception without any perceiver and pure action without any doer. Thus, just as the dream images vanish upon waking up, the false self-images of the past vanish upon the dawn of wisdom. And the pure presence of God as our true Self radiates from the Heart. In this way, Sanatkumara summarizes all of Vedanta succinctly for Prthu, who devoutly abides by these teachings and gets liberated.

न यस्य चित्तं बहिरर्थविभ्रमं तमोगुहायां च विशुद्धमाविशत् ।
यद्भक्तियोगानुगृहीतमञ्जसा मुनिर्विचष्टे ननु तत्र ते गतिम् ॥
Bh 4.24.59

na yasya cittaṁ bahirarthavibhramaṁ tamoguhāyāṁ cha viśhuddhamāviśhat
yadbhaktiyogānugṛhītamañjasā munirvichaṣhṭe nanu tatra te gatim

The meditative devotee whose mind is neither distracted by external objects nor loses itself in drowsiness, being pure and blessed with loving devotion, easily and certainly succeeds in realizing God's true nature.

It is commonly observed in any form of meditation, whether it be focused on an object of meditation such as chanting of mantra, watching the breath or on the very subject of who is meditating, the two most important obstacles are distracting thoughts and drowsiness leading to sleep. The distracting thoughts rise due to the impressions in memory of past experiences that are stored as associated with the false ego. Drowsiness and sleep rise due to the dullness of the mind born out of having too much activity and food. The truly meditative devotee is free of both these distractions by keeping the mind very alert. This requires consuming moderate, balanced and pure food as well as not engaging in unnecessary activities either outwardly or through inner chatter and not running after external experiences which are fleeting and leave strong impressions on the mind. When one is alert and free of these tendencies, then the mind is pure and free of both these obstacles, making it conducive for the mind to be single pointed and blessed with loving devotion to realize the Absolute.

श्रेयसामिह सर्वेषां ज्ञानं निःश्रेयसं परम् ।
सुखं तरति दुष्पारं ज्ञाननौर्व्यसनार्णवम् ॥ Bh 4.24.75

*shreyasāmiha sarveshāṁ jñānaṁ niḥshreyasaṁ param
sukhaṁ tarati dushpāraṁ jñānanaurvyasanārṇavam*

Of all the blessings here, the greatest is spiritual wisdom that bestows supreme beatitude. The one who sails in the boat of wisdom easily crosses over the ocean of misery which is otherwise most difficult to cross.

The material world is compared to an ocean of misery because of the inherent impermanence of everything, which causes suffering when one is attached to it. It is said that just as an alert serpent grabs and gobbles up a rat, the divine energy as Time eats up everything when one least expects. Therefore, the wisdom that liberates one from this fear of dissolution is to be free of all attachment to the impermanent by seeing everything as the ever-changing dance of the Eternal Being. Thus, true wisdom is not acquiring knowledge through books but the inner realization that God alone exists in all the various forms. Krishna instructs in the Gita too that a truly wise one is he who surrenders unto Him seeing only the Supreme Being everywhere (*bahūnāṁ janmanāmante jñānavān māṁ prapadyate / vāsudevaḥ sarvam iti sa mahātmā sudurlabhaḥ*—BG 7.19). Such wisdom is true *jnana* or wisdom which is non-different from true *bhakti* or surrender to the Divine and it is the boat that carries us over the ocean of impermanent existence.

स्वं लोकं न विदुस्ते वै यत्र देवो जनार्दनः ।
आहुर्धूम्रधियो वेदं सकर्मकमतद्विदः ॥ Bh 4.29.48

svaṁ lokaṁ na viduste vai yatra devo janārdanaḥ
āhurdhūmradhiyo vedaṁ sakarmakamatadvidaḥ

Those with their understanding clouded speak of the Vedas as purely ritualistic and are not aware of the true essence of the Vedas whose main purpose is Self-realization by recognizing the Supreme Being as the only Truth.

Vedas have three portions broadly speaking—*karma kānda* (fruitive rituals), *upasana kānda* (prayers) and *jnana kānda* which is the direct teaching of Self-realization also called as Vedanta. Of these, the fruitive rituals cause one to get caught in a false sense of doership and cause/effect determinism, and a desire for various pleasures. There are many who associate Vedas only with such fruitive rituals and ignore the true essence of Vedas which is to realize the Supreme Being. This is condemned in this verse just as Krishna does clearly in the Gita: "Those who are drawn to the flowery words of Vedas that speak of rites and rituals are caught in desire of heavenly pleasures for enjoyment and opulence. Enslaved by such rites, they have no chance of a resolute mind. Therefore, transcend the portion of Vedas that speak of the three gunas and rise above all dualities." (BG 2.42–45). Here, Bhāgavatam emphasizes the realization of the Supreme Being, Janardana or the One who protects everyone devoted to Him, and not engaging in desire laden rituals, as the true purpose of Vedas.

गृहेष्वाविशतां चापि पुंसां कुशलकर्मणाम् ।
मद्वार्तायातयामानां न बन्धाय गृहा मताः ॥ Bh 4.30.19

gṛheṣvāviśatāṁ chāpi puṁsāṁ kuśhalakarmaṇām
madvārtāyātayāmānāṁ na bandhāya gṛhā matāḥ

Even living as a householder, if one engages in auspicious activities, dedicates them to God and spends spare time in discussions and inquiries of the Absolute Truth, that householder life is not considered a source of bondage.

Normally the householder's life keeps one busy with various activities related to family and work responsibilities which makes one prone to the sense of doership with its desires, fears, worries and anxieties. However, it doesn't mean one has to abstain from all activities or simply look to escape from them because wherever one goes, one cannot run away from the mind which alone carries the seeds of desires and fears. Therefore, the way shown here is to purify the householder's life so that it does not become a source of bondage. It begins with spending spare time in Satsang or association that uplifts us into discussing and inquiring about the Absolute Truth of the Supreme Being. That leads to lack of interest in unnecessary activities, engaging more in auspicious activities and dedicating them to God without any sense of expectation of results which brings forth peace. Krishna says in the Gita as well that the one who does his prescribed duties without desire for its fruits is the true renunciate and Yogi, not the one who prematurely disengages from activities (*anāśhritaḥ karmaphalaṁ kāryaṁ karma karoti yaḥ / sa sannyāsī cha yogī cha na niragnir na chākriyaḥ*—BG 6.1).

तज्जन्म तानि कर्माणि तदायुस्तन्मनो वच: ।
नृणां येनेह विश्वात्मा सेव्यते हरिरीश्वर: ।। Bh 4.31.9

tajjanma tāni karmāṇi tadāyustanmano vacaḥ
nṛṇāṁ yeneha vishvātmā sevyate haririśhvaraḥ

That birth, those actions, that period of life, that mind and that speech alone is worth in this world, through which the Supreme Being and the Soul of the Universe, Hari, is resorted to.

As the last teaching of the fourth skandha, Narada instructs that whether one has great birth and lineage, long span of life, learning, asceticism, flowery speech, talents, penetrating intellect, strength of body, keenness of the senses, practice of Yoga, knowledge of the scriptures etc., all of these are of no avail if one is caught in the ignorance of the false ego. He states that the greatest blessing and the true purpose of all other blessings, is to realize the Absolute Truth, that the beloved Self of all living entities is the One Supreme Being. This frees one from greed, envy, hate, anger and all the negative qualities that are all rooted in the false ego. And thus, it enables one to live a truly peaceful and contented life with kindness toward all, which cannot be attained through pride of learning, affluence or pedigree. The perfection of human life is to transcend the separative identification and realize the all-pervading Supreme Being, Hari—meaning the One who takes away the ego.

FIFTH CANTO
Cosmic Order

न तस्य कश्चित्तपसा विद्यया वा न योगवीर्येण मनीषया वा ।
नैवार्थधर्मैः परतः स्वतो वा कृतं विहन्तुं तनुभृद्विभूयात् ॥ Bh 5.1.12

*na tasya kaśhchittapasā vidyayā vā na yogavīryeṇa maniṣhayā vā
naivārthadharmaiḥ parataḥ svato vā kṛtaṁ vihantuṁ tanubhṛd
vibhūyāt*

**No embodied being is capable of undoing what has been
ordained, through asceticism or erudition, through
Yogic power or intellectual acumen, through affluence or
religious merit, by oneself or by the help of another.**

When one is purely caught in the material conception of cause
and effect, then one feels that one is entitled to a particular
result as an effect, based on putting in the effort which is
deemed as the sole cause. But life teaches through various
events that one's effort is not the sole cause and there are
many other hidden causes that apparently happen by chance
and end up influencing the result, in totally unexpected
ways. Thus, when one's false sense of individualism and pride
in self-effort goes away, there is an acknowledgment of the
mysterious hand of the Universe in every action. This might
still lead one to believe that one can influence this mysterious

power through various spiritual practices. One might take up asceticism, develop Yogic powers (*siddhis*), increase one's affluence or merit, use one's intellectual acumen to decode the mysteries of the Universe and so on, all with the intent of influencing the results. But one will find that no matter what powers or faculties one develops, the infinite Cosmic Intelligence has its own ways and events unfold as ordained, regardless of one's desires. When this is realized fully, then true equanimity dawns where one puts in the necessary effort but accepts the results as ordained by the unitary Divine Power. This is the true spirit of karma yoga.

कर्माशयं हृदयग्रन्थिबन्धमविद्ययासादितमप्रमत्तः ।
अनेन योगेन यथोपदेशं सम्यग्व्यपोह्योपरमेत योगात् ॥
Bh 5.5.14

karmāśhayaṁ hṛdayagranthibandham avidyayāsāditam apramattaḥ
anena yogena yathopadeśhaṁ samyagvyapohyoparameta yogāt

Remaining vigilant every moment as instructed, one ought to completely shake off the knot of egotism in the heart which causes bondage due to ignorance as the storehouse of all latent desires.

The knot of egotism is the false identification with the body and mind, with its various memories and images as "me." The cause for all bondage is due to this ignorant identification with the mental images coming from the past and getting caught in desires, fears, judgments and so on. As we go through the day, if we remain vigilant of the voice in our head every moment, we will notice that most perceptions and activities are colored by being identified with the image as "me." The image might be associated with one's body, relations, work, religion, nation or even one's spiritual journey. The image unconsciously takes over as "me" and provides a filtered commentary on what's being perceived or acted upon. To be vigilant is to be aware of this inner voice every moment as it rises and it dissolves in the very light of awareness. This dissolution of identification with a self-image is the cutting of the knot of egotism. When this knot is removed, then one abides as simply Awareness with no illusion of an individual perceiving or acting. There is only the holistic perception that action is done by the Divine Power.

गुरुर्न स स्यात्स्वजनो न स स्यात् पिता न स स्याज्जननी न सा स्यात् ।
दैवं न तत्स्यान्न पतिश्च स स्यान्न मोचयेद्यः समुपेतमृत्युम् ॥
Bh 5.5.18

gururna sa syātsvajano na sa syāt pitā na sa syājjananī na sā syāt daivaṁ na tatsyānna patiśhcha sa syānna mocayedyaḥ samupetamṛtyum

If one is unable to help liberate from the fear of death, such a Guru is no Guru, such a relation is no relation, such a father is no father, such a mother is no mother, such a deity is no deity, such a husband is no husband.

The Divine Avatar in the form of Rshabha instructs his son Bharata and other princes as well as his subjects on the main duty of a king, a father, a Guru or relation which is to guide them toward God-realization. If the subjects of a king or the children of a father or the pupils of a Guru are ignorant, they ought to be instructed patiently and even if they don't listen, one has to persist with the teaching. However, if they are not able to guide one toward the highest purpose of human life, then such a Guru, relation, father, mother, husband are of no value at all, even though each of these relationships is highly regarded. As an example, Bali Maharaja ignored his own Guru Shukracharya when he advised against surrendering to the Lord. Similarly, Prahlada went against his father Hiranyakashipu, Bharata against his mother Kaikeyi, Vibhishana against his elder brother Ravana and the Gopis of Vrndavana were drawn away from their husbands. Thus, we see the truth of this verse illustrated in each of these episodes in Bhāgavatam to reveal that even the most revered relationship can be given up, if it is an obstacle to God-realization.

स्थौल्यं कार्श्यं व्याधय आधयश्च क्षुत्तृड् भयं कलिरिच्छा जरा च ।
निद्रा रतिर्मन्युरहंमदः शुचो देहेन जातस्य हि मे न सन्ति ।।
Bh 5.10.10

sthaulyaṁ kārśhyaṁ vyādhaya ādhayaśhcha kṣhuttṛḍ bhayaṁ kalirichchhā jarā cha
nidrā ratirmanyurahaṁmadaḥ śhucho dehena jātasya hi me na santi

Being stout or lean, having ailments, worries, hunger, thirst, fear, strife, desire, old age, sleep, pleasure, anger, vanity of ego, grief—all these appear only in the body and mind, not in the pure Self.

Bharata, the son of Rshabha, ruled righteously for a long time and hence the land came to be known as Bharat. Then he retired to the woods by an Ashram to dedicate himself to meditation and devotion. He, however, gets attached to a little deer that distracts him from his purpose, showing the great peril of attachment. He is eventually reborn as Jadabharata who due to his past life austerities, is now fully Self-realized right from birth. He lives as an Avadhoota (fully liberated sage) moving around freely. Once the king of the region, Rahugana, who is on his way to visit a sage, without recognizing Jadabharata's greatness, orders him to carry his palanquin and chastises him for not doing his work properly despite being stout. Jadabharata calmly replies to the king that whatever the king calls him—stout, lean, tired, hungry—as well as any other attributes of the body or the mind do not apply to his true nature as Pure Awareness. This response jolts the king to the realization that he is no ordinary person, and he asks for instruction on Self-realization which results in a profound discourse by Jadabharata.

क्षेत्रज्ञ आत्मा पुरुष: पुराण: साक्षात्स्वयंज्योतिरज: परेश: ।
नारायणो भगवान् वासुदेव: स्वमाययाऽऽत्मन्यवधीयमान: ।।
Bh 5.11.13

kshetrajña ātmā purushah purānah sākshātsvayamjyotirajah pareshah
nārāyano bhagavān vāsudevah svamāyayātmanyavadhīyamānah

He who illuminates this body, the very Self of all, the most ancient, self-effulgent, unborn, controller of all known as Narayana is the Supreme Being, the all-pervading Vāsudeva, who enters the hearts of all by His own Maya.

Jadabharata proceeds to instruct Rahugana with great precision on the wisdom of Self-realization. He reveals that the Supreme Being is not just within us but also without, thus all-pervading. It is the mind that creates the illusion of a separate self as "me," thus creating division and resulting in lust, anger, greed etc. The mind comes into contact with various sensations through the senses and due to predisposition, multiplies into diverse thoughts and desires. However, if one can remain totally aware of the movements of the mind without getting identified with it, it is revealed that this awareness is unaffected by the activities of the mind. The very Awareness is realized as our true Self which is common to all, free of any adjuncts, ever-present, self-effulgent and all-pervading. The Supreme Being is referred to as Bhagavan Narayana who is the all-pervading Vāsudeva. As the air enters the breath of all, it is said that He enters the hearts of all beings as the Pure Awareness.

ज्ञानं विशुद्धं परमार्थमेकमनन्तरं त्वबहिर्ब्रह्म सत्यम् ।
प्रत्यक् प्रशान्तं भगवच्छब्दसंज्ञं यद्वासुदेवं कवयो वदन्ति ॥
Bh 5.12.11

jñānaṁ viśhuddhaṁ paramārthamekamanantaraṁ
tvabahirbrahma satyam
pratyak praśhāntaṁ bhagavachchhabdasaṁjñaṁ yadvāsudevaṁ
kavayo vadanti

Pure Consciousness alone is the nature of the Supreme Being, who is absolute, one without a second, with no inside or outside, all perfect, immutable and the very meaning of the word "Bhagavan" and called by the sages as Vāsudeva.

Jadabharata further instructs on the very nature of the Supreme Being. First, he points out that all material forms from the body to earth to all the elements are just made of subtle atoms as constituent factors which are brought forth by the inconceivable energy that underlies all of matter. And this energy is constantly in flux thus all of matter is of an ephemeral nature. But the very source of this material energy is Pure Consciousness that alone pervades the whole Universe. Just as space is said to be inside the room whereas the room itself is contained in space, similarly the Supreme Being of the nature of Pure Consciousness is said to be within the body, but the very body is contained within Pure Consciousness. Therefore, there is no question of inside or outside to the Absolute Truth, which is unchanging, ever peaceful and unaffected by the happenings of the universe just as the light that illuminates a room is unaffected by the activities in the room. This Absolute Truth who is all-pervading and hence known as Vāsudeva is what is signified by the word Bhagavan. Thus, Jadabharata gives the most perfect definition of God, not as a mental projection, not separated by time or space, but the very essence of each one of us here and now.

यत्रोत्तमश्लोकगुणानुवादः प्रस्तूयते ग्राम्यकथाविघातः ।
निषेव्यमाणोऽनुदिनं मुमुक्षोर्मतिं सतीं यच्छति वासुदेवे ॥
Bh 5.12.13

yatrottamaśhlokaguṇānuvādaḥ prastūyate grāmyakathāvighātaḥ
niṣhevyamāṇo'nudinaṁ mumukṣhormatiṁ satīṁ yachchhati
vāsudeve

In the assembly of the exalted are held discourses on the excellence of the Supreme Being, which shuts out

talk of worldly matters. By listening to such discourses every day, the pure mind of the seeker of liberation gets focused on the all-pervading Lord.

After describing the true nature of God as the essence of our very existence, Jadabharata now describes the easiest way to realize the Supreme Being is simply being in the assemblies where discourses are held on His excellence. He says such association with devotees is superior to any austerity, asceticism, ritual, charity, studying Vedas, honoring nature etc. While all these practices have their own merits, what is emphasized here is the supreme efficacious association of those devoted to the Supreme Being. When we come together in such an assembly, unlike other practices where the mind is found to wander, the mind is automatically focused to be meditative. Such assembly has no room for worldly stories, gossip and other mundane topics but focuses solely on the transcendental truth of the Supreme Being who pervades the whole universe and hence called Vāsudeva. Therefore, a taste for Satsang is the surest sign of Grace as it removes the taste for temporal affairs and situates the mind in a serene, pure state that is most conducive for liberation.

स्वस्त्यस्तु विश्वस्य खल: प्रसीदतां ध्यायन्तु भूतानि शिवं मिथो धिया।
मनश्च भद्रं भजतादधोक्षजे आवेश्यतां नो मतिरप्यहैतुकी ॥
Bh 5.18.9

swastyastu vishvasya khalaḥ prasīdatāṁ dhyāyantu bhūtāni shivaṁ mitho dhiyā
manashcha bhadraṁ bhajatādadhokṣhaje āveśhyatāṁ no matirapyahaitukī

May there be well-being throughout the universe. May the wicked be pacified. May all beings be good to each other. May the mind always be in auspiciousness. May the intellect be immersed in motiveless love for the Transcendent.

This is a sublime prayer of the great devotee Prahlada whose story comes in detail later in the seventh skandha. Prahlada reflects the state of a true Bhagavata whose every thought, word and action is only for the welfare of the whole universe. The normal prevalent state of most beings identified with their body, mind, relations and possessions is always motivated by what's in it for me. Whereas the state of a realized being is a spontaneous expression of how to serve. It is spontaneous due to total absence of separation through the vision of seeing the entire universe as the Cosmic body of the Supreme Being. So, the prayer is selfless, only for the welfare of all and especially of those who are caught in the ego. The entire attitude of this prayer is captured by the last word *ahaituki*, which means motiveless. Freedom from all selfish motives, including seeking liberation and thus being totally surrendered to the Supreme Being, is the mark of a true Bhagavata that Prahlada is the perfect example of.

यत्सङ्गलब्धं निजवीर्यवैभवं तीर्थं मुहुः संस्पृशतां हि मानसम् ।
हरत्यजोऽन्तः श्रुतिभिर्गतोऽङ्गजं को वै न सेवेत मुकुन्दविक्रमम् ॥
Bh 5.18.11

*yatsangalabdham nijaviryavaibhavam tirtham muhuh
samsprśhatām hi mānasam
haratyajo'ntah shrutibhirgato'ngajam ko vai na seveta
mukundavikramam*

Entering through the ears into the mind of the one who repeatedly listens in the company of devotees to the uniquely glorious and purifying accounts of the Supreme Being, the Unborn takes away the impurities of the listener.

Of all the various practices that one can take on to realize the Absolute Truth, Bhāgavatam gives the highest place to Satsang or right association with devotees and repeatedly emphasizes it as the foundation for one's realization. In the right association, the ears get the nectar of wisdom and devotion without any effort, and it gently enters the mind to purify it by removing the false notions and superimpositions due to various attachments to ephemeral phenomena. This causes one to lose interest in mundane affairs and take delight in listening to the glory of the Supreme Being—referred to in this verse as Mukunda or the bestower of liberation. Thus, one gets free of the false ego and realizes the true essence of one's being as divine. Therefore, resorting to holy association with curiosity and openness is all that is necessary to be free of false identities that bring about suffering and to be established in freedom and unconditional love toward all.

न यत्र वैकुण्ठकथासुधापगा न साधवो भागवतास्तदाश्रयाः ।
न यत्र यज्ञेशमखा महोत्सवाः सुरेशलोकोऽपि न वै स सेव्यताम् ॥
Bh 5.19.24

*na yatra vaikuṇṭhakathāsudhāpagā na sādhavo
bhāgavatāstadāśhrayāḥ
na yatra yajñeśhamakhā mahotsavāḥ sureśhaloko'pi na vai sa
sevyatām*

That region, be it the abode of the ruler of the heavens, ought not be resorted to, where the nectar of the accounts of the Supreme Being does not flow, where there are no saintly devotees abiding, where there is no sacrifice performed and where festive celebration of the Lord doesn't happen.

Just as the company of saintly beings gives the nectar of wisdom and devotion effortlessly, the place bereft of such company takes us away from our true Self. When we listen to the pastimes of the Supreme Being who bestows freedom from suffering (Vaikuntha) and when we have the company of saintly devotees who take delight in this nectar through listening and sharing discourses, singing the divine names and abiding in the sacred silence, the mind gets uplifted to the same wavelength. Such association brings about the natural letting go of "me" and "mine" which is the true meaning of sacrifice—to make the presence sacred by offering the false ego to the fire of wisdom. Gathering thus in the sacred Presence and honoring the Divine is the true purpose of all festivities and celebrations. All other festivities bereft of the Divine are like decorating a corpse as Bhāgavatam declares later (*yās tadviraktāḥ shavashobhanā matāḥ*—Bh 10.38.12). Therefore, just as one ought to seek holy association, one ought to either avoid association with the worldly minded or even better, elevate such association with Divine Presence which is true service.

SIXTH CANTO
Divine Grace

पतितः स्खलितो भग्नः सन्दष्टस्तप्त आहतः ।
हरिरित्यवशेनाह पुमान्नार्हति यातनाः ॥ Bh 6.2.15

patitaḥ skhalito bhagnaḥ sandaṣṭastapta āhataḥ
haririt yavaśenāha pumānnārhati yātanāḥ

One who chants Hari or any other name of the Supreme Being even involuntarily while falling down, stumbling, bitten or injured, is not caught in the web of suffering.

The sixth skandha begins with the story of Ajamila which brings out the Grace of the Holy Names of Bhagavan. Parikshit asks Shuka Brahmam on the best atonement for sinful deeds as the various atonements usually done don't seem to remove the seed for future sinful actions. Shuka Brahmam responds that indeed the only true atonement for all sins is through Self-realization, by surrendering unto the Supreme Lord and taking the Holy Name. He then narrates the story of Ajamila, who originally being a pious person, due to attraction to a lewd woman fell from his position and engaged in many sinful activities. He named his last son Narayana and at the moment of death, had the good fortune of calling out his son's name aloud. That invoked the messengers of the Supreme Being to counter the messengers of Death who'd come to take him for punishment for his sinful actions. The messengers of the Lord pointed out that Ajamila had atoned for all his sins by uttering the most auspicious Holy Name "Narayana" and therefore ought to be released from the noose of death. The messengers of Death deferred to the messengers of the Lord, Ajamila was restored to his former self and the messengers of Bhagavan disappeared. Ajamila couldn't believe the great blessing he had been bestowed with, though most undeserving. Filled with gratitude and resolve to completely turn his life around, he departed to Haridwar and engaged in a dedicated life of devotion and surrender. Thus, the power of Grace of both the Holy Name and the momentary Satsang he had with the Lord's messengers is revealed by this episode. Krishna reveals the significance of chanting the Holy name in the Gita by saying, "Of all sacred rituals, I am the chanting of the Name" (*yajñānāṁ japayajño'smi*—BG 10.25).

यं वै न गोभिर्मनसासुभिर्वा हृदा गिरा वासुभृतो विचक्षते ।
आत्मानमन्तर्हृदि सन्तमात्मनां चक्षुर्यथैवाकृतयस्ततः परम् ॥
Bh 6.3.16

yaṁ vai na gobhirmanasāsubhirvā hṛdā girā vāsubhṛto
vichakṣhate
ātmānamantarhṛdi santamātmanāṁ
chakṣhuryathaivākṛtayastataḥ param

Even as colors that are seen cannot perceive the faculty of vision that is the seer, the mind or organs of action, intellect or speech cannot perceive the Seer of all living beings, dwelling in their very heart.

The messengers of Death report to Yama, the deity presiding over Death, about being overruled by the messengers of the Lord and ask for clarification. Yama, a fully enlightened being, gives beautiful instructions on the Supreme Being and says those surrendered unto all-pervading Timeless Supreme Being are freed of bodily sense of "me" and not under the purview of Time and hence Death itself. He tells them Death only has control over those who are attached to the body and mind that are changeful and bound by Time. All those who are caught in identification with the three modes of Sattva, Rajas and Tamas are subject to the cycle of birth and death. However, if one recognizes the very Seer of the modes of nature as the true Self, then he is freed from the noose of Yama. This recognition of the Seer is not through the help of mind or intellect or speech which are themselves only the seen, just as objects of sight such as colors cannot perceive the eyes that see them. Therefore, it is not by knowing but by surrendering unto the Source and abiding in Him that one can recognize the true Seer.

यस्मिन्यतो येन च यस्य यस्मै यद्यो यथा कुरुते कार्यते च ।
परावरेषां परमं प्राक् प्रसिद्धं तद् ब्रह्म तद्धेतुरनन्यदेकम् ॥
Bh 6.4.30

yasmin yato yena cha yasya yasmai yadyo yathā kurute kāryate cha
parāvareṣhāṁ paramaṁ prāk prasiddhaṁ tad brahma taddheturananyadekam

Wherever, with whatever motive, by whatever means,
for whatever purpose, whatever work that whoever does

however or is prompted to do, all that has its cause only as the Infinite Being, one without a second.

This is another comprehensive verse of Bhāgavatam that brings out very poetically the truth that all might of all kinds have only one Source, in the Supreme Being also called the Almighty. The source of all intelligence and energy from a subatomic particle to a super galactic cluster and beyond can all be reduced to one unitary Power which is the holy grail of science as well. The very substrate from which this unitary Power comes forth is called the Infinite Being or Brahman. Seen another way, the world is experienced only as perception through subject and object interaction. Subject as I, object as the other, the space and time in between subject and object—everything is only based on perception. And every perception is in Awareness and made of Awareness, just as every ocean wave is in water and made of water. Therefore, the world being nothing other than perception and perception being nothing other than Awareness, everything here is Awareness, which is the nature of the Infinite Being, Brahman. This is the direct pointer of the Vedic aphorism *"sarvam khalvidam brahman"* (Everything here is Brahman). This beautiful verse of Bhāgavatam brings out the essence of this aphorism by asserting that every action in every possible way has as its only cause as Brahman.

अस्तीति नास्तीति च वस्तुनिष्ठयोरेकस्थयोर्भिन्नविरुद्धधर्मणो: ।
अवेक्षितं किञ्चन योगसाङ्ख्ययो: समं परं ह्यनुकूलं बृहत्तत् ॥
Bh 6.4.32

astīti nāstīti cha
vastuniṣhṭhayorekasthayorbhinnaviruddhadharmaṇoh

avekṣitaṁ kiñchana yogasāṅkhyayoḥ samaṁ paraṁ hyanukūlaṁ bṛhattat

Through the apparently distinct and contradictory approaches of affirming and negating the manifest existence, the two ways of surrender and wisdom both profess abidance in the same one Truth which is acceptable to both as the Transcendent Infinite Being.

In this profound verse, Bhāgavatam removes all dispute between bhakti and jnana by establishing the apparently contradictory approaches as equally valid means for abidance in the same Absolute Truth. It uses the word Yoga to refer to the way of surrender and Sankhya to refer to the way of wisdom through self-inquiry. In the way of surrender, everything in the manifest existence is affirmed as an expression of the all-pervading Cosmic Intelligence that comes forth from the Supreme Being who is the Source of all and thereby one is freed of egoic attachments and abides in the Absolute Truth. In the way of wisdom, everything in the manifest existence is negated as "not true, not true" (*neti neti*) due to their impermanence and what remains is the Pure Awareness in which all of existence comes and goes, which is realized as the only abiding Truth and one again is freed of egoic attachments and abides in the Absolute Truth. Thus, the approach of affirming or negating existence both lead to the realization of the same Infinite Being who both pervades and transcends all of existence.

न नाकपृष्ठं न च पारमेष्ठ्यं न सार्वभौमं न रसाधिपत्यम् ।
न योगसिद्धीरपुनर्भवं वा समञ्जस त्वा विरहय्य काङ्क्षे ॥
Bh 6.11.25

na nākapṛṣhṭhaṁ na cha pārameṣhṭhyaṁ na sārvabhaumaṁ na rasādhipatyam
na yogasiddhīrapunarbhavaṁ vā samañjasa tvā virahayya kāṅkṣhe

I crave neither the highest heavenly regions nor the abode of Brahma nor sovereignty over the entire earth or extra-terrestrial regions, nor superhuman powers nor even liberation from rebirth, if separated from You, O storehouse of all grace.

This is one of the most beautiful verses of Bhāgavatam, for its poetic alliteration as well as its profound expression of divine love. And most surprisingly, it comes from a demon called Vrtrasura, thus revealing that anyone and everyone is within the ambit of grace. Vrtra comes to fight Indra, the head of the demigods, knowing full well that Indra is blessed with a divine weapon, impossible to overpower. A fierce battle then ensues between the troops of Indra and Vrtra. When Vrtra sees his troops lose and flee the battlefield, he shows great courage and fights on. Finally, he encounters Indra directly and realizing that he is about to be slain as ordained, Vrtra reveals his heart as a completely surrendered devotee and fully ready to embrace his destiny. He first chastises Indra for being arrogant about his powers, saying that the Lord does not bestow powers and riches to those exclusively devoted to Him as it only causes pride and fear. He instead frustrates the efforts of His devotees in gaining worldly riches and such frustration is to be inferred as His grace. Then he offers a heartfelt prayer to the Lord accepting his death fully, asking that if he is to be reborn, may that be as only the servant of His servants (*dāsānudāso bhavitāsmi bhūyaḥ*). With no desire for any power, riches or even freedom from rebirth, he prays to the Supreme Being to never be separated from Him through the false ego of "me" but ever surrendered unto Him.

अजातपक्षा इव मातरं खगाः स्तन्यं यथा वत्सतराः क्षुधार्ताः ।
प्रियं प्रियेव व्युषितं विषण्णा मनोऽरविन्दाक्ष दिदृक्षते त्वाम् ॥
Bh 6.11.26

ajātapakṣhā iva mātaraṁ khagāḥ stanyaṁ yathā vatsatarāḥ kṣhudhārtāḥ
priyaṁ priyeva vyuṣhitaṁ viṣhaṇṇā mano'ravindākṣha didṛkṣhate tvām

As a fledgling bird in the nest eager for its mother bird, as young calves tormented with hunger yearning for milk from the mother cow's udders, as a lover suffering from separation while longing for her beloved to return home, O lotus-eyed Lord, my mind is keen to behold You.

Vrtra continues with his most moving expression of divine love in another heartfelt prayer. Each example he gives here is most appropriate to bring forth his single-pointed, exclusive longing for the Supreme Being. With each metaphor, the sense of longing progressively increases in intensity, from that of a newborn bird to that of a young calf which is more sentient to the peak of a lover, pining in separation with all her being as will be shown later by the Gopis of Vrndavan. Vrtra and Indra then engage in a fierce battle and even after losing his arm, Vrtra fights valiantly and makes Indra fall down on the ground. Exhorting Indra to get up to engage in a fair battle again, Vrtra instructs that everything happens as ordained by the Lord and not recognizing that He alone is the cause of all powers, potencies and life itself, only the ignorant consider themselves as the cause of their actions. He tells Indra to see that everything is subject to the control of God as a wooden puppet is to its showman and to regard all blessings in the form of life, affluence, fame and power and their contraries as ordained by the Lord. One has to accept victory and defeat, fame and infamy, life and death with equanimity. Indra gets up and glorifies Vrtra for his amazing wisdom and devotion in the heat of the battle, then engages in the fight with great respect and eventually as ordained, he kills Vrtra. Upon dying, an effulgence from his heart (*atmajyoti*) issues forth and merges into the Supreme Being while the sages and demigods glorify Vrtra for his pure devotion as everyone looks on with wonder.

यथा प्रयान्ति संयान्ति स्रोतोवेगेन बालुका: ।
संयुज्यन्ते वियुज्यन्ते तथा कालेन देहिन: ॥ Bh 6.15.3

yathā prayānti saṁyānti srotovegena bālukāḥ
saṁyujyante viyujyante tathā kālena dehinaḥ

As sand particles come together and drift apart in a river due to the current of a stream, so are embodied beings brought together and separated by Time.

Upon listening to the narration of Vrtrasura's sublime wisdom and surrender, Parikshit asks Shuka Brahmam, despite being a demon, how Vrtra had such unflinching devotion which is rare even among the saintly. Shuka Brahmam responds by narrating a story of King Chitraketu who was a prosperous ruler of a huge kingdom with great wealth, power and many wives but no children and in spite of all the opulence was very depressed. Sage Angira once came to his kingdom and upon being implored by the king to satisfy his burning desire to have a child to continue the dynasty, the sage shows the way for the king to have a son, while warning him that the son will bring great joy and great grief. And sure enough, first there is great joy and festivity upon the principal queen giving birth to a son. But that makes the other queens extremely envious, and they do the unthinkable act of poisoning the young prince to kill him. As prophesied by the sage, the king now falls into an ocean of grief and is unable to move. To give him consolation, sage Angira comes with Narada to visit the king. He first imparts the wisdom of impermanence of everything by pointing out that just as sand particles or leaves float together for some time in a river and then part due to a wave, people come together and part due to Time. It is seen everywhere that families get separated due to children growing up and leaving the house, let alone extreme situations such as the king faced. So, no matter what, Time always takes people away in different directions and to therefore not be attached to any relation or situation is the beginning of wisdom.

भूतैर्भूतानि भूतेशः सृजत्यवति हन्ति च ।
आत्मसृष्टैरस्वतन्त्रैरनपेक्षोऽपि बालवत् ॥ Bh 6.15.6

bhūtairbhūtāni bhūteśhaḥ sṛjatyavati hanti cha
ātmasṛṣhṭairasvatantrairanapekṣho'pi bālavat

It is the Lord of the created beings who though Unborn and Unchanging, like a child engaged in a play, creates, sustains and destroys living entities out of Himself and therefore the embodied entities are never independent.

The two sages Angira and Narada, out of their immense compassion, impart the highest wisdom to Chitraketu to bestow Grace and to bring him out of grief. They point to him that it is only due to delusion that one gets attached to the body, relations, wealth etc. which are all impermanent by nature. Everything belongs to the Lord who creates, preserves and dissolves by His energy. The example of a play is given which is also known as *lila*. Just as even a human play is created, sustained and dissolved by a director with various characters all doing their part according to the script, the Divine play is scripted perfectly by the Cosmic Director. Thus, there is no individual "me" or "mine" associated with the body, all being only the energy of the Supreme Being. So, there is no independence within the body/mind which is conditioned by nature and nurture as ordained. True independence lies only in recognizing that our very essence is not the body/mind but pure Awareness that is untouched by the activities of the body/mind. Chitraketu is thus instructed to recognize the illusory nature of all worldly relations, objects and ideas, and realize the abiding essence as the Supreme Being who alone is permanent.

अयं हि देहिनो देहो द्रव्यज्ञानक्रियात्मकः ।
देहिनो विविधक्लेशसन्तापकृदुदाहृतः ॥
तस्मात् स्वस्थेन मनसा विमृश्य गतिमात्मनः ।
द्वैते ध्रुवार्थविश्रम्भं त्यजोपशममाविश ॥ Bh 6.15.25-26

ayaṁ hi dehino deho dravyajñānakriyātmakaḥ
dehino vividhakleśhasantāpakṛdudāhṛtaḥ
tasmāt svasthena manasā vimṛśhya gatimātmanaḥ
dvaite dhruvārthaviśhrambhaṁ tyajopaśhamamāviśha

If one regards oneself as the body consisting of gross elements, senses of perception and organs of action, then it causes afflictions and misery of various kinds. Therefore, inquire with a calm mind as to the true nature of the Self and abide in peace giving up attachment to the duality of the world.

The body is made of both gross and subtle elements which are described in five layers (*koshas*) by the Upanishads. First is the physical body made up of food (*annamaya kosha*) which is the gross matter. Second is the energy body (*pranamaya kosha*) which is responsible for all the activities of the body such as blood circulation, hunger, thirst, digestion etc. Third is the mind (*manomaya kosha*) made of memories, desires and other mental impressions. Fourth is the intellect (*vijnanamaya kosha*) which is the ability to perceive and discern. Fifth is the subtle seed of the ego (*anandamaya kosha*) also known as the causal body from which every other kosha springs forth. If we identify ourselves with any of these layers as our "self," it is known to cause misery due to their impermanent nature. The physical body, the energy, the mind, the intellect and the ego are all well known to be a source of afflictions in the form of sickness and ailments, mental anxieties and depression etc. So, one has to inquire calmly to recognize the unchanging pure Awareness that underlies and illuminates all these layers of the body that are ever in flux. This leads to being free of identification with the body/mind as oneself and realization of our ever-peaceful true nature.

एष नित्योऽव्ययः सूक्ष्म एष सर्वाश्रयः स्वदृक् ।
आत्ममायागुणैर्विश्वमात्मानं सृजते प्रभुः ॥ Bh 6.16.9

*esha nityo'vyayaḥ sūkṣhma esha sarvāśhrayaḥ svadṛk
ātmamāyāguṇairviśhvamātmānaṁ sṛjate prabhuḥ*

The apparent individual is only an expression of the eternal, undecaying, unmanifest, self-effulgent, ground of all existence that manifests itself in the form of the universe by its own power.

The various individual beings relate to each other as kinsmen and adversaries, sometimes with the same beings as friends and at times as enemies over time. Just as various ornaments each with its own unique name, form and characteristics manifest from the same gold that is ever the same despite the apparent multiplicity of ornaments, so do various beings such as humans, animals and other forms manifest from the same Absolute Being who remains unaffected by the apparent multiplicity of individuals. If one gets caught in the name, form and characteristics of the ornament, one loses sight of the underlying gold. Similarly, if one gets caught in the apparent differences among various beings, each uniquely manifested by the power called Maya inherent in the Absolute Being, then one loses sight of the underlying oneness of all beings. If we focus instead on the very sense of existence that springs spontaneously in one's heart, then we connect to the very Source of existence and see everyone with equal vision.

परमाणुपरममहतोस्त्वमाद्यन्तान्तरवर्ती त्रयविधुरः ।
आदावन्तेऽपि च सत्त्वानां यद् ध्रुवं तदेवान्तरालेऽपि ॥
Bh 6.16.36

*paramāṇuparamamahatostvamādyantāntaravartī trayavidhuraḥ
ādāvante'pi cha sattvānāṁ yad dhruvaṁ tadevāntarāle'pi*

The Supreme Being exists prior to the subtlest atom, pervades all the intermediate stages too and exists after the dissolution of the infinite universe. That which is at the beginning and the end alone is certainly there in the middle.

If we look with discernment, it's clearly seen that everything is in constant flux every moment, including every thought, every perception and every cell, every atom, every particle. Everything is impermanent, including the idea of impermanence, which is only a concept that comes and goes, because nothing takes any fixed shape even for a moment to become impermanent. As the ancient teacher Gaudapada has observed, "That which was not and that which will not be, does not even exist now." Everything that seems to appear doesn't have any substantive existence. But underlying these ever-changing appearances is the Source of all, who alone abides prior to creation, during existence and after dissolution. This Source is realized as our true Being, the very light of Awareness that shines forth in each living entity as the pure sense of existence. To not be caught in fleeting self-images of the mind but to recognize and abide in the unchanging Source in our heart is true devotion.

गुणप्रवाह एतस्मिन् कः शापः को न्वनुग्रहः ।
कः स्वर्गो नरकः को वा किं सुखं दुःखमेव वा ॥ Bh 6.17.20

guṇapravāha etasmin kaḥ śāpaḥ konvanugrahaḥ
kaḥ svargo narakaḥ ko vā kiṁ sukhaṁ duḥkhameva vā

In this flow of material energy, what is a curse and what is a blessing? What is heaven and what is hell? What is joy and what is sorrow?

Upon the instructions of the sages Angira and Narada, Chitraketu was freed of all attachments and committed himself to focused meditation and eventually had direct experience of the Divine. He then roamed around the earth freely without any sense of bondage with great Yogic powers. On one occasion, he went to Mount Kailasa, and there he saw Shiva instructing many sages while His consort Parvati was seated on His lap. In a momentary lapse into egoic conditioning, Chitraketu criticized Shiva for embracing Parvati in an open assembly. This made Mother Parvati pronounce a curse that Chitraketu shall be born as a demon, for the great transgression of insulting Shiva, the most auspicious of the auspicious. Instantly, Chitraketu realized his folly created due to a momentary lack of alertness and accepted the curse with equanimity. He bowed to Mother Parvati saying, what is the difference between blessing and curse or pleasure and pain which keeps alternating in this world. He was born as the demon Vrtrasura filled with sublime devotion as already seen. Shuka Brahmam thus connects the story of Chitraketu to the question of Parikshit on how Vrtrasura had such uncommon devotion though being a demon, while also instructing that one has to be very alert every moment regardless of past realization as the ego can trap one instantly.

SEVENTH CANTO
Highest Dharma

आसीनः पर्यटन्नश्नन् शयानः प्रपिबन् ब्रुवन् ।
नानुसन्धत्त एतानि गोविन्दपरिरम्भितः ॥ Bh 7.4.38

āsīnaḥ paryaṭannaśhnan śhayānaḥ prapiban bruvan
nānusandhatta etāni govindaparirambhitaḥ

Sitting or walking, eating or drinking, lying down or speaking, Prahlada was never conscious of anything else except being ever in the constant embrace in his heart with the Lord Govinda.

In response to Parikshit's question on the mystery behind the Lord's descent to kill demons, Shuka Brahmam starts to narrate a sacred dialogue between King Yudhishthira and Sage Narada. Yudhishthira asks Narada about the story of Hiranyakashipu and his son, the glorious devotee Prahlada. Narada starts by recounting how Hiranyakashipu was filled with rage at the slaying of his brother Hiranyaksha by Varaha Avatar. So, he ordered his demoniac forces to unleash terror on earth by destroying anyone engaged in any religious activity. At the same time, he went into his inner quarters where his family was grieving over his brother's death and preached words of wisdom about the impermanence of the world and the eternality of the soul. Thus, he demonstrated how words mean nothing if the heart is not transformed. Hiranyakashipu then decides to become invincible to get his revenge with the Lord. So, he went to Mount Mandana and engaged in intense austerities to please Brahma who appeared before him to grant him a boon. Knowing that Brahma will not grant immortality directly, Hiranyakashipu asked for a very clever boon that he shall have no death from any created being, through any weapon, during day or night, inside or outside, on earth or in air. And he had all his requested boons conferred upon him by Brahma. Thus, feeling invincible, he ruled earth and heaven with an iron fist, intoxicated with power and causing immense harm. All the sages appealed to the Supreme Being who assured them that the vile demon would be destroyed when he harms his own child, the divine Prahlada. Sure enough, the son born to him as Prahlada grows up to be a saintly child with ecstatic devotion, manifesting all qualities of the highest form of divine love as described in this verse.

स यदानुव्रतः पुंसां पशुबुद्धिर्विभिद्यते ।
अन्य एष तथान्योऽहमिति भेदगतासती ॥ Bh 7.5.12

sa yadānuvrataḥ puṁsāṁ paśhubuddhirvibhidyate
anya eṣha tathānyo'hamiti bhedagatāsatī

Only the Grace of the Supreme Being removes the false notion in men that "he is other than I" due to bodily identification which is a beastly way of living.

Prahlada grows up to be devoted to the sages, rich in character, true to his word, with senses regulated, seeing all as his own self and beloved to all. Ever happy to serve others, unperturbed at heart and free of any craving, he lived with equanimity and sublime devotion. He was always only conscious of the Supreme Being Sri Hari, singing, dancing, remembering and ever abiding in divine love. Hiranyakashipu, wanting Prahlada to be like other demons, sent him to a school to be taught in the worldly ways by his chosen teachers. But Prahlada showed no interest whatsoever in the education that keeps one in ignorance. Instead, he boldly proclaimed that one has to always take refuge in the Supreme Being which alone prevents one's fall into darkness. He told his teachers that it is the beastly way to simply identify with the body and engage in mere survival, reproduction and sense gratification. The true purpose of human life awakens by the Grace of God and enables one to transcend bodily divisions to see everyone as an expression of the One Supreme Source.

श्रवणं कीर्तनं विष्णो: स्मरणं पादसेवनम् ।
अर्चनं वन्दनं दास्यं सख्यमात्मनिवेदनम् ॥
इति पुंसार्पिता विष्णौ भक्तिश्चेन्नवलक्षणा ।
क्रियेत भगवत्यद्धा तन्मन्येऽधीतमुत्तमम् ॥ Bh 7.5.23-24

shravaṇaṁ kīrtanaṁ viṣṇoḥ smaraṇaṁ pādasevanam
archanaṁ vandanaṁ dāsyaṁ sakhyam ātmanivedanam
iti puṁsārpitā viṣṇau bhaktiśchennavalakṣaṇā
kriyeta bhagavatyaddhā tanmanye'dhītamuttamam

To listen, glorify, contemplate upon, serve, worship, offer obeisances, dedicate all actions, cultivate friendship and surrender everything unto the Supreme Being—such devotion as marked by any of the above nine

features toward the all-pervading Lord, I deem to be the highest form of learning.

When Hiranyakashipu summons Prahalda again after another stint in the demoniac school to find out what he learned there, Prahlada fearlessly declares that the highest form of learning is to engage in nine forms of devotional service. Each of the nine ways of devotion that Prahlada enumerates is powerful enough that if one engages fully with one's heart in any one of them, it is enough to attain perfection. Here is the list in detail with an exemplar for each of these ways of devotion:

1. Listening about Him (*śhravaṇaṁ*)—this includes listening to stories, discourses, names and praises about Him. Parikshit, the listener of Bhāgavatam, is the prime example. Without even having a sip of water, he listened for seven days and nights to Srimad Bhāgavatam with keen interest.

2. Glorifying Him(*kīrtanaṁ*)—this includes speaking and singing about His glories and chanting the names. Prime example is Shuka Brahmam who sang Srimad Bhāgavatam for seven days and nights and when it was over left the place immediately without waiting for any accolades.

3. Remembering Him (*viṣhṇoḥ smaraṇaṁ*)—this includes always reflecting upon what is listened to, contemplating about Him and meditating upon Him. Prime example is Prahlada, who from the time he was in his mother's womb was thinking constantly of Hari and when the Lord appeared as Narasimha and asked for a boon his only ask was that he should remember Hari forever.

4. Serving His Lotus Feet (*pādasevanam*)—this includes serving His form, His devotees, the rivers that flow from His feet. Prime example is Mahalakshmi who ever serves Sri Hari's lotus feet.

5. Worshiping His deity form (*archanam*)—this includes worshiping in temples and doing fire sacrifices (*yajna*). Prime example is Prthu Maharaja who did ninety nine grand sacrifices in a desireless manner

6. Offering obeisances unto Him (*vandanam*)—this includes falling prostrate in front of the temple deity, great sages and Bhagavatas. Akrura is the prime example who was sent by Kamsa to bring Krishna from Vrndavana to Mathura, but being a pure devotee, he fell prostrate upon seeing the footprints of Krishna near the banks of Yamuna.

7. Dedicate all actions to Him (*dāsyam*)—this includes ever being ready to serve by dedicating all actions to Him. Prime example is the famous one of Hanuman, who proclaimed loudly that he is ever the servant of his most beloved Lord Ram and dedicated every moment to serve Him.

8. Seeing Him as our only true friend (*sakhyam*)—this includes having a mood of closeness and not distant awe toward Him. Prime example is Arjuna who was the dear friend of Krishna and was always in intimate reverent friendly affection with Krishna.

9. Surrendering body, mind and soul to Him (*ātmanivedanam*)—this includes being ready to give up everything for His sake. Prime example is Maharaja Bali who gave up his own head to Lord Trivikrama to keep his word.

मतिर्न कृष्णे परतः स्वतो वा मिथोऽभिपद्येत गृहव्रतानाम् ।
अदान्तगोभिर्विशतां तमिस्रं पुनः पुनश्चर्वितचर्वणानाम् ।।
Bh 7.5.30

matir na kṛṣhṇe parataḥ svato vā mitho'bhipadyeta gṛhavratānām
adāntagobhirviśhatāṁ tamisraṁ punaḥ
punaśhcharvitacharvaṇānām

The mind of those attached to worldly activity falls into a repeated cycle of suffering as the unregulated senses engage in chewing over the same chewed fare again and again. So their mind does not get drawn to Krishna, either by itself or even through others exhorting them or both.

The Upanishads point out that it is the mind alone that is the cause for both bondage and liberation (*mana eva manuṣhyānam kāranam bandha mokṣhayoh*). When the mind is drawn to worldly activity due to attachment to various desires, then the senses are unregulated like unruly horses going where they please, indulging in momentary gratification resulting in suffering. Thus, this cycle of indulgence and suffering repeats itself again and again over the same set of experiences. The expression "chewing over the already chewed" (*punaḥ punaśhcharvitacharvaṇānām*) used by Prahlada is very pointed and powerful because it is the same indulgences that the mind gets drawn to repeatedly causing addictive patterns, whether it be food or drugs or media consumption or a relationship, all of which result in increasing suffering over time. Even after experiencing the suffering that inevitably comes from indulgence, the mind gets drawn to seeking the same pleasure again helplessly, thus chewing over the already chewed repeatedly. Such a mind is unable to be drawn to the Supreme Lord (*matir na kṛṣhṇe*) by itself and even if someone points out, it is met with resistance thus making it very hard to break the pattern of the mind. Therefore, it is important to be very alert to the ways of the mind and not get pulled into its vortex but instead keep the mind and the senses regulated which alone leads to a purposeful and peaceful living.

कौमार आचरेत्प्राज्ञो धर्मान्भागवतानिह ।
दुर्लभं मानुषं जन्म तदप्यध्रुवमर्थदम् ॥ Bh 7.6.1

kaumāra ācharetprājño dharmānbhāgavatāniha
durlabhaṁ mānuṣhaṁ janma tadapyadhruvamarthadam

In this human life, a wise one ought to live in accordance with Bhagavata Dharma (the way of God-realization) right from childhood. Human birth is rare and also transient, so it ought to be used meaningfully.

Prahlada instructs on the need to take up spiritual wisdom right from childhood rather than waiting until one is old. It is commonly believed by many that one can immerse oneself in worldly attachments and activities through childhood and adult life, while leaving the spiritual pursuit for old age. However, due to a lifelong pursuit of worldly desires and the infirmity of the body due to old age, one is unable to summon the focus or the energy necessary for self-inquiry. Furthermore, the purpose of spiritual wisdom and self-inquiry is not for some after-life deliverance as commonly misunderstood, but to live life as it unfolds now sanely, fearlessly and freely with peace and love. Therefore, one ought to take up as soon as possible this wisdom of God-realization that awakens the heart to unconditional love. Else life is frittered and wasted away in pointless pursuits only to realize that decades have flown by, death is on its way, and the mind is still attached. Adi Shankara thus exhorts in Bhaja Govindam, "O fool! Give up your thirst for material wealth and with dispassion in the mind, abide in Truth." (*mūḍha jahīhi dhanāgama tṛṣhṇāṃ kuru sadbuddhim manasi vitṛṣhṇām*). A wise man ought to strive for this state of blessedness while the body and mind are sound, and also impart this to children at a young age. That is true education that makes them flower into divine beings.

न ह्यच्युतं प्रीणयतो बह्वायासोऽसुरात्मजाः ।
आत्मत्वात्सर्वभूतानां सिद्धत्वादिह सर्वतः ॥ Bh 7.6.19

na hyachyutaṁ prīṇayato bahvāyāso'surātmajāḥ
ātmatvātsarvabhūtānāṁ siddhatvādiha sarvataḥ

Indeed there is no exertion needed in being devoted to and realizing the Immortal Lord as He is the very Self of all created beings and fully present here and everywhere.

Only when there is separation in time and space to attain anything, there is a need for exertion to do so. What Prahlada declares here is that the Supreme Being is the very Self of each of us and present everywhere, therefore there is no exertion involved in God-realization if we recognize this simple and yet profound Truth. If we perceive the ever-changing nature of the body, the life energy, the mind and the intellect and negate them as not the real self, then what remains is the conscious presence that spontaneously shines forth in the heart as "I am." This is the presence of God within every living entity and thus Prahlada states that He is the true Self of all. When we recognize this truth that the very conscious presence is even closer than one's breath because it is aware of the very breath, then that presence is realized as God abiding in our heart as Krishna reveals in the Gita (*sarvasya chāham hridi sannivishtah*—BG 15.15). Therefore, to abide in the presence of God in our heart here and now is true devotion and Self-realization, which is available to everyone directly, if we remain alert.

केवलानुभवानन्दस्वरूप: परमेश्वर: ।
माययान्तर्हितैश्वर्य ईयते गुणसर्गया ॥
तस्मात्सर्वेषु भूतेषु दयां कुरुत सौहृदम् ।
भावमासुरमुन्मुच्य यया तुष्यत्यधोक्षज: ॥ Bh 7.6.23-24

kevalānubhavānandasvarūpah parameśhvarah
māyayāntarhitaiśhvarya īyate guṇasargayā
tasmātsarveṣhu bhūteṣhu dayām kuruta sauhṛdam
bhāvamāsuramunmuchya yayā tuṣhyatyadhokṣhajah

The Supreme Lord is of the nature of Pure Consciousness and Bliss, though His divinity is concealed by Maya which gives rise to the material creation. Therefore, give up the demoniac disposition and be compassionate and friendly toward all living entities, whereby the Lord is pleased.

The demoniac disposition is one caught in the separative sense of "me" and "mine," thus looking at everyone and everything with the attitude of "what's in it for me." The divine disposition is to look with eyes of compassion and friendliness by recognizing the common Source, of which everyone and everything is a unique expression. It is through the clear perception that every created being from the smallest ant to the mightiest of all, in all material things made of the five gross elements, and in the Cosmic Intelligence that directs them all, abides the one and only transcendent Supreme Being, the imperishable Lord of all (*eka eva paro hyātmā bhagavān īshvaro'vyayaḥ*—Bh 7.6.21). He pervades the whole universe as the subject and the object of all perceptions. Any sense perception brings forth the duality of the perceiver and the perceived, and we identify as the perceiver to see the perceived as the other. Whereas the truth is that the very perceiver rises forth spontaneously from the all-pervading Cosmic Intelligence, as do the perceived objects. Therefore, seeing both the apparent subject and object as an expression of the Supreme Being removes the sense of otherness and brings forth compassion and friendliness towards all. That is true devotion which pleases the all-pervading Absolute Being.

आत्मा नित्योऽव्यय: शुद्ध एक: क्षेत्रज्ञ आश्रय: ।
अविक्रिय: स्वदृग् हेतुर्व्यापकोऽसङ्ग्यनावृत: ॥ Bh 7.7.19

ātmā nityo'vyayaḥ śhuddha ekaḥ kṣhetrajña āshrayaḥ
avikriyaḥ svadṛg heturvyāpako'saṅgyanāvṛtaḥ

The Supreme Self is eternal, undecaying, pure, one without a second, knower of all activities, substrate of all, changeless, self-effulgent, the primal cause, all-pervading, unattached and free of material covering.

After emphasizing the importance of listening with an earnest and sincere attitude that makes wisdom and devotion take root in the heart, Prahlada describes the essence of Truth succinctly through twelve transcendent characteristics that help one to be free of the false notions of "me" and "mine" springing from ignorance. Everything that is manifest is subject to Time and goes through birth, growth and decay while the Supreme Self is untouched by Time. Therefore, anything within the purview of Time is not eternal, goes through decay, gets impure due to mixing with other elements, is found to be diverse, is an object of knowledge, is dependent on the ground of existence, is ever-changing, is not known by itself, is within the cycle of cause and effect, is limited, is attached to form and is inert, being made of matter. Because the Supreme Self as the true Seer of all is outside the purview of Time, it has the opposite characteristics of each of the above, being transcendent to Time, as listed in this verse. Thus, by negating everything within the purview of Time including the body, mind, intellect and all other possessions, one can recognize one's true nature as the very ground of existence that is unchanging, fully aware and ever complete.

एवं निर्जितषड्वर्गैः क्रियते भक्तिरीश्वरे ।
वासुदेवे भगवति यया संलभ्यते रतिः ॥ Bh 7.7.33

evaṁ nirjitashaḍvargaiḥ kriyate bhaktirīśhvare
vāsudeve bhagavati yayā saṁlabhyate ratiḥ

**Devotion to the all-powerful Supreme Being Vāsudeva
is practiced by subduing the six hindrances, and such
devotion blooms forth as unconditional love.**

Prahlada continues by instructing that the very seed of ignorance has to be burned which is the true meaning of Yoga (*bījanirharaṇaṁ yogaḥ*—Bh 7.7.28) and it removes attachment to material nature made of the three gunas within the purview of Time. And of the many devices available for achieving this purpose, the most efficacious is to awaken devotion in the heart for the Supreme Being Vāsudeva who pervades everywhere. This can be accomplished by serving one's Guru and abide by his teachings, by fellowship with other devotees, by reverentially listening about the Supreme Being and His pastimes, by an attitude of humble worship of the Divine and most importantly, serving all living entities with the clear perception that Bhagavan resides in all of them (*hariḥ sarveṣhu bhūteṣhu bhagavān āsta īśhvaraḥ*—Bh 7.7.32). This helps subdue the six hindrances which are lust, anger, greed, pride, delusion and envy. It also implies regulating the six senses including the mind. Thus, true devotion flowers in the heart and expresses itself as unconditional love for all.

नालं द्विजत्वं देवत्वमृषित्वं वासुरात्मजाः ।
प्रीणनाय मुकुन्दस्य न वृत्तं न बहुज्ञता ॥
न दानं न तपो नेज्या न शौचं न व्रतानि च ।
प्रीयतेऽमलया भक्त्या हरिरन्यद् विडम्बनम् ॥ Bh 7.7.51-52

nālaṁ dvijatvaṁ devatvamṛshitvaṁ vāsurātmajāḥ
prīṇanāya mukundasya na vṛttaṁ na bahujñatā
na dānaṁ na tapo nejyā na śhauchaṁ na vratāni cha
prīyate'malayā bhaktyā hariranyad viḍambanam

Not through belonging to the class of the twice born or the Devas or the Rishis, not by having good character or great learning, not by engaging in charity or austerities or worship, not by observing sacred vows, not even by maintaining purity of the body and mind, can one please the Supreme Being. He is pleased only through unalloyed loving devotion. All else is mere show.

Prahlada first describes the true signs of one fully surrendered to the Supreme Being as one who has a loving heart, whose voice chokes up with tears upon hearing or singing the names and glories of the Supreme Being, who may sit in meditation silently sometimes or chant loudly other times but whose mind is ever fixed on the Lord as the very Self. Thus, his bonds are removed, ignorance and latent desires are burned, and his body and mind are fully in tune with the Divine. This is the mark of highest devotion and wisdom, that removes the separative identity and puts an end to all suffering. Such devotion requires no exertion, no materials, no paraphernalia but only a loving heart. Whereas, all other activities, religious or secular, involve great exertion and require various articles and yet are all ephemeral in nature, causing attachment and eventual suffering. Therefore, Prahlada exhorts everyone to worship with all of one's heart the Supreme Being who is the very Self of all, called here as Mukunda, the one who bestows liberation (*mukti*) by removing the false ego. Such worship is available to anyone regardless of their birth, learning, ability to engage in charitable acts and elaborate rituals, sacred vows etc. What's more, all such activities, devoid of pure devotion in the heart, are a mere show that have the opposite effect of boosting the ego and strengthening bondage. Therefore, Prahlada with great compassion simplifies the entire process to the single commandment of loving God with all of one's heart as the innermost essence of our very being, which is the first and the last step in the journey of Self-realization.

एतावानेव लोकेऽस्मिन्पुंसः स्वार्थः परः स्मृतः ।
एकान्तभक्तिर्गोविन्दे यत्सर्वत्र तदीक्षणम् ॥ Bh 7.7.55

etāvāneva loke'sminpuṁsaḥ svārthaḥ parahsmṛtaḥ
ekāntabhaktirgovinde yatsarvatra tadīkshaṇam

Exclusive devotion to the Supreme Lord Govinda is the same as beholding Him in every living entity and this alone is declared to be the highest purpose of man in this world.

Prahlada concludes his instructions by beautifully bringing out the true fruit of devotion to the Lord as compassion and unconditional love toward all living entities. The very sense of our existence that spontaneously rises forth as "I am" in the heart is the presence of God which is the same sense of existence in every living entity. While each living entity is different from another in the aspects of bodily features and all other faculties, the one common unifying factor is the sense of existence itself as "I am." Thus, by freeing oneself of all false identifications of the body and the mind, when one recognizes this pure existence as "I am" and surrenders it to the Supreme Source, then one perceives the same sense of existence in every living entity as coming from the same Source. This is to see God everywhere. As Krishna says in the Gita, "The one who sees Me everywhere and sees everything in Me never loses sight of Me and I never lose sight of him" (*yo māṁ paśhyati sarvatra sarvaṁ cha mayi paśhyati / tasyāhaṁ na praṇaśhyāmi sa cha me na praṇaśhyati*—BG 6.30). Such vision of sameness is true devotion that beholds Him in all creatures and unconditionally loves everyone as the presence of God. This is the highest purpose of human life.

सत्यं विधातुं निजभृत्यभाषितं व्याप्तिं च भूतेष्वखिलेषु चात्मनः ।
अदृश्यतात्यद्भुतरूपमुद्वहन् स्तम्भे सभायां न मृगं न मानुषम् ॥
Bh 7.8.18

satyaṁ vidhātuṁ nijabhṛtyabhāṣitaṁ vyāptiṁ cha
bhūteṣhvakhileṣu chātmanaḥ
adṛśhyatātyadbhutarūpamudvahan stambhe sabhāyāṁ na mṛgaṁ
na mānuṣham

To substantiate the utterance of His dear devotee and His presence in all objects, the Lord appeared in a pillar in the court, assuming a wonderful form that was neither a lion nor a man.

Alarmed at hearing the instructions of Prahlada exhorting pure devotion to the Lord, the teacher of the demon boys reported the matter to Hiranyakashipu who summoned Prahlada and reproached him harshly, asking by whose might had he violated the authority of his father, the undisputed emperor. Prahlada replied calmly to his father that not only he, but the king and everyone else functions only by the might of the one omnipresent, omnipotent Supreme Lord and appealed to his father to give up his demoniac disposition. This enraged Hiranyakashipu further, who thundered at his son while pointing at a pillar, "Where is this Lord you talk of? If he is omnipresent, why is he not seen in this pillar?" While Prahlada pointed to the subtle energy of the Supreme Being that pervades the whole universe and is beyond sense perception, the gross materialistic mind believes only in the deluding senses as its authority. Therefore, to substantiate even at that level, the Lord took the most terrifying form of man-lion as Narasimha (*nṛsiṁharūpastadalaṁ bhayānakam*—Bh

7.8.20) and appeared bursting out of the pillar with a loud explosion. The demon ran toward him to fight, only to die like a moth in a flame. Lord Narasimha killed him in the form of a man-lion at dusk with bare nails, putting the demon on His lap at the doorstep. In this manner every boon the demon asked for was satisfied—of not being killed by man or animal, not during day or night, not by any weapon, not on earth or in air and not inside or outside, illustrating that however sophisticated a plan the ego makes, it will be thwarted by the Divine.

यस्मिन्यतो यर्हि येन च यस्य यस्माद् यस्मै यथा यदुत यस्त्वपरः परो वा ।
भावः करोति विकरोति पृथक्स्वभावः सञ्चोदितस्तदखिलं भवतः स्वरूपम् ॥ Bh 7.9.20

yasminyato yarhi yena cha yasya yasmād yasmai yathā yaduta yastvaparaḥ paro vā
bhāvaḥ karoti vikaroti pṛthak svabhāvaḥ sañchoditastadakhilaṁ bhavataḥ svarūpam

Whatever being, high or low, possessing whatever nature, wherever and from whatever motive, whenever, with whatever instrument, from whatever source, prompted by whoever and howsoever way he produces or transforms anything, whatever the thing produced or transformed—all that is You alone.

After the demon is slain by the ferocious man-lion form of the Lord as Narasimha, the whole world that was cast under a dark shadow due to the evil Hiranyakashipu celebrated with an outburst of joy and the sky showered down flowers. All the demigods and celestial beings assembled to glorify the Lord in his furious and terrifying form, but none dared to approach Him seated on the royal throne. Even the divine consort Lakshmi did not dare go near, bewildered by this unseen form. Brahma, realizing that Prahlada alone could pacify the Lord, asked him to approach the Lord. Prahlada immediately did so and offered His obeisances, and the Lord placed His lotus hand on Prahlada's head that instantly bestowed him with direct wisdom of the Supreme Being. Prahlada then humbly offered that he is utterly incapable of appropriately glorifying the Supreme Lord of infinite prowess but went on to utter the most beautiful prayer. He affirmed that the only qualification needed to realize the Supreme Being is pure loving devotion, which alone enables one to see that everything, everywhere, every moment in every form doing every little thing is all an expression of the Supreme Source. Or put simply, the highest form of devotion and wisdom is to recognize that God alone is.

तस्मादमूस्तनुभृतामहमाशिषोऽज्ञ आयुः श्रियं
विभवमैन्द्रियमाविरिञ्च्यात् ।
नेच्छामि ते विलुलितानुरुविक्रमेण कालात्मनोपनय मां
निजभृत्यपार्श्वम् ॥ Bh 7.9.24

tasmādamūstanubhṛtāmahamāśhiṣho'jña āyuḥ śhriyaṁ
vibhavamaindriyamāviriñchyāt
nechchhāmi te vilulitānuruvikrameṇa kālātmanopanaya māṁ
nijabhṛtyapārśhvam

I do not covet blessings sought normally by embodied beings such as long life, wealth, glory and comforts, not even mystic powers, because all of these are crushed by

You in the form of Time. Therefore, my only prayer is to always place me by the side of Your devotees.

Prahlada continues his prayers by saying that more than wealth, pedigree, learning, strength, intelligence and endeavor, it is only the devotion in the heart that pleases God. This devotion has its highest expression as unconditional love for all beings by seeing the Divine within everyone. The one who possesses such devotion and love is situated in the highest plane, whatever other qualifications he lacks. And the one who lacks it falls due to inordinate pride from all his other qualifications. The easiest way to tide over all obstacles and be situated in this plane of devotion and wisdom is by enjoying the fellowship of enlightened beings who have fully surrendered to God. All other boons such as long life, riches and glory which people crave are all swept away by Time inevitably. By recognizing the unsubstantial nature of all worldly enjoyments, the only prayer worth asking for is to be in holy company with true devotees that removes all inner impediments due to the ego and makes one's life a sublime expression of love.

प्रायेण देव मुनयः स्वविमुक्तिकामा मौनं चरन्ति विजने न परार्थनिष्ठाः ।
नैतान्विहाय कृपणान्विमुमुक्ष एको नान्यं त्वदस्य शरणं भ्रमतोऽनुपश्ये ॥ Bh 7.9.44

prāyeṇa deva munayaḥ svavimuktikāmā maunaṁ charanti vijane na parārthaniṣṭhāḥ
naitānvihāya kṛpaṇānvimumukṣa eko nānyaṁ tvadasya
śharaṇaṁ bhramato'nupaśhye

The ascetics desirous of their own liberation generally practice silent meditation in solitude as they do not care about others. However, I do not desire to be liberated alone, leaving behind the miserable beings who have no other haven than You to be free of suffering.

Prahlada expresses his heart of compassion toward all beings in this prayer, in gratitude for the grace bestowed upon him by the celestial sage Narada. He remembers that even though born to a demoniac father, he was favored by Narada who instructed him on the highest wisdom of Self-realization through loving devotion and thus saved him from falling headlong into suffering due to excessive attachment to worldliness. Narada taught Prahlada that the Supreme Being alone constitutes the entire universe in its beginning, middle and end and therefore any notion of separative identity as "me" and "mine" is meaningless and illusory. This seed of wisdom and devotion alone sprouted forth in Prahlada into total surrender and blessedness; therefore he expresses that it is only appropriate to similarly share this wisdom with people who are otherwise drawn to hellish existence due to unregulated mind and senses. Thus, Prahlada makes the most powerful case for always being a vehicle of compassion toward those even the least bit willing to listen, so that the grace of the exalted would descend upon them.

यदि दास्यसि मे कामान्वरांस्त्वं वरदर्षभ ।
कामानां हृद्यसंरोहं भवतस्तु वृणे वरम् ॥ Bh 7.10.7

*yadi dāsyasi me kāmānvarāṁstvaṁ varadarṣhabha
kāmānāṁ hṛdyasaṁrohaṁ bhavatastu vṛṇe varam*

If You are inclined to bestow any boon upon me, O Chief among bestowers, I solicit from You this boon alone that no desire may ever sprout in my heart.

After Prahlada offers his heart melting prayers, the Lord, highly pleased, tells him to ask for any boon he desires. But even on being tempted with boons that are so alluring to anyone, Prahlada does not hanker after them, being exclusively devoted. He prays to not be tempted with such prospects as one who seeks worldly blessings from God is not a devotee, but only in business (*yasta āśhiṣha āśhāste na sa bhṛtyaḥ sa vai vaṇik*—Bh 7.10.4). Therefore, he says, if at all any boon has to be bestowed, let it be that there is no desire to ask for anything ever, being fully content with what is ordained and ever beholding only the Divine everywhere. Bringing out Prahlada's unparalleled greatness, the Lord Himself blesses him with all benedictions and declares that Prahlada will be the perfect model for all devotees (*bhavān me khalu bhaktānāṁ sarveṣhāṁ pratirūpadhṛk*—Bh 7.10.21). Thus, concludes the most auspicious episode of Lord Narasimha that is ever glorified as one of the principal ten Avatars of the Lord of the universe, Keshava, taking the form of half-man, half-lion (*keśhava dhṛta narahari rūpa jaya jagadīśha hare*—Dashavatara Stotra).

नत्वा भगवतेऽजाय लोकानां धर्मसेतवे ।
वक्ष्ये सनातनं धर्मं नारायणमुखाच्छ्रुतम् ॥ Bh 7.11.5

natvā bhagavate'jāya lokānāṁ dharmasetave
vakṣhye sanātanaṁ dharmaṁ nārāyaṇamukhācchrutam

Bowing down to the Supreme Being, who is the Unborn and the protector of righteousness among people, I shall expound on the Eternal Sanatana Dharma as heard from the mouth of Narayana.

Narada gives an exposition on Sanatana Dharma or the Eternal Way of living that upholds righteousness and makes life conducive for Self-realization. This is not a sectarian way of living for any particular group of people but the universal way of living that is applicable across all races, nationalities and other societal divisions. The Source and sustenance of all of life is the Absolute Being who is Unborn, Unmanifest and Unchanging. Therefore, Narada begins his discourse on Dharma by offering his obeisances unto the Source of Dharma itself (*dharmamūlaṁ hi bhagavān*—Bh 7.11.7). Then he lists the virtues that comprise the essence of Dharma, chief among them being truthfulness, compassion, simplicity, purity, equanimity, discernment, regulation of the mind and the senses, peacefulness, discipline, charity, honesty, contentment, silence, self-inquiry and devotion to the Supreme Being. Thus, he makes clear that anyone who lives by these virtues is a true claimant to living by the principles of Sanatana Dharma.

यस्य यत्लक्षणं प्रोक्तं पुंसो वर्णाभिव्यञ्जकम् ।
यदन्यत्रापि दृश्येत तत्तेनैव विनिर्दिशेत् ॥ Bh 7.11.35

yasya yallakshaṇaṁ proktaṁ puṁso varṇābhivyañjakam
yadanyatrāpi dṛśhyeta tattenaiva vinirdiśhet

If what has been declared to be the characteristics of a particular propensity is perceived in one even if born in a

family of another propensity, then that takes precedence regardless of birth.

After describing the foundation of dharma, Narada goes on to describe the four predominant propensities among people that are characterized by:

1. Those drawn to study and teaching of knowledge in various domains or those who perform religious rituals
2. Those drawn to administration or being warrior like with a martial spirit, valor and fortitude
3. Those drawn to trade, business, farming etc. with dexterity to acquire wealth
4. Those drawn to serve the society with humility and loyalty.

Narada makes it very clear in this verse that these propensities are to be determined by the characteristics perceived in a person and not by the family one belongs to. This is exactly as Krishna declares in the Gita that the four propensities are to be known by qualities and activities (*chāturvarnyam mayā shrshtam guna karma vibhāgashah*—BG 4.13). Thus, there is no scriptural validation for the corruption that has crept into society over centuries of one's propensity being attributed to birth as a permanent division. Every propensity is noble and conducive for living together in harmony and journeying toward Self-realization.

एवं विधो ब्रह्मचारी वानप्रस्थो यतिर्गृही ।
चरन्विदितविज्ञान: परं ब्रह्माधिगच्छति ॥ Bh 7.12.16

evaṁ vidho brahmachārī vānaprastho yatirgṛhī
charanviditavijñānaḥ paraṁ brahmādhigachchhati

Following the rules of conduct laid down for each stage of life and having come to know what ought to be known, a student, a householder, an anchorite or a renunciate realizes the transcendent Absolute.

After describing the four propensities among people, Narada next describes the four stages of life as the natural progression that people go through:

1. The student life which ought to be marked by sincere study with affection and reverence toward the teacher, moderate in diet, simple living with mind and senses regulated and focused on learning with emphasis on Self-knowledge.
2. The householder life where one gets married, has children, sets up a house, supports the family through work without any sense of doership and also generously provides for people in the remaining three stages.
3. The retired anchorite life where one is freed of householder responsibilities, enters a retired life, simplifies lifestyle and diet, and lives an ascetic life focused on meditation, learning, sharing the knowledge and giving back.
4. The renunciate stage that one may enter the life of a roaming recluse with no fixed abode, living on alms, ever turned toward the Absolute Being with no attachment to anything material, ever peaceful and imparting wisdom and grace wherever one goes. Narada again makes it clear that every stage of life is

perfect in its own way. One can realize the Supreme Being while living in any stage of life and act without the egoic identification, thereby abiding in the transcendent Absolute throughout the journey of life, living with awareness and devotion.

नाहं निन्दे न च स्तौमि स्वभावविषमं जनम् ।
एतेषां श्रेय आशासे उतैकात्म्यं महात्मनि ।। Bh 7.13.42

nāhaṁ ninde na cha staumi svabhāvaviṣhamaṁ janam
eteṣhāṁ śhreya āśhāse utaikātmyaṁ mahātmani

I neither condemn nor praise people who are of diverse dispositions due to their nature. I only wish them the highest well-being in the form of being one with the Supreme Spirit.

This is the expression of the highest wisdom of the one ever abiding in the vision of the Absolute as the source and the sustenance of all beings and thereby friendly to all, ever peaceful and free of desire or fear. Both bondage and liberation are perceived as ultimately illusory, and one remains unconcerned about life or death. Not caught in partial causes, one does not engage in any arguments and does not even show any outward sign of being enlightened. The futility of endeavoring to attain more than what is necessary for material existence is recognized and everything is accepted with total contentment, whatever comes one's way. Unaffected by criticism or flattery as Krishna says in the Gita (*tulya nindāstutiḥ*—BG 12.19), one neither criticizes nor flatters people by recognizing that the diverse dispositions of the three gunas that make up Prakrti is what acts in the various ways. Thus, one never feeds the false separative ego by attributing blame or credit, instead only sees everyone as an expression of the Divine and wishes the same state of benediction for all beings. This is the perfection of human life, to live in total freedom and unconditional love toward all beings.

भावाद्वैतं क्रियाद्वैतं द्रव्याद्वैतं तथात्मनः ।
वर्तयन्स्वानुभूत्येह त्रीन्स्वप्रान्धुनुते मुनिः ॥ Bh 7.15.62

bhāvādvaitaṁ kriyādvaitaṁ dravyādvaitaṁ tathātmanaḥ
vartayansvānubhūtyeha trīnsvapnāndhunute muniḥ

By recognizing the non-duality of existence, activity and matter, the contemplative one shakes off the three dreams of daily living.

The three dreams of daily living refer to the three states of waking, dream and deep sleep. All three states are equated to a dream because ultimately, they are all fleeting and have no permanent basis to them. To shake off attachment to these three alternating states as oneself, is by recognizing the ever-present non-duality in existence, activity and matter. Non-duality in existence (*bhava advaita*) is recognized by contemplating upon the substantial unity of cause and effect as for instance, while thread is said to be the cause of cloth, in reality cloth is nothing but thread. Non-duality in activity (*kriya advaita*) is recognized by contemplating upon the spontaneous nature of all activities of body, speech and mind through a combination of complex physiological processes with no sense of doership. Non-duality in matter (*dravya advaita*) is recognized by identifying that all matter comprising the bodies of one's own, relations and all embodied beings are made of the same essence. Thus, by perceiving the non-dual Truth that underlies all existence, activity and matter, one is free of the false sense of separative identity that is imagined as journeying through time and the timeless pure being is revealed as our true Self.

EIGHTH CANTO
Cycles of Time

आत्मावास्यमिदं विश्वं यत् किञ्चिज्जगत्यां जगत् ।
तेन त्यक्तेन भुञ्जीथा मा गृधः कस्यस्विद्धनम् ॥ Bh 8.1.10

ātmāvāsyam idaṁ viśhvaṁ yat kiñchijjagatyāṁ jagat
tena tyaktena bhuñjīthā mā gṛdhaḥ kasyasviddhanam

Whatever exists in the world is all pervaded by the one true Self. Therefore, live content with what is assigned to you and do not covet the wealth of anyone else.

This verse is a beautiful mirror of the first verse of Isha Upanishad that begins with *īśhāvāsyamidaṁ sarvaṁ*. While the Upanishad verse says that the entire world is pervaded by God (*īśhā*), this Bhāgavatam verse says the entire world is pervaded by the one true Self (*ātmā*), thus making clear that to realize God is to realize our true Self. Every animate life form in this world is made of matter exhibiting energy and tremendous intelligence, as seen from small ants with their foraging skills and swarm intelligence to the human body with 40 trillion cells each engaging in various complex processes. The energy and the intelligence exhibited in animate beings demonstrates a perfect order that is far beyond what thought can ever understand. All this is pervaded by the Cosmic intelligence that makes everything function harmoniously. Thus, every human faculty—the body, the energy, the mind, the intellect—are all expressions of the same universal intelligence. And the very awareness within that underlies all our faculties is the nature of the Supreme Being and hence our true Self. We falsely identify ourselves with our physical, mental or intellectual faculties as "me" and "mine" without recognizing the perfect intelligence pervading every cell of the body that makes these faculties manifest. The Source of this all-pervading Cosmic intelligence is what we call God who is found to be the very order of the universe. Thus, by performing duties without attachment or proprietorship, living with contentment and free of covetousness, one can realize God as the very ground of existence and the power of all our actions.

क्षेत्रज्ञाय नमस्तुभ्यं सर्वाध्यक्षाय साक्षिणे । पुरुषायात्ममूलाय मूलप्रकृतये नमः ॥ Bh 8.3.13

kshetrajñāya namastubhyaṁ sarvādhyakshāya sākshiṇe
puruṣhāyātmamūlāya mūlaprakṛtaye namaḥ

Obeisances to the knower of all activities of all living entities, the supreme controller and the knower of all, the source of all embodied beings and the root of all manifest intelligence.

This is a beautiful prayer offered by Gajendra, the king of elephants. In a beautiful mountainous island, there lived Gajendra, the king of elephants, with his herd and lording over the whole region with strength and vigor. One day, as he was sporting in the waters of a beautiful lake, suddenly he was caught by an alligator and unable to free himself. Nobody else from his family or friends could come to his rescue and only watched helplessly while he struggled in pain. In that moment of utter despair, the seed of devotion from his past awoke in him and he turned to the Supreme Lord to take refuge. Settling his mind in the heart with clarity, Gajendra offered a most sublime prayer of surrender to the Lord, describing with great depth and love the infinite glory of the Supreme Lord, who bestowed His Grace by descending in His transcendent form to kill the alligator. This story symbolizes egoic identification with power, wealth, family etc. through Gajendra who is caught in the noose of death as Time which is the alligator. And when he surrenders to the Supreme Being, the wisdom of Sudarshana Chakra cuts Time itself and bestows the realization of the Timeless Eternal Being as our true Self.

अविक्रियं सत्यमनन्तमाद्यं गुहाशयं निष्कलमप्रतर्क्यम् ।
मनोऽग्रयानं वचसानिरुक्तं नमामहे देववरं वरेण्यम् ॥ Bh 8.5.26

*avikriyaṁ satyamanantamādyaṁ guhāśhayaṁ
niṣhkalamapratarkyam
mano'grayānaṁ vachasāniruktaṁ namāmahe devavaraṁ
varenyam*

We bow to the Supreme Being, who is changeless, ever true, infinite, most ancient, dwelling in the heart, unconditioned, incomprehensible through reasoning, quicker than mind, indescribable through speech and most worthy of being sought for.

This verse marks a prayer offered by Brahma as part of another highly symbolic episode of Bhāgavatam—the churning of the ocean to get nectar. In the ever-ongoing battle between good and evil represented by the demigods and the demons with each side alternately gaining an upper hand as part of the divine play. At one such time, the Devas are thoroughly defeated by the demons, and they seek refuge in Brahma, who in turn offers a beautiful prayer of total surrender to the Supreme Being, describing Him as the only unchanging truth beyond all dualities including good and evil. He is ever present in the heart and yet beyond the reach of reason, speech and mind as the Upanishads declare (*yato vācho nivartante aprāpya manasā saha*). So, it is not by logic but by surrender that one realizes the Truth. After Brahma offers this beautiful prayer of surrender, the Supreme Being instructs the demigods to not fight but engage with the demons and together churn the ocean of milk, taking Mount Mandara as the churning rod and the serpent Vasuki as the churning rope to bring out the nectar. And when the mountain is found to be unstable while churning, the Lord descends as Kurma (Tortoise) to provide stability at the base of the mountain under water. This whole episode is symbolic of the need to not identify with one's good or bad qualities as "mine" by feeling proud of good qualities or struggling to overcome bad qualities, but to inquire into the common ground with the churn of self-inquiry. And what brings stability in our self-inquiry is Grace, symbolized by Kurma Avatar who supports the entire churning.

देवदेव महादेव भूतात्मन् भूतभावन ।
त्राहि न: शरणापन्नांस्त्रैलोक्यदहनाद् विषात् ॥ Bh 8.7.21

devadeva mahādeva bhūtātman bhūtabhāvana
trāhi naḥ śharaṇāpannāṁstrailokyadahanād viṣhāt

O God of all gods, O Mahadeva, the Protector of all, the very Self of all created beings, save us who have sought refuge in you from this poison that is burning all the three worlds.

When the churning of the ocean proceeds as instructed, what first issues forth are not the nectar as expected but a most deadly poison called Halahala. Seeing that unbearable poison spreading in all directions with tremendous force and finding no protection, all the beings involved in the churning got terrified and sought protection from Lord Shiva, the ever auspicious. Lord Shiva out of his infinite compassion consumes all the poison which is retained in His throat, and it becomes a blue garland, thus getting the name Neelakantha (blue-throated). To protect the afflicted is the duty of one with any power to do so and Lord Shiva sets the highest example in this regard. Also, this whole episode is symbolic of how meditation and self-inquiry will bring to the surface all the subconscious negative tendencies, desires and fears which seem terrifying and can drown one in negativity. But if we surrender all that negativity to the Lord, then He takes them away completely. And only then comes out the nectar of Self-realization which is true peace, happiness and unconditional love for all beings.

तं वटुं वामनं दृष्ट्वा मोदमाना महर्षयः ।
कर्माणि कारयामासुः पुरस्कृत्य प्रजापतिम् ॥ Bh 8.18.13

taṁ vaṭuṁ vāmanaṁ dṛṣṭvā modamānā maharṣayaḥ
karmāṇi kārayāmāsuḥ puraskṛtya prajāpatim

Greatly rejoicing to see the Lord in the form of Vamana, eminent sages headed by father Kashyapa performed the sacred initiation rites with due ceremony.

Parikshit asks the reason why the Lord came as a dwarf boy (Vamana) to ask for three paces of land from Bali. Shuka Brahmam begins by recounting how Bali served his Guru Shukracharya so humbly that he was bestowed with all his spiritual energy. Thus, greatly empowered, Bali laid siege on Indra's heaven causing the Devas to abandon the city of heaven (Amaravati) and Bali ruled heaven and earth with blessings from his Guru. The mother of the Devas Aditi was very perturbed by this and pleaded with her husband, the sage Kashyapa, to help her children, the Devas. After smiling at such bondage due to affection that causes suffering, the sage taught Aditi the most powerful observance called Payovrata which involves living only on milk for twelve days in the bright fortnight of Phalguna and engaging in very simple daily prayers to Deity and/or sacred fire, followed by serving a milk-based preparation to all assembled. Aditi observed Payovrata very sincerely as instructed by her sagely husband Kashyapa. And accordingly, the Lord blessed her with the boon that He shall take Avatar as her son Vamana to fulfill her desire of restoring her sons, the Devas, to the heavenly abode.

यद्युत्तमश्लोक भवान् ममेरितं वचो व्यलीकं सुरवर्य मन्यते ।
करोम्यृतं तत्र भवेत् प्रलम्भनं पदं तृतीयं कुरु शीर्ष्णि मे निजम् ॥
Bh 8.22.2

yadyuttamaśhloka bhavān mameritaṁ vacho vyalīkaṁ suravarya manyate
karomyṛtaṁ tanna bhavet pralambhanaṁ padaṁ tṛtīyaṁ kuru śhīrṣhṇi me nijam

O Illustrious One, if You wonder whether the vow made by me is untrue, I shall presently fulfill it as I never intended to deceive You. Pray, place Your third footstep on my head.

The Lord appeared as the son of Aditi and Kashyapa as a dwarf boy, Vamana. He went to Bali's sacrifice where everyone was completely overwhelmed by His radiance. Being offered to ask for any boon by Bali, Lord Vamana asked Bali for three paces of land. Bali agreed and was about to offer the boon when his Guru Shukracharya objected by revealing to Bali that the one who has come as the dwarf was none other than the Supreme Being and He would snatch away everything with His three strides. Bali respectfully disregarded his own Guru because he had given his word already to Vamana and now it had to be kept all the more so, knowing that it is Bhagavan. Once Bali solemnized his offering, Bhagavan took His Cosmic Form as the Infinite Lord and with one stride, measured all of earth with the subterranean regions and a second stride covered all of heaven. Now with not an atom left for the third stride and being tested by the Lord as to where it can be placed, Bali in a sublime act of self-surrender offered his head for the third step in order to keep his word to Bhagavan. In the first two strides, Bali gave all his possessions and for the third stride, he offered himself, the possessor. This is the ultimate act of self-surrender for which Bali is always remembered. Then Bhagavan revealed His Grace by showing that He had enacted this pastime only to reveal the greatness of Bali's composure and supreme surrender under unparalleled adversity.

NINTH CANTO
Chronicles of the Divine

स वै मन: कृष्णपदारविन्दयोर्वचांसि वैकुण्ठगुणानुवर्णने ।
करौ हरेर्मन्दिरमार्जनादिषु श्रुतिं चकाराच्युतसत्कथोदये ॥
मुकुन्दलिङ्गालयदर्शने दृशौ तद्भृत्यगात्रस्पर्शेऽङ्गसङ्गमम् ।
घ्राणं च तत्पादसरोजसौरभे श्रीमत्तुलस्या रसनां तदर्पिते ॥
पादौ हरे: क्षेत्रपदानुसर्पणे शिरो हृषीकेशपदाभिवन्दने ।
कामं च दास्ये न तु कामकाम्यया यथोत्तमश्लोकजनाश्रया रति: ॥
Bh 9.4.18–20

sa vai manaḥ kṛṣhṇapadāravindayorvachāṁsi
vaikuṇṭhaguṇānuvarṇane
karau harermandiramārjanādiṣhu śhrutiṁ
chakārāchyutasatkathodaye
mukundaliṅgālayadarśhane dṛśhau
tadbhṛtyagātrasparśhe'ṅgasaṅgamam
ghrāṇaṁ cha tatpādasarojasaurabhe śhrīmattulasyā rasanāṁ
tadarpite
pādau hareḥ kṣhetrapadānusarpaṇe śhiro
hṛṣhīkeśhapadābhivandane
kāmaṁ cha dāsye na tu kāmakāmyayā
yathottamaśhlokajanāśhrayā ratiḥ

**Ambarish fixed his mind on the lotus feet of Krishna.
His speech was used only to recount the virtues of the**

Lord. His hands were used in cleaning the temples and other services. His listening was directed only toward the excellent stories of the Immortal One. His vision was only engaged in seeing Deities and the temples of Lord Mukunda. His sense of touch was employed only to serve the limbs of the devotees. His sense of smell was directed only toward the fragrance of the blessed Tulasi leaves offered to the lotus feet of the Lord. He tasted only food offered to the Lord. His feet were only used to walk toward places sacred to Hari. His head always bowed to the feet of the Lord of all senses. Thus, he only sought to serve the Lord and to have love for the devotees of the Lord of excellent renown.

Ambarish was a king in the line of Ikshwaku, the same lineage in which later Bhagavan would descend as the glorious Avatar of Sri Ram. Ambarish is an exemplar of how one can be engaged in the world fully as a king and yet be totally devoted to the Lord. Rather than trying to control the senses and the mind which always involves struggle due to the natural tendency of the senses and the mind to go outward toward the sense objects and thoughts, Ambarish shows the way of effortlessly regulating the senses and the mind by dedicating all of them in the service of the Lord. This is the way shown by Bhāgavatam to live a life of true Yoga by sublimating the senses and the mind toward transcendental activities. If we see the omnipresent Lord in everyone and everything, then we can live in the mood of serving Him through every interaction. Further, we can engage each sense toward its natural object while also connected to the Lord, thus elevating and purifying them. For instance, rather than controlling the propensity to listen to music, one can listen to heartfelt kirtans sung out of true devotion. If there is a propensity to travel, it can be used to go to sacred places and be in holy company. Impulse to activity can be used purely in the mood of service rather than for any personal gratification. Thus, Ambarish shows the sublime way of transcending material living by simply transmuting the activities of the senses and the mind.

अहं भक्तपराधीनो ह्यस्वतन्त्र इव द्विज ।
साधुभिर्ग्रस्तहृदयो भक्तैर्भक्तजनप्रिय: ॥ Bh 9.4.63

aham bhaktaparādhīno hyasvatantra iva dvija
sādhubhirgrastahṛdayo bhaktairbhaktajanapriyaḥ

My heart is possessed completely by My pious devotees for whom I am the only Beloved, so I am subject to their control and not independent.

Ambarish was a supreme devotee, a Maha Bhagavata, who lived in total surrender to Bhagavan, engaged all his senses in adoring Him and ruled his kingdom without the slightest trace of attachment and led his subjects toward devotion. Therefore, he was always protected by Bhagavan's Sudarshana Chakra which symbolizes the power of wisdom. Once sage Durvasa came to visit as Ambarish was about to break Ekadashi fast and was welcomed with great honor by Ambarish. Yet the sage took offence for a minor issue of how the fast was broken by Ambarish and cursed him to be killed. While Ambarish remained calm in the face of the dreadful curse, the ever-protective Sudarshana Chakra removed the curse and further, started to chase Durvasa himself. After fleeing everywhere with his mystical powers to escape the burning heat of Sudarshana and not finding refuge anywhere,

Durvasa finally went to Vaikuntha to surrender to the Lord Himself. But to the great wonder of Durvasa, the all-powerful Lord beautifully expressed His utter inability to help, saying that when it comes to His pure devotees, He is bound by their love (*bhakta parādhīna*) and not independent to act. He Himself and His consort Sri are secondary to the pure devotees for whom Bhagavan is the only refuge, He asked the sage, how can I ever forsake those who have surrendered everything unto Me? The devotees have fastened their hearts on Me and look upon everyone with the same eyes (*samadarshanāḥ*), thus keeping me bound in their love. Therefore, Bhagavan told the sage that the only way out for Durvasa is to seek forgiveness from Ambarish, the very pure devotee that he had offended.

साधवो हृदयं मह्यं साधूनां हृदयं त्वहम् ।
मदन्यत् ते न जानन्ति नाहं तेभ्यो मनागपि ॥ Bh 9.4.68

sādhavo hṛdayaṁ mahyaṁ sādhūnāṁ hṛdayaṁ tvaham
madanyat te na jānanti nāhaṁ tebhyo manāgapi

Pious ones are My very heart, and I am the very heart of the pious. They do not know anything dearer than Me, and I do not know anything dearer than them.

The pious ones (*sadhu*) are those fully established in the realization that nothing exists separate from God. Therefore, their devotion is completely free of any desire unlike the devotion of those caught in egoic identification. In the Gita, Krishna describes four types of devotees—the ones in distress, those who desire worldly possessions, seekers of knowledge and the realized ones established in wisdom (*ārto jijñāsur arthārthī jñānī cha*—BG 7.16). The first three types of devotion are tainted with selfish motives—whether it be removal of suffering, attainment of material wealth or even acquisition of knowledge. Whereas the fourth and the highest type of devotion is motiveless, exclusive devotion that recognizes the all-pervasive nature of God as the only Truth and therefore free of any selfish desire whatsoever. Thus, Krishna declares in the very next verse, "Among all these types of devotees, I consider the *jñānīs* to be the highest, being situated in true wisdom with single pointed, steadfast devotion. I am very dear to them, and they are very dear to Me" (*teṣhāṁ jñānī nityayukta ekabhaktir viśhiṣhyate / priyo hi jñānino'tyartham ahaṁ sa cha mama priyaḥ*—BG 7.17). That is what is indicated in this Bhāgavatam verse as well that the pure realized sadhu is the very heart of Bhagavan and Bhagavan is the very heart of the realized being because he only sees God in everyone and everything and as his own true Self. He doesn't know anything dearer than God and such a surrendered devotee's welfare is taken care of by the Divine as there is none dearer to Him.

अहो अनन्तदासानां महत्त्वं दृष्टमद्य मे ।
कृतागसोऽपि यद् राजन् मङ्गलानि समीहसे ॥ Bh 9.5.14

Ah, the glory of the devotees of the Infinite Being has been seen by me today in that you strive for the good even of those who have wronged you.

As directed by Bhagavan, Durvasa came right back to Ambarish to ask for his forgiveness and to be saved from the scorching heat of Sudarshana. The sage clasped the feet of Ambarish who was much embarrassed due to his humility and had not registered any negative feeling in his heart in the first place. Ambarish instantly offered a beautiful prayer to Sudarshana, who honored the devotion of Ambarish and withdrew, thus Durvasa was rid of the burning heat. Being supremely gratified and moved by the greatness of Ambarish, Durvasa glorified Ambarish who epitomizes the highest state of devotion to the all-pervading Infinite Being. Such a devotee is full of compassion for everyone and helps anyone in misery, while not expecting any credit or letting any pride enter his mind. He keeps his thought, word and deed ever pure and only strives to serve everyone, seeing the presence of God everywhere. Thus, the blessed story of Ambarish represents the highest perfection of human life that can be actualized here and now, and this is the central message of Bhāgavatam.

साधवो न्यासिन: शान्ता ब्रह्मिष्ठा लोकपावना: ।
हरन्त्यघं तेऽङ्गसङ्गात् तेष्वास्ते ह्यघभिद्धरि: ॥ Bh 9.9.6

sādhavo nyāsinaḥ śhāntā brahmiṣhṭhā lokapāvanāḥ
harantyaghaṁ te'ṅgasaṅgāt teṣhvāste hyaghabhiddhariḥ

Pious beings who are free of egoic attachments, ever peacefully abiding in the Supreme Being and capable of purifying the whole world shall wash off the sins of Ganga through the very contact of their body with the waters, for in their heart dwells the Supreme Lord Hari who removes all sins.

Shuka Brahmam continues with the account of the illustrious dynasty of Ikshvaku. One of them is King Sagara who once embarked on a grand Vedic ritual called *ashwamedha yajna* to establish his sovereignty. The sacrificial horse of the *yajna* that is free to roam about, went to the Ashram of the great sage Kapila. Sagara's sons who went looking for the horse committed a transgression against the sage due to which they were burned to ashes. It was revealed then that for the liberation of the deceased and the well-being of the kingdom, the ashes had to be washed by bringing the sacred waters of Ganga to earth. After many attempts by successors such as Anshuman and Dilip, King Bhagiratha, a descendant, was able to bring Ganga down to earth through his severe penance. Pleased with his penance, Mother Ganga revealed herself and told him that she is happy to descend onto earth, but she had a reservation that people would constantly wash off their sins in her waters which will pollute her. Bhagiratha reassured her that though people may wash off their sins in her waters, there will also be many great beings, Bhagavatas, the sages abiding in Brahman (*brahma niṣhṭhā*) who'd also take a dip in her waters and thereby sanctifying and renewing her every time. Thus, Ganga was pacified on this count, and the glory of the true devotees was brought out, in that the most sacred Ganga who purifies everyone else is herself purified by the pure devotees.

धारयिष्यति ते वेगं रुद्रस्त्वात्मा शरीरिणाम् ।
यस्मिन्नोतमिदं प्रोतं विश्वं शाटीव तन्तुषु ॥ Bh 9.9.7

dhārayiṣhyati te vegaṁ rudrastvātmā śharīriṇām
yasminnotamidaṁ protaṁ viśhvaṁ śhāṭīva tantuṣhu

Lord Shiva, the very Self of all, by whom this whole universe is woven, like a cloth woven from threads, will bear the force of Ganga as she descends onto earth.

Ganga then puts forth another reservation to Bhagiratha that her force of descent would be so fierce that it would pierce earth unless someone is able to stem her flow and release her gently. Knowing that only Lord Shiva is powerful enough to sustain that force, Bhagiratha prayed to Shiva who is the essence of the universe just as threads are the essence of cloth. While cloth comes in many names and forms, their very essence is simply thread. Similarly, this universe is filled with many names and forms and yet their very essence is Shiva who is pure Consciousness. After being propitiated by Bhagiratha thus, Shiva agreed to bear Ganga's force and accepted her onto His hair locks to release her gently onto earth. Symbolically, Ganga represents *jnana* (wisdom) of God-realization, and such sacred knowledge is so powerful that it must be received only through the Guru represented by Shiva (*sadāshiva samārambhām*) for mortals to be able to absorb it. Thus, Bhagiratha, with tremendous effort for which he became synonymous (*bhagiratha prayatnam*), brought Ganga to the earthly plane as a blessing for not only his ancestors, but for all of posterity.

तस्यापि भगवानेष साक्षाद् ब्रह्ममयो हरि: ।
अंशांशेन चतुर्धागात् पुत्रत्वं प्रार्थित: सुरै: ।
रामलक्ष्मणभरतशत्रुघ्ना इति संज्ञया ॥ Bh 9.10.2

tasyāpi bhagavāneṣha sākṣhād brahmamayo hariḥ
aṁśhāṁśhena chaturdhāgāt putratvaṁ prārthitaḥ suraiḥ
rāmalakṣhmaṇabharataśhatrughnā iti saṁjñayā

As prayed for by celestial beings, the Supreme Lord Hari Himself who is the all-pervading pure Brahman, took Avatar as Rama, the son of Dasharatha, along with His

expansions with the names of Lakshmana, Bharata and Shatrughna.

Going through the lineage of Ikshwaku, Shuka Brahmam now comes to the blessed Avatar of Rama. When unrighteousness becomes overpowering on Earth due to various demoniac rulers, it causes great disharmony to all elements of nature. Then the guardian deities of nature symbolized by celestial beings pray for order to be restored. Accordingly, the Supreme Being descends to protect the righteous, annihilate the wicked and re-establish dharma as Krishna says in the Gita (*paritrāṇāya sādhūnāṁ vināśhāya cha duṣhkritām / dharma sansthāpanārthāya sambhavāmi yuge yuge*—BG 4.8). In keeping with this eternal principle, when the forces of unrighteousness headed by Ravana gained ascendancy, the most divine Avatar of Sri Rama happened along with His expansions as the blessed brothers Lakshmana, Bharata and Shatrughna. Shuka Brahmam then tells Parikshit the entire story in the form of the chronicle of the Beloved Husband of Sita, that has already been narrated in detail by the great sage Valmiki. And since Parikshit has listened to the wonderful narration of Ramayana time and again, Shuka Brahmam only gives a brief summary of the grand epic, going through all the six major portions, namely *bāla kānda, ayodhyā kānda, āranya kānda, kishkindhā kānda, sundara kānda, yuddha kānda.* Thus, Bhāgavatam describes the entire journey of Rama and Sita as a short and sweet summary from the birth of Rama, to getting married to Sita and being asked to go to the forest, to Sita being abducted by Ravana, to Rama getting the help of the monkeys to find Sita, to Hanuman's divine mission as the messenger of Rama, to the final battle between Rama and

Ravana and the most auspicious coronation of Rama along with Sita in Ayodhya.

नमो ब्रह्मण्यदेवाय रामायाकुण्ठमेधसे ।
उत्तमश्लोकधुर्याय न्यस्तदण्डार्पिताङ्घ्रये ॥ Bh 9.11.7

namo brahmaṇyadevāya rāmāyākuṇṭhamedhase
uttamaśhlokadhuryāya nyastadaṇḍārpitāṅghraye

Hail to Sri Ram, who is ever devoted to the wise sages, the foremost among those of excellent renown, whose wisdom knows no obstruction and whose lotus feet are worshiped by the ever peaceful.

After summarizing the events of the entire Ramayana, Shuka Brahmam gives a beautiful description of the most auspicious event of Rama's ascension to the throne (*pattābhishekam*). Having heard from Hanuman of Sri Rama's impending arrival back to Ayodhya with Sita and Lakshmana after victory over Ravana, Bharata placed on his head the wooden sandals of Rama and accompanied by ministers, priests and citizens, proceeded to welcome his brother Rama in the midst of songs, musical instruments, chants of Vedas, chariots of gold decked with colorful flags, warriors, traders, dancers, all celebrating the arrival. Upon meeting Rama, with eyes full of tears, Bharata dropped down at His feet. Rama held Bharata in His arms for a long time, bathing him with tears of love. Then Rama offered His greetings to everyone there who were ecstatic upon seeing Him, dancing joyfully waving their upper clothes and showering flowers. Bharata held His sandals. Vibishana and Sugriva waved a fan on either side. Hanuman held a white umbrella. Shatrughna held His bow and quiver full of arrows. Sita held a pot with waters from all sacred rivers. Angada took His sword. Jambavan carried His shield of gold. And surrounded by them all, the Lord shone like a full moon among stars and hence called Ramachandra. Rama entered the festive city, greeted His stepmothers first, then His own mother and His teachers. Upon seeing Him, everyone rose up like the dead came back to life and bathed Him with a flood of tears. Sage Vasishta unraveled His matted locks and bathed Him with waters brought from various oceans and rivers. He was then clad in a beautiful attire, adorned with garlands of flowers and ornaments. His divine consort Sita and His brothers were also elegantly dressed and well adorned. After His brothers offered their obeisances, then Lord Sri Rama with His divine consort Sita and blessed by all the sages and worshiped by all Devas, ascended to the throne of Ayodhya.

पुरुषो रामचरितं श्रवणैरुपधारयन् ।
आनृशंस्यपरो राजन् कर्मबन्धैर्विमुच्यते ॥ Bh 9.11.23

puruṣho rāmacharitaṁ śhravaṇairupadhārayan
ānṛśhaṁsyaparo rājan karmabandhairvimuchyate

Anyone who treasures the narrative of the pastimes of Ram through listening with love will be situated in peace and freed from the shackles of karmic bondage.

The entire narrative of Ramayana not only brings forth loving devotion in the hearts of the listeners but is also deeply symbolic of the inner journey toward freedom from egoic bondage. Sita represents the soul that is one with the Divine, Rama, in the paradise of no conflict Ayodhya (a place with no *yuddha* or conflict). The Divine couple aided by the intellect to discern, Lakshmana, descend into the jungle of suffering, *samsara* or creation. There the ten-headed Ravana symbolizing the ten senses (five for perception—sight, sound, taste, smell and touch and five for action—speech, hold, movement, procreation and excretion) invokes desire for the golden deer of material pleasure. That lures the soul away from the Divine, as she ignores the line of discernment drawn by the intellect. What results is the imprisonment in the hellish existence that is Lanka. The soul deeply repents and pines for union with the Divine who sets forth to reclaim the soul back from the clutches of evil. And the key instrument of the Divine in this sacred journey is the monkey mind that is now totally surrendered and therefore of unbelievable potential to remove all obstacles, represented by Hanuman. The hellish existence that is Lanka has as its reigning quality passionate desire (*rajas*) embodied by Ravana alongside sloth (*tamas*) and goodness (*sattva*) embodied by the two brothers Kumbhakarna and Vibhishana respectively. While sloth remains by the side of desire, goodness tries to offer counsel and upon being spurned, renounces desire to surrender to the Divine. Once Hanuman sets fire to Lanka, i.e. the totally surrendered mind of the soul burns desire, the outcome of the final war is already determined showing the supremacy of Sundara Kandam. The concluding war and the final victory (observed on *Vijayadashami*) of Rama over Ravana has its own tremendous significance and unsurpassed grandeur, symbolizing the inner struggle that every serious seeker wages. In the war, Rama beheads Ravana repeatedly only for another head to come up ad infinitum just as thoughts keep springing up one after another. Finally, Rama aims directly for the heart rather than chopping every head that comes up signifying the need for the seeker to not control each separate thought but to go to the very source of thought as "I," rising in the heart. And with the final victory comes the joyous reunion and the coronation of Rama with Sita in Ayodhya, symbolizing the ascent of the soul back to the throne of the Divine.

न जातु काम: कामानामुपभोगेन शाम्यति ।
हविषा कृष्णवर्त्मेव भूय एवाभिवर्धते ॥ Bh 9.19.14

na jātu kāmaḥ kāmānāmupabhogena śhaṁyati
haviṣhā kṛṣhṇavartmeva bhūya evābhivardhate

The craving for sense gratification with the enjoyment of sense objects never ceases, it only causes it to grow even stronger like fire that is fed with fuel.

The one who is bound by the cords of desire and attachment never feels satiated, no matter how much sense enjoyment is experienced. One gets only deluded by its charm and fails to recognize the true Self that is free of all experiences. It is said all the wealth, all the pleasures, all the power that exists on earth cannot yield satisfaction to the mind of a man caught in lust and greed. One mistakenly thinks that one can satisfy his desire by indulging in them, thus exhausting them, but in actuality indulgence in desires only acts like fuel for the fire of desire and makes them burn stronger. Only when one stops entertaining the false notion of separative identification of the body and the mind as "me," the pull of desires for objects and experiences ceases. Therefore, one seeking true happiness ought to simply be rid of the thirst for pleasure which only produces pain and drains the body and the mind of its vitality. Only then one can have the correct vision that everything is divine and be free of seeking pleasure or validation from others and make every moment sacred by giving unconditional love to all.

न कामयेऽहं गतिमीश्वरात् परामष्टर्द्धियुक्तामपुनर्भवं वा ।
आर्तिं प्रपद्येऽखिलदेहभाजामन्तःस्थितो येन भवन्त्यदुःखाः ॥
Bh 9.21.12

na kāmaye'haṁ gatimīśhvarāt
parāmaṣhṭarddhiyuktāmapunarbhavaṁ vā
ārtiṁ prapadye'khiladehabhājāmantaḥsthito yena
bhavantyaduḥkhāḥ

I do not seek from the Lord even the highest position of perfection with eightfold Yogic powers or liberation from the cycle of birth and death. I only want to feel the heart of every embodied being and take on their suffering so that they may be relieved of it.

Bhāgavatam gives an account of a great devotee called Rantideva who shows that true devotion is immense compassion for all those suffering. Rantideva lived with great contentment subsisting on whatever was available, always ready to help others by giving away all that he had without minding any personal hardships. Once he was put to test by the Divine to reveal his supreme glory. He had fasted for forty-eight days without taking any food and on the forty-ninth day, he was about to break the fast with a preparation made of milk and clarified butter. As he was about to partake of the offering, a sage came asking for food and Rantideva gladly gave a portion of the food. Then came a worker and he was also given a portion of the food. Finally, as the last portion alone remained to be eaten, a stranger came with his dogs saying that they were hungry and Rantideva without hesitation gave away the remaining food. He only saw the Supreme Being in all and therefore joyfully gave away without worrying about himself. His only prayer was that he may ever be able to help those in suffering by taking on their suffering, rather than having any personal motive including mystical powers, liberation etc. This very spirit of giving rejuvenated his body and there was no exhaustion, weariness or weakness in him. Then it was revealed that the three beings who came in the form of the sage, the worker and the dog owner were none other than Brahma, Vishnu and Shiva. He was thus fully blessed for his unparalleled spirit of generosity that Maya would simply dissolve and not have any effect on him whatsoever. Thus, Rantideva shows us the secret to make human life sublime—seeing the Divine in all and serving all every moment without seeking anything for personal gain.

यदा यदा हि धर्मस्य क्षयो वृद्धिश्च पाप्मनः ।
तदा तु भगवानीश आत्मानं सृजते हरिः ॥
न ह्यस्य जन्मनो हेतुः कर्मणो वा महीपते ।
आत्ममायां विनेशस्य परस्य द्रष्टुरात्मनः ॥ Bh 9.24.56-57

yadā yadā hi dharmasya kṣhayo vṛddhiśhcha pāpmanaḥ
tadā tu bhagavānīśha ātmānaṁ sṛjate hariḥ
na hyasya janmano hetuḥ karmaṇo vā mahīpate
ātmamāyāṁ vineśhasya parasya draṣhṭurātmanaḥ

Whenever there is a decline of virtue and increase of sinful activities in the world, the Supreme Being manifests Himself at that time. Being the unattached

seer who is Transcendent, there is no other cause for His appearance and actions other than His own potency.

After recounting the entire lineage of the Lunar Dynasty and the descendants of Yadu, Shuka Brahmam toward the very end of ninth Skandha, comes to the blessed couple of Devaki and Vasudeva and briefly introduces the most complete Avatar of Krishna by stating that Bhagavan appeared as the eighth son of the blessed couple. Shuka Brahmam gives the outer purpose of the Supreme Avatar by beautifully echoing the famous verse of Bhagavad Gita where Krishna Himself declares that whenever there are a fall of true religious values and the rise of vice and irreligion, He appears to restore order (*yadā yadā hi dharmasya glānirbhavati bhārata / abhyutthānam adharmasya tadātmānaṁ sṛjāmyaham*—BG 4.7). Also, unlike all living entities who are born into a given circumstance and start engaging in actions as imposed by the Divine Will, in the case of the Supreme Being who is the eternal Light in the hearts of all and the very source of the Divine Will, His appearance and actions are out of His own potency and His will to sport to bestow Grace.

यन्मायाचेष्टितं पुंसः स्थित्युत्पत्त्यप्ययाय हि । अनुग्रहस्तन्निवृत्तेरात्मलाभाय चेष्यते ॥ Bh 9.24.58

yanmāyācheshṭitaṁ puṁsaḥ sthityutpattyapyayāya hi anugrahastannivṛttterātmalābhāya cheṣyate

The activity of His Maya brings forth the birth, sustenance and dissolution of the living entities, while His Grace brings forth Self-realization and the cessation of the cycle of suffering.

The entire manifestation of the universe and every single living entity in this world goes through the same three stages of creation, sustenance and dissolution. These three activities are carried forth by the divine energy (Maya) of the Supreme Being through the Cosmic Intelligence that pervades the whole universe. Further, there is the deluding potency of Maya that binds living entities into a false sense of self associated with the body and caught in separation that causes desire, fear and suffering. But the very same divine energy also brings Grace (*anugraha*) by which true wisdom is bestowed, that there is no separate individual but only the Divine taking on all the forms and acting through each one. This brings about Self-realization which is the recognition that we don't exist as separate individuals but are only expressions of the One Supreme Being who is our true Self. Thus, Self-realization is the same as God-realization and that happens through Grace. While the outer purpose of the Avatar of the Supreme Being was described as establishing dharma, the inner purpose is hinted here as bestowing Grace that leads to God-realization and that is, in fact, the most important purpose of the Avatar of the Supreme Being, especially as Krishna in His most complete form.

कलौ जनिष्यमाणानां दुःखशोकतमोनुदम् ।
अनुग्रहाय भक्तानां सुपुण्यं व्यतनोद् यशः ॥
यस्मिन् सत्कर्णपीयुषे यशस्तीर्थवरे सकृत् ।
श्रोत्राञ्जलिरुपस्पृश्य धुनुते कर्मवासनाम् ॥ Bh 9.24.61-62

kalau janishyamāṇānāṁ duḥkhaśhokatamonudam
anugrahāya bhaktānāṁ supuṇyaṁ vyatanod yaśhaḥ
yasmin satkarṇapīyuṣhe yaśhastīrthavare sakṛt
śhrotrāñjalirupaspṛśhya dhunute karmavāsanām

In order to shower His Grace on the devotees and drive away the sorrow, grief and ignorance of everyone for all of posterity, He spread far and wide His most sacred glory. Listening to His glory which flows like a stream of nectar to the ears of the righteous, one shakes off all bondage in the form of attachment to desires.

Shuka Brahmam now elaborates upon the inner and the most important purpose of the Avatar of Krishna. Destroying the wicked and protecting the virtuous can be accomplished even by forces of nature and events without the need to descend into the world of matter. So that is only the apparent outer purpose of the Avatar. The true purpose is to assume divine names and forms and perform various pastimes that turn places into sacred pilgrimage spots, thereby bestowing Grace to all of posterity. Simply listening to the sweet names and the enchanting pastimes, beholding the divine forms and visiting the hallowed, holy places removes the false attachments and ignorance from the mind, fills the heart with divine love and situates one in freedom from desires and fears. This is the true purpose of the Avatar. Shuka Brahmam concludes the ninth skandha by giving a teaser of the most delightful and charming Avatar of Krishna, summarizing all His activities in just two short verses. Having heard this, Parikshit being the most perfect listener will draw out all the details of the various pastimes of Krishna, which forms the most glorious tenth skandha of Bhāgavatam.

TENTH CANTO
Nectar of Pastimes

सम्यग्व्यवसिता बुद्धिस्तव राजर्षिसत्तम ।
वासुदेवकथायां ते यज्जाता नैष्ठिकी रतिः ॥
वासुदेवकथाप्रश्नः पुरुषांस्त्रीन् पुनाति हि ।
वक्तारं प्रच्छकं श्रोतॄंस्तत्पादसलिलं यथा ॥ Bh 10.1.15-16

samyagvyavasitā buddhistava rājarṣisattama
vāsudevakathāyāṁ te yajjātā naiṣṭhikī ratiḥ
vāsudevakathāpraśnaḥ puruṣāṁstrīn punāti hi
vaktāraṁ pracchakam śrotॄṁstatpādasalilaṁ yathā

One's mind has arrived at the right conclusion when abiding devotion has sprung up in the heart to listen to the pastimes of Krishna. Any inquiry about these pastimes purifies the three people involved—speaker, questioner and listener, just as the waters of Ganga touched by the Lord's feet purifies everyone.

The tenth canto of Bhāgavatam is known as that which stills the mind (*nirodha skandha*). Interestingly, the entire tenth canto is a detailed account of all the activities of the Supreme Avatar of Krishna from His appearance in Mathura to the sweet, mischievous pastimes in Vraja to the return to Mathura and onto the opulent reign at Dwaraka. And yet by simply listening to these pastimes along with the sweet exchanges of the various devotees of Krishna in various moods (*rasa*) of friendly, parental or conjugal love, the mind is effortlessly stilled and the lotus of one's heart blooms in devotion. Parikshit listened to the teaser by Shuka Brahmam at the end of the ninth canto of Krishna Avatar for which he had been waiting so eagerly. So, he begins the tenth canto by asking Shuka Brahmam to narrate in great detail the deeds performed by the Supreme Being, appearing in the Yadu clan. Being pleasing to the ears as well as the mind, these pastimes are sung even by those totally detached from worldly pursuits. Parikshit, being the grandson of Arjuna who was a dear friend of Krishna, who had life saved in the womb of his mother by Krishna, expresses his utmost keenness to listen to the entire account of the pastimes. Only when the listener is so keen to absorb, the speaker is filled with the joy of sharing. Thus, Shuka Brahmam upon hearing the great enthusiasm expressed by Parikshit joyfully begins by first praising Parikshit for being a great listener whose mind is pure and whose heart is full of devotion. He adds that just as Ganga purifies anyone who comes in contact with her through the ages, the very inquiry of Parikshit will purify not only him but also anyone who speaks or listens to Bhāgavatam for all of posterity.

भगवानपि विश्वात्मा विदित्वा कंसजं भयम् ।
यदूनां निजनाथानां योगमायां समादिशत् ॥ Bh 10.2.6

bhagavānapi viśhvātmā viditvā kaṁsajaṁ bhayam
yadūnāṁ nijanāthānāṁ yogamāyāṁ samādiśat

The Supreme Lord, who is the Self of the Universe, knowing the fear of the Yadus from Kamsa, instructed Yogamaya.

Upon being asked by Parikshit to elaborate in great detail every single aspect of the glorious pastimes of Krishna right from His divine appearance, Shuka Brahmam begins with the story of Vasudeva and Devaki getting married. After the wedding, Devaki's cousin Kamsa is told by a heavenly voice that he shall be killed by the eighth son of Devaki. As he proceeds to kill his own sister, Vasudeva intervenes and offers to give their sons to Kamsa as they are born. And Kamsa, possessed by evil, kills the first six sons of Vasudeva and Devaki. Kamsa also causes tremendous fear among the Yadus by persecuting them. Under these circumstances, Bhagavan will proceed to descend first through His expansion as Balaram and then Himself as Krishna (*kṛṣhṇastu bhagavān svayam*—Bh 1.3.28). He shall do so through His energy as the Divine Mother known as Yogamaya —she who is responsible for all activities of the universe in the form of creation, sustenance and dissolution, for the ignorance that causes individual beings to be caught in the false ego and for the Grace that brings forth the realization that it is the play of the Divine. It is the Divine Mother who will now make perfect arrangements for Krishna to appear and execute the most charming and wonderful pastimes that will all be beautifully described in this canto by Shuka Brahmam.

नामधेयानि कुर्वन्ति स्थानानि च नरा भुवि ।
दुर्गेति भद्रकालीति विजया वैष्णवीति च ॥
कुमुदा चण्डिका कृष्णा माधवी कन्यकेति च ।
माया नारायणीशानी शारदेत्यम्बिकेति च ॥ Bh 10.2.11-12

nāmadheyāni kurvanti sthānāni cha narā bhuvi
durgeti bhadrakālīti vijayā vaiṣhṇavīti cha
kumudā chaṇḍikā kṛṣhṇā mādhavī kanyaketi cha
māyā nārāyaṇīśhānī śhāradetyambiketi cha

People will worship Yogamaya as the Divine Mother in various places on earth with various divine names such as Durga, Bhadrakali, Vijaya, Vaishnavi, Kumuda, Chandika, Krishna, Madhavi, Kanyaka, Maya, Narayani, Ishani, Sharada and Ambika.

Krishna instructs Yogamaya to proceed to Vraja enriched by cows and cowherds. There, in Nanda's Gokula resides Rohini, another wife of Vasudeva. Devaki has her seventh child in the womb as the expansion of Bhagavan known as Sesha or Balaram that is to be transferred to the womb of Rohini. He tells her He himself shall be born as the eighth son of Devaki with His full divine potencies while Yogamaya shall be born as the daughter of Nanda and his blessed wife Yashoda. Thus, instructing Yogamaya to prepare perfectly for His appearance, the Supreme Being glorifies the Divine Mother who is His own energy as worshippable in so many divine names across earth. Thus, as mentioned in this verse, She is worshiped with various names in various places such as Durga in Kashi, Bhardrakali in Avanti, Vijaya in Odisha, Vaishnavi in Jammu, Sharada in Kashmir, Kanyaka in Kanyakumari, Mahalakshmi in Maharashtra and so on. Each name signifies one of the many potencies of the Divine Mother who is the energy (*shakti*) of the entire universe and bestower of Grace that awakens wisdom and divine love.

सत्यव्रतं सत्यपरं त्रिसत्यं सत्यस्य योनिं निहितं च सत्ये ।
सत्यस्य सत्यमृतसत्यनेत्रं सत्यात्मकं त्वां शरणं प्रपन्नाः ॥
Bh 10.2.26

satyavrataṁ satyaparaṁ trisatyaṁ satyasya yoniṁ nihitaṁ cha satye
satyasya satyamṛtasatyanetraṁ satyātmakaṁ tvāṁ śharaṇaṁ prapannāḥ

We surrender unto You, who is of truthful vow, the transcendent truth, the truth of all three states, the source of truth, the truth of the five elements, the truth of all truths, vision (seer) of truth and the very essence of truth.

After the auspicious appearance of Balaram as the elder brother, Krishna entered the womb of Devaki, causing her to glow radiant, having now turned into a temple of the Lord. Brahma and the devatas come in a subtle form to offer their prayers to Krishna even before He is born. In this beautiful verse, they glorify the essence of the Supreme Being through various nuances of one beautiful word—truth (*satyam*). He is the one of truthful vow in every sense and His Supreme vow that He always keeps is that anyone who surrenders unto Him completely is liberated (*sarvadharmān parityajya mām ekaṁ śharaṇaṁ vraja / ahaṁ tvāṁ sarvapāpebhyo mokshayiṣhyāmi mā śhuchaḥ*—BG 18.66). He is the truth that transcends all of time and space, all of material energy. He is the truth that pervades all three states of waking, dream and deep sleep, all three tenses of past, present and future and all three qualities of *sattva, rajas, tamas*. He is the truth that pervades all the five elements of space, air, fire, water and soil. He is the truth of all truths in that everything that appears as true is only relative within time and space and observer dependent, whereas the underlying truth of all truths is the substrate which is free of the observer and the observed. His vision is alone truthful, being pure awareness untainted by the limited senses. Therefore, His very essence is Truth.

एकायनोऽसौ द्विफलस्त्रिमूलश्चतूरसः पञ्चविधः षडात्मा ।
सप्तत्वगष्टविटपो नवाक्षो दशच्छदी द्विखगो ह्यादिवृक्षः ॥
Bh 10.2.27

ekāyano'sau dviphalastrimūlaśchatūrasaḥ pañchavidhaḥ shadātmā
saptatvagashṭaviṭapo navāksho daśhachchhadī dvikhago hyādivṛkshaḥ

The beginningless tree of creation has indeed one ground, two fruits, three roots, four tastes, five means of perception, six states, seven layers of bark, eight branches, nine hollows and ten leaves with two birds sitting on it.

In this beautiful verse, Bhāgavatam describes various aspects of our embodied existence through the ascending order of natural numbers. The ground of existence is the one all-pervading cosmic intelligence. The two fruits of existence are pleasure and pain. The three roots are the three modes of nature—*sattva, rajas, tamas.* The four tastes are the four human pursuits—virtue (*dharma*), wealth (*artha*), gratification (*kāma*) and liberation (*moksha*). The five means of perception are the five senses of sight, sound, smell, taste and touch. The six states of embodied life are birth, existence, growth, maturity, decay and destruction. The seven layers of bark are the seven bodily constituents—skin, blood, muscle, fat, bone, marrow and the generative fluid. The eight branches are the five gross and three subtle elements—soil, water, fire, air, space, mind, intellect and memory. The nine hollows are the nine openings—two eyes, two ears, two nostrils, mouth, rectum and the genitals. And the ten leaves are the ten vital airs passing through the body. In this tree of the embodied being, are found sitting two birds—the apparent individual as the false sense of self and the pure Awareness as the true Self of all. Thus, every aspect of the embodied living is all an expression of and illuminated by the One Supreme Being who is the only Truth of all of existence.

येऽन्येऽरविन्दाक्ष विमुक्तमानिनस्त्वय्यस्तभावादविशुद्धबुद्धयः ।
आरुह्य कृच्छ्रेण परं पदं ततः पतन्त्यधोऽनादृतयुष्मदङ्घ्रयः ॥
Bh 10.2.32

ye'nye'ravindākṣha
vimuktamāninastvayyastabhāvādaviśhuddhabuddhayaḥ
āruhya kṛchchhreṇa parampadaṁ tataḥ patantyadho'nādṛtayuṣh
madaṅghrayaḥ

Those who tread the path of dry knowledge and regard themselves as liberated, but whose mind is impure due to not being fully surrendered to Your lotus feet, fall down from their position even if they attain a high state.

If one does not recognize that the entire tree of existence as the phenomenal universe is only an expression of the Supreme Being who is the cause and its support, then the vision is clouded by seeing the One as many. Then taking ourselves to be separate, we are caught in desires of various kinds. But finding all of them to be finite and not ultimately fulfilling, we turn toward the Infinite. As we do so, the one who is endowed with true wisdom surrenders the very false self that seeks to realize God. Thereby freed of all suffering of mundane existence, one lives in unconditional love toward all beings by seeing only Bhagavan everywhere. But if one seeks to realize the Truth by engaging only in dry knowledge and intellectual speculation, trying to figure it all out as it were, then one is always frustrated with these attempts. Clear conceptual knowledge in the mind may make one regard oneself as liberated but without wisdom flowering in the heart, one is prone to falling down from whatever state one has attained through strenuous mental efforts. Therefore, Bhāgavatam repeatedly instructs us to never engage in mere intellectual gymnastics through textual knowledge but surrender the very sense of "me" to the One source who alone exists.

निशीथे तम उद्भूते जायमाने जनार्दने ।
देवक्यां देवरूपिण्यां विष्णुः सर्वगुहाशयः ।
आविरासीद् यथा प्राच्यां दिशीन्दुरिव पुष्कलः ॥ Bh 10.3.8

nishīthe tama udbhūte jāyamāne janārdane
devakyāṁ devarūpiṇyāṁ viṣṇuḥ sarvaguhāśhayaḥ
āvirāsīd yathā prāchyāṁ diśhīnduriva puṣhkalaḥ

At midnight, enveloped in thick darkness, the Supreme Being who is the in-dweller of all hearts manifested Himself in His fullness through Devaki who looked divine herself, even as the full moon appears in the eastern horizon.

The delightful hour of Krishna's descent approached on the eighth day (*aṣhtami*) of the lunar cycle as the star Rohini was at the ascendant. The whole land was filled with blessings, and the skies became clear of clouds even though it was the rainy season. All the rivers flowed exuberantly, ponds bloomed with lotuses, birds and bees made pleasing sounds, a gentle breeze from the Yamnua river brought in a waft of sweet fragrance, all the saintly beings became cheerful while the demoniac beings felt suddenly depressed. In such an auspicious hour at the stroke of midnight, the Supreme Being Vishnu who is all pervading as the in-dwelling Presence in the heart cave of all living beings and who is known as Janaradana, the one who destroys the wicked, protects the devotees made His divine descent as Krishna through Devaki and shone bright as the full moon in the eastern sky.

तमद्भुतं बालकमम्बुजेक्षणं चतुर्भुजं शङ्खगदाद्युदायुधम् ।
श्रीवत्सलक्ष्मं गलशोभिकौस्तुभं पीताम्बरं सान्द्रपयोदसौभगम् ॥
Bh 10.3.9

*tamadbhutaṁ bālakamambujekṣhaṇaṁ chaturbhujaṁ
śhaṅkhagadādyudāyudham
śhrīvatsalakṣhmaṁ galaśhobhikaustubhaṁ pītāmbaraṁ
sāndrapayodasaubhagam*

That extraordinarily wonderful child appeared with lotus-like eyes, endowed with four arms, wielding uplifted weapons and emblems such as a conch, a mace and a discus, bearing on His bosom the mark of Srivatsa, clad in yellow silk, with the complexion of a thick cloud.

Appearing as the Supreme Being, Krishna first reveals His transcendental form to His parents Vasudeva and Devaki before withdrawing it to take the form of a newborn baby. His transcendental, four-armed form carrying a conch, a mace, a discus and a lotus flower, is highly symbolic. The conch when blown gives the sound of Om which is the primordial sound that brings forth the five elements, hence Krishna's conch is called *panchajanya* (that which brings forth the five). The mace (*gada*) symbolizes the hard knocks that life gives us in the form of suffering and challenges us to wake up from the slumber of ignorance. The discus (*sudarshana*) represents the unstoppable wheel of time that destroys everything material while providing refuge to those who surrender to the Timeless. The lotus flower (*padma*) symbolizes the awakened heart that is surrendered. With these divine emblems, Krishna makes His appearance on Earth in the most wonderful (*adhbutam*) manner and will go on to execute wonderful pastimes, bringing delight to one and all.

विदितोऽसि भवान् साक्षात्पुरुषः प्रकृतेः परः ।
केवलानुभवानन्दस्वरूपः सर्वबुद्धिदृक् ॥ Bh 10.3.13

vidito'si bhavān sākṣhāt puruṣhaḥ prakṛteḥ paraḥ
kevalānubhavānandasvarūpaḥ sarvabuddhidṛk

You have been directly known as the Supreme Being who is transcendent to all of the material energy. The absolute experience of happiness is Your very essence, being the seer of all minds.

After beholding the splendorous form of Krishna, Father Vasudeva recognized Him to be none other than the Supreme

Being. Thus, all his fears that Kamsa might kill this son melted away instantly and he was filled with pure joy and wonder. He proceeded to glorify his own son with a pure mind as the Supreme Being who is the embodiment of Pure Consciousness, untouched by the material energy. Having evolved the entire universe made of the three gunas by His own material energy, He remains unaffected by it just as the sun remains unaffected by all the activities of the solar energy. Just as space seems to be within a room even though the room is contained within space, He seems to be within the hearts of living entities as the in-dwelling Awareness, though in fact all living entities and the entire universe appear and dissolve within Him. Similarly, now He seems to have appeared within the prison cell while in truth, the distinction of inside and outside does not exist in Him. Vasudeva thus beautifully glorifies with profound wisdom and devotion, the essence of the Supreme Being who has now descended to protect the righteous, destroy the wicked and bestow His Grace to all.

रूपं यत् तत् प्राहुरव्यक्तमाद्यं ब्रह्म ज्योतिर्निर्गुणं निर्विकारम् ।
सत्तामात्रं निर्विशेषं निरीहं स त्वं साक्षाद् विष्णुरध्यात्मदीपः ॥
Bh 10.3.24

rūpaṁ yat tat prāhuravyaktamādyaṁ brahma jyotirnirguṇaṁ nirvikāram
sattāmātraṁ nirviśeṣhaṁ nirīhaṁ sa tvaṁ sākṣhād vishṇuradhyātmadīpaḥ

You are the all-pervading Vishnu, the illuminating Presence within all living entities, the indefinable, unmanifest, primordial, pure Consciousness, free of any

limiting attributes, unqualified, unchanging Supreme Brahman.

After the father Vasudeva glorifies Krishna upon His appearance, the Mother Devaki too, perceiving all the auspicious signs in her son, is freed of all fears of Kamsa and offers this profound prayer to Krishna with a radiant smile. The entire essence of the Upanishads is brought forth in this beautiful prayer to Krishna describing Him as beyond all definitions of mind or speech, the Unborn, who is the ground for the play of birth and death, the original cause of all causes, who has no material qualities, One who transcends time and space, therefore is free of all changes as the Infinite Being known as Brahman. The universe evolves out of Him bringing forth time and space and merges back unto Him upon dissolution. When one is freed of the false identification with the body and the mind that appear within time and space as "me," one is freed of the fear of death by recognizing that the essence of oneself and everyone, everything is none other than the eternal Supreme Being, thus realizing that God Alone Is.

कालेन स्नानशौचाभ्यां संस्कारैस्तपसेज्यया ।
शुध्यन्ति दानै: सन्तुष्या द्रव्याण्यात्मात्मविद्यया ।। Bh 10.5.4

kālena snānashauchābhyāṁ samskāraistapasejyayā
shudhyanti dānaiḥ santuṣhṭyā dravyāṇyātmātmavidyayā

The body gets purified through bathing, washing and observing sacred rituals. The mind gets purified through austerity, worship, charity and contentment. And the Self is revealed as pure through Self-knowledge.

After the prayers offered by Vasudeva and Devaki to His transcendental form, Krishna transforms into a baby. And as per the arrangement of Yogamaya, everyone is put into the deep sleep of Yoganidra and Vasudeva carries Krishna across Yamuna to Gokul where Yashoda has given birth to a baby girl, Yogamaya Herself at the same time. So Vasudeva leaves Krishna with the blessed couple of Nanda and Yashoda and brings back Yogamaya to Mathura. The spell of Yoganidra is then removed and Kamsa comes to kill this baby girl too. However, She slips out of him instantly, reveals Her true form, warns Kamsa that his killer is elsewhere, and disappears. Kamsa, now terribly confused and afraid, releases Vasudeva and Devaki. His evil counselors advise to kill all the babies born in the last ten days and he commands accordingly, thus ensuring his own imminent destruction. Meanwhile Baby Krishna is in Nanda's Gokula and there is a great celebration (Nandotsava) for the newborn. Nanda arranges for the purification ritual, giving generous gifts to everyone. Here Shuka Brahmam notes that the body needs to be kept pure by external cleansing rituals while the mind needs to be kept pure too by living an austere and simple life, giving generously and being content, all of which Nanda exemplifies. And such purity of body and mind enables awakening through direct Self-knowledge to the pure vision of the Self as the all-pervading Supreme Being.

नूनं ह्यदृष्टनिष्ठोऽयमदृष्टपरमो जनः ।
अदृष्टमात्मनस्तत्त्वं यो वेद न स मुह्यति ॥ Bh 10.5.30

nūnaṁ hyadṛṣhṭaniṣhṭho'yamadṛṣhṭaparamo janaḥ
adṛṣhṭamātmanastattvaṁ yo veda na sa muhyati

Indeed, every living entity lives as per what is ordained by the unseen hand of destiny. The one who knows that his embodied existence is entirely as ordained by destiny does not get deluded.

After organizing the grand celebration upon the birth of baby Krishna, Nanda comes to Mathura to pay his annual taxes to Kamsa and there he meets Vasudeva. Having come to know that Kamsa has killed the first six sons of Vasudeva, Nanda shares in the grief of Vasudeva and consoles him that in fact everything happens as ordained and accepting what has happened is to be free of delusion. Suffering is mainly due to resistance to happenings of past, present and future. All regret, anger, anxiety etc. are only due to resistance, which is based on an underlying desire that things can be different from what they are. But time always unfolds perfectly, no matter how unpleasant or pleasant it may seem, as ordained by the Divine. Therefore, one ought to put one's best effort into any given moment while accepting whatever happens as the perfect dispensation of Providence. This is the essence of karma yoga that brings forth right action as an expression of one's fullest potential while remaining free of any expectations and therefore peaceful within.

येन येनावतारेण भगवान् हरिरीश्वरः ।
करोति कर्णरम्याणि मनोज्ञानि च नः प्रभो ॥
यच्छृण्वतोऽपैत्यरतिर्वितृष्णा सत्त्वं च शुद्ध्यत्यचिरेण पुंसः ।
भक्तिर्हरौ तत्पुरुषे च सख्यं तदेव हारं वद मन्यसे चेत् ॥
Bh 10.7.1–2

yena yenāvatāreṇa bhagavān haririśhvaraḥ
karoti karṇaramyāṇi manojñāni cha naḥ prabho

yachchhṛṇvato'paityaratirvitṛṣhṇā sattvaṁ cha
śhuddhyatyachireṇa puṁsaḥ
bhaktirharau tatpuruṣhe cha sakhyaṁ tadeva hāraṁ vada
manyase chet

The exploits of the Supreme Lord Hari, through all His Avatars, are so charming to the ear and appealing to the mind. Simply listening to the narration of the activities of the Lord causes dissatisfaction and cravings to disappear, the mind gets purified, devotion, flowers, and friendship with His devotees become firmly established.

Soon after the celebration of Krishna's appearance in Gokula, a demoness called Putana comes disguised as the most beautiful woman with the intent to kill Krishna by poisoning Him through her milk. Instead, she gets killed as Krishna sucks her life out effortlessly. She gets liberated in the process simply due to contact with Krishna. Narrating this wonderful episode, Shuka Brahmam adds, if a demoness got the same destiny that saints would, then how much more easily would one who has sincere devotion to Krishna realize the highest state. He adds that all suffering out of ignorance is totally removed for those who look upon Krishna as their Beloved. Parikshit, upon listening to the first of the many wonderful exploits of Krishna, expresses his great joy on receiving such nectar that makes the mind still, the heart flower in devotion and great love to spring forth for all devotees who share in this joy. Pleased by the enthusiasm of Parikshit, Shuka Brahmam continues with the narration of the pastimes of how a demon called Shakatasura who hid in a chariot with the intent to crush Krishna was also liberated by Krishna simply kicking the chariot. Then Trnavrta came in the form of a whirlwind, picked Krishna up into the skies but got choked by Krishna and fell down dead, to be liberated. While performing such miraculous feats, Krishna was also not causing any sense of awe in Yashoda and Nanda who were overjoyed that Krishna was magically saved each time and looked upon Him as their child who needed protection, thus enhancing their sweet mood of parental love (*vātsalya rasa*).

येऽसूयानृतदम्भेर्षाहिंसामानविवर्जिताः ।
न तेषां सत्यशीलानामाशिषो विफलाः कृताः ॥ Bh 10.7.13

ye'sūyānṛtadambhershāhimsāmānavivarjitāḥ
na teshāṁ satyashīlānāmāshisho viphalāḥ kṛtāḥ

The benedictions uttered by the truthful ones who are free from envy, dishonesty, arrogance, hypocrisy and violence never go in vain.

With the protective mood of parental love, Nanda wanted to remove any evil omens that were causing such demons to come and harm Krishna. So he organized a ceremony where oblations were offered to the sacred fire and Vedic hymns were chanted by the Brahmana priests. Here, Shuka Brahmam notes that what is paramount in such ceremonies and what truly makes the benedictions and blessings come true is the quality of those who chant these mantras. As Narada described in the seventh skandha, it is by the qualities and not by birth that one can be called a Brahmana. And here it is defined as the absence of the opposite, negative qualities—totally being free of comparison and envy, not speaking any untruths, being free of arrogance and hypocrisy and not having violence even in thought. Only when such truthful ones conduct *yajna* and pronounce benedictions, true blessings manifest for everyone.

महद्विचलनं नृणां गृहिणां दीनचेतसाम् ।
निःश्रेयसाय भगवन्कल्पते नान्यथा क्वचित् ॥ Bh 10.8.4

mahadvichalanaṁ nṛṇāṁ gṛhiṇāṁ dīnachetasām
niḥśhreyasāya bhagavan kalpate nānyathā kvachit

The moving about of exalted beings is directed toward no other purpose than the supreme good of men who are otherwise attached to their households and distressed in mind.

Garga Rishi, the family priest of the Yadus, came to Nanda's Vraja to do the formal naming ceremony of Krishna and Balaram. Nanda welcomed him with delight, offered his respect and asked him of the purpose of his visit, noting that a great being like Garga is concerned only with the benefit of others. While those caught in worldly attachments always look for "what's in it for me" in every interaction, the liberated beings only serve others with love. Garga replied that he came to do the formal naming ceremony and it was done in the auspicious cow-pen, to not draw any unwanted attention. Garga formally gave the names Balaram (delights all with great strength) and Krishna (of dark complexion). He further hinted that Krishna is equal to Narayana (*nārāyaṇasamo guṇaiḥ*—Bh 10.8.19) in all virtues, opulence, fame and glory. Garga Rishi then left for Mathura, having delighted and blessed Nanda through the naming ceremony.

ततस्तु भगवान् कृष्णो वयस्यैर्व्रजबालकैः ।
सहरामो व्रजस्त्रीणां चिक्रीडे जनयन् मुदम् ॥ Bh 10.8.27

tatastu bhagavān kṛshṇo vayasyairvrajabālakaiḥ
saharāmo vrajastrīṇāṁ chikrīḍe janayan mudam

In the course of time, Krishna along with Balaram, began to sport with the boys of Vraja, bringing delight to the women of Vraja.

Krishna and Balaram first began to sport crawling on their knees with tinkling bells around their anklets on the grounds of Vraja, bringing great delight to mothers Yashoda, Rohini and all the women of Vraja. Then starting to walk, Krishna started to engage in boyish pranks along with Balaram. The women of Vraja would joyfully complain that Krishna untethered their calves, pulled the other boys into their pranks, stole and ate the curds and butter stored in their homes, and fed it to them and the monkeys while pretending to be innocent in front of Yashoda. Listening to these complaints, Yashoda would look at the charming face of Krishna who looked at her with apparently fearful eyes causing her to laugh. The women of Vraja also took great delight by being in His company in the guise of reporting complaints. Thus, everyone in Gokula was immersed in Divine bliss, being drawn to the Supreme Being with such intense love that effortlessly removed all traces of ego and situated them in pure joy.

सा तत्र ददृशे विश्वं जगत्स्थास्नु च खं दिशः ।
साद्रिद्वीपाब्धिभूगोलं सवाय्वग्नीन्दुतारकम् ॥ Bh 10.8.37

sā tatra dadṛshe viśhvaṁ jagatsthāsnu cha khaṁ diśhaḥ
sādridvīpābdhibhūgolaṁ savāyvagnīndutārakam

Inside the Lord's mouth, Yashoda beheld the entire universe consisting of the moving and the unmoving, space, directions, all of earth with mountains, islands, oceans, wind, fire, moon, and the stars.

One day, while at play, the boys headed by Balaram complained to Yashoda that Krishna had eaten dirt. When chastised for doing so, Krishna replied innocently that everyone was simply lying and Yashoda can check His mouth herself. When asked to open his mouth, she beheld the most astonishing vision of the entire universe made of the three gunas with all its modifications, within the tiny mouth of Krishna. Further, she saw within that vision of the entire earth, the land of Vraja including herself looking into Krishna's mouth. She was seized with great wonder as to whether it was some grand delusion of her mind. She bowed down mentally to the Supreme Being who can never be understood by the mind, intellect or the senses. After bestowing this momentary vision of the Infinite to the blessed Yashoda, Krishna's divine Maya ensured that she was drawn immediately into maternal love that looked upon Him, who is glorified by all the Vedas, Upanishads and systems of Yoga, simply as her own dear son.

न चान्तर्न बहिर्यस्य न पूर्वं नापि चापरम् ।
पूर्वापरं बहिश्चान्तर्जगतो यो जगच्च यः ॥
तं मत्वात्मजमव्यक्तं मर्त्यलिङ्गमधोक्षजम् ।
गोपिकोलूखले दाम्ना बबन्ध प्राकृतं यथा ॥ Bh 10.9.13-14

*na chāntarna bahiryasya na pūrvaṁ nāpi chāparam
pūrvāparaṁ bahiśchāntarjagato yo jagachcha yaḥ
taṁ matvātmajam avyaktam martyaliṅgamadhokṣhajam
gopikolūkhale dāmnā babandha prākṛtaṁ yathā*

There is no inside or outside, before or after with respect to the Supreme Being who exists in all of space and all of time, being the universe Himself. Yet the unmanifest Lord who is beyond senses appeared as a human child and Yashoda, regarding Him as her own son, proceeded to tie Him like an ordinary naughty child to a wooden mortar with a rope.

One day, while Mother Yashoda was churning butter, Krishna came to her, hungry for milk. She fed Him as he lay on her lap, but she suddenly remembered the milk boiling on the stove, so she put him down and went in haste to take care of the milk, before finishing the feeding. Krishna feigned anger upon being left in the middle of his feeding and taking a piece of stone, He broke a pot of curds. Then he went to an interior room of the house to steal and eat butter. Yashoda came back to find the pot of curds broken and Krishna standing on an overturned wooden mortar eating butter and sharing it with a monkey. As Yashoda sneaked on him from behind with a rod in her hand, Krishna got down and ran away as if afraid. Yashoda caught hold of Him, who is elusive for even the greatest Yogi attempting to reach Him through meditation. Casting her rod away, Yashoda then sought to bind Him with a rope. Shuka Brahmam here notes the beauty of this pastime in which the Supreme Being who is beyond time and space and from whom they come forth is sporting as a mere child afraid of His mother attempting to bind Him with a rope.

एवं सन्दर्शिता ह्यङ्ग हरिणा भृत्यवश्यता ।
स्ववशेनापि कृष्णेन यस्येदं सेश्वरं वशे ॥
नेमं विरिञ्चो न भवो न श्रीरप्यङ्गसंश्रया ।
प्रसादं लेभिरे गोपी यत्तत्प्राप विमुक्तिदात् ॥
नायं सुखापो भगवान्देहिनां गोपिकासुतः ।
ज्ञानिनां चात्मभूतानां यथा भक्तिमतामिह ॥ Bh 10.9.19-21

evam sandarshitā hyanga hariṇā bhṛtyavaśhyatā
svavaśhenāpi kṛṣhṇena yasyedam seśhvaram vaśhe
nemam viriñcho na bhavo na śrīrapyangasamśhrayā
prasādam lebhire gopī yattatprāpa vimuktidāt
nāyam sukhāpo bhagavān dehinām gopikāsutaḥ
jñāninām chātmabhūtānām yathā bhaktimatāmiha

Thus, Krishna demonstrated His amenability to be controlled by His devotees despite being the Master of the entire Universe. Neither Brahma nor Shiva nor Lakshmi received such Grace from Him as the cowherd woman Yashoda. Krishna, the son of Yashoda, is not easily accessible to anyone identified with the body or with dry knowledge of scriptures or with other attempts to realize Him as for those who are filled with loving devotion.

When Yashoda proceeded to bind Krishna around His belly with a rope, it fell short by two inches. Yashoda then connected another rope to it to make it longer and still found the combined rope to be two inches short. Then she joined yet another rope and no matter how many ropes she added, it kept falling two inches short. Finally, she gave up and only smiled at her own frustration and amazement at the inability to bind Little Krishna, while other cowherd women watched this play with wonder amid laughter. Perceiving the exertion and the surrender of His mother, Krishna then allowed Himself to be bound by Yashoda out of compassion. This episode is highly symbolic of how all the attempts to realize God through one's own efforts always falls short until one surrenders unto Him completely and only then Grace is bestowed by which one realizes God's presence in the Heart. While even Lakshmi serves His lotus feet with great reverence, the simple cowherd woman Yashoda, out of pure maternal love, was able to bind the Supreme Being as a child, demonstrating that the pure heart of a devotee can control the very controller of the Universe. He is easily available to those who approach Him with pure love, rather than those who attempt to realize Him through dry knowledge or philosophical speculation. This whole pastime of Krishna being bound by a rope (*dama*) around His belly (*udara*) has resulted in another auspicious name for the Lord as Damodara, a very special name that invokes the Grace of the Supreme Being.

साधूनां समचित्तानां मुकुन्दचरणैषिणाम् ।
उपेक्ष्यैः किं धनस्तम्भैरसद्भिरसदाश्रयैः ॥ Bh 10.10.18

sādhūnāṁ samachittānāṁ mukundacharaṇaiṣhiṇām
upekṣhyaiḥ kiṁ dhanastambhairasadbhirasadāśhrayaiḥ

Saintly beings, endowed with equanimity and desiring only the lotus feet of the Supreme Being, have nothing to do with those who are proud of their wealth and attached to sense gratification.

After being tied by the rope to the wooden mortar as Damodara, Yashoda went back to her household duties. Krishna then noticed a pair of giant trees and crawled between them. Long ago, the two sons of Kubera on account of their arrogance, being inebriated with wine and blind with lust, had disrespected Sage Narada who then pronounced a curse that they would turn into trees. On their repentance, they were assured that Krishna himself would liberate them. Being attached to the bodily identification and drunk with the pride of wealth as exhibited by the sons of Kubera, only brings forth lust, greed and other vices. The ones who are full of arrogant pride of wealth do not recognize the value of association with the saintly beings who are ever equanimous and fully surrendered to Mukunda (One who bestows liberation). The saintly beings too stay away from the ones caught in vanity and hubris but show compassion for their ignorance. Hence Narada, while pronouncing the curse, also declared that they would be restored back to their original form by Krishna when loving devotion awakened in their hearts. Thus, even the curse of a sage is only for the purpose of bestowing Grace and is a blessing in disguise.

देवर्षिर्मे प्रियतमो यदिमौ धनदात्मजौ ।
तत्तथा साधयिष्यामि यद् गीतं तन्महात्मना ॥ Bh 10.10.25

devarṣhirme priyatamo yadimau dhanadātmajau
tattathā sādhayiṣhyāmi yad gītaṁ tanmahātmanā

(Krishna said to Himself), "Since the celestial sage Narada is dear to Me, I shall redeem the two sons of Kubera as has been prophesied by the great soul."

The two sons of Kubera by the curse of Narada, which was really a blessing, stood as trees for a long time in the sacred land of Vraja, right in the courtyard of the house of Nanda and Yashoda until Krishna crawled in His divine form of Damodara with a wooden mortar tied to His waist. He positioned the mortar between the two trees and pulled it with great force that uprooted the trees and restored the two sons of Kubera to their original form to fulfill the prophecy of the great sage and devotee Narada. Such is the power of a fully surrendered sage that God feels obliged to keep the word of the sage. Even though the two Yaksha boys had not engaged in any spiritual practices to merit such a blessing, they were still given the highest benediction of the direct vision (*darshan*) of Krishna simply by the Grace of Narada.

वाणी गुणानुकथने श्रवणौ कथायां हस्तौ च कर्मसु मनस्तव पादयोर्नः ।
स्मृत्यां शिरस्तव निवासजगत्प्रणामे दृष्टिः सतां दर्शनेऽस्तु भवत्तनूनाम् ॥ Bh 10.10.38

vāṇī guṇānukathane śhravaṇau kathāyaṁ hastau cha karmasu manastava pādayornaḥ
smṛtyāṁ śhirastava nivāsajagatpraṇāme dṛṣhṭiḥ satāṁ darhśane'stu bhavattanūnām

Let our speech be employed in recounting Your glories, our ears in hearing Your stories, our hands in doing Your work, our mind in the contemplation of Your lotus feet, our head in bowing to the whole world which is Your abode and our sight in beholding sages who are Your very embodiment.

The two Yakshas, Nalakubara and Manigriva, regaining their original form and freed of all pride upon directly beholding Krishna, offered a beautiful prayer to Him, the Supreme Being who is the greatest Yogi of all. They recognized Him as both the unmanifest Source and the manifest universe and the One controller of the body, mind, senses of all. They saw Him as Time itself and the allpervading and imperishable Vishnu, the Supreme Ordainer (*tvameva kālo bhagavān viṣhṇuravyaya īśhvaraḥ*—Bh 10.10.30). The unmanifest Source alone comes forth in the form of subtle divine energy (*prakrti*) made of the three gunas and as the Cosmic Intelligence (*mahat tattva*) that brings forth the mind, intellect and the senses which are hence incapable of grasping Him, their very Source. The Yakshas simply surrendered unto Him as the all-pervading Infinite Being Vāsudeva who cannot be known by those caught in self-identification as "me." Thus, glorifying Krishna as the embodiment of Supreme auspiciousness, well-being and peace, and also expressing gratitude to the great sage Narada for bestowing such causeless mercy, the Yakshas uttered this universal prayer that may all our faculties of speaking, seeing, listening, working, thinking be ever engaged in perceiving, glorifying and serving the One all-pervading Lord appearing as infinite names and forms.

दर्शयंस्तद्विदां लोक आत्मनो भृत्यवश्यताम् ।
व्रजस्योवाह वै हर्षं भगवान् बालचेष्टितैः ॥ Bh 10.11.9

darśhayaṁstadvidāṁ loka ātmano bhṛtyavaśhyatām
vrajasyovāha vai harṣhaṁ bhagavān bālacheṣhṭitaiḥ

Demonstrating to those who know Him, that He is subject to the will of His devotees in this world, the Lord indeed brought joy to Vraja through His childhood sports.

Growing up in the land of Vraja, Krishna would dance to the tune of the loving cowherd women whenever they asked Him to do so. When asked to sing, He would sing at the top of His voice. If asked to carry a wooden seat or a pair of sandals or anything else needed by the cowherd women, Krishna gladly did so. Thus, it is said that He behaved like a puppet wholly subject to the will of the Gopis. Herein lies the greatness of pure devotion that the Supreme Being, who is puppet master for the whole Universe where everything from the smallest atom to the largest galaxies move as ordained by Him, takes this sweet form to let His devotees be His puppet master. Later too, when He acted as a messenger for Yudhishthira or a charioteer for Arjuna, it was as if He forgot His Lordship and simply acted according to the command of His devotees. Thus, Krishna demonstrates throughout His Avatar, the highest principle of unconditional love and service, that makes even God dance to the tune of the devotee.

वृन्दावनं गोवर्धनं यमुनापुलिनानि च ।
वीक्ष्यासीदुत्तमा प्रीती राममाधवयोर्नृप ॥ Bh 10.11.36

vṛndāvanaṁ govardhanaṁ yamunāpulināni cha
vīkṣhyāsīduttamā prītī rāmamādhavayornṛpa

At the sight of Vrndavana, Govardhana and the sandy banks of Yamuna, both Balaram and Krishna were filled with supreme joy.

Krishna was engaged in the sweetest of pastimes in Gokul, giving great joy to all the cowherd men and women, especially Yashoda and Nanda. Along with Balaram, Krishna would go out to play with friends daily while Yashoda and Rohini would call out to them to come eat food and derive immense joy from such maternal love. After some time, the elders decided to move from Gokul to Vrndavan which is a forest along Yamuna, to be away from the demons of Kamsa. Seeing the forests of Vrndavan and the nearby mountain Govardhan as well as the beautiful banks of Yamuna gave immense joy to Krishna and Balaram as these locations would witness the most wondrous pastimes in the coming years. Gradually, Krishna and Balaram grew up to be old enough to take the calves to pasture along with their friends. By now, a couple of demons found their way to Vrndavana. First came Vatsasura in the form of a calf and then Bakasura in the form of a huge crane bird. and were killed. Like moths coming to a flame, they were both easily disposed of by Krishna.

एवं सम्मोहयन् विष्णुं विमोहं विश्वमोहनम् ।
स्वयैव माययाजोऽपि स्वयमेव विमोहितः ॥ Bh 10.13.44

evaṁ sammohayan viṣṇuṁ vimohaṁ viśhvamohanam

svayaiva māyayājo'pi svayameva vimohitaḥ

Trying to delude the all-pervading Lord who enchants the whole universe, Brahma stood deluded himself.

Once Krishna went for a picnic with all the cowherd boys in the forests of Vrndavan. The boys had a good time with Krishna as their intimate friend. A demon named Aghasura came there to kill Krishna and took the form of a huge python with his mouth wide open that looked like the opening of a cave. The boys went inside to explore and fainted from his poison. Krishna noticed this and tore apart the mouth to kill the demon. A light from the demon's being came forth and merged into the transcendental body of Krishna, thereby liberating the demon to the great wonder of everyone. After Aghasura was liberated, Brahma wanted to test Krishna and stole the calves first and then the boys away and hid them in a cave. Krishna Himself expanded as all the boys and the calves and going back home, pleased all the respective parents with unbounded joy. When Brahma came back after a year had passed, he was given a vision of the Supreme Being Narayana having taken the form of boys and calves for a whole year, thus revealing that as everyone and everything, God alone is. Learning this most profound lesson while attempting to test the Divine, Brahma fell at the feet of Krishna to offer his prayers.

श्रेयःसृतिं भक्तिमुदस्य ते विभो क्लिशयन्ति ये केवलबोधलब्धये ।
तेषामसौ क्लेशल एव शिष्यते नान्यद् यथा स्थूलतुषावघातिनाम्
॥ Bh 10.14.4

shreyaḥsṛtiṁ bhaktimudasya te vibho kliśhyanti ye
kevalabodhalabdhaye
teshāmasau kleśhala eva śhiṣyate nānyad yathā
sthūlatuṣhāvaghātinām

For those who take pains to attain spiritual enlightenment that is devoid of loving devotion, the fountainhead of all blessings, such effort proves to be wasted exertion similar to pounding mere husk.

After being humbled, Brahma begins his prayers to Krishna by first expressing the inability of the mind to comprehend the essence of the Supreme Being who is of the nature of Truth, Consciousness and Bliss. Those who attempt to understand through the mind and the intellect, through study, through abstractions and speculations, always find it elusive and all their efforts lead nowhere. The only understanding that is necessary in the realm of spiritual wisdom is that it can never be understood by the mind. As succinctly declared by Ramana Maharshi, to know it is simply to be it. The Upanishads declare too: "Truth cannot be attained by the study of the Vedas, or by intelligence, or by much hearing of sacred books. It is attained by him alone whom It chooses and to such a one, It reveals Its own essence." (*nāyamātmā pravachanena labhyo na medhayā na bahunā śhrutena / yamevaiṣha vṛṇute tena labhyaḥ tasyaiṣha ātmā vivṛṇute tanūm svām*—Mundaka Upanishad 3.2.3). Thus, it is Grace that reveals the essence of Truth and that happens through surrender of the false "me." Such surrender is the essence of loving devotion which is the recognition that through all names and forms as apparent self and the others, God alone exists.

तथापि भूमन्महिमागुणस्य ते विबोद्धुमर्हत्यमलान्तरात्मभिः ।
अविक्रियात् स्वानुभवादरूपतो ह्यनन्यबोध्यात्मतया न चान्यथा ॥
Bh 10.14.6

tathāpi bhūmanmahimāguṇasya te
viboddhumarhatyamalāntarātmabhiḥ
avikriyāt svānubhavādarūpato hyananyabodhyātmatayā na
chānyathā

The glory of the Supreme Being devoid of all attributes can be realized by the pure hearted who have turned within, free of objectification, through direct perception by dissolving the mind into the mold of the Self, as the self-effulgent being.

This verse beautifully describes the very essence of God-realization, which is the same as Self-realization, as being free of subject-object relationship. The mind that is externalized is always identifying with various images, ideologies and concepts as the subject "me" and through the prism of this assumed subjectivity, processes the objective world of things, ideas and relationships. Then at some point, the mind realizes the impermanent and deeply dissatisfying nature of the ever-fleeting objective world of both the gross and the subtle, which causes the mind to seek that which is permanent and unchanging. Yet here too, the mind can instantly reify this eternal Truth that is God into an idea, an image, a concept based on acquired knowledge and projected experiences. Thus, the same subject-object relationship continues in a different garb, with the mind still identified as the "me" that wants to have the experience of God or Self-realization, which only proves elusive and frustrating. Therefore, the pointer here is to turn the mind within by freeing itself of every acquired false identity, however pious it may seem, and thereby empty and dissolve the mind totally in the Beingness which is the self-effulgent presence of God where there is no subject-object relationship anymore.

अज्ञानसंज्ञौ भवबन्धमोक्षौ द्वौ नाम नान्यौ स्त ऋतज्ञभावात् ।
अजस्रचित्यात्मनि केवले परे विचार्यमाणे तरणाविवाहनी ॥
Bh 10.14.26

ajñānasaṁjñau bhavabandhamokṣhau dvau nāma nānyau sta ṛtajñabhāvāt
ajasrachityātmani kevale pare vichāryamāṇe taraṇāvivāhanī

Bondage and liberation are both merely names given through ignorance. In relation to the absolute transcendent Self that is Truth and Consciousness, bondage and liberation have no existence, just as day and night have no existence from the perspective of the sun.

The feeling of bondage rises out of false separation as "me." The body, the senses and the intellect function with an innate intelligence that is coming forth from the source of all energy that is divine. Every cell in the body has its own intelligence with which it functions each moment. The various complex physiological processes of the bodily organs, the tremendous precision of sense perceptions, the faculties of the brain such as memory and logical ability are all functioning spontaneously without any separate identity as "me." And yet, due to ignorance, there is an assumption of a separate self which attaches to the body, the senses, the intellect and their activities as "mine." This illusion of me and mine creates a false separation from the one divine energy that is animating all of the universe. It is this sense of separation that feels limited and in bondage and therefore seeks liberation. Hence the feeling of bondage and the desire for liberation are only due to the false separation rising out of ignorance. From the perspective of the One divine energy which has as its substrate the very ground of Being as Pure Consciousness, there is no separation whatsoever, and nobody in bondage or seeking liberation. So, when one inquires as to whether there is actually a separate self or "me" by turning within, it is found to be non-existent. This is true surrender, to not take false ownership of the activities of the body and the mind but recognize that everything happens only by the Intelligence of the all-pervading one Supreme Being.

तावद् रागादयः स्तेनास्तावत् कारागृहं गृहम् ।
तावन्मोहोऽङ्घ्रिनिगडो यावत् कृष्ण न ते जनाः ॥ Bh 10.14.26

tāvad rāgādayaḥ stenāstāvat kārāgṛham gṛham
tāvanmoho'ṅghrinigaḍo yāvat kṛṣhṇa na te janāḥ

As long as one has not surrendered unto You, worldly desires act as thieves that rob the peace, the house is like a prison and attachments to people and things act as shackles.

The sense of bondage that is felt due to worldly desires, emotional attachments to people, home and things are all only due to the false sense of ego as "me" and "mine." Even if one attempts to escape from one's duties, relations or home, one would feel the same sense of bondage because the cause lies within, not without. It is ignorance and not outer circumstance that is the cause of bondage. Therefore, one can remain free inwardly wherever one is, by removing the ignorance with the light of wisdom in the recognition that the Divine alone expresses as everyone and everything, thus being empty of the "me." Just as a cup emptied of its contents reveals the fullness of space, the emptiness of "me" reveals the wholeness of the Divine here and now. Therefore, rather than complain about the outer situation of one's work, family, house etc. and relegating the spiritual journey to a future projected time when one will be supposedly free, it is important to inquire now and be free of the false ego wherever one is.

तस्मात् प्रियतमः स्वात्मा सर्वेषामपि देहिनाम् ।
तदर्थमेव सकलं जगदेतच्चराचरम् ॥ Bh 10.14.54

tasmāt priyatamaḥ svātmā sarveshāmapi dehinām
tadarthameva sakalaṁ jagadetachcharācharam

One's own Self is supremely dear to all embodied beings. The whole of creation made of the animate and the inanimate is loved for the sake of the Self alone.

While one may consider one's progeny, wealth etc. as dear to oneself, in reality they are all dear only because they are connected to oneself. It is the love for oneself that gets superimposed on one's children, house, position etc. This conception of oneself is the root I-thought associated with the body found in every embodied being. This I-thought is found to come up spontaneously in every living entity that acts as the impetus for survival and reproduction, nurturing one's offsprings etc. In human beings, this I-thought rises spontaneously for the same purpose but due to the faculty of thought, this self-consciousness gets superimposed onto not only children or possessions, but talents, ideologies, nationalities, religions etc., causing immense division, conflict and suffering. Human beings are caught in the I-thought that has taken on a monstrous proportion, robbing the peace from within. The way to transcend it is by turning the very faculty of thought toward its Source and recognizing that everything rises spontaneously from the one all-pervading Cosmic Intelligence. This frees one from the very root I-thought and empty of the false "me," one abides as the wholeness of Being, the true Self of all. From this wholeness of Being, arises all energy that is matter and manifests as all things, mobile and immobile, starting with one's body including the root I-thought. Therefore, one can directly perceive that what is truly dear to one as the Self is the very source of the I-thought which is the Ground of Being and the true essence of God. This is true Self-realization which is non-different from God-realization that nothing exists other than God (*bhagavadrūpam akhilaṁ nānyad vastviha kiñchana*—Bh 10.14.56).

अनुग्रहोऽयं भवतः कृतो हि नो दण्डोऽसतां ते खलु कल्मषापहः ।
यद् दन्दशूकत्वममुष्य देहिनः क्रोधोऽपि तेऽनुग्रह एव सम्मतः ॥
Bh 10.16.34

anugraho'yaṁ bhavataḥ kṛto hi no daṇḍo'satāṁ te khalu kalmaṣhāpahaḥ
yad dandaśhūkatvamamuṣhya dehinaḥ krodho'pi te'nugraha eva sammataḥ

Any punishment to the wicked wipes out their sins and as such, it is a boon conferred by You. Your wrath is regarded by us as only another form of Grace that has rid the serpent of all sins.

One day, when Krishna went with all the boys to Yamuna, the cows and the cowherd boys drank the waters of Yamuna that had been poisoned by a serpent called Kaliya who had taken abode in Yamuna. Krishna by His mystic powers revived the cows and the cowherds who had fallen and then entered Yamnua to rid the sacred river of the poisonous serpent. He proceeded to subdue the serpent by dancing on top of the hundred hoods of Kaliya, crushing them under the force of His feet. Whichever hood of the serpent His leg landed on, poison was forced out of it as the serpent vomited copious amounts of blood. Distressed to see the serpent sinking under the weight of Krishna, the wives of Kaliya approached Krishna with bowed heads and offered a prayer by first recognizing that Kaliya being punished in this way is a blessing to remove the pride of the serpent. This episode is very symbolic, as the hundred hoods of Kaliya represent the ten senses (five senses of perception and five of action) going out in ten directions (four cardinal, four ordinal, above and below) filled with the poison of the ego and the Lord dancing upon the hundred hoods represents a great suffering or calamity that strikes the outgoing impulse of sense gratification, removing the poisonous attachment of the ego. Thus, as the wives of Kaliya point out in this prayer, every punishment meted out by the Divine in the form of suffering is only Grace in disguise as it removes false attachments and turns one toward the Truth.

ज्ञानविज्ञाननिधये ब्रह्मणेऽनन्तशक्तये ।
अगुणायाविकाराय नमस्तेऽप्राकृताय च ॥ Bh 10.16.40

jñānavijñānanidhaye brahmaṇe'nantaśhaktaye
aguṇāyāvikārāya namaste'prākṛtāya cha

Obeisances to the treasure trove of pure wisdom and realization, the Absolute with infinite powers, transcending all qualities, unchanging and untouched by material nature.

The wives of serpent Kaliya continue their prayers to Krishna by offering Him obeisances as the Supreme Being, the substrate of all the elements, eternally existing as the cause of all causes, appearing as Time, the material and efficient cause of the Universe, the various elements and the corresponding senses that perceive them, the subtlest all-pervading essence and yet appearing with form to bring forth loving devotion. Upon the heartfelt prayers, Krishna lets go of the serpent as its poison is already removed and banishes him to the ocean. Thus, the waters of Yamuna were again rendered pure for everyone to bathe and use. The inner meaning of subduing but not killing the serpent Kaliya is that one need not shut off the senses completely, but only ought to regulate them to be free of the poison of the ego, so that they can fall into their natural harmonious functioning.

गिरयो वर्षधाराभिर्हन्यमाना न विव्यथु: ।
अभिभूयमाना व्यसनैर्यथाधोक्षजचेतसः ॥ Bh 10.20.15

girayo varshadhārābhirhanyamānā na vivyathuḥ
abhibhūyamānā Vyasanairyathādhokṣhajachetasaḥ

Even though struck with heavy downpour by rain-bearing clouds, the mountains do not feel the least bit agitated just as those who are absorbed in the Transcendental Being are not affected even if overwhelmed with calamities.

The monsoon season with thundering skies commenced in Vrndavan causing nature to flourish abundantly. Śhuka Brahmam describes this with great poetic beauty using similes that also bring forth Self-knowledge. The sky was covered with lightning, thunder and clouds, like wisdom is obscured by the qualities of sattva, rajas and tamas. Huge clouds poured down water to bring joy, akin to the compassionate ones who pour out wisdom to relieve suffering. Fireflies were shining while the clouds covered the moon and the stars, just as false gurus flourish when ignorance clouds people's judgment. Frogs started croaking in unison after being quiet all day, just like pupils chant Vedas in the evening after learning all day. Small streams overflowed unchecked, just as men with little knowledge upon suddenly finding riches run behind the senses with no regulation. All the land looked charming with fresh water, just as devotees who look charming with the radiance of the ever-fresh wisdom. Rivers were turbulent like an immature Yogi agitated upon contact with sense objects. Tracks were hidden with overgrown grass as the highest teaching gets obscured over time. Peacocks rejoiced in dance upon the advent of rain just as the distressed people would rejoice upon seeing a true devotee. In such opulent environs of Vrndavan, Krishna walked through the forests with his friends, took shelter in caves during heavy downpour, sat on green meadows surrounded by the cowherd boys and cows, and played His rapturous flute that brought delight to all beings.

वृन्दावनं सखि भुवो वितनोति कीर्तिं यद्
देवकीसुतपदाम्बुजलब्धलक्ष्मि ।
गोविन्दवेणुमनु मत्तमयूरनृत्यं प्रेक्ष्याद्रिसान्ववरतान्यसमस्तसत्त्वम्
॥ Bh 10.21.10

vṛndāvanaṁ sakhi bhuvo vitanoti kīrtiṁ yad
devakīsutapadāmbujalabdhalakṣhmi

govindaveṇumanu mattamayūranṛtyaṁ
prekṣhyādrisānvavaratānyasamastasattvam

Vrndavan enhances the glory of the Earth, being graced by the lotus feet of Krishna and hearing the music of the flute played by Him and seeing the peacocks dancing enraptured by the music, all creatures in the mountain Govardhana remain still.

Hearing the music of the flute (*venugānam*) of Krishna that kindled love in their heats, the Gopis of Vraja found themselves entranced and drawn to His exquisite form adorned with a crest of peacock feathers, wearing a garland of flowers and a golden silk cloth, with His graceful walk that left footprints in the soft sands of Vrndavan. The Gopis discussed among themselves the great fortune of everyone and everything associated with Krishna, starting with the flute that touched the lips of Krishna, the bamboo trees that the flute was made from, the river whose waters nourished those trees and all the animals and inhabitants of Vraja who get to listen to this enchanting music. They surmised that the cows, birds and all other beings that remained still while listening to the music like Yogis in trance must have been sages before. Even the clouds were doing the service of being an umbrella from the scorch of the sun and the glorious mountain of Govardhana was the foremost witness to this utmost captivating, divine music of Krishna.

कात्यायनि महामाये महायोगिन्यधीश्वरि ।
नन्दगोपसुतं देवि पतिं मे कुरु ते नमः॥ Bh 10.22.4

kātyāyani mahāmāye mahāyoginyadhīśvari
nandagopasutaṁ devi patiṁ me kuru te namaḥ

O Mother Katyayani! O Mahamaya—great deluding potency, possessed of infinite Yogic powers as the Supreme Ruler of the Universe, please make Krishna my consort. My obeisances unto You.

Being enchanted by the divine form, the nectarean music and the blissful pastimes of Krishna, the Gopis of Vraja were drawn to Him in the most intimate and sweetest mood of devotion (*mādhurya rasa*) to be their consort. So in the next winter season during the month of *Mārgashirsha* (December/ January), each one of them took a vow to go to Yamuna early in the morning, to take a dip in the cold waters and pray to the Divine Mother to have Krishna as her consort for an entire month. At the end of the month of rising early, bathing and singing the praises of Krishna, on the full moon day, Krishna Himself came to the banks of Yamuna to reward their sincere prayers. First, He tested them by taking away their clothes as the Gopis while they bathed and climbed a tree out of their reach and asked them to come out of the water to get their clothes. After great hesitation, they fully surrendered by letting go of all shame to appear before Krishna. Then, He told them to their great joy that their prayer to have Him as their consort would be granted in the next autumn season. This episode of taking away the clothes before bestowing Grace is symbolic of getting rid of all attachments and being stripped of the clothing of "me" worn by us, for the realization of the all-pervading Beloved. This sacred month-long observance of the Gopis was later emulated by Godha Devi also known as Andal in the famous *Tirupāvai* with the same mood of waking early every morning in the winter month of *Margashirsha* to bathe and offer prayers to Krishna with total self-surrender.

पश्यतैतान् महाभागान् परार्थैकान्तजीवितान् ।
वातवर्षातपहिमान् सहन्तो वारयन्ति नः ॥ Bh 10.22.32

*pashyataitān mahābhāgān parārthaikāntajīvitān
vātavarṣhātapahimān sahanto vārayanti naḥ*

Look at these highly blessed trees that live solely for others. By enduring storms, showers, sunshine and snow, they offer protection to us who seek shelter under them.

Accompanied by the cowherd boys, Krishna wandered in the forests playing His flute. Once when Krishna was sitting with the cowherd boys under the shade of a tree that shielded them from the scorching rays of the sun, He pointed out the selfless service that trees offer in all seasons, whether it be hot, cold, rainy or windy. They also offer themselves as fuel for fire after they are dead. Thus, they are a means of subsistence for all beings through their leaves, flowers, fruits, roots, shade, bark and wood. This is the essence of a perfect life for every human being to emulate and offer service to others constantly through one's body, mind, speech, wealth and one's very existence. There is also the beautiful symbolism of Krishna's flute that produces exquisite music. Just as the flute becomes an instrument for His divine music by being hollow and empty within, when we remain empty of the ego, free of its false sense of "me" and "mine," then the body and the mind become perfect instruments for the Divine energy to flow through.

नासां द्विजातिसंस्कारो न निवासो गुरावपि ।
न तपो नात्ममीमांसा न शौचं न क्रियाः शुभाः ॥
तथापि ह्युत्तमःश्लोके कृष्णे योगेश्वरेश्वरे ।
भक्तिर्दृढा न चास्माकं संस्कारादिमतामपि ॥ Bh 10.23.42-43

nāsāṁ dvijātisaṁskāro na nivāso gurāvapi
na tapo nātmamīmāṁsā na śhaucaṁ na kriyāḥ śhubhāḥ
tathāpi hyuttamaḥśhloke kṛṣhṇe yogeśhvareśhvare
bhaktirdṛḍhā na cāsmākaṁ saṁskārādimatāmapi

Without being endowed with any qualifications such as observing sacred rites, study of scriptures, austerities, inquiry, virtuous activities, etc., the wives of the priestly Brahmanas had unswerving devotion to Krishna of excellent renown who is the master of all Yogas. But the husbands lacked such devotion despite possessing all those qualifications.

Once while roaming the forests of Vrndavan, the cowherd boys got very hungry. So, Krishna asked them to go to a nearby sacrificial hall to ask for food from the priestly Brahmanas engaged in fruitive sacrifices. The Brahmanas ignored the request of the cowherd boys, being engaged in their rituals. The boys went back and reported this to Krishna. With a knowing smile, Krishna then asked the boys to go to the priestly Brahmanas' wives who were separately engaged in cooking food for the sacrifice. When the boys did so, the wives were elated to know that Krishna had asked for food. Knowing that the purpose of all Vedic sacrifices is only to recognize the Supreme Being who has appeared as Krishna, they were very glad to not only give all the food but also started to go themselves to give the food to Krishna. Upon seeing this, their husbands, fathers etc. who were engaged in the sacrifice tried to stop them, but they paid no heed abandoning their family connections seeking the presence of Krishna. Very pleased at their absolute loving devotion, Krishna bestowed His full Grace upon them and gave them leave to go back. By then, the priestly Brahmanas realized their folly and had now awakened to true wisdom of realizing Krishna as the Supreme Beloved. They rued their ignorance despite all their scriptural knowledge and ritualistic activities, while their wives without any such knowledge had their hearts filled with divine love. So the Brahmanas glorified Krishna for executing this wonderful pastime of asking for food and teaching them the valuable lesson of opening their hearts while also revealing the greatness of their wives.

गोवर्धने धृते शैले आसाराद् रक्षिते व्रजे ।
गोलोकादाव्रजत्कृष्णं सुरभिः शक्र एव च ॥ Bh 10.27.1

govardhane dhṛte śhaile āsārād rakṣhite vraje
golokādāvrajatkṛṣhṇaṁ surabhiḥ śhakra eva cha

When Govardhana Mountain was lifted and held up by Krishna and Vraja was protected from torrential rain, Indra along with the celestial cow Surabhi of Goloka sought Krishna to offer prayers.

Once Krishna saw all the cowherd men headed by Father Nanda preparing for a major sacrifice ritual to worship Indra, the god of rain. Krishna told them that there was no need to worship any such partial deity as every created entity functions according to their nature and does their duty as ordained. He logically pointed out that since the duties of the cowherds were supported by cows and Govardhana Mountain, they could instead just worship them rather than any demigod. Accordingly, the whole of Vrndavan celebrated the cows and performed Govardhana Puja which was all arranged to curb Indra's pride. Predictably Indra got angry as his worship was stopped, and he sent down a torrential downpour to flood Vraja to show his power. When sought as refuge, Krishna effortlessly lifted Govardhana and gave shelter to all the residents of Vrndavan and cows for a whole week. Indra with his pride curbed, approached Krishna to offer his apology and prayers by recognizing the falsity of his sense of doership and that indeed everything happens only as ordained by the Supreme Being.

न खलु गोपीकानन्दनो भवान् अखिलदेहिनामन्तरात्मदृक् ।
विखनसार्थितो विश्वगुप्तये सख उदेयिवान् सात्वतां कुले ॥
Bh 10.31.4

na khalu gopīkānandano bhavān akhiladehināmantarātmadṛk
vikhanasārthito viśhvaguptaye sakha udeyivān sātvatāṁ kule

You are not a mere son of a cowherd woman. Being the seer of the inner sense of the mind of all embodied beings, You appeared in the clan of the Yadus for the protection of the universe.

On a beautiful autumn full moon night (Sharad Purnima), Krishna played His enchanting flute that kindled divine love and drew all the Gopis to the forest from their homes, leaving whatever they were doing. Krishna first teased them by asking them to go back to their homes which only heightened the intensity of longing for the Gopis to be with

Krishna that they expressed in a heartfelt prayer. Then as He obliged each of them by embracing them to begin the most intimate and mysterious Rāsa Lila, the Gopis momentarily got proud of their special association with Krishna. Sending this He instantly disappeared from their midst as the Gopis searched for Him in the forest. They traced the footprints of Krishna in the forest lit brightly by the soothing rays of the moon for some distance, but the footprints disappeared into the thick woods leaving the Gopis distraught. Then the Gopis, dearly missing their most Beloved Krishna, assembled on the riverbank of Yamuna together and poured their hearts out in the most sublime song of exquisite Sanskrit poetry called the Gopi Gitam, which contains this beautiful verse.

रासोत्सवः सम्प्रवृत्तो गोपीमण्डलमण्डितः ।
योगेश्वरेण कृष्णेन तासां मध्ये द्वयोर्द्वयोः ॥ Bh 10.33.4

rāsotsavaḥ sampravṛtto gopīmaṇḍalamaṇḍitaḥ
yogeśhvareṇa kṛṣṇhena tāsāṁ madhye dvayordvayoḥ

Then commenced the festive dance of Rāsa Lila with a circle of the Gopis and Krishna, the Master of Yogas, appearing in many identical forms between every two Gopis.

After the outpouring of the Gopi Gitam where the intense longing was expressed by the Gopis so beautifully, Krishna re-appeared in their midst and enraptured them all with His smiling lotus-like countenance. Their bliss knew no bounds as they surrounded Him and embraced Him with love on the moonlit banks of Yamuna. They shed their agony of separation upon His re-appearance. After comforting them with His charming words, Krishna started the most blessed dance of Rasa Lila with the Gopis. This is the pinnacle of the most intimate form of devotion described by Shuka Brahmam in a very heart melting way to bestow Grace and engender devotion in the hearts of all beings for all of posterity. Also, the episode of the Gopis feeling pride upon embracing Krishna, only to see Him vanish instantly, and yearning with great longing to get His vision again is highly symbolic. One who has a glimpse of the Infinite in total stillness in meditation may then feel proud due to ego coming back to claim it as its experience, only to find that the glimpse doesn't come back. Only after intense yearning that removes the false ego, the stillness of the Infinite again reveals Itself.

एवं ब्रुवाणा विरहातुरा भृशं व्रजस्त्रियः कृष्णविषक्तमानसाः ।
विसृज्य लज्जां रुरुदुः स्म सुस्वरं गोविन्द दामोदर माधवेति ॥
Bh 10.39.31

evaṁ bruvāṇā virahāturā bhṛśhaṁ vrajastriyaḥ
kṛṣhṇaviṣhaktamānasāḥ
visṛjya lajjāṁ ruruduḥ sma susvaraṁ govinda dāmodara
mādhaveti

The women of Vraja, sorely afflicted at the thought of separation from Krishna, cried loudly while casting away all bashfulness, "O Govinda, O Damodara, O Madhava!"

Every day as Krishna took the cows to graze on the Govardhan mountain, the Gopis missed Him dearly and awaited His return every evening. They sang the most exquisite poetry in the mood of separation, in pairs of verses called Yugala Gitam, increasing their love for Krishna every day. As time passed this way, Narada went to Kamsa to reveal the exact whereabouts of Krishna as he foresaw the end of Kamsa was near. Enraged to hear this, Kamsa sent Akrura to Vrndavan to bring Krishna and Balaram to Mathura, foolishly thinking that he could kill Them without realizing that he is inviting his own death. Akrura left for Vrndavan in intense devotion, filled with immense gratitude for the causeless mercy of being able to have the unique blessing of beholding Krishna. He envisioned the most blessed scene with tears rolling as he proceeded to Vrndavan. Upon reaching, he rolled in the sands of Vrndavan in ecstasy on seeing the footprints of Krishna. As he reached the courtyard of Nanda by sunset, he was blessed by a vision of Krishna and Balaram which was beyond anything he had imagined. At Nanda's home, he was extended supreme hospitality by Krishna Himself along with Balaram in the most loving way. Akrura conveyed the message of Kamsa to bring Krishna and Balaram to Mathura. They both smiled knowingly that this was Kamsa inviting his own death. Nanda made plans for all the cowherd men to accompany Krishna and Balaram with Akrura to Mathura. Upon hearing this, the Gopis were crestfallen. They cried all night in separation and poured their hearts out in the most moving way, unable to bear the coming departure of Krishna in the morning. This heart-rending cry of "Govinda, Damodara, Madhava" by the Gopis still resonates as the refrain in many beautiful devotional songs of Krishna.

स नित्यदोद्विग्नधिया तमीश्वरंपिबन्नदन्वा विचरन् स्वपन् श्वसन् ।
ददर्श चक्रायुधमग्रतो यत-स्तदेव रूपं दुरवापमाप ॥ Bh 10.44.39

sa nityadodvignadhiyā tamīśhvarampibannadanvā vicaran svapan śhvasan

*dadarśha chakrāyudhamagrato yatastadeva rūpaṁ
duravāpamāpa*

With a mind full of fear, Kamsa visualized the Lord with every breath; while drinking, speaking, walking or lying down, he was bestowed liberation upon being slain by Krishna.

Akrura took Krishna and Balaram to Mathura and en route, as he stopped to offer prayers by the banks of Yamuna, Akrura was blessed inside the waters of Yamuna with the most ecstatic vision of Krishna and Balaram appearing as Narayana and His thousand headed snake Adi Sesha. Upon reaching Mathura, Krishna and Balaram entered the city majestically with all the residents flocking to get their divine vision. As they wandered, Krishna readily bestowed grace upon a humble weaver and a florist as they offered what they had in service of Krishna with devotion. They then met a hunchback woman who too humbly offered exquisite sandal pastes to Krishna and was straightened into a beautiful lady. Krishna soon afterwards, entered the amphitheater with Balaram where a wrestling bout was scheduled the next day and broke the huge bow kept there for display. The sound of the crash reached the ears of Kamsa in the palace who felt great fear in his heart. The next day, Kamsa took his seat in the wrestling arena. Krishna came with Balaram to the amphitheater and saw a massive elephant Kuvalayapida at the gate, being instigated to attack Krishna. Effortlessly killing the charging elephant, Krishna entered the wrestling arena along with Balaram, causing everyone in the galleries to be completely captivated and discuss among themselves the glory of Krishna. Krishna and Balaram then wrestled Chanura and Mushtika respectively and killed them to the delight of all the spectators. Kamsa got enraged and ordered that Nanda be arrested and Vasudeva be killed. Instantly Krishna jumped onto the royal dais, dragged Kamsa down and killed him with a mighty blow to the great joy of the entire kingdom. Because of his constant contemplation on Krishna due to fear till the very moment of death, Kamsa was liberated upon being slain, what to speak then of those who contemplate upon Him with love.

दृष्टं श्रुतं भूतभवद् भविष्यत्स्थास्नुश्चरिष्णुर्महदल्पकं च ।
विनाच्युताद् वस्तु तरां न वाच्यं स एव सर्वं परमात्मभूतः ॥
Bh 10.46.43

drshtam shrutam bhūtabhavad
bhavishyatsthāsnushcharishnurmahadalpakam cha
vināchyutād vastu tarām na vāchyam sa eva sarvam
paramātmabhūtaḥ

Nothing that is seen or heard, that is past, present or future, that is immobile or mobile, that is huge or tiny, can be said to be separate from the Infinite Lord, who alone is everything and the only Truth.

After liberating Mathura, Krishna first honored His parents Vasudeva and Devaki and then installed Ugrasena as the king of Mathura and brought the entire Yadu clan back to Mathura. He requested Nanda to head back to Vrndavan, while expressing His profound love for Nanda, Yashoda and all the cowherd men and women. Thereafter, Krishna and Balaram went to the Gurukul of Sandipani to learn all the arts and sciences. Sometime later, Krishna sent His dear friend Uddhava to Vrndavan with His message to the beloved parents and Gopis. Uddhava first met Nanda and Yashoda, who gave him a warm welcome and inquired fondly about Krishna. Uddhava replied by first glorifying their unconditional love for Krishna and explained to them the true essence of Krishna as not just their beloved son but the Supreme Being and the teacher of all, who sees everyone as the same. He described Krishna as the material and efficient cause of the universe, who also abides in the hearts of all as life-giving energy while taking on this human semblance as their beloved son. In this way, he removed their grief of separation from Krishna by assuring them that indeed nothing exists apart from Him and therefore they can never be away from Krishna who pervades all of time and space, everyone and everything, being the only Truth that there is.

सर्वात्मभावोऽधिकृतो भवतीनामधोक्षजे ।
विरहेण महाभागा महान्मेऽनुग्रहः कृतः ॥ Bh 10.47.27

sarvātmabhāvo'dhikṛto bhavatīnāmadhokṣhaje
virahena mahābhāgā mahānme'nugrahaḥ kṛtaḥ

The Gopis had developed whole-hearted love for the Transcendental Being, due to the intense feeling of separation. And by witnessing such unparalleled love, Uddhava felt bestowed with Grace.

After his night-long discussions with Nanda, Uddhava went to Yamuna the next morning for his ablutions and met the Gopis by the river. After ascertaining that Uddhava was sent by Krishna, they poured their hearts out in the agony of separation from Krishna. The principal Gopi, Radha, in a poetic lament expressed her sorrow over Krishna's absence as an ode to a black bee flying among the flowers on the riverbank. While acknowledging His inescapable allure, Radha contrasted with the Gopis' intense single pointed devotion to Krishna and His seeming abandonment just as the bee leaves the flower after drinking honey for a while. In this way, Radha and the Gopis revealed their unwavering love of Krishna despite the distance and wondered whether He remembered them. Uddhava was moved by the Gopis' selfless devotion and praised their intense love, which transcended all ordinary relationships and norms. Uddhava then relayed Krishna's message that He is always with them, emphasizing both His omnipresence and the eternal nature of their connection, and also that the separation of the Gopis was meant only to intensify their longing, taking them to the summit of unconditional love. Uddhava glorified the Gopis for such exclusive devotion, which surpasses not only the saints and sages, but even the divine consort Lakshmi. Deeply moved, Uddhava expressed his yearning to be born as a creeper in Vraja that would be graced to receive the dust of the Gopis' feet. He spent a long time thus basking in the divine love of the Gopis in Vrndavan and finally returned to Mathura with a full heart and renewed devotion to Krishna.

तस्मादि्सृज्याशिष ईश सर्वतो रजस्तम:सत्त्वगुणानुबन्धना: ।
निरञ्जनं निर्गुणमद्वयं परं त्वां ज्ञाप्तिमात्रं पुरुषं व्रजाम्यहम् ॥
Bh 10.51.57

tasmādvisṛjyāśhiṣha īśha sarvato
rajastamaḥsattvaguṇānubandhanāḥ
nirañjanaṁ nirguṇamadvayaṁ paraṁ tvāṁ jñāptimātraṁ
puruṣhaṁ vrajāmyaham

Rejecting all blessings that are in the field of the relative and associated with the qualities of Sattva, Rajas and Tamas, I take refuge only in the Supreme Being of the nature of pure consciousness, free from the taint of Maya, beyond all qualities and one without a second.

Jarasandha, the father-in-law of Kamsa, came with a huge army to besiege Mathura to exact revenge for Kamsa's death. Krishna along with Balaram effortlessly killed the entire army but spared Jarasandha. He came back seventeen times with a huge army and each time, they killed the army but spared him. Then another evil king called Kālayāvana came to attack Mathura at the same time that Jarasandha was about to attack the eighteenth time. Krishna decided it was time to move and establish the city of Dwaraka in the west coast of Bharat and transferred the entire population of Mathura to Dwaraka by His Yogamaya. Krishna then came out of Mathura unarmed in front of Kālayāvana and mysteriously started running which caused Kalayavana to chase Krishna into a cave. There, Kālayāvana got burned to ashes by Muchukunda who was given a boon to sleep undisturbed for helping the *devas* in a battle a long time ago. Muchukunda then offered beautiful prayers to Krishna, reflecting on how humans are deluded by Maya, identify with the body and chase temporary pleasures including all worldly and even heavenly desires that are impermanent and pointless. He expressed that the highest blessing is *satsang* (association with saints) that helps one recognize and take refuge in the essence of Being as eternal. Krishna, pleased with his purity and renunciation, bestowed Grace upon Muchukunda.

भगवान् भीष्मकसुतां रुक्मिणीं रुचिराननाम् ।
राक्षसेन विधानेन उपयेम इति श्रुतम् ॥ Bh 10.52.18

bhagavān bhīṣmakasutaṁ rukmiṇīṁ rucirānanām
rākṣasena vidhānena upayema iti śrutam

Lord Krishna married Rukmini, the one with a lovely countenance and the daughter of Bhishmaka, by taking her away from rival suitors by force.

Rukmini, an expansion of Lakshmi, longed to marry Krishna based on just hearing His glories. But Rukmini's five brothers wanted to get her married to Shishupala, who hated Krishna. So, Rukmini sent Krishna an endearing letter through a sagely being, expressing her yearning heart with a specific plan for Krishna to carry her away. Krishna accordingly mounted a chariot to go to Vidarbha to claim Rukmini as He too longed to marry her. Meanwhile, her father had made elaborate arrangements for the grand wedding with Sishupala, and Rukmini hoped that Krishna had received her letter. Krishna right on time reached Vidarbha and first sent a message to Rukmini that He would certainly marry her, to allay her fears. Then on the morning of the wedding, as per the plan given by Rukmini, as she came out of the temple of Mother Parvati after offering prayers of gratitude, Krishna came in His chariot and carried Rukmini away in an instant as all the kings and armies of the bridegroom family and friends watched. Soon the armies of the enemy king pursued a chase behind Krishna's chariot but were decimated by the mighty army of Balaram who came to assist Krishna. Rukmini's eldest brother Rukmi alone pursued Krishna and Rukmini and engaged in a duel with Krishna. He was about to be killed but was spared by Krishna upon Rukmini's intervention. Balaram then gave Rukmini instructions to be free of attachment by teaching her Self-knowledge. After reaching Dwaraka, the grand wedding of Krishna with Rukmini took place to the delight of all. This entire episode apart from being very dramatic and absorbing is also steeped in symbolism. Rukmini represents the apparent individual trapped by the five senses, her five brothers. These senses want to bind the "me" to worldly life, represented by their preferred bridegroom Shishupala (taking care of children). Rukmini's exclusive devotion to Krishna signifies total surrender to the Supreme Being, rejecting sensory attachments. Krishna taking her to Dwaraka by defeating everyone represents Grace that comes forth to liberate by removing illusion.

तं विलोक्याच्युतो दूरात् प्रियापर्यङ्कमास्थितः ।
सहसोत्थाय चाभ्येत्य दोर्भ्यां पर्यग्रहीन्मुदा ॥ Bh 10.80.18

tam vilokyāchyuto dūrāt priyāparyankamāsthitaḥ
sahasotthāya chābhyetya dorbhyām paryagrahīnmudā

Krishna, who was seated on the couch with His consort Rukmini, upon seeing His old friend Sudama from a distance, suddenly rose from His seat and advanced towards Sudama to joyously hug him.

There was a dear friend of Krishna from His days with Guru Sandipani called Sudama, a Brahmana abiding in the wisdom of the Infinite Brahman and free of all attachments. Living in abject poverty and always dressed in tattered clothes, he was also known as Kuchela. He was asked by his wife to approach his childhood friend Krishna now ruling Dwaraka with all opulence to relieve their suffering. Though Sudama was not inclined to ask anything from Krishna, he accepted her proposal only to get the *darshan* of Krishna and set off for Dwaraka, taking a humble gift of beaten rice. Upon reaching Dwaraka, he was welcomed by Krishna with great love and honor, much to the surprise of everyone in the palace including His consort Rukmini. Krishna seated him in His own couch and gave him the highest respect, served him and started reminiscing about their days at Gurukul, much to the joy of Sudama. Then Krishna asked Sudama playfully as to what he got for Him and despite his reluctance to reveal the modest gift he had got, Krishna took the beaten rice and ate it joyfully. Sudama soon after left with a contented heart without ever asking anything of Krishna. But when he returned home, he couldn't recognize his own house which had now transformed into an opulent palace with unimaginable wealth by Krishna's grace. Upon beholding the drastically changed circumstance just due to contact with his beloved friend, Sudama accepted the wealth too with the same equanimity as the prior poverty. He remained humble and devoted, never attached to his newfound wealth and ever with the realization that true wealth lies in loving devotion to the Infinite Being.

यस्याहमनुगृह्णामि हरिष्ये तद्धनं शनै: ।
ततोऽधनं त्यजन्त्यस्य स्वजना दुःखदुःखितम् ॥
स यदा वितथोद्योगो निर्विण्ण: स्याद् धनेहया ।
मत्परै: कृतमैत्रस्य करिष्ये मदनुग्रहम् ॥ Bh 10.88.8-9

yasyāham anugrhṇāmi hariṣhye taddhanaṁ śhanaiḥ
tato'dhanaṁ tyajantyasya svajanā duḥkhaduḥkhitam
sa yadā vitathodyogo nirviṇṇaḥ syād dhanehayā
matparaiḥ krtamaitrasya kariṣhye madanugraham

Upon whom I bestow my grace; I gradually deprive him of all his wealth. Then the relatives and friends of such a poverty-stricken man abandon him. In this way he suffers one distress after another. And when he becomes completely frustrated in his attempts to acquire wealth, he seeks only to associate with My transcendent being and I bestow My complete grace upon him.

While grace normally is construed as associated with what is deemed to be positive outcomes or pleasant situations in life, this beautiful verse reveals that the most profound manifestation of grace comes through the most challenging situations in life. When one faces acute setbacks in life whether it be in finances, profession, relationships or health, it acts as the most powerful catalyst to be freed of the unconscious attachment to the "me" in all those spheres of life. All the discourses on the impermanence of phenomena and therefore the need for detachment hardly has any impact until one is actually face to face with the reality of impermanence. Thus, Krishna here explains that when grace is bestowed, it is done so not by giving but taking away. When one is stripped of possessions of any kind, it is revealed as to who among one's family or friends truly loves unconditionally as opposed to loving wealth, status or other external factors. In moments of utter desperation, if one is fortunate to come in contact with the highest pointer of our true nature and association with beings abiding in Truth, then one can turn around one's entire life instantaneously to being free of any identification with egoic attachments of any kind and live in the freedom of total aliveness and unconditional love. Thus, when we face any hardship, instead of complaining or wallowing in self-pity or victim mentality, one can see it as the highest form of

grace that opens a portal to the most precious treasure trove
of divine love.

ELEVENTH CANTO
Final Teachings

कायेन वाचा मनसेन्द्रियैर्वा बुद्ध्यात्मना वानुसृतस्वभावात् ।
करोति यद् यत् सकलं परस्मै नारायणायेति समर्पयेत्तत् ॥
Bh 11.2.36

kāyena vāchā manasendriyairvā buddhyātmanā
vānusṛtasvabhāvāt
karoti yad yat sakalaṁ parasmai nārāyaṇāyeti samarpayettat

Whatever one does with the body, speech, mind, senses, intellect or anything else of one's nature, let it all be offered to the Supreme Being.

An account of the great Avatar of Rshabha who embodied renunciation and his many pious sons including Bharata who later became Jadabharata was given earlier in the fifth canto. Among the sons of Rshabha were also nine great sages whose teachings are now given in the beginning of the eleventh canto. First among them is Kavi who shows the way of true happiness through freedom from doership in this famous verse which also is found with slight modification in the Vishnu Sahasranamam and in Krishna's teaching in the Bhagavad Gita: "Whatever you do, eat, sacrifice, gift or perform as austerity, do everything as an offering unto

Me." (*yatkaroṣhi yadaśhnāsi yajjuhoṣhi dadāsi yat / yattapasyasi kaunteya tatkuruṣhva madarpaṇam*—BG 9.27). Whatever is done by the various faculties of the body happens through the divine intelligence that pervades the whole body. Every cell, every organ, every system of the body functions harmoniously to produce action—whether it be thought, speech or movement. But the false sense of ownership of the action as mine results in attachment, pride, guilt etc. and results in suffering. So, if one simply remains aware of this sense of doership rising and sees the corruption it brings, then the very awareness dissolves the sense of doership and all actions are surrendered to the Source from which they emanate. Doing so ensures one does not fall prey to the false notion of self as the body which is the trap of Maya and instead remains in discernment and loving devotion to the all-pervading Supreme, that removes the dream of duality and bestows fearlessness.

सर्वभूतेषु यः पश्येद् भगवद्भावमात्मनः ।
भूतानि भगवत्यात्मन्येष भागवतोत्तमः ॥ Bh 11.2.45

sarvabhūteṣhu yaḥ paśhyed bhagavadbhāvamātmanaḥ
bhūtāni bhagavatyātmanyeṣha bhāgavatottamaḥ

One who is the foremost among devotees sees the one Supreme Being as the true Self within all living entities and all the living entities as abiding within the one Supreme Being.

The next among the nine sages, known as Hari, declares that the highest devotee (*Bhagavatottama*) is one who sees the Supreme Being in all creatures and all creatures in Him. Just as all the five elements are within the body and the body itself is contained within the planet made of the five elements, the indwelling and the all-pervading essence within and around all living entities is the Divine. Thus, seeing everyone, everything, everywhere as Divine is the sign of highest devotion. Whereas the second level of devotion is to treat devotees with friendliness, the ignorant with compassion and enemies with indifference, thus still perceiving distinction between beings. And the third level is to see the Divine only in images or temples but not in others. The highest devotee is never overwhelmed by the dualities of life such as desire and fear, birth and death, richness and poverty etc. Just as eating food satisfies the taste, removes hunger and nourishes the body all at the same time, the one who sees the Supreme Being alone everywhere is filled with devotion, wisdom and detachment all at the same time. Thus, he is freed of all cravings, never identifying with the body or grades in society, race, or stage of life. He makes no distinction between others, seeing everyone with an equal eye and is always serene. His presence cools the passions and fears of others, much like the moon cools the earth and he abides in the Divine at all times with unwavering devotion.

इति भागवतान् धर्मान् शिक्षन् भक्त्या तदुत्थया ।
नारायणपरो मायामञ्जस्तरति दुस्तराम् ॥ Bh 11.3.33

iti bhāgavatān dharmān śhikṣhan bhaktyā tadutthayā
nārāyaṇaparo māyāmañjastarati dustarām

By understanding and living as per the Bhagavata Dharma, the pure devotee easily crosses the unfathomable Maya.

The next two sages, Antariksha and Prabuddha, describe the nature of Maya and the way to overcome it. Maya is the energy that not only brings forth the entire manifest creation of the animate and the inanimate through the various elements of nature but also creates the false sense of egoic identification in humans that causes desire and fear. The way to overcome the suffering caused due to the ego is through discernment that any attempt to gain happiness in the outer realm only leads to impermanent and ultimately contrary results. One then approaches a wise preceptor to get a direct pointer on the nature of the true all-pervading, unitary Self of all. This will enable one to get detached from frivolous pursuits, gain the association of devotees in Satsang, have love and compassion toward all beings, be established in purity, endurance, sincerity, regulation of the senses and speech, be content, and free of the sense of "me" and "mine." Living such a life of clarity and love is the essence of Bhagavata Dharma that makes one easily free of the shackles of Maya.

नैतन्मनो विशति वागुत चक्षुरात्मा प्राणेन्द्रियाणि च यथानलमर्चिषः स्वाः ।
शब्दोऽपि बोधकनिषेधधतयात्ममूलमर्थोक्तमाह यदृते न निषेधसिद्धिः ॥ Bh 11.3.36

naitanmano viśhati vāguta cakṣhurātmā prāṇendriyāṇi cha
yathānalamarchiṣhaḥ svāḥ
śhabdo'pi bodhakaniṣedhatayātmamūlamarthoktamāha yadṛte na
niṣhedhasiddhiḥ

Just as sparks cannot illuminate the fire from which they come forth, the mind, speech, intellect, life energy and the senses cannot grasp the Source from which they

**come. The revealed word of Vedas too makes no positive
assertion about this very Source from which they come
forth. However, no negative description would be
possible if there were no ultimate Reality.**

The next sage, Pippalayana, describes the very essence of the
Supreme Reality as the causeless primordial cause of creation,
sustenance and dissolution of the universe that brings forth
all sentient beings. It alone animates the functioning of the
body, mind, senses and intellect which are only like tiny
sparks coming from a huge fire. Any attempt through the
mind or the intellect to understand or experience God is as
futile as sparks trying to illuminate the fire. That's why the
Vedas do not describe the Source in any positive terms but
only through negation such as Unborn, Infinite, Unchanging.
However, these very negative descriptions clearly indicate
that the limitations of the born, finite and changing are not
present in the ultimate Reality which is the only eternal
refuge as beautifully captured by the Buddha: "If there were
not the Unborn, Unformed, Unmanifested, there would be no
escape from the world of the born, formed, manifested." This
Absolute Truth is beyond birth and death, growth and decay,
unaffected, omnipresent and pervading all states of existence
and one with a pure heart that is totally purged of the false
notion of me sees it as clearly as daylight.

परोक्षवादो वेदोऽयं बालानामनुशासनम् ।
कर्ममोक्षाय कर्माणि विधत्ते ह्यगदं यथा ॥ Bh 11.3.44

*parokṣhavādo vedo'yaṁ bālānāmanuśhāsanam
karmamokṣhāya karmāṇi vidhatte hyagadaṁ yathā*

The Vedas have a deeper import than what the words apparently convey. Their real purpose is to bestow freedom from doership of actions, but they entice the ignorant with attaining heavenly realms through actions, just as a child is given sweets before swallowing a medicine.

The next sage, Avirhotra, describes the true purpose of Vedas that have three portions broadly speaking—karma kanda, upasana kanda and jnana kanda. The karma kanda portions are about fruitive rituals, the upasana kanda is a collection of samhitas (prayers) and the jnana kanda also called as Vedanta is the direct teaching of Self-knowledge. While the prayers of upasana kanda is considered as good discipline for bringing purity that leads to awakening of Self-knowledge, the rituals of karma kanda can cause one to be trapped in a false sense of doership and cause/effect determinism, and a desire for various pleasures, both earthly and heavenly. Krishna too warns in the Gita against getting caught in the words of the Vedas that put forth such temptations: "Those who are drawn to the flowery words of Vedas that speak of rites and rituals are caught in desire of heavenly pleasures for enjoyment and opulence. Enslaved by such rites, they have no chance of a resolute mind. Transcend the portion of Vedas that speak of the three gunas and rise above all dualities" (BG 2.42–45). Therefore, the key import of Vedas is to transcend the letter and realize the spirit which is to awaken to the realization that the Divine alone exists here and now.

यो वा अनन्तस्य गुणाननन्ताननुक्रमिष्यन् स तु बालबुद्धिः ।
रजांसि भूमेर्गणयेत् कथञ्चित् कालेन नैवाखिलशक्तिधाम्नः ॥
Bh 11.4.2

yo vā anantasya guṇān anantānanukramiṣhyan sa tu bālabuddhiḥ
rajāṁsi bhūmergaṇayet kathañchit kālena
naivākhilaśhaktidhāmnaḥ

One who seeks to enumerate the infinite qualities of the Infinite Lord is indeed of puerile understanding. One may even possibly count the particles of dust on earth, but not the excellences of the omnipotent Supreme Being.

The next sage, Drumila, upon being asked about the various Avatars of the Supreme Being, states that indeed it is impossible to enumerate them as they are uncountable (*avatārā hyasaṅkhyeyā hareḥ*—Bh 1.3.26). First describing that the entire Universe made of the five elements constitutes His body and therefore the whole of creation can be said to be His Avatar, then Drumila describes some of the Avatars of the Supreme Being such as the sages Narayana and Nara, Dattatreya, Rshabha, Hayagriva and followed by the well-known principal ten Avatars known as Dashavatar. The next sage Chamasa reiterates that the true purpose of the Vedas is to realize the all-pervading Supreme Lord within all beings. Scholarly study bereft of this realization only leads to pride, delusion, and indulgence in base desires. Rituals and scriptural learning become futile if they don't awaken humility, detachment, and recognition of the divine in all. Finally, the last sage Karabhajana describes that in the four yugas namely Satya, Treta, Dwapara and Kali, the Lord is worshiped through meditation, sacrifice, deity worship, and chanting of His names, the last being the sweetest way of simply taking the holy names with motiveless love that bestows realization of the highest wisdom.

शुद्धिर्नृणां न तु तथेड्य दुराशयानां विद्याश्रुताध्ययनदानतपःक्रि याभिः ।
सत्त्वात्मनामृषभ ते यशसि प्रवृद्धसच्छ्रद्धया श्रवणसम्भृतया यथा स्यात् ॥ Bh 11.6.9

*shuddhirnṛṇāṁ na tu tathedya durāshayānāṁ vidyāshrutādhyaya
nadānatapaḥkriyābhiḥ
sattvātmanām ṛṣhabha te yashasi pravṛddhasachchhraddhayā
shravaṇasambhṛtayā yathā syāt*

More than reading scriptures or engaging in rituals, charity and austerities, the efficacious way for purification of mind and realizing You is by constantly hearing Your glory and contemplating on You alone which removes all the cravings.

As Krishna's earthly Avatar neared its end, Brahma and other Devas descended to offer their prayers to Krishna, recognizing that the purpose of His Avatar to relieve Earth's burden and re-establish righteousness had been fulfilled. They glorified Krishna as the eternal, blissful Supreme Being, untouched by the three gunas, beyond creation and destruction, the source of time, the five elements, and all intelligence. Praising the simple contemplation of His pastimes being more powerful than all the rituals and scholarly study of scriptures, they proclaimed that His long earthly stay of 125 years had accomplished its purpose. Krishna affirmed in response and added that one final act remained—the destruction of the Yadava clan that had grown arrogant. He recounted the curse of the sages, who were insulted by the prank of an arrogant Yadava, which would result in an iron pestle becoming the cause for ruin. And despite attempts to destroy the pestle, its fragments would return as instruments of the Yadavas' downfall and only after that, Krishna would depart Earth. Krishna then gathered the Yadavas, warning them of grave omens, and instructed them to go to the sacred land of Prabhasa for purificatory rituals. As preparations began, Krishna's devoted friend Uddhava alone realized the deeper significance of the events unfolding, he approached Krishna for His final instruction, and thus began the divine discourse known as the Uddhava Gita.

नाहं तवाङ्घ्रिकमलं क्षणार्धमपि केशव ।
त्यक्तुं समुत्सहे नाथ स्वधाम नय मामपि ।। Bh 11.6.43

nāhaṁ tavāṅghrikamalaṁ kshaṇārdhamapi keśhava
tyaktuṁ samutsahe nātha svadhāma naya māmapi

I cannot bear separation from You even for half a second, Oh Keshava. Therefore, kindly take me as well with You to Your abode.

Uddhava, with a heart full of devotion and reverence, approached Krishna, the Master of Yoga and first noted that Krishna, though fully capable, had chosen not to revoke the curse of the sages, instead letting the events unfold as ordained and would soon leave the Earth after the destruction of the Yadavas. Unable to bear the impending separation, Uddhava pleaded with deep yearning to not be left behind. He recalled the countless moments they had shared—sitting, walking, eating—as every part of his life had been infused with Krishna's presence. He recounted that the garlands he wore, the sandal paste he used, and the food he ate were all sanctified by Krishna's touch. So, he appealed as to how he could live without Krishna, when even those who had merely heard His stories remained forever drawn to Him. His only desire was to love Krishna, to remember His smile and glances, and to speak of His divine deeds. Hearing this heartfelt outpouring of Uddhava, Krishna was very pleased and imparted His final and most intimate teachings of the Uddhava Gita.

दोषबुद्ध्योभयातीतो निषेधान्न निवर्तते ।
गुणबुद्ध्या च विहितं न करोति यथार्भक: ।। Bh 11.7.11

doshabuddhyobhayātīto nishedhānna nivartate
gunabuddhyā cha vihitaṁ na karoti yathārbhakaḥ

He who has transcended the duality of good and evil does not engage in prescribed duties because of any injunctions nor refrain from wrong doing. He just acts spontaneously like a child without any calculations.

Krishna began his instructions to Uddhava by summarizing the highest essence of Self-knowledge. He told Uddhava to be free of all attachments and fix the mind only on the Divine, seeing everyone with an equal eye. Whatever is perceived by the mind through the senses is only a projection of the very same mind based on its knowledge and therefore illusory in nature. The one with an unsteady mind gets attached to the transient phenomena and perceiving diversity develops the duality of good and evil with its judgments as well as prescribed and prohibited actions. But when one sees everything as the play of the Divine, one is free of the false notion of multiplicity of selves and realizes the one true Self of all as the Supreme Being. Then one is not acting out of the acquired memory of what is right and wrong, but out of the vision of love and compassion that comes out of being free of the false ego. Such a being acts spontaneously like a child and is incapable of doing anything wrong. He who has a clear realization of this wisdom is alone a true friend of all beings, full of peace, beholds the entire universe as Divine and never undergoes any sorrow.

प्रायेण मनुजा लोके लोकतत्त्वविचक्षणाः ।
समुद्धरन्ति ह्यात्मानमात्मनैवाशुभाशयात् ॥ Bh 11.7.19

prāyeṇa manujā loke lokatattvavichakṣhaṇāḥ
samuddharanti hyātmānamātmanaivāśhubhāśhayāt

In this world, those who engage in inquiring into the true nature of the world lift themselves up by their own efforts and rid themselves of cravings that are unwholesome.

Uddhava appealed to Krishna as the embodiment and fountainhead of Yoga and as the refuge to get over the difficulty of renouncing attachments for those caught in the notion of me and mine through ignorance. Krishna replied with great clarity that the only way to lift oneself out of ignorance is by one's own vigilance and not looking for help outside. The true guide is within us and present in all forms without, if we observe with clarity and learn through direct perception and inference. The way of inquiry into oneself (jnana yoga) and the surrender of doership of actions (karma yoga) both clearly enable one to perceive the Divine as one's own Self. This is the unique blessing of human life, to be vigilant and discover the Supreme Being who cannot be perceived through secondhand knowledge of the intellect but only through direct insight from within.

सन्ति मे गुरवो राजन् बहवो बुद्ध्युपाश्रिताः ।
यतो बुद्धिमुपादाय मुक्तोऽटामीह तान् शृणु ॥ Bh 11.7.32

santi me guravo rājan bahavo buddhyupāśhritāḥ
yato buddhimupādāya mukto'ṭāmīha tān śhṛṇu

Many are my preceptors selected by keen observation, acquiring wisdom from them, I wander freely in the world.

To elaborate upon the theme of finding one's Guru in all forms by observing keenly, Krishna narrated to Uddhava the story of the sage Dattatreya who shared with King Yadu the twenty-four Gurus he learnt from through clear perception. Twenty-four, being the number of hours in a day, it also symbolizes that one can learn throughout the day by being alertly aware of the outer environs and the inner responses to them. Here is a summary of the twenty-four Gurus of Dattatreya and the key lessons he learned from each of them.

1. **Earth**—Endurance in the face of abuse, offering support to all without complaint, and serving others selflessly like mountains and trees that provide herbs, shade and shelter.
2. **Air**—Living freely and lightly, taking in only what is essential for survival, and remaining unaffected by the environment, whether fragrant or foul.

3. **Sky (Space)**—Being all-pervading, unlimited, untouched by changes, and unaffected by cloud or dust particles that float in it.
4. **Water**—Being clear, pure, gentle, and refreshing, offering inner and outer cleansing, quenching thirst, nourishing, and purifying all.
5. **Fire**—Equal in its treatment of all offerings, retaining its essential heat regardless of form, and symbolizing the ascetic who digests all experiences while burning past and future attachments.
6. **Sun**—Accepting offerings only to return them at the right time, like the sun absorbs water to release it as rain and reflecting the truth that the same reality appears different in many bodies.
7. **Dove**—Blind attachment to family and offspring leads to grief and destruction, as shown by the story of the entire dove family perishing in the hunter's trap due to emotional entanglement.
8. **Python**—Not chasing after food but happy with whatever comes on its own and resting peacefully in true contentment.
9. **Ocean**—Unshakable calm regardless of whether rivers flow in or dry up, represents even-mindedness amid gain or loss, joy or sorrow.
10. **Moth**—The pursuit of attraction driven by uncontrolled desire ignited by mere appearance like the moth running to the flame leads to its destruction.
11. **Bee**—The wise collect knowledge from various sources without harming any, just as a bee collects honey from various flowers gently.
12. **Honey Gatherer**—The labor of bees in storing the honey is all taken away in one instant by the honey

gatherer, showing the futility of hoarding wealth as it will be snatched away one day.

13. **Elephant**—The desire for physical contact can be a trap, just as the elephant is caught by its longing to touch the she-elephant placed by hunters as bait.

14. **Deer**—The lure of sound can destroy discretion, like the deer caught by a hunter's sweet music, revealing how indulgence in sense pleasure leads to bondage.

15. **Fish**—The uncontrolled craving for taste is the most difficult to overcome, as the fish rushes to the baited hook, sealing its own fate.

16. **Pingala (Prostitute)**—A single night of unfulfilled desire led to sudden awakening, as she realized the futility of false hope and turned inward in detachment and devotion to the Supreme.

17. **Osprey (Bird of prey)**—Possessing what others desire invites conflict, and peace is gained by giving up attachment, as seen when the osprey having a prey in its mouth is mobbed by other birds but finds relief when it drops the prey.

18. **Child**—Freedom from pride, honor, and anxiety enables spontaneous joy and play, as both the guileless child and the realized sage live free of the ego.

19. **Maiden**—Solitude brings peace, while even the company of two leads to noise and disturbance, as shown by the girl who removed her bangles one by one to finally just having only one to avoid making sound.

20. **Arrow Maker**—Deep concentration arises from single-pointed focus, like the craftsman who became oblivious even to a royal procession while absorbed in shaping arrows.

21. **Serpent**—An ascetic must avoid fixed dwellings and remain silent and unbound, just as a snake uses another's burrow and quietly moves from place to place.
22. **Spider**—The universe arises from and dissolves into the one Self, just as a spider spins a web from its own body and swallows it back after play.
23. **Wasp**—Constant focus, even through fear, transforms one's being, as the larva becomes the wasp itself through intense attention.
24. **Body**— Awareness of the body's impermanent, fragile, and ever-changing nature brings forth renunciation and shows that unregulated senses drag a person in conflicting directions, wasting the rare human birth.

अमान्यमत्सरो दक्षो निर्ममोदृढसौहृदः ।
असत्वरोऽर्थजिज्ञासुरनसूयुरमोघवाक् ॥ Bh 11.10.6

amānyamatsaro dakṣho nirmamo dṛḍhasauhṛdaḥ
asatvaro'rthajijñāsuranasūyuramoghavāk

One ought to be free from pride, envy, sloth and attachment, be firmly devoted to the teacher, be keen on inquiring into oneself, never find faults and never indulge in useless talk.

After describing the importance of being a light unto oneself and through observation, finding the teacher and teaching in all forms every moment of the day, Krishna emphasized to Uddhava the importance of detachment by keenly noticing how the actions of those blindly attached to sense gratification always produce the contrary result of misery. Due to taking as real the sense of diversity projected by the mind which is no different from what is perceived in a dream, one gets caught in the false identification with the body and mind as well as "me" and "mine." This results in pride, envy, possessiveness, fault finding etc. Therefore, if one is deeply devoted to the teaching that points to Truth and remains alert and attentive, then one is free of the sense of "mine" (*nirmama*) that removes all such negative qualities. One then sees that the same Divine manifests uniquely in all beings, just as the same fire takes the shape of different logs that are burned. Realizing this wisdom dispels the illusion of the false, separate self that is the root of the apparent cycle of rebirth. Krishna further says, when one contacts the highest teaching, it is similar to two pieces of wood rubbing against each other to produce the fire of Self-knowledge. Uddhava is also instructed on the wrong notion of seeking heaven and its pleasures to escape the fear of death as all such realms are only projections of thought and temporary in nature. Therefore, the right way to be free of all illusion and fear is to transcend the false notion of multitude of souls as self and others, whereby only the unbroken flame of the Divine shines.

बद्धो मुक्त इति व्याख्या गुणतो मे न वस्तुतः ।
गुणस्य मायामूलत्वान्न मे मोक्षो न बन्धनम् ॥ Bh 11.11.1

baddho mukta iti vyākhyā guṇato me na vastutaḥ
guṇasya māyāmūlatvānna me mokṣo na bandhanam

The characterization of being bound or liberated is only determined by the identification with the gunas (modes of nature) and has nothing to do with the Divine

essence that is ever free of Maya and has no bondage or liberation.

The three gunas (*sattva, rajas, tamas*) underlie all actions of body and mind, but when one falsely identifies with the qualities as "me," one is said to be in bondage and when that identification is dropped, one is said to be liberated. Yet in reality, this bondage and liberation are only apparent, as there is nobody who is entangled except the imaginary sense of self as me. This is similar to the sun's reflection in a pot of water, wherein when the water has ripples, the reflection seems to dance, but the sun itself is unaffected. To illustrate, Krishna invokes the image of two birds perched on a tree. One bird eats the fruits of action and is subject to pleasure and pain, while the other merely watches, unattached, and remains undisturbed. The first bird represents the ignorant, who are identified with body-mind, while the second bird is the enlightened one that abides as the pure Being. All actions are really the gunas acting on gunas, the seeming doer is illusory. So, the wise one lets the body and mind function as per the gunas while remaining unaffected, like the sky is unperturbed by passing clouds. The wise one acts without any identification, transcending good and evil, unaffected by praise or blame and seeing the same essence everywhere. The company of such a wise being lifts everyone out of the net of delusion through compassion, equanimity, purity and love.

न रोधयति मां योगो न साङ्ख्यं धर्म एव च ।
न स्वाध्यायस्तपस्त्यागो नेष्टापूर्तं न दक्षिणा ॥
व्रतानि यज्ञश्छन्दांसि तीर्थानि नियमा यमाः ।
यथावरुन्धे सत्सङ्गः सर्वसङ्गापहो हि माम् ॥ Bh 11.12.1-2

na rodhayati mām yogo na sānkhyam dharma eva cha
na svādhyāyastapastyāgo neshtāpūrtam na dakshiṇā
vratāni yajñaśhchhandāmsi tīrthāni niyamā yamāḥ

Neither practicing Yoga nor learning the Sankhya philosophy nor following the various codes of Dharma nor studying the scriptures nor austerities nor renunciation, nor pouring oblations into the sacred fire nor works of charity nor fasts nor worship of deities nor muttering mantras nor going to holy places of pilgrimage nor observing injunctions help one realize the Divine as much as Satsang which puts an end to all attachments.

The constant fellowship of the wise bestows Grace effortlessly while all the various practices, observances, study etc. involve great effort and yet do not have the same potency as Satsang. Krishna gave the examples of so many beings of different classes, such as Prahalada, Bali, Sugreeva, Hanuman, Vibhishan, Vrtrasura, who had all realized the highest state, because of Satsang and nothing else, even though they did not study any scriptures, did not go to any holy places, did not observe any sacred vows etc. Further Krishna gave the example of the Gopis of Vrndavan who had attained Him purely by their mood of love, again without austerities or scriptural study. He recalled how their hearts pined with separation when He departed to Mathura, how they remembered the nights of *rasa leela* and held Him exclusively in their thought, merging into Him as rivers into the ocean. These women, aglow with devotion, did not analyze or meditate on His nature, yet through surrender they reached the Supreme. So, Krishna urged Uddhava to renounce all do's and don'ts—even renounce the idea of renunciation itself—and simply surrender wholeheartedly. Just as a garment is nothing but the cotton threads from which it is woven, the universe is nothing but the essence of the Divine. All the seven chakras, all levels of speech (*para, pashyanti, madhyama, vaikhari*), every action, perception, and cognition are nothing but His manifestation. Krishna illustrated a metaphorical cosmic tree whose roots (virtue and sin), stalks (gunas), branches (elements), leaves (sense-objects), and nest (heart) symbolize the universe. In that nest sit two birds: one, the false ego, flitting and eating fruits; the other, pure awareness, simply watching. The ego is chasing pleasure and going through suffering, while the true Self abides undisturbed. To be free of the ego and to rest in the purity of the Divine, Krishna enjoins Uddhava to engage in Satsang and see all as Bhagavan alone, thus letting the actions of the body/mind fall into their right place.

आगमोऽप: प्रजा देश: काल: कर्म च जन्म च ।
ध्यानं मन्त्रोऽथ संस्कारो दशैते गुणहेतव: ॥ Bh 11.13.4

āgamo'paḥ prajā deśhaḥ kālaḥ karma cha janma cha
dhyānaṁ mantro'tha saṁskāro daśhaite guṇahetavaḥ

Scripture, water, people, place, time, work, birth, contemplation, mantra, and rites—these ten factors are contributory to the growth of a *guna*.

The three modes (gunas) of nature—*sattva* (purity), *rajas* (passion), and *tamas* (ignorance)—belong only to matter while the true Being remains untouched by them. By taking recourse to *sattva*, one can be free of *rajas* and *tamas*, and flower in devotion, love and virtue while removing unrighteousness and dissolving darkness. And then, *sattva* itself melts into simply Being. Krishna explained the ten factors associated with each of the gunas that contribute to their growth—scripture, water, people, place, time, work, birth, contemplation, mantra, and rites. It is fairly clear that the quality of people we associate with, place of dwelling, time of the day, nature of one's work occupation etc. all have a strong impact on the qualities that the mind imbibes and therefore one has to be very discerning with these factors. What's less obvious but equally critical is that even scriptures, mantras, rites etc. are of these three types. Therefore, it is just as important to be discerning with so-called religious activities that lead to sectarian identification, desire for worldly goals etc. and recognize that true religion is only to connect with the eternal Source of life itself.

मनसा वचसा दृष्ट्या गृह्यतेऽन्यैरपीन्द्रियै: ।
अहमेव न मत्तोऽन्यदिति बुध्यध्वमञ्जसा ॥ Bh 11.13.24

manasā vacasā dṛṣhṭyā gṛhyate'nyairapīndriyaiḥ
ahameva na matto'nyad iti budhyadhvamañjasā

Realize through inquiry into Truth that whatever is grasped by the mind, expressed through speech or perceived through vision and other sense faculties is all only the Divine and nothing else.

When Uddhava asked why people still gravitate toward sense-objects despite their transitory nature, Krishna said that it arises from the perverted sense of self as "me" rising in the heart, which gives birth to ignorance and leads to misjudgment, desire, and wrong action. The discerning person realizes these impulses as springing from the false "me." withdraws the mind, steadies the breath, and peacefully abides in Being. And thus, one recognizes that every perception, cognition, speech and action is nothing other than Him. Only the mind binds itself to sense objects, and this attachment disturbs the body, but pure Awareness remains ever untouched. By seeing this clearly, one is freed of false identification with body, mind, and sense objects, and stands anchored in the unchanging truth. The three states of waking, dream and deep sleep belong to the mind alone but through false identification with the mind, one feels subject to them. Even while awake, the one bound by ego sleeps to reality just as one dreaming, and perceives divisions in people, places and time due to seeing oneself and others as separate. All suffering, unrighteousness and evil spring only from this false identification. The sword of wisdom cuts through this delusion of many selves and reveals that all is the one Supreme Being. Then any desire that surfaces up, vanishes without taking root and one remains unbothered about even one's body, just as an intoxicated person remains unaware of his clothes falling off. In such a being who has transcended all three gunas and rests in the Divine as one's true heart, equanimity, detachment and all virtues spring forth effortlessly.

सर्वासामपि सिद्धीनां हेतुः पतिरहं प्रभुः ।
अहं योगस्य साङ्ख्यस्य धर्मस्य ब्रह्मवादिनाम् ॥ Bh 11.15.35

sarvāsāmapi siddhīnāṁ hetuḥ patirahaṁ prabhuḥ
ahaṁ yogasya sāṅkhyasya dharmasya brahmavādinām

The Source, the Custodian and the Controller of all *siddhis* (yogic powers) as well as the essence of Yoga,

Sankhya, Dharma and the Vedas, am I, the Supreme Being.

Krishna then outlined eighteen distinct *siddhis* that can be perfected through yoga. The first eight—*aṇimā, mahimā, laghimā, prapti, prākāmya, īshitā, vashitā, kāmāvasāyitā*—are the primary perfections. These eight correspond respectively to shrinking the body to atomic minuteness (*aṇima*), expanding to gigantic proportions (*mahimā*), rendering the body weightless (*laghimā*), access to all sensory faculties across creation (*prapti*), fulfillment of any pleasure (*prākāmya*), control over Maya (*īshitā*), non-attachment to sense pleasures (*vashitā*) and access to any experience that is sought (*kāmāvasāyitā*). The remaining ten secondary siddhis include freedom from hunger and thirst, clairvoyance at great distances, rapid movement of mind and body, shapeshifting, entering other bodies, leaving the body at will, witnessing celestial pastimes, fulfilling any desire, and universal dominion. Beyond these eighteen lie further siddhis such as omniscience (knowing past, present, future), immunity to dualities like heat and cold, mind-reading, mastery over elemental forces, invincibility, and more. All these powers emerge through deep meditation on the Divine. Yet Krishna made it clear that though yogis might manifest such powers, the wise treat these siddhis as only distractions. True perfection lies not in miraculous feats but in surrendering to the Divine, seeing Him as the source, sustainer, and controller of all perfections, and transcending the false ego to abide in the Supreme Being.

अहमात्मोद्धवामीषां भूतानां सुहृदीश्वरः ।
अहं सर्वाणि भूतानि तेषां स्थित्युद्भवाप्ययः ॥ Bh 11.16.9

aham ātmoddhavāmīṣhāṁ bhūtānāṁ suhṛdīśhvaraḥ
ahaṁ sarvāṇi bhūtāni teṣhāṁ sthityudbhavāpyayaḥ

I am the Self, the Friend and the Controller of all living entities. I am all beings as well as their creation, sustenance and dissolution.

After listening to the teachings of Krishna thus far, Uddhava glorifies Krishna as the Infinite Brahman with no beginning or end, unobscured by Maya (*tvaṁ brahma paramaṁ sākṣhād anādyantamapāvṛtam*—Bh 11.16.1), who is extolled by the true knowers of Vedas. And since He cannot be known or perceived as the inner essence, Uddhava asked Krishna to reveal His powerful manifestations by which He can be known. In response, Krishna recalls that Arjuna asked the same question on the battlefield of Mahabharat and reveals to Uddhava the majestic display of His opulences (*vibhutis*) as described in Chapter 10 of Bhagavad Gita. He first emphatically states that the most intimate opulence is being the Self, the friend and the sovereign cause of all beings. He is also the Cosmic Intelligence (*mahat*), Time, equilibrium of the gunas and the mind. He is the sacred syllable Om among mantras, Gayatri among Vedic meters, Vishnu among Devas, Narada among sages, Garuda among birds, Prahlada among Asuras, Ganga among rivers, lion among animals, fig among trees, Sun among the luminous, Himalaya among abodes, Skanda among generals, Hanuman among monkeys, courage of the courageous, strength of the strong and the defining principle of every sense faculty, every element and every mode of nature. All these wondrous manifestations are only to beckon one to pure devotion. By regulating mind, speech, and breath, and fixing attention solely on Him, one realizes that everything is His expression and nothing exists apart from Him.

ज्ञानविज्ञानसंसिद्धाः पदं श्रेष्ठं विदुर्मम ।
ज्ञानी प्रियतमोऽतो मे ज्ञानेनासौ बिभर्ति माम् ॥ Bh 11.19.3

jñānavijñānasaṁsiddhāḥ padaṁ śreṣhṭhaṁ vidurmama
jñānī priyatamo'to me jñānenāsau bibharti mām

Only those perfected beings abiding in true wisdom and realization know My supreme glory. The realized one sees Me alone by his realization and thus the most dear to Me.

Krishna declares that the perfection of wisdom and devotion is the recognition of the One all-pervading Supreme Being as the only Truth behind all fleeting phenomena. True wisdom is not dry logical reasoning but only that which culminates in loving devotion, whereby the world of diversity is seen as a mere phantom appearance of the one underlying essence. Hence, what is indicated by wisdom is not scholarship but direct insight into Truth that requires one to inquire within. No amount of asceticism, prayers, pilgrimages, charity, rituals and other outer activities can bring forth the purity that the inner light of wisdom can. Only by realizing the falsity of "me" and "mine," one is freed of all desires including the desire for liberation. Such a state of total desirelessness bestows one with unconditional love toward all beings and freedom from all suffering. This brings forth naturally, and not through cultivation, all auspicious qualities such as peace, wholesome speech, detachment, modesty, silence, fearlessness, purity, austerity, contentment, sense regulation, freedom from praise or blame and all righteousness.

भिद्यते हृदयग्रन्थिश्छिद्यन्ते सर्वसंशयाः ।
क्षीयन्ते चास्य कर्माणि मयि दृष्टेऽखिलात्मनि ॥ Bh 11.20.30

bhidyate hṛdayagranthiśhchhidyante sarvasaṁshayāḥ
kshīyante chāsya karmāṇi mayi dṛṣṭe'khilātmani

The knot in the heart is cut asunder, all doubts resolved and the entire stock of karma burned the very instant one realizes the Self of the Universe.

The root of all karma is the false sense of doership which has its source, the knot in the heart felt as I-thought. This separative sense of identification with the body and the mind as "me" results in one taking ownership of the actions and the results, imagining oneself to be the doer and the experiencer. There is thus hankering and despair, excitement and depression, happiness and sadness alternating constantly, causing restlessness and misery. When one inquires within and recognizes the falsity of the sense of "me" by seeing that actions take place according to the modes of nature that function perfectly on their own as an expression of the Cosmic Intelligence, then one recognizes the one Supreme Being who is the Self of the Universe as the true doer and experiencer of all actions. This realization cuts the knot in the heart, removes all doubts in the mind and brings forth lightness and clarity. This results in total desirelessness where one does not seek anything, including even liberation. Such complete desirelessness is declared to be the greatest and the most supreme benediction (*nairapekṣhyaṁ paraṁ prāhuḥ*—Bh 11.20.35), whereby one totally accepts life as it unfolds without resistance and simply lives in freedom.

नायं जनो मे सुखदुःखहेतुर्न देवतात्मा ग्रहकर्मकाला: ।
मन: परं कारणमामनन्ति संसारचक्रं परिवर्तयेद् यत् ॥
Bh 11.23.43

nāyaṁ jano me sukhaduḥkhaheturna devatātmā
grahakarmakālāḥ
manaḥ paraṁ kāraṇamāmananti saṁsārachakraṁ parivartayed
yat

Neither people nor any deity nor the true Self nor the stars nor karma nor time is responsible for joy and sorrow but one's mind alone is the cause.

It is the normal tendency to blame someone—whether it be other people, deities, astrological positions, karma, etc.—for one's problems and challenges. But in reality, it is one's own mind that is responsible for all of one's actions and the results thereof. So if one stops blaming others or circumstances but completely accepts whatever is ordained as one's own responsibility, then one will not dissipate energy in looking for excuses, wallowing in victimhood, resisting the situation. Instead, by total acceptance of whatever difficulties arise, there is tremendous energy available to act and address the situation. It is the mind driven by the three gunas of *sattva, rajas, tamas* alone that generates various experiences, while the pure Being remains unaffected. Mistaken identification with the mind causes one to be swayed by the experiences and lose objectivity. The entire discipline of yoga—yama and niyama (do's and don'ts), devotion, purity, charity, truthfulness, nonviolence, austerity, and study—is meant only to regulate the mind so that it no longer is swayed by desire and aversion. When the mind is regulated, no circumstance can disturb its peace; when unregulated, it creates endless agitation and projects the illusion of an external cause for suffering. Just as one limb does not blame another for injury, the wise recognize that all apparent agents and experiences arise from the same divine ground. To ascribe joy or sorrow to others is ignorance born of separation. Understanding this, one ceases to blame anyone or anything outside but acts with full responsibility while being free within through total acceptance of what is.

द्रव्यं देश: फलं कालो ज्ञानं कर्म च कारक: ।
श्रद्धावस्थाकृतिर्निष्ठा त्रैगुण्य: सर्व एव हि ॥ Bh 11.25.30

dravyaṁ deshaḥ phalaṁ kālo jñānam karma cha kārakaḥ
shraddhāvasthākrtirnishthā trai-guṇyaḥ sarva eva hi

Substance, abode, result, time, knowledge, action, agent, conviction, consciousness, form and destiny are all constituted of the three gunas alone.

The three gunas—*sattva, rajas, tamas*—govern all activity of the body and mind. Sattva embodies purity, clarity, contentment, truth, compassion, and discipline. Rajas manifests as restlessness, desire, pride, and attachment to action and reward. Tamas appears as delusion, lethargy, fear, and cruelty. All three bind the soul through identification with the body and the I-thought. Even Sattva, though luminous, still sustains subtle attachment to virtue and peace. When Rajas predominates, the mind is agitated by craving and dissatisfaction. When Tamas prevails, it is clouded by confusion and inertia. These modes permeate all aspects of life—substances, knowledge, action, food, joy, place, and temperament—appearing as purity, passion, or dullness in each. But the gunas belong to Prakriti alone, the field of mind and matter, and not to the pure Being, which is beyond all modes. Through sattva, one refines the mind and transcends rajas and tamas and ultimately rises beyond Sattva itself. Such transcendence comes through surrender to the Divine, acting without attachment to results, and recognizing all phenomena as expressions of the one eternal Being.

ततो दुःसङ्गमुत्सृज्य सत्सु सज्जेत बुद्धिमान् ।
सन्त एवास्य छिन्दन्ति मनोव्यासङ्गमुक्तिभिः ॥ Bh 11.26.26

tato duḥsaṅgamutsṛjya satsu sajjeta buddhimān
santa evāsya chhindanti manoVyasaṅgamuktibhiḥ

Eschewing evil company, the prudent one ought to associate only with the righteous, as they cut asunder the deep attachment of his mind by their pointers.

Keeping the company of the wise brings liberation, for only they can sever the deep bonds of attachment. Such saintly beings are free from craving and ego, serene, equal toward all beings, unaffected by opposites such as pleasure and pain, and unattached to possessions. Their hearts rest solely in the Divine. In their company, the sacred stories, teachings, and glories of the Supreme are joyfully discussed, purifying the mind and awakening devotion. Through their Satsang, reverence and love for the Divine naturally blossom, bringing peace, purity, and fulfillment. In contrast, association with the impure, driven by sense pleasure and delusion, binds one to ignorance and suffering. Therefore, the company one keeps determines one's inner state—bondage or freedom. Just as food sustains the body, the saints sustain the one seeking liberation. While the sun grants outer sight, the wise ones bestow inner vision that never fades. They are the true refuge for those drowning in worldly existence, embodying truth, love, and peace—verily the presence of the Divine itself. To seek their company is to awaken to wisdom and liberation, where the heart flowers in love towards all and nothing remains to be attained.

परस्वभावकर्माणि न प्रशंसेन्न गर्हयेत् ।
विश्वमेकात्मकं पश्यन् प्रकृत्या पुरुषेण च ॥ Bh 11.28.1

parasvabhāvakarmāṇi na praśhaṁsenna garhayet
viśhvamekātmakaṁ paśhyan prakṛtyā puruṣeṇa cha

Seeing the whole Universe brought forth by Cosmic Intelligence as one indivisible Whole, one ought to neither praise nor condemn the nature or the actions of others.

As we reach the concluding portions of Uddhava Gita, Krishna points out that the entire universe is one indivisible expression of Consciousness, non-dual reality. The apparent split between the seer and the seen arises only due to identification with the false sense of "me." In truth, seeing, hearing, and doing simply happen as the play of the Infinite, without a doer. This natural wholeness is lost when the notion of "I" arises, and with it comes the urge to know, experience, and possess. Even the desire to experience or know God arises from this same sense of separation, for to experience something implies a division between the experiencer and the experienced. Since everything is already Divine, there is none outside it to experience it. When this fallacy is seen, the false sense of separation dissolves, and what remains is self-luminous and whole. In this recognition, there is no cause for praise or blame, pride or guilt, for all actions arise from the same intelligence that moves everything. To praise or condemn is to assume separation and doership, which sustains ignorance. When this illusion ends, everything is seen as the spontaneous play of the One, flowing effortlessly in its own perfection.

आत्मैव तदिदं विश्वं सृज्यते सृजति प्रभुः ।
त्रायते त्राति विश्वात्मा ह्रियते हरतीश्वरः ॥ Bh 11.28.6

ātmaiva tadidaṁ viśhvaṁ sṛjyate sṛjati prabhuḥ
trāyate trāti viśhvātmā hriyate haratīśhvaraḥ

The Universe is non-different from the Supreme Being who is the creator and the created, the sustainer and the sustained, the destroyer and the destroyed.

The Infinite can never be grasped by thought or speech, for whatever the mind captures is only a fragment and therefore unreal. The mind, by its very nature, operates from separation—it first creates the notion of "me" apart from what is, and from that limited position tries to comprehend the boundless. This effort is futile, for the finite can never comprehend the Infinite. When it is seen that the finite is but an expression of the Infinite, all distinctions dissolve and only the Infinite remains. Perceptions and actions then are seen simply as the movement of the Infinite itself, with no individual perceiver or doer. When the false sense of "me" is emptied, what shines forth is the pure intelligence that alone exists as all. That one Consciousness is simultaneously the creator and the created the protector and the protected, the destroyer and the destroyed. There is no division between God and creation, for the divine alone appears as everything. Like a spider spinning a web out of itself and withdrawing it again, the Infinite projects the universe from its own being, sustains it, and reabsorbs it—all as a spontaneous play of its own nature.

यथा हिरण्यं स्वकृतं पुरस्तात् पश्चाच्च सर्वस्य हिरण्मयस्य ।
तदेव मध्ये व्यवहार्यमाणं नानापदेशैरहमस्य तद्वत् ॥ Bh 11.28.19

yathā hiraṇyaṁ svakṛtaṁ purastāt paśhchāchcha sarvasya hiraṇmayasya
tadeva madhye vyavahāryamāṇaṁ nānāpadeśhairahamasya tadvat

Just as the gold that exists prior to, after dissolving and while in the shape of the ornaments is called by different names, so does the Supreme Being exist before and after the universe and also as the universe called by different names.

So long as one identifies with the body, mind and senses as "me" due to lack of discernment, pleasure and pain keep alternating. Even though the Infinite Being alone exists, the false identification causes one to experience suffering, excitement, fear, anger, greed and delusion, just as one dreaming while asleep experiences various emotions in the dream as if real. But just as waking up from the dream ends the experiences of the dream, awakening to one's true nature as Pure Being cuts the identification with the sense of "me" and ends suffering. Then it is clearly seen that just as gold remains the same in its essence before, during and after being shaped into ornaments, the Infinite Being remains the same in the beginning, middle and end of all experiences. Any effect is non-different from its cause in its essence which pervades it. All types of furniture though called by many names are essentially wood, all ornaments though called by many names are essentially gold, and similarly all forms of the universe though called by many names are essentially the Supreme Being. Being free of identification with form, which is an ever-changing phenomenon, one realizes and abides as the unchanging luminous essence that is ever free.

अयं हि सर्वकल्पानां सध्रीचीनो मतो मम ।
मद्भावः सर्वभूतेषु मनोवाक्कायवृत्तिभिः ॥ Bh 11.29.19

ayaṁ hi sarvakalpānāṁ sadhrīchīno mato mama
madbhāvaḥ sarvabhūteṣhu manovākkāyavṛttibhiḥ

To look upon all beings as Myself through all activities of mind, speech and body is the highest of all disciplines.

At the end of Uddhava Gita, after listening to the entire discourse, Uddhava asks Krishna for the simplest and most direct way to abide in truth. He observes that those proud of their spiritual knowledge fall into the trap of the ego, while true wisdom lies in surrendering completely to Krishna, the Supreme Being who is both within and without. Pleased by Uddhava's sincerity, Krishna answers compassionately and summarizes the entire teaching. He says the easiest way to realize Him is to dedicate all thoughts, actions, and intentions to Him alone. By constantly remembering Him, surrendering the mind and intellect, engaging in actions for His sake, seeking the company of the pious and celebrating the Divine through song, dance, art, and devotion, one can turn every activity into a remembrance of the Supreme and purify one's heart. One then perceives Krishna everywhere, just as the all-pervading space. Seeing all beings—wise or ignorant, kind or cruel, human, animal, or even inanimate—as His own expression, one becomes free from fault-finding, rivalry, pride, and blame. In this vision of unity, all doubts dissolve and one realizes the all-pervading Brahman as the only truth. This is the wisdom of the wise, the essence of all Vedanta, and the direct way to liberation.

य एतदानन्दसमुद्रसम्भृतं ज्ञानामृतं भागवताय भाषितम् ।
कृष्णेन योगेश्वरसेविताङ्घ्रिणा सच्छ्रद्धयासेव्य जगद् विमुच्यते
॥ Bh 11.29.48

ya etadānandasamudrasambhṛtaṁ jñānāmṛtaṁ bhāgavatāya bhāṣhitam
kṛṣhṇena yogeśhvarasevitāṅghriṇā sachchhraddhayāsevya jagad vimuchyate

The one who tastes with reverence, even a little of the nectar of wisdom churned out of the ocean of bliss and taught to the great devotee Uddhava by Krishna, the Lord of all Yogis, not only liberates oneself but the world at large gets liberated through the fellowship.

After completing the entire discourse of Uddhava Gita over 24 chapters of the eleventh canto of Bhāgavatam, Krishna declares that the aforesaid teaching covers the entire range of Vedanta in a nutshell in a lucid way and grasping this fully, one can be free of all doubts and be liberated here and now. Krishna thus assures that the one who treasures this dialogue between Him and Uddhava will certainly recognize the hidden meaning of the Vedas which is the realization of the Infinite Brahman, and anyone who shares it or listens to it with reverence, free of hypocrisy and pride, will get purified and enlightened by this lamp of wisdom. Hearing this benediction, Uddhava is moved to tears and choked with emotion offers his obeisances to his beloved friend Krishna as the greatest Yogi of all (*namo'stu te mahāyogin*). Krishna then instructs Uddhava to proceed to the hallowed Badarikashrama (Badrinath) and spend the rest of his days there in the bliss of Self-realization.

भगवान् पितामहं वीक्ष्य विभूतीरात्मनो विभुः ।
संयोज्यात्मनि चात्मानं पद्मनेत्रे न्यमीलयत् ॥ Bh 11.31.5

bhagavān pitāmaham vīkṣhya vibhūtīrātmano vibhuḥ
samyojyātmani chātmānam padmanetre nyamīlayat

Casting His glance upon the divine beings and fixing His mind on His own essence, the all-pervading Lord closed His lotus eyes.

After Uddhava's departure, Parikshit asked Shuka Brahmam about Krishna's final act—how the Yadavas met their end and how the Lord Himself left the earth. Shuka says, as foretold by sages, evil omens appeared in Dwaraka, and Krishna led the Yadavas to Prabhasa to perform sacred rites. However, under the influence of Krishna's own Divine Will, overcome by delusion, having drunk intoxicating liquor, they fought among themselves with blades that had sprung from the cursed iron pestle. The entire Yadu clan destroyed itself in the terrible civil war. Balaram then sat in meditation by the sea and departed, merging into the Supreme. Krishna walked to a peepal tree, now sat all alone in serene majesty, radiant like a dark rain cloud, having executed the most festive pastimes for a full span of 125 years. A hunter named Jara, mistaking His foot for a deer, shot an arrow that fulfilled the sages' prophecy. Krishna forgave the hunter pleading with remorse for his apparent transgression and instead only bestowed Grace upon him. Finally, surrounded by unseen celestial beings, Krishna closed His lotus eyes and ascended to His eternal realm, thus having concluded His earthly pastimes. This also marked the end of Dwapara Yuga and the onset of Kali Yuga.

TWELFTH CANTO
Epilogue

विद्यातपःप्राणनिरोधमैत्रीतीर्थाभिषेकव्रतदानजप्यैः ।
नात्यन्तशुद्धिं लभतेऽन्तरात्मा यथा हृदिस्थे भगवत्यनन्ते ॥
Bh 12.3.48

vidyātapaḥprāṇanirodhamaitrītīrthābhiṣhekavratadānajapyaiḥ
nātyantaśhuddhiṁ labhate'ntarātmā yathā hṛdisthe
bhagavatyanante

One's mind does not become as purified through knowledge, austerities, breath control, friendliness, going to sacred waters, observing vows, charity or chants, as it does when the Infinite Being is enshrined in the heart.

Shuka Brahmam begins the twelfth skandha by first describing in detail the various evils of Kali Yuga. The word *kali* means conflict and therefore it signifies the period when people are engaged in various conflicts due to egoic identification. It causes a decline of righteousness, truth, purity, forgiveness, compassion and also life energy and bodily strength. People become more obsessed with wealth, status, trickery and lust, as bigotry, hypocrisy, impiety and pretentious scholarship rule the roost. Without recognizing the impermanence of all possessions, everyone gets attached to acquiring more, resulting in conflicts of all kinds—between nations, religions, families and within households. However, despite all these evils, Shuka Brahmam assures that even in the worst of times, the one who inwardly abides in the Infinite Being, remains serene and unaffected. One can be free even in the most conflict-riven age of Kali, not by outer demonstrations of religiosity and virtue which strengthen the false division of the separate ego, but by fully recognizing the presence of the Divine in the heart as pure Awareness.

नित्यो नैमित्तिकश्चैव तथा प्राकृतिको लय: ।
आत्यन्तिकश्च कथित: कालस्य गतिरीदृशी ॥ Bh 12.4.38

nityo naimittikaśhchaiva tathā prākṛtiko layaḥ
ātyantikaśhcha kathitaḥ kālasya gatirīdṛśhī

The four types of dissolution are the continuous, occasional, elemental and eternal. Such is the course of Time.

Shuka Brahmam then describes the four kinds of dissolution, or *pralaya,* explaining the nature of Time that moves in endless rhythms starting from the smallest division as the movement of an atom to huge cycles known as *yugas* and *kalpas.* The first type of dissolution, *nitya pralaya,* is the continuous, moment-to-moment dissolution of all matter, as everything is in perpetual change and decay. Nothing remains the same even for a moment as there is constant flux of every manifest phenomenon. The second type of dissolution, *naimittika pralaya,* is the occasional dissolution that happens at the end of each *kalpa*—a thousand cycles of the four *yugas*—when all realms disappear and rest as the night of the creative energy Brahma to awaken again for the next *kalpa*. After thousands of such *kalpas*, the elemental dissolution called the *prakritika pralaya*, also known as the great dissolution, *maha pralaya*, occurs, when even the primordial nature dissolves back into the Unmanifest. All elements—soil, water, fire, air, space, and the subtle principles—merge back into their source, leaving only pure potentiality. Yet even this state is not final, for creation emerges again in a new cycle. Beyond these three types of dissolution that happen in time, there is the fourth type of dissolution which is known as *ātma pralaya*, or the dissolution of the false ego. It is the dissolving of the false sense of "me" and "mine," through wisdom and grace, revealing the one Supreme Being as the sole reality. Thus, the first three types of dissolution happen within Time, while *ātma pralaya* transcends Time—it happens only in the eternal now, when the illusion of separation ends and only the Supreme remains.

अहं ब्रह्म परं धाम ब्रह्माहं परमं पदम् ।
एवं समीक्ष्य चात्मानमात्मन्याधाय निष्कले ॥ Bh 12.5.11

aham brahma param dhāma brahmāham paramam padam
evam samīkṣhya chātmānamātmanyādhāya niṣhkale

Abide in the Truth that I am non-different from the Infinite Being, that is the Supreme Refuge and the transcendental state of being. Thus, realizing your true nature, you will be free of death.

In his final discourse to Parikshit, Shuka Brahmam summarizes the entire Bhāgavatam by revealing its essence—that only the Supreme Being, the soul of the universe, truly exists. He instructs the king to give up the delusion of death, for what dies is only the body composed of the three *gunas*, while the eternal Self is neither born nor dies. He explains that all creation is like a dream or a mirage of the mind, transient and illusory, while the Self remains untouched, just as space inside a pot remains unchanged whether a pot is intact or broken. Death, therefore, is only the dissolution of form, not of essence. The Pure Being appears to manifest through countless forms yet remains one and undivided. Shuka Brahmam urges Parikshit to relinquish all attachment to body, family, lineage etc. and abide as the infinite Self—limitless, self-effulgent, and beyond all change. He tells him that the prophesied serpent's bite can burn only the body, not the real Self. By recognizing the true essence of one's very existence as the one Supreme Being, one is free from fear and duality. Shuka Brahmam thus compassionately concludes his teachings that spanned 18,000 verses and gives the entire essence of all Vedas, which not only liberated Parikshit, but remains as a beacon of light for countless generations.

सिद्धोऽस्म्यनुगृहीतोऽस्मि भवता करुणात्मना ।
श्रावितो यच्च मे साक्षादनादिनिधनो हरिः ॥ Bh 12.6.2

siddho'smyanugrhīto'smi bhavatā karuṇātmanā
shrāvito yachcha me sākṣhādanādinidhano hariḥ

The purpose of life stands accomplished, and one is filled with Grace by hearing from the compassionate teacher, this discourse on the Supreme Being who has no beginning or end.

Having heard the entire discourse of the great sage Shuka Brahmam who saw the whole universe within him and looked upon all with love, Parikshit expresses his gratitude with joined palms. He glorifies the power of Grace coming forth from exalted beings such as Shuka Brahmam who have completely surrendered unto the Immortal Lord and it is Grace that poured out as this entire Purana which speaks only of the illustrious Supreme Being, Hari. Now fully suffused with divine wisdom that gives fearlessness, Parikshit boldly declares that he is not afraid of the snake Takshaka or any other agency of death, since he has realized eternal oneness with the Infinite Brahman. He seeks permission to sit silently in meditation as he is about to give up his body as prophesied, now that the seed of ignorance has been obliterated by the revelation of Shuka Brahmam. Thus, addressed by the king and his purpose accomplished, the divine sage Shuka Brahmam silently got up and left without waiting for any acknowledgement from the large gathering there, exemplifying perfection as the speaker. Then, Parikshit with all doubts resolved and free of all attachments, sat down by Ganga in total stillness. As prophesied, the most venomous snake Takshaka came to inject poison into the body of the royal sage Parikshit whose mortal remains were reduced to ashes. Everyone assembled there witnessed this most glorious and graceful departure of Parikshit with wonder and offered showers of flowers and praises.

परं पदं वैष्णवमामनन्ति तद् यत्रेति नेतीत्यतदुत्सिसृक्षव: ।
विसृज्य दौरात्म्यमनन्यसौहृदा हृदोपगुह्यावसितं समाहितै: ॥
Bh 12.6.32

param padam vaiṣhṇavamāmananti tad yanneti
netītyatadutsisṛkṣhavaḥ
visṛjya daurātmyamananyasauhṛdā hṛdopaguhyāvasitam
samāhitaiḥ

Yogis who are free of the false identification with the body as me, and of the sense of mine with regard to those connected with the body, and are exclusively devoted to God, and who therefore reject every transient phenomenon as not true, embrace with their heart the supreme essence of the all-pervading Lord and abide in the transcendental state of Vishnu.

The great enchanting potency of Maya makes living beings that are His own manifestations fall foul to their fellow beings under the force of passions such as anger, greed and envy. This power of Maya repeatedly flashes in the mind as judgments about others and vanishes only when the true Self is realized through inquiring within. When one is thus freed of the grip of Maya, there is no room for the warfare of words and labels, nor does the mind remain caught in various machinations and doubts. Then, there does not exist any karma due to freedom from the sense of doership or any association with the fruits thereof. Such is the nature of the God-realized being who is neither capable of being opposed by anyone nor capable of opposing anyone. Therefore, a true Yogi revels in the bliss of unconditional love toward all and free from all fears, is not bothered by praise or insult and never shows disrespect or hostility toward anyone. Such is the transcendental state of Vishnu (*param padam vaiṣhṇavam*) that is free of the notions of "me" and "mine."

स्वधाम्रो ब्राह्मण: साक्षाद् वाचक: परमात्मन: ।
स सर्वमन्त्रोपनिषद्वेदबीजं सनातनम् ॥ Bh 12.6.41

svadhāmno brahmaṇaḥ sākṣhād vāchakaḥ paramātmanaḥ
sa sarvamantropaniṣhadvedabījaṁ sanātanam

The sound OM is directly expressive of its Source, the Supreme Being. It is the hidden meaning and the eternal seed of all mantras, Upanishads and the Vedas.

The primordial creative energy in the very beginning came forth as the sacred sound OM, by focusing on which Yogis shake off all impurities of the mind. Its origin is the Unmanifest and is the source of all that is manifest, including speech in the form of Vedas. It flashes in the heart upon meditation revealing the true nature of the Infinite Being. It consists of three parts (A, U, M) which signifies the threefold gunas (sattva, rajas, tamas), three primary Vedas (Rig, Yajur and Sāma), three realms of existence (bhuḥ, bhuvaḥ, swaḥ) and the three states of existence (wakefulness, dream and deep sleep). Out of the sacred sound OM, came all alphabets and the entire revelation of the Vedas that were later divided into Samhitas, Upanishads etc. and passed on from generation to generation through various sages and their pupils. Then the great sage Vyasa organized and classified the multitudes of mantras into four distinct groups, namely Rig, Yajur, Sāma and Atharva, and imparted them respectively to four of his foremost pupils, namely Paila, Vaishampāyana, Jaimini and Sumantu. Following that, Vyasa composed the Puranas and taught them to Romaharshana. The Puranas, eighteen in number of which this glorious Bhāgavatam is the crown jewel, deal with topics such as creation, time, dynasties, divine stories and the way to liberation. Thus, the entire Vedic cannon has come forth to bring spiritual illumination to all and has its root in the sacred sound OM.

किं वर्णये तव विभो यदुदीरितोऽसुः संस्पन्दते तमनु वाङ्मनइन्द्रियाणि ।
स्पन्दन्ति वै तनुभृतामजशर्वयोश्च स्वस्याप्यथापि भजतामसि भावबन्धुः ।। Bh 12.8.40

kiṁ varṇaye tava vibho yadudīrito'suḥ saṁspandate tamanu vāṅmanaindriyāṇi
spandanti vai tanubhṛtāmajaśharvayośhcha svasyāpyathāpi bhajatāmasi bhāvabandhuḥ

How can one glorify the Supreme Being? It is due to Him alone that the vital air, speech, mind, the senses of perception and the organs of action all function in the embodied beings. He is the true friend of anyone who surrenders unto Him.

The great sage Marandeya's story appears toward the very end of Bhāgavatam as the final illustration of a supreme Bhagavata who embodies the perfect harmony of wisdom, devotion and dispassion. Born in a line of sages, Markandeya took to austerity even as a youth. Clad in bark and deer skin with matted locks, carrying a staff and rudraksha beads, he lived in simplicity, worshiping the Supreme Being as all forms: the sacred fire, the sun and the moon, his Guru, the sages, and his own inner self. Inwardly absorbed, he transcended ignorance, ego, and fear by abiding in unwavering meditation. Frightened by such steadfastness and with an intention to interrupt it, Indra sent the sweet allure of Apsaras with Cupid and the season of spring to tempt him amid the beauty of the Himalayan slopes. But Markandeya remained still, his mind unmoved like a steady flame in windless air. Realizing his glory, the tempters withdrew, and the heavens themselves bowed to his purity. Then Nara and Narayana—the twin forms of the Supreme Being—appeared before him in radiant splendor. Overwhelmed with devotion, Markandeya offered heartfelt prayers, hailing Bhagavan as the source of speech, breath, mind, and all beings, the one reality manifesting and dissolving all of creation like a spider spinning and withdrawing its web. He declared that no refuge exists for the deluded apart from the Lord, whose lotus feet dissolves all impurities and fear. Renouncing every sense of "me" and "mine," he offered himself completely, recognizing Narayana as the inner controller, the very universe, the Guru of all, the essence of all the Vedas, and the supreme truth beyond all thought and form.

प्रागुत्तरस्यां शाखायां तस्यापि ददृशे शिशुम् ।
शयानं पर्णपुटके ग्रसन्तं प्रभया तमः ॥ Bh 12.9.21

prāguttarasyāṁ śhākhāyāṁ tasyāpi dadṛśhe śhiśhum
śhayānaṁ parṇapuṭake grasantaṁ prabhayā tamaḥ

Upon a branch of the tree located in the north-east, Markandeya saw an Infant lying in a hollow leaf and the darkness was swallowed up by the effulgent radiance of that Divine Child.

Markandeya was offered any boon he desired, due to his steadfast meditation, purity of mind, asceticism, mastery of the Vedas and Self-abidance. Humbled, Markandeya declared that the vision of the Lord alone was the highest blessing. Yet, when pressed to ask for something, he wished to witness the extent of the Lord's Maya—the mysterious power through which the universe of infinite diversity appears. He was granted the wish to be revealed someday soon. The sage then returned to his meditative life, seeing the Lord in fire, sun, moon, earth, air, and all beings, ever overwhelmed with devotion. Then one evening as he was meditating on the banks of a river, a furious wind sprang up, frightful clouds flashed with lightning and volleys of rain poured down. Soon the whole earth was submerged in a deluge, and the sage was tossed around by the waves and the violent wind. He was engulfed in total darkness and drifted along helplessly for what seemed like ages in the raging sea, exhausted, oppressed by hunger, thirst and assailed by aquatic creatures. He suddenly saw a radiant banyan tree upon a patch of earth, and on its leaf lay the Divine Infant Krishna— shining like an emerald with a lotus-like face, charming eyes and a bright smile, pulling one of His feet into his mouth, sucking His big toe. The sage was suddenly freed of all fatigue and enraptured approached Him and was drawn into the Infant's breath, where he beheld the entire universe—mountains, oceans, beings, time, and even his own hermitage. This vision of the Divine Infant floating on the banyan leaf is invoked in the famous prayer, Bala Mukunda Ashtakam. Then, in an instant, the sage emerged again and the Child, the tree, the deluge all vanished, and he found himself back at his hermitage. The power of Maya was thus revealed to him, that all of creation is but a divine vision—seemingly real in experience, yet dreamlike in essence.

नमः शिवाय शान्ताय सत्त्वाय प्रमृडाय च ।
रजोजुषेऽप्यघोराय नमस्तुभ्यं तमोजुषे ॥ Bh 12.10.17

namaḥ śhivāya śhāntāya sattvāya pramṛḍāya ca
rajojuṣhe'pyaghorāya namastubhyaṁ tamojuṣhe

**Obeisances to the Supreme Lord Shiva, who is
all-auspicious and all-peaceful, embodiment of *sattva*
that delights all, appearing as *rajas* though never
frightful and assuming *tamas* though never deluded.**

After beholding the vastness of the deluding potency of Maya,
Markandeya realized how even the most learned can fall prey
to this delusion, without total surrender to the Supreme Being.
Then, as he sat poised and composed in deep meditation, Lord
Śhiva and His consort Parvati saw him. Pleased to see his
total stillness like a motionless sea, Mother Parvati wanted to
bestow a blessing upon him. Shiva said to her the sage would
not desire any blessing, not even liberation, as he is free of
the false sense of separation through total devotion and then
approached him simply for the joy of meeting a pious being.
Entering the sage's heart through Yogamaya, Shiva revealed
the radiant three-eyed form, clad in tiger skin, holding a
trident and drum. Markandeya bowed down and worshiped
Shiva, by invoking the auspicious five syllable mantra *namaḥ
śhivāya*, which appears at the very culmination of Bhāgavatam.
Shiva praised Markandeya's purity, tranquility, detachment,
love and devotion, and declared that even sacred waters and
holy temples purify only over time, but the very sight of a
true sage purifies instantly. Markandeya humbly offered his
prayers to Shiva as the embodiment of Truth, untouched
by illusion like the waker unaffected by his dream. Shiva

then blessed him with unwavering devotion, eternal youth, freedom from death and Self-realization. Thus, ends the most auspicious story of the great sage Markandeya, the only sage after whom another entire Purana is named.

मृषा गिरस्ता ह्यसतीरसत्कथा न कथ्यते यद् भगवानधोक्षज: ।
तदेव सत्यं तदुहैव मङ्गलं तदेव पुण्यं भगवद्गुणोदयम् ॥
तदेव रम्यं रुचिरं नवं नवं तदेव शश्वन्मनसो महोत्सवम् ।
तदेव शोकार्णवशोषणं नृणां यदुत्तम:श्लोकयशोऽनुगीयते ॥
Bh 12.12.48-49

mṛṣhā girastā hyasatīrasatkathā na kathyate yad
bhagavānadhokṣhajaḥ
tadeva satyaṁ taduhaiva maṅgalaṁ tadeva puṇyaṁ
bhagavadguṇodayam
tadeva ramyaṁ ruchiraṁ navaṁ navaṁ tadeva śhaśhvan manaso
mahotsavam
tadeva śhokārṇavaśhoṣhaṇaṁ nṛṇāṁ
yaduttamaḥśhlokayaśho'nugīyate

The utterances and discussions whose theme is not the transcendent Supreme Being are false and ignoble. On the other hand, those utterances which speak and glorify the Supreme Being alone are truthful, blessed, sacred, auspicious, the fountainhead of divine qualities, pleasant, the source of ever-fresh delight, the perennial source of celebration to the mind and the remover of the ocean of grief for all beings.

Sūta Maharshi now comes to the conclusion of the entire narration of Bhāgavatam that is the most worthy of reading or listening, for it celebrates the Supreme Being Narayana who is the refuge of all. It reveals the mystery of the transcendent Brahman and the means of realization through wisdom, devotion and dispassion (*jnāna, bhakti, vairāgya*). As part of the conclusion, Sūta beautifully summarizes the contents of the entire Bhāgavatam covering all the twelve skandhas:

Skandha 1: Narada's story and inspiration to Vyasa to compose Bhāgavatam and Parīkshit's curse that leads to the seven-day dialogue with Śhuka Brahmam.

Skandha 2: The entire teachings summarized by Shuka Brahmam including the all-pervading Cosmic form, enumeration of the various Avatars and the distilled essence of Vedanta in four verses (*chatuḥśhlokī*).

Skandha 3: Vidura's inquiry to Maitreya who expounds upon the nature of creation, an account of Varaha Avatar rescuing the earth and Kapila's teachings on Sankhya.

Skandha 4: The hubris of Daksha being humbled, the profound devotion of Dhruva and the rule of pious King Prthu and his descendants.

Skandha 5: Rshabha's supreme renunciation, the story of Jadabharata emphasizing dispassion and freedom that transcends all injunctions and a description of various realms of the universe.

Skandha 6: Divine Grace shining through the redemption of Ajamila and the devotion of the demon Vṛtrāsura and his previous life as Chitraketu.

Skandha 7: The most sublime devotion and teachings of Prahlāda and the appearance of Narasimha heralding the triumph of devotion over tyranny.

Skandha 8: Deliverance of the elephant Gajendra, symbolic churning of the milk ocean and the supreme surrender of Bali to Vamana Avatar.

Skandha 9: An account of the royal lineage with righteous rulers such as Ambarish, culminating in the blessed story of Sri Ram.

Skandha 10: The heart of Bhāgavatam that narrates the appearance and nectar-like pastimes of Krishna along with Balaram through Vrndavan, Mathura and Dwaraka.

Skandha 11: Krishna's final teachings to dear friend Uddhava on Self-knowledge and devotion, known famously as Uddhava Gita.

Skandha 12: The conflict-prone nature of Kali Yuga, Parīkshit's blessed liberation and the divine vision of the sage Markandeya.

यं ब्रह्मा वरुणेन्द्ररुद्रमरुतः स्तुन्वन्ति दिव्यैः स्तवैर्वेदैः
साङ्गपदक्रमोपनिषदैर्गायन्ति यं सामगाः ।
ध्यानावस्थिततद्गतेन मनसा पश्यन्ति यं योगिनो यस्यान्तं न विदुः
सुरासुरगणा देवाय तस्मै नमः ॥ Bh 12.13.1

yaṁ brahmā varuṇendrarudramarutaḥ stunvanti divyaiḥ
stavairvedaiḥ sāṅgapadakramopaniṣhadairgāyanti yaṁ sāmagāḥ
dhyānāvasthitatadgatena manasā paśhyanti yaṁ yogino
yasyāntaṁ na viduḥ surāsuragaṇā devāya tasmai namaḥ

Obeisances to the Supreme Being, who is adored through divine hymns by all the deities, who is glorified by the musical chants of Sāma Veda and in various branches of Vedas and the Upanishads, who is perceived by the Yogis

**through their still mind in meditation, and yet whose
actual truth is unknowable to gods and demons alike.**

This is a famous prayer appearing toward the end of Bhāgavatam
glorifying the Supreme Being who is the sole subject matter
of the entire twelve cantos of this Purana. Hence it is declared
that reading this work has the same reward as studying all
the Vedas whose purpose is to ultimately bring out the all-
pervading Absolute that Bhāgavatam makes accessible in the
sweetest way. Reading or listening to Bhāgavatam alone with
a calm and collected mind confers the highest benediction
and rids one of ignorance. Any composition that elaborates
upon the Infinite Being, even if faulty in diction, is revered
by saints as opposed to eloquent speech that wallows only in
worldly matters. Bhāgavatam is perfect in both its essence and
expression, bringing out the highest Truth through moving
stories and flawless poetry that transports the listener to
inner peace and divine bliss. It celebrates Hari, the Remover
of Ignorance, at every step through every episode, more than
any other work. And it has come through the Self-realized
sage Shuka Brahmam, ever abiding in bliss and graciously
revealing the highest truth that wipes out the suffering of all.

सर्ववेदान्तसारं यद् ब्रह्मात्मैकत्वलक्षणम् ।
वस्त्वद्वितीयं तन्निष्ठं कैवल्यैकप्रयोजनम् ॥ Bh 12.13.12

*sarvavedāntasāraṁ yad brahmātmaikatvalakshaṇam
vastvadvitīyaṁ tanniṣhṭhaṁ kaivalyaikaprayojanam*

**This Bhāgavatam is the sum and substance of the whole
of Vedanta and has as its defining feature, the oneness of
the apparent individual with the Absolute. It elaborates**

upon the non-dual essence and has liberation as its only purpose.

There are eighteen primary Puranas in total, each with thousands of verses, for a combined grand total of four hundred thousand verses. However, Bhāgavatam alone with its 18,000 verses sits as the crown jewel among them all and contains the quintessence of all the Vedas and Puranas. It was graciously revealed by the Supreme Being out of compassion to Brahma before he set about the task of creation. It is adorned in the beginning, middle and the end with various legends and accounts that illustrate the glory of loving devotion and dispassion. It is filled with nectar-like stories describing the pastimes of the Lord and moving tales of many great Bhagavatas. And through every one of these accounts, Bhāgavatam brings forth only the all-pervading Truth without a second (*advitīyam*), the unborn and indescribable ground of all appearance. What seems to be a universe of multiplicity is only an expression of the non-dual Divine. Thus, it brings out the distilled essence of Vedanta which is the heart of the Upaniṣhads that the apparent individual is non-different from the Absolute. Therefore, the purpose of Bhāgavatam is *kaivalya*—freedom from the ignorance of false separation as "me" to the recognition that **God Alone Is.**

निम्नगानां यथा गङ्गा देवानामच्युतो यथा ।
वैष्णवानां यथा शम्भुः पुराणानामिदं तथा ॥ Bh 12.13.16

nimnagānāṁ yathā gaṅgā devānāmachyuto yathā
vaiṣhṇavānāṁ yathā śhambhuḥ purāṇānāmidam tathā

Bhāgavatam occupies the same place of pride among the Puranas as the holy Ganga among the rivers, Achyuta among the deities and Shiva among the Vaishnavas.

Bhāgavatam is celebrated as the supreme (Maha) Purana, the one before which all other Puranas fade as stars upon sunrise. It presents the cream of the Upanishads and a perfect synthesis of philosophy, devotion, cosmology and stories of sages and Avatars. So, it is said that all the other Puranas spread their luster in an assembly of the righteous only so long as the glorious Bhāgavatam is not presented. Ganga is the most sacred among all rivers. Achyuta is the Immortal Supreme Being, the Absolute among the worshippable. Shiva being the first Guru is the greatest Vaishnava—the one fully abiding in and therefore non-different from the all-pervading Vishnu. Kashi is unsurpassed among holy places. Similarly, Bhāgavatam is unexcelled among all scriptures. Hence, Bhāgavatam is praised as the greatest gift that can be given, for it is a form of Kṛishṇa Himself that is accessible to the heart and mind, guiding one directly to the realization of the eternal, non-dual Truth. Through every teaching and every prayer, it points to the illusion of separation as an individual and the only abiding Reality as the all-pervading Absolute, thus revealing the ever-shining light of freedom of Being.

श्रीमद्भागवतं पुराणममलं यद्वैष्णवानां प्रियं यस्मिन्
पारमहंस्यमेकममलं ज्ञानं परं गीयते ।
तत्र ज्ञानविरागभक्तिसहितं नैष्कर्म्यमाविष्कृतं तच्छृण्वन् सुपठन्
विचारणपरो भक्त्या विमुच्येत्रर: ॥ Bh 12.13.18

*śrīmadbhāgavatam purāṇamamalam yadvaiṣṇavānāṁ priyaṁ
yasmin pāramahaṁsyamekamamalam jñānam param gīyate*

tatra jñānavirāgabhaktisahitaṁ naishkarmyamāvishkṛtaṁ
tachchhṛṇvan supaṭhan vichāraṇaparo bhaktyā vimuchyennaraḥ

The glorious Bhāgavatam is free of any blemish and beloved of the devotees, for it glorifies only the Absolute Truth that is ever pure. It expounds upon true wisdom, detachment, devotion and bestows freedom from doership. One who devoutly listens to it, carefully reads it and contemplates upon it is certain to be liberated.

As a summary glorification of Bhāgavatam, this famous verse refers to it as ever pure and free of taint (*amalam*), ever dear to all devotees for it brings forth the sweet mood of devotion that erases the false ego and is ever celebrated as the highest exposition of Truth (*pāramahamsyam*). It is a sacred confluence of wisdom (*jnāna*), dispassion (*vairāgya*) and devotion (*bhakti*). And through this confluence, it brings freedom from doership of actions (*naishkarmyam*). Therefore, a sincere study and contemplation of the message contained herein is sufficient to free one of the illusory separation as an individual and realize the Oneness of the all-pervading Absolute.

कस्मै येन विभासितोऽयमतुलो ज्ञानप्रदीपः पुरा तद्रूपेण च
नारदाय मुनये कृष्णाय तद्रूपिणा ।
योगीन्द्राय तदात्मनाथ भगवद्रातय कारुण्यतस्तच्छुद्धं विमलं
विशोकममृतं सत्यं परं धीमहि ॥ Bh 12.13.19

kasmai yena vibhāsito'yamatulo jñānapradīpaḥ purā tadrūpeṇa
cha nāradāya munaye kṛṣhṇāya tadrūpiṇā
yogīndrāya tadātmanātha bhagavadrātāya

*kāruṇyatastachchhuddhaṁ vimalaṁ viśhokamamṛtaṁ satyaṁ
paraṁ dhīmahi*

**We meditate upon the pure, spotless, eternal,
transcendent Absolute, that is untouched by sorrow.
This incomparable light of wisdom was first revealed
to Brahma, who taught Narada, who then instructed
Vyasa, who taught his son Shuka, the greatest among all
Yogis, who in turn narrated to Parikshit with immense
compassion, this Supreme Truth that we meditate upon.**

Bhāgavatam concludes by invoking the same beautiful
expression with which it began in the very first verse—*satyam
param dhīmahi*. It is an invocation of the Highest Truth that has
been passed down through the disciplic succession through
Brahma, Narada, Vyasa and Shuka Brahmam who narrated it
in seven days to the saintly king Parikshit. The king was first
saved while in the womb by Krishna and finally liberated while
awaiting his death by listening to Bhāgavatam. Sūta listened to
that narration of Shuka Brahmam to Parikshit and recounted
it exactly as he had listened to the Rishis of Naimisharanyam.
The only subject matter of Bhāgavatam through the entire
twelve cantos that cover various topics, stories and teachings
is always to point to the pure eternal Truth (*satyaṁ*) that frees
one from suffering. It awakens unwavering devotion to the
all-pervading Bhagavan Vasudeva, the seer of all, who taught
this Purana in the most concise form to Brahma upon creation.
And this majestic work of 18,000 verses culminates with the
triumphant declaration that all suffering is alleviated, and
one is freed of all sins that have their root only in ignorance
by meditating upon the Supreme Being Hari to whom I offer
obeisances—*namāmi hariṁ param.*

Thus concludes the glorious Bhāgavata Mahā Purāṇa, also known as the Paramahamsa Samhita, composed by the great sage Vyasa consisting of eighteen thousand verses in twelve cantos.

हरिः ॐ तत् सत्
hariḥ om tat sat

ABOUT
RED MOUNTAIN ASHRAM

Named after the sacred Arunachala—the "unmoving stillness" symbolizing the dawn of wisdom—**Red Mountain Ashram** is a dedicated sanctuary for the teachings of self-inquiry and surrender as revealed by Ramana Maharshi. Our vision is to disseminate these profound teachings, fostering a space where people of all backgrounds engage in a daily rhythm of inquiry, meditation, and service.

This mission is anchored in both in-person and online programs, ranging from daily meditations to immersive retreats designed to bring about stillness, clarity, and purposeful action each moment, here and now.

For more information on our programs and to join our community, please visit **RedMountainAshram.org**